Joe Weider

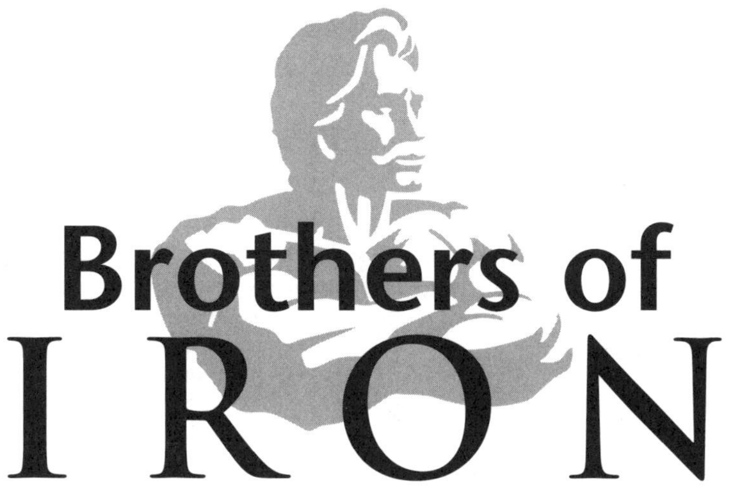

Brothers of IRON

JOE WEIDER
BEN WEIDER
WITH MIKE STEERE

SportsPublishingLLC.com

ISBN-10: 1-59670-124-2
ISBN-13: 978-1-59670-124-3

Photos provided by Weider Health and Fitness.

Publishers: Peter L. Bannon and Joseph J. Bannon Sr.
Senior managing editor: Susan M. Moyer
Acquisitions editor: Mike Pearson
Developmental editor: Erin Linden-Levy
Art director: K. Jeffrey Higgerson
Dust jacket design: Dustin J. Hubbart
Interior layout: Dustin J. Hubbart
Photo editor: David Marsh

Sports Publishing L.L.C.
804 North Neil Street
Champaign, IL 61820
Phone: 1-877-424-2665
Fax: 217-363-2073
SportsPublishingLLC.com

Printed in the United States of America

Library of Congress Cataloging-in-Publication Data

Weider, Joe.
Brothers of iron / Joe Weider, Ben Weider with Mike Steere.
p. cm.
Includes index.
ISBN-13: 978-1-59670-124-3 (hard cover : alk. paper)
ISBN-10: 1-59670-124-2 (hard cover : alk. paper)
1. Bodybuilders--Canada--Biography. 2. Brothers--Canada--Biography. 3. Weider, Joe. 4. Weider, Ben, 1923-. I. Weider, Ben, 1923-. II. Steere, Michael. III. Title.
GV545.5.W43 2006
796.41'092--dc22
[B]

2006023062

With deepest gratitude and love, we dedicate this book to our parents, Anna and Louis Weider.

Ten Predictions
About Bodybuilding

(as they appeared in the July 1950 issue of *Your Physique*)

by Joe Weider

1. I PREDICT that civilization will speed up in every phase, and that the stresses and strains on mankind will continue to increase.

2. I PREDICT that the resulting increase in mental and physical illness will force the world to recognize the importance of systematic exercise and physical activities.

3. I PREDICT that bodybuilding will become the chief form of systematic exercise and physical activity, and that it will come to be looked upon as one of the greatest forces in the field of preventive medicine.

4. I PREDICT that a full realization of the importance of muscular development will sweep the world, and the sport of bodybuilding will grow by leaps and bounds.

5. I PREDICT that the basics of good bodybuilding—which include a balanced diet, adequate sleep, plenty of fresh air, ample sunshine, and regular workouts—will become basics of living.

6. I PREDICT that bodybuilding will become the stepping-stone to every other sport and physical activity.

7. I PREDICT that the art of relaxation, one of the fundamentals in bodybuilding, will become more and more important as tensions increase, and that relaxation will be universally taught and advocated.

8. I PREDICT that bodybuilding will spread to every corner of the world and that it will one day be recognized as the king of all sports and physical activities.

9. I PREDICT that those who practice bodybuilding will live healthier, happier and more useful lives.

10. I PREDICT that bodybuilding will one day become one of the greatest forces in existence, and that it may be hailed as the activity that actually saved civilization from itself.

CONTENTS

FOR JOE

Years before I met him in person, Joe Weider changed my life. I'll never forget the first time I picked up one of Joe's muscle magazines. I was just a boy in a little village in Austria, and I barely knew what bodybuilding was, but when I looked at the pictures of great bodybuilders I saw my destiny. I was inspired to become a great champion myself.

From the magazines I learned about Joe, the Trainer of Champions, a man bigger and more powerful in our sport than the fantastic muscle men in the pictures. He personally showed the greats how to train and how to eat correctly and do all the things it takes to get stronger and healthier and build an outstanding physique. Millions of people all around the world became Joe's pupils by reading his magazines and following his teachings, and I became one of those millions. The magazines gave me direction and inspired me to work out five hours a day and push myself to the limit. And the Weider magazines became like how-to manuals for my entire life. They showed me where I wanted to go. To America. To California. I made a promise to myself that one day I would come here to train in the same gyms as such great California bodybuilders as Larry Scott and Dave Draper. And after I left bodybuilding I would stay and become a leading man in Hollywood and then serve the public.

Thanks to Joe Weider I could keep all the promises that I made to myself. When I came to America in 1968, Joe became my sponsor and coach and inspiration and mentor. One word sums up Joe's role in my life—father. After my own father passed away Joe more than filled the gap. Joe is a brilliant man, and he understood me and took all my ambitions very seriously and helped me in every way he could. Not only did he show me how to build my muscles and succeed in our sport, he showed me how to fulfill my role as a champion and do well in business. He even opened my eyes to beauty and the finer things in life like artwork and antiques. Joe's generosity to me knew no bounds. I honestly don't know where I'd be or what I'd be doing if Joe had not come into my life. From the day I entered public service and politics, Joe has contributed generously to my campaigns, all the way through my ballot initiative for school programs, the recall campaign where I first won office, and, now, my re-election campaign. And he has always stood behind me, giving moral support that means the world to me.

What Joe gave to me, in terms of knowledge and encouragement and inspiration, he really gave to the entire world. And what he did for me, he did for millions upon millions of individuals. My work has taken me all around the world, and absolutely everywhere I have gone, I've seen Joe's picture and heard people honor and revere his name. I just got back from an official trip to China, and people there came up to me with old copies of Joe's magazines for me to autograph. Over and over they asked me questions about Joe. What was it like to train with him? What's he like in person? Are he and I close friends? Back in the 1980s when I first shot a film in Moscow, I went to Red Square and Russian people crowded around me asking me all about Joe. In African villages in the middle of nowhere I saw pictures from Joe's magazines up on the walls of houses made out of mud. The men there had primitive weights made out of junk, but they were Weider pupils just like I once was back in Austria. And bodybuilding, as taught by Joe, gave them a sense of pride in accomplishment and hope.

As Joe showed me and millions of others, you build much more than muscles when you build your body. In fact, muscles and the strength to lift heavy weights are almost beside the point. The strength and the power that really matter are inside. Bodybuilding has a tremendous impact psychologically. When you pick up a weight and start exercising, it's impossible to feel hopeless or helpless. From one workout to the next, even from one rep to the next, you feel your body changing. And if you can change your body, you can change other things.

Joe Weider picked up a weight when he was 13 years old, and he went on to change the entire world.

The amazing and inspirational life stories that Joe and his brother Ben tell in this book show you the incredible changes they brought about. Starting with nothing but Joe's ideas and his vision, the Weider brothers brought bodybuilding out of the shadows and built it into a major international sport. And Joe taught the world that resistance training to build strength and muscles—bodybuilding—is for everybody. Everybody. Young or old, casual exerciser or serious competitive athlete, you will be happier and healthier and do your job better if you work out with weights or resistance machines. Nobody would argue with such a statement now, but Joe had to fight tooth and nail for 60 years to bring the truth about bodybuilding to light. Now athletes in every single sport lift weights and build their bodies, as do members of the United States Armed Forces. On my many visits to American military bases, more than I can count, I've always seen Joe's magazines in barracks and in weight rooms. Not only are the soldiers and sailors and airmen fans of Joe and bodybuilding enthusiasts, they do strength conditioning as part of their military training. Bodybuilding makes stronger, better fighting men. As Joe writes in this book, movie stars and celebrities are bodybuilders, too. In fact, people everywhere look better and feel better because of the pioneering work of Joe Weider. For that we all owe him thanks. And for what Joe gave to me personally, I owe all the thanks I can give.

—Governor Arnold Schwarzenegger
Sacramento, California

BEN WEIDER, SPORTSMAN AND GENTLEMAN

During my long tenure as president of the International Olympic Committee (1980-2001), I met many people of accomplishment and merit. Among them, Ben Weider made the deepest and most lasting impression on me for his great love of sport, his love and amazing capacity for work, and also for his great love of world history.

As a sports leader, Ben has tirelessly championed the cause of bodybuilding. He is the founding president of the International Federation of Bodybuilders, which, under his leadership, has grown into one of the largest sports federations, with 173 member nations and participation in most of the IOC-recognized Games, such as the Asian Games and World Games. During my IOC presidency it was my great pleasure to grant the IFBB provisional IOC recognition.

Besides earning his sport acceptance and great popularity worldwide, Ben and his brother Joe Weider built international industries based on bodybuilding, fitness, and health.

In his avocation as a pre-eminent Napoleonic historian, Ben was able to prove, after long research, that emperor Napoleon Bonaparte was a victim of poisoning, not cancer as previously believed.

In our many meetings together, Ben Weider always came meticulously prepared and wasted not a moment of my limited time. I am sure that he always conducts himself with the same focus, discipline, and energy.

Hereby, I testify to my friendship and admiration for this great man called Ben Weider. Those who do not know him personally, as I do, will enjoy and profit by meeting him and learning his life story in this book.

—Juan Antonio Samaranch
Marques de Samaranch

AUTHOR'S NOTE

By Ben Weider

Montreal, 2006

It takes two hands to clap, and it takes two brothers, Joe Weider and Ben Weider, to tell the story you're about to read. We chose to write a two-man autobiography as partner-authors, some chapters by Joe, others by me, to make our book as true to the way we live and work as a book could possibly be. We have been a team since the end of World War II, when it was my good fortune and my privilege to join with Joe and work to advance his great visions for bodybuilding, fitness, and the health and well-being of the entire world. Even though we've been many miles apart for almost 60 years—Joe in New York, then California, me in Montreal—Joe has been by my side, and I by his, every day of our lives. Our shared mission and our mutual respect and trust—and our love—wipes away the miles.

Because Joe is the founding genius and creative engine of our enterprises, you'll read more of his words than mine. But I daresay the tale would be incomplete without my own account of how I have carried the Weider vision to the world, fighting for—and winning—respect and official recognition for bodybuilding (including Olympic recognition), the Holy Grail of my own lifelong quest as founding president of the International Federation of Body Builders, which I still lead. Once far outside the mainstream of athletics, our sport now has 173 national federations spanning every continent and region. It takes a realist to make dreams real and a diplomat to persuade the world that it needs to change—such is my role, and I'm deeply proud of it.

First, though, comes the visionary. Our story begins with Joe...

CHAPTER ONE

BORN WITH A BARBELL IN MY HANDS

Joe Weider

I don't have many clear memories from my childhood because I wasn't such a happy kid. The story of my arrival in this world gives you a good idea why.

The nurse showed me to my mother, who was worn out from the labor, and she smiled and went to sleep. Later somebody brought me back so my mother could hold me, but she pushed me away.

"This isn't my baby!" she yelled.

"Of course it's your baby," my father and everybody told her.

"No, I had I girl. I saw with my own eyes. Bring me my girl!"

When Ma got an idea in her head—even a wrong idea because she was woozy—you couldn't talk her out of it. And when she got upset, there was no soothing or reasoning. She was a force of nature, like a hurricane, and you just waited for the trouble to blow over. Eventually she calmed down and accepted that she had given birth to me.

I was never her baby, though.

I came up the hard way, in the hardest of times. My family lacked for money and all the things it bought beyond the bare necessities. My brother Ben and I had no opportunity to go to high school. But the only thing missing that really hurt me was the lack of my mother's love.

What the child needs but doesn't get, he searches for his whole life.

What my mother really yelled was, *"Das is nisht mein kint!"*

At home we spoke Yiddish, the language of the Ashkenazic Jews who lived in Eastern Europe. My father was born in 1885, my mother a few years later, in Kurov, a little town near Lublin in southeastern Poland that then belonged to Czarist Russia. Pa's Hebrew name was *Arieh*, or "Lion," which would have been a good name for me. In Canada he became Louis, but friends from Europe still used his everyday Jewish name, *Leb,* "Lion" in both Yiddish and German. Yiddish is mostly a dialect of Medieval German, which the Jews spoke when they lived along the River Rhine. They went east after King Casimir the Great of Poland invited them to settle and help to civilize his country. That was in the fourteenth century, so my family lived in Eastern Europe for something like 500 years—until they either left like my parents or the Nazis wiped them out like they wiped out all my relatives in Poland, including my grandfather, Moishe Weider. He was in his eighties then, as I am now.

As soon as I got out of the house and learned English, I was ashamed that we spoke Yiddish at home. All kids of immigrants feel that way because they want so much to blend in. I was never ashamed of my background, though. There are tribal Jews and religious Jews. I have been both, except for a few years when Adolph Hitler and the things he did in Europe made me doubt God. I have never doubted since, although I am not what you would call an observant Jew, in terms of going to temple and praying and keeping kosher. But all my life I was—and I am—a proud Jew.

A child could never understand and the child inside still can't, but as I got older I came to see why my mother made so many difficulties for me. She had nothing but trouble where she came from, and she knew she deserved a better life.

Her name before she married was Anna Nudelmann. She was the most beautiful girl in the *shtetl,* the Jewish community, with strong straight features and blue eyes that she passed on to me. At 5 feet, 6 inches she towered above other women, who were tall if they stood 5 foot 3. But her family was as poor as the Weiders. People like that were lucky if they ate meat once a week and had their own outhouse instead of a ditch.

My mother's father was a pious man but also a tyrant at home. This explains why Ma was so independent in matters of faith and everything else. She set religious rules aside and never let anybody, man or woman, tell her what to do. And she, too, hungered for motherly love. Her mother died when she was only 12 or 13 years old. Almost immediately her father found a younger woman, who told him she'd never marry a man with more than three children. Since he had four kids, he made my mother go away and hide. After the wedding my mother came home but then left again on her own because her new stepmother was so cruel to her. To survive she took a job as a seamstress in town where she made friends with many Polish people. Her association with the Gentiles drove her father crazy, but she didn't care. Her friends protected her when mobs came and raised hell with the Jews. Such *pogroms,* which occurred so the peasants could take out their frustrations in a way that didn't bother the ruling class, happened every few years.

Through all the misery, my mother carried herself like a queen. And she was like a queen in Canada, where life was better but still tough. Once I visited Poland and saw all around me women who walked the earth with great power and grace. They stood strong and proud, with beautiful upright posture. Almost every one of them reminded me of my mother.

When my mother was 16, my Grandfather Nudelmann arranged for her to be married to a younger man who knew the Torah and the Jewish laws backward and forward. My mother said she would marry only for love. The man she finally chose was tall and good-looking and as unlike her father as a man could possibly be. That was my father, the most mild and gentle and loving human being I ever knew. Even now, the memory of him and his goodness brings tears. My brother Ben, in whose arms Pa died, gets too emotional to speak of his passing, which happened on January 11, 1951.

People who felt sorry for my father because of the way my mother treated him were wrong. There was cosmic justice and balance in their union, because opposites complete each other. What one lacks, the other provides. People who called my father a saint were wrong, too. He was just a man who followed his nature—as my mother followed hers. Hers was to exert her will, and his was to love. Pa adored his wife and family and did everything he could to show us how he felt.

I have beautiful memories of my parents in the living room in the evenings, my father reading to my mother from the newspapers. He had to give her the news in Yiddish because she never learned more than a few words of English. If he had the money, my father would have lavished presents on all of us. Instead, his gifts were gestures of love. I'd wake up and find my shoes shined and my clothes pressed because he did such things while we slept. To me he was like Moses or Jesus Christ—he showed what perfect love looked like in human form.

Don't be so surprised that I just brought Jesus into my story. I understand more about Christianity than most Christians. All my life I have studied the lives and philosophies of men with powerful new ideas that changed the world. A revolutionary must learn from other revolutionaries. You cheat yourself of knowledge if you're afraid to face evil, so I also made serious studies of Vladimir Lenin and Josef Stalin and even Adolph Hitler. Jesus, of course, comes down on the side of good. He can't be blamed for all the vicious things done in his name.

My parents got married in 1905 or 1906, a time when the regime stirred up more and more *pogroms* because the rage of the downtrodden people was getting out of hand. Persecuting the Jews did nothing to stop the coming Russian Revolution, but it made life more dangerous and miserable for people like my parents.

Things got even tougher for them in 1907 when Czarist officers came to town and forced my father into the army. Pa served a few years in a horse-drawn artillery unit in the Ukraine. He later showed me a lump where a horse had kicked him in the head and told how a priest splashed him with holy water during a blessing of the troops. The water went into his eyes, but he didn't dare wipe it off or even blink for fear of offending the Christians. My mother said she lost three babies in those early years of marriage. Two, she told us, were stillborn because of malnutrition. One lived for two months but starved after my mother's breasts dried up because she had so little to eat.

Finally, in about 1911, my parents got a chance to go to North America. My father went first under the sponsorship of his cousin Sender Goldstein, who was doing well for himself in Montreal. The rules said that sponsors could bring only immediate family, so Pa came over as Louis Goldstein. Later he brought his own younger brother, who called himself Philip Goldstein. Uncle Philip got restless and moved to New York City and kept the name Goldstein. So did Pa, until my mother got mad at the Goldsteins and decided to get rid of their name. She had to go to court to legally change the name back to Weider.

I'm sure I would have done just as well—my brother, too—as Joe Goldstein and Ben Goldstein. But our real family name was a better fit for the Weider lifetime mission. Think of the way it hits the ears and the eyes. Joe Weider truly sounds like the Trainer of Champions, the Master Blaster. The letters look powerful on Weider weight plates, resistance machines, supplements that make you stronger—and, of course, on all my magazines.

In Montreal my father took a job in a garment factory that his cousin arranged for him. He lived in a miserable little room and saved, by nickels and dimes, for my mother's passage from Europe.

"Be patient, we'll be together soon," he wrote in letters.

You know by now how patient she was. Ma came up with her own way to get cash for her steamship ticket. She brought action against her stepmother, claiming ownership of a pearl necklace that her real mother had left to her but her stepmother had kept. The *shtetl* elders who judged such things ruled that her claim was just and valid. As soon as she got the necklace, she sold it and traveled across Europe with a man on his way to join relatives in the Canadian province of Manitoba. At Antwerp, Belgium, they boarded a filthy, crowded immigrant ship. In the two weeks it took to reach Halifax, Nova Scotia, my mother came down with a terrible fever, probably typhoid, that damaged her hearing. It was partial deafness that kept her from learning English, because she couldn't pick up the sounds of new words.

Ma got off the train from Halifax at the old Windsor Station in Montreal. She showed my father's address to a representative of the Canadian Jewish Congress who took her across the city by streetcar. Pa had no idea she was coming. I'm sure she looked like death warmed over from the trip and sickness, but to him she appeared like an angel from heaven. He cried from happiness, and Ma yelled at him for letting her stay in Poland so long.

My parents took a little apartment on the east side of town. My father continued to eke out a living in the *shmata,* the rag trade, which made a few Jews rich from the sweat of thousands of others just off the boat. Pa hated the garment factories with all his heart, but that was the only work he ever did.

Ma got pregnant and gave birth to a baby boy named Jakob who got sick and died when he was about two months old. In 1916 my older brother Louis was born. He was the first of us to live past infancy, but a cloud soon came over this happiness. As a child, Louis came down with a bad cold that got worse. Penicillin or antibiotics would have cured him right away, but they weren't yet available, and he developed rheumatic fever that damaged his heart and made him sickly all his life. He was dead before he was 30.

Next I came along, but I can't tell you when I was born, because nobody could tell me. My birthday was said to be November 29, which is when I celebrate it, but nobody knew for sure. Ma had a rough idea, remembering that I was born just before Hanukkah. Nothing was on paper, though, because the rabbi's records burned in a fire and we never found government documentation. I'm not sure of the year, either. When I applied for United States citizenship, I found a school record that said I was born in 1920. Other records said 1922—but who cares? A year or two, this way or that, doesn't mean a thing.

In a personal history like this, there's a time that's more important than the day and year of birth. It could be 10 or 20 or even 40 years earlier. This time is the formative period of your parents or whoever raised you. Their thoughts and habits surround you and shape you. They're all you know in your first years, but they come from a time gone by when you were only an egg. I just told you about my parents' time, because it was my time, too. I was shaped by their experiences in the early 1900s when things were even worse than during the Great Depression, which would be my own formative period.

Never forget: You came into the world stuck in somebody else's past. You should pay attention to the previous generation, because you're in it.

The world is even more stuck in the past than individual people are. When I started to develop my ideas on muscle building and fitness and health, the prevailing wisdom was 40 years, maybe even 50 years, out of date. Coaches trained their athletes, if you could call it training, based on information and techniques from the turn of the century. The respected medical authorities, men in their sixties whose ideas about health and exercise were formed when they were in medical school, who never tested their ideas because they didn't think exercise was worthy of scientific study, had to pass the torch to clear the way for new thinking.

When people say somebody was ahead of his time, they really mean that he managed to catch up to the time he lived in. To do that, the guy had to fight tooth and nail. I know, because I had to.

Every three years another child was born into our family—Louis, me, Ben, and Freda. First we lived in an apartment on Henri-Julien Street, and after that in a house at 4466 Colonial Avenue. That house, which had a rental flat upstairs, was the first property my parents ever owned and my home from my ninth year until my twenties when I moved to the U.S. It is the only home my mind goes back to when I think of home.

Back then, Montreal had about 59,000 Jews, the majority from overseas. Practically all of them lived northeast of downtown in a corridor along St. Lawrence Boulevard, which everybody called The Main. Our house, a couple blocks east of The Main and a half-block south of Mount Royal Boulevard, was right in the heart of things. If you went outside and smelled all the families' cooking and the odors from the factory a few doors down where they made pickles and smoked meat—the Montreal equivalent of pastrami—and if you listened to the neighbors and watched them, you were as much in the Old World as the New. The immigrants brought so much of their homelands with them that we lived in a transplanted European ghetto.

This little world of ours straddled the line between two bigger worlds. To the west were the English, to the east the French Canadians. Of the 800,000-some people who lived in the city, about two-thirds were French speakers. The rest spoke English, the language of the Anglo-Protestant elite who ran things. Plutocrats, I would call them. New immigrants learned English rather than French, because that was the language for getting ahead.

The dominant groups also brought along their ancestral homelands. The upper crust acted more proper and polished and above-it-all than lords and ladies back in England. The French, who had been in Canada since the 1600s, were more like peasants from an earlier century. Kids who came around to make trouble yelled *Moodgie Jweef!*—their way of pronouncing *Maudits Juifs!* They meant "Dirty Jews!" but the first word translates as "cursed," in the Biblical sense of damned for all eternity. A lot of the French swear words were really old-time church words. Quebec was more Catholic than France had been for 200 years, and the priests still stirred up bad feelings against the Jews.

Our old neighborhood, like New York's Lower East Side, became a breeding ground for genius of all kinds and an important part of the national history and culture. The writers Saul Bellow, Mordecai Richler, and Leonard Cohen grew up along The Main, as did musicians and artists and doctors and millionaires and business magnates. Our ruling wealthy dynasty was the Bronfman family, who started making whiskey just before alcoholic drinks were outlawed in the U.S. in 1919. By the time Prohibition ended in 1933, the Bronfmans had made their first fortune from booze that was smuggled across the border. In the 1940s one of the Bronfman girls got the hots for me. More about this later.

You can fight the past, as I did, and still love tradition.

People in the neighborhood looked out for each other like their ancestors since time immemorial. When somebody got sick, neighbors came and took turns nursing and cooking, cleaning, minding the kids. They worked together and took care of everything. In springtime, families gathered with clothes their kids outgrew and stuff they didn't need any more and swapped it around. Sometimes Ma took me to neighbors with bigger kids, and I tried on their old clothes. If I could wear them, they were mine, and then Ma would give away the things I outgrew. Now and again a better-off family got rid of their curtains. Pa, who had skills from his work, took them and made dresses for my sister.

There was so much life out on the street. People buying, selling, talking, laughing. And every house was full of life. I can't tell you where we put everybody—parents, children, relatives who sometimes stayed with us. Since there were tenants upstairs, we only had the first floor, which had two small bedrooms, a front room, a sort of dining room leading back to the kitchen, and the bathroom way in back. The backyard was a tiny patch of dirt with the lane (our word for alley) behind it. If you put a young couple and a kid or two in there now, they'd cry about needing more room. But we didn't feel crowded, and we didn't complain.

The family feeling went up and down our street. If you wanted to visit or borrow something, you just went to somebody's door and knocked. If you wanted to talk, somebody would listen. I was poor then, and I left and got rich, but right now, remembering the way things were on Colonial Avenue, I feel loss more than gain. You could sit in one of these great, big California houses with palm trees and swimming pools 'til hell froze over, waiting for somebody to ring the bell and say, "I just came over because I felt like talking." If you went next door and said, "Hey, we made too much food tonight, why don't you eat with us?" the neighbors would think you lost your mind.

The women ran our communal society, and on our block Ma was boss of the women. I remember all the neighbor ladies sitting around our table, talking and eating little snacks and sweets that Ma set out. She loved to entertain and show off what a great cook and hostess she was. But when she heard somebody stretching the truth or speaking nonsense, Ma came down like a ton of bricks, yelling at some poor lady, "Stop talking silliness! You're breaking my head!"

The women kept coming around, though, because they looked up to her.

And I loved having them in the house. *"Kum, Yossele,"* they'd say, using the pet name that meant Little Joey, and they'd pass me from lap to lap and kiss me and fuss over me. Later I heard that I was the smartest, best little boy. I brought cookies if somebody asked and did other things grownups requested. I got a lot of tenderness and affection from those neighbor ladies, as if I had a houseful of aunties.

For a few years I had a real aunt in the house; Sarah, my mother's younger half-sister. My mother, who had bonded with her new half-siblings even though she fought with the parents, brought Sarah over from Poland the way Pa brought his brother Philip over. Considering what would happen, my parents really saved my aunt and my uncle's lives, but of course nobody knew that yet. Sarah was so sweet and motherly. She'd play with me for hours and take me into the little day bed she slept in and hold me. She really loved me. All those women loved me, which is why, I think, I've always gotten along so well with women and why I appreciate and understand them better than most other men.

When I was in my late thirties and living in New York City, I had a dream.

All I could see was an arm, a woman's arm, but powerful like the arm on a statue of a warrior goddess. I flinched away because I was scared it would strike out at me.

A psychoanalyst I saw for a while told me the arm represented my mother. I could have saved my money and skipped that session—Who else would it be? Ma went around the house with a leather belt around her neck. If one of us got rowdy and loud or didn't do what she said right that minute, she'd lash out—WHACK! with the belt, just like that, and never even bat an eye.

I see now that Ma needed order and peace to do all her work, but I never appreciated getting hit. When I was 14 or so, I finally put a stop to it. By that time I was getting muscles and confidence because I'd started my weight training. One day Ma raised the belt, and I grabbed it and told her the next time she tried to use it on me, I'd use it on her.

From then on, when trouble came up, Ma told my father to speak to me. He never raised his voice, but his words of loving reason and concern were more powerful than a thousand leather straps. I would have done anything, anything in the world, not to hurt or disappoint him.

After I stood up for myself, my mother would tell people: Don't bother arguing or fighting with Joe—he'll just fight back harder.

Ma said this, too: If you go to Joe and talk nicely, he'll give you the shirt off his back.

To be fair to my mother, we all depended on her discipline and inner strength. Every day was a struggle to stretch the little bit of money Pa earned to feed us and keep a nice home. And Ma gave me great and powerful gifts. She showed me how to live with strength and determination and do what's right.

One of my first clear memories, which seems like part of my life and not just a story, comes from my sixth or seventh year. I went to the grocery store with a shopping list from my mother along with another kid whose mother sent him for groceries. Neither of us took cash because neighborhood merchants did business on the cuff. They had to give credit because people's money would run out when the men had no work.

I gave our list to the grocer. Fine, no problem, he said. But he handed back my friend's list. The grocer said he would fill my order because my mother always paid as soon as Pa got his paycheck, but he cut off my friend's family because his mother was so unreliable.

Ma's reputation in the neighborhood was solid gold. Years later I met a man who said his father owned the shoe store where Ma shopped. She bought our shoes on time, like everybody else, but the man said she paid off her debt like nobody he ever saw. Other women would whine and ask for extensions, but Ma marched in and laid down 50 cents every week, on the button, with her head held high. That made a lasting impression, the man said.

It made a lasting impression on me, too. My businesses, like all businesses, would have their ups and downs. When things were at their worst, people told me to declare bankruptcy and start over debt-free, but I wouldn't do it. I honored all my obligations, paid back every penny I owed, because I was too proud not to. I owe that to my mother.

Back when my wife, Betty, and I were first going out and getting to know each other, she was very shocked that I couldn't name a single one of my teachers or classmates or say much of anything about my years at Bancroft Elementary School. She could name all of her teachers, grade by grade, and recall her classmates and all kinds of little incidents from her early schooling.

This shows one of the things I learned about women from observation and understanding: They have better memories. This is because they live much more in the present and pay attention to day-to-day happenings. And it all sticks in their minds. Men remember less because they notice less. The present and past don't matter so much because they live looking into the future, figuring out what's coming up and what they're going to do. I know this is true for me. All the looking back and remembering that I'm doing right now does not come naturally to me.

I did pretty well in grade school, the only formal schooling I got. I was a quiet, serious kid who never made trouble and was dreamy and imaginative. Already the world in my head, full of my own ideas and images, was as interesting as everybody else's world.

By the fourth or fifth grade we were going into the Great Depression, which hit Montreal hard. Some of those years Pa worked only a few months, and I provided some small change for the family by delivering newspapers. I had three routes. Before school I delivered one of the New York papers and then at lunchtime took around *The Gazette,* one of Montreal's English dailies. After school I delivered a French evening paper, *La Presse.* In the upper grades, I also got a job at a corner newsstand.

That far north, winter days are very short, so I was out delivering papers before daylight and after dark in temperatures down to 30 below or even colder. The newsstand felt colder than the paper routes because I wasn't moving so much. I was a skinny kid, and I'd wear a mask on my face and pack my clothes with newspapers for extra insulation. My gloves had the fingertips cut off so I could handle coins and make change.

My brother Ben and I made a joke out of the cold. When we both worked on the streets, wearing woolen masks that got icy from our breathing, somebody asked how we managed to communicate. We said the words we spoke all winter froze solid but then thawed out in springtime, so we heard each other loud and clear.

Picture two hands rendered in pencil lines and shadowing. They press together side by side, just a little bit cupped, with the palms facing you. The point of view is like seeing your own hands, except the tips of the fingers become factory chimneys belching out plumes of smoke. The smoke isn't really smoke, though. It takes on the shape of men, powerful working men, creating things like cars, planes, ships, and locomotives. All is in motion, swirling and filling the sky above the hands.

I did that drawing in art class during my last year at Bancroft School and called it *The Industrial Age*.

The subject came from history class, but I don't know why it inspired such fantastic images for me.

My art teacher, who was not a young woman, had a matronly, kindly look and manner that I liked, and she was always very attentive and encouraging. When she first saw my drawing, she put a hand to her face and looked like she wanted to cry. She asked how I created such a thing, and I told her I just saw it in my mind and drew it.

My teacher sat down by me and took my hands and said, "Talent like yours must not go to waste. Promise me, Joe, that you will be an artist."

I didn't say anything because I was so surprised.

"Please, Joe," the teacher said, "Make me this promise. You must be an artist."

"Yes," I said, "I promise."

The teacher called in the principal who admired my drawing and took it away, and I never saw it again.

I kept my promise in ways my teacher and I never imagined, devoting my life to artistry and creativity in images, graphic design, writing, and the living human physique. But when I was young I felt like I broke the promise because I couldn't go on to art school or any kind of school. After the seventh grade I left the education system for good and found full-time work to help support my family. In three years my brother Ben would do the same.

Not a year after I made the promise, I saw my art teacher out on the street. Before she saw me, I ran into a building and hid. I would have died of shame if my teacher saw what I was doing, which was pulling a wagon loaded with groceries. Six days a week, eight o'clock in the morning to eight at night, to midnight or even later on Fridays and Saturdays, I worked as a delivery boy for Badler's Groceries, a store about a mile from home that had customers all over the city. Old Man Badler treated me like dirt—although his wife and brother were nice—and paid me two bucks a week. If I'd let him, he would have chiseled me out of that, trying to dock me for bruising bananas and other nonsense. But I was glad to have that job, and I worked my butt off to keep it.

You could say my real education began there. Even a lousy job like delivering groceries was an education in work. I learned how to push myself and overcome exhaustion. At one or two in the morning I'd be asleep on my feet, but then I'd splash cold water on my face and pull one more wagonload of groceries out onto the street.

I'm not singin' you the blues. I'm just telling how I got to be who I am. People who have tried to explain all the things Joe Weider did forget one simple thing—work. Nobody ever outworked me. Not when I was 12, or 32, or 60. I became the Trainer of Champions because I knew how to inspire great bodybuilders like Reg Park, Dave Draper, Arnold Schwarzenegger, Franco Columbu, Lou Ferrigno, and dozens of other guys to work harder than they ever thought they could. With my Weider Principles of Training, I taught them how to work smart, too. Sweating, straining, and wearing yourself out in the gym are just wasted effort, not work, unless you accomplish something. Work brought me success in publishing, too. I always worked harder and longer than the people who worked for me, and I knew how to get the best work out of them. A lot of guys I hired were characters and oddballs and kids off the street that no other magazine publisher would touch, but I saw the good work they could do.

Note to parents: You've got to make your kids work. I don't care if it's mopping floors, cutting grass, cleaning pools, or making hamburgers. Trying to win your child's love by buying him cars, ski trips and what-all, you betray and hurt him because he won't learn the value of money. Worse than that, he won't learn his own value and fulfill his personal potential. Easy-come, easy-go is an education in worthlessness. And you can't do anything of significance if you're afraid of work.

My real intellectual education also began after I left school. I was frightened of being ignorant and left behind, so I studied the writings of philosophers and great thinkers—Nietzsche, Freud, Schopenhauer, Marx, and so on. I did much more than just suck up what I read. I examined everything, testing it with my own reason and writing out commentaries and criticisms that deepened my understanding and also protected my independence. I worried that someone else's brilliance would absorb me, so I did the absorbing, questioning every sentence and deciding what meaning, if any, it had for me. I think I learned more, faster, than any school kid my age because I didn't have teachers to simplify the ideas and spoon-feed me and slow me down. A school kid could finish his homework and go out with his friends, but I was so ravenous for knowledge that I read and wrote every free minute I had.

My studies kept my mind alive, and they gave me comfort and hope. I remember coming to a chapter written by the German philosopher Schopenhauer where he asked, "What is an intelligent man?" He said it had nothing to do with years of university study and professorships and that sort of thing. Those are the marks of learned men, whose heads are full of other people's ideas but who are not necessarily creative or brilliant. A truly smart man, Schopenhauer wrote, studies humanity on his own, watching other people and what they do and trying to understand their character. This made me feel good because I realized that poverty really didn't mean I had to be poor in knowledge. I could sharpen and improve my mind all on my own.

Pulling my grocery wagon actually made me more of a creative thinker. Every day I walked through the same neighborhoods, seeing the same buildings, with nobody to talk to. To keep from going crazy, I lived in my mind and dreamed up wonderful adventures. Sometimes I was a ship's captain fighting pirates, a brilliant police detective, bold explorer, brave aviator, and on and on. My fantasies were different from other kids', I think, because they were less about killing the bad guys and more about protecting and rescuing people and doing good for the world. And my stories were very long and complicated, more like whole books and movies than simple make-believe. I'd come back to them and work on the plots and characters and even visualize the imaginary worlds.

To this day I do what I did delivering groceries. All my life I've had the ability to go into a contemplative state and see, whole and complete, very complicated things that don't yet exist. In publishing I could close my eyes and see an entire magazine—cover art and teaser lines, inside layouts and ads, all the way to the back page. I always saw projects, beginning to end, before I started them. A good imagination is better than any amount of calculating, weighing possibilities, kicking ideas around at meetings, market studies, and other BS like that. You don't have to stop and waste a lot of time considering things, because you know, just know, in your heart and your guts, what needs to be done. People used to be amazed how fast I made creative decisions, which were usually right, but they would have understood if they could see what I saw.

Sometimes, out on the streets, I came across things of beauty and grace. I'd go out of my way to walk through the wealthy neighborhoods in the hills near Mount Royal, the mountain that overlooks all of Montreal, where the streets were steep and winding and the biggest houses looked like estates and manors in England. Everything seemed so elegant and perfect, down to the little details on the houses and lawns and flowers. Then I'd walk back into the city on Sherbrooke Street and stop to admire the English people coming and going at the entrance of the Ritz, the most elegant hotel in the city. The doorman liked me and let me stand and watch. To the gentlemen and their ladies I was invisible, like a bug, but I admired those people greatly. I especially liked watching the English women, dressed so stylishly and moving like swans, talking and laughing with smooth, perfect voices that sounded like music. And I loved the way the men helped them out of cars, gave them their arms and treated them so graciously, as if they were princesses. Those people were never loud or rude, not even to servants like their drivers and the doorman and bellmen. I memorized what they did and practiced saying things like, "Please, after you, I insist," and "How lovely you look, my dear."

Even as a younger boy I liked formality and imitated it. At age 8 or so, I saw a movie about German aristocrats and then went around standing stiff and straight, making little bows of respect to people, and clicking my heels.

Newsmen and magazine writers always overemphasize the rough parts of my youth. We didn't have war in the streets, and guys didn't beat me up every time I went out the front door. It is true that I, like every other Jewish kid, took a lot of crap. But mostly it was like barking dogs—you'd heard it so long you barely noticed. Once in a while somebody shoved me around and we fought, but that didn't happen often. Generally I saw trouble coming and knew how to avoid it and go about my business. I never was scared out on the street, but I was realistic.

As I got older and reached the age where physical dominance and power really matter, the situation made me more and more frustrated and furious. I got sick and tired of putting my head down and walking away to avoid trouble. I wanted *it* to avoid *me*. I wanted to stand up to bullies and jerks and make them leave me alone, once and for all.

I wanted to defend myself.

I wanted to look like I could defend myself, too.

But I was too skinny.

At age 13, I was 5 feet, 6 inches tall and shooting up toward my adult height of 5 foot 11. But I only weighed about 110 pounds. Skin and bones, that's all I was—I needed to get some muscle.

Wrestling, I thought, could be the answer. Training would build me up, and I could use the moves I learned on the street. I could just see myself throwing a headlock on some loudmouth and twisting him like a pretzel until he begged for mercy.

I went to a Y where they had wrestling, but the coach took one look at me, laughed, and said forget it. He told me I was so thin I'd get hurt.

Had I been in that guy's shoes, I would have seen a kid with desire, guts, and athletic potential worth developing, and I would have trained that kid. I did, in fact, have a talent for wrestling. In a few years I'd be going to the mat with bruisers and street toughs 10 years older than I was, just for the fun of it, and I'd tie them in knots.

The coach was a jerk. I was just a kid, though, and getting turned down hurt.

About the same time I thought about broadening my opportunities. I knew that my seventh-grade education wasn't going to get me anywhere, but I couldn't quit work to finish high school. Trade school looked like a good possibility, even though the thought of working at a trade made me sick at heart. That didn't seem much better than Pa's factory job, but Ma pestered me to find a skill so I could make a decent living, and I didn't see any alternative. When I went to inquire at the trade school office, a man told me I couldn't even apply without two years of high school.

That turndown crushed all my hope. All I wanted in the world was the power to do something, anything, to change my circumstances, but I felt completely powerless. No door was going to open for me, not even a crack.

In the worst moments, depression came over me. I felt ugly, worthless, and all alone. I wanted to die. But I was too strong to give in to moods like that, so I picked myself up and went on working and improving my mind.

Reading as much as I did, I went through a lot of books. I was a pest at the public library and spent a lot of time looking for cheap used books in a store a few blocks from home that sold reading matter of all kinds. I forget what philosophy or history I was looking for the day I saw some old issues of a magazine called *Strength*. Out of curiosity I picked one up and opened it.

Instantly I was mesmerized. Among articles about exercise, healthy eating, and so forth, there were pictures of men with muscles more powerful and impressive than I'd ever imagined. The men lifted enormous weights or posed to show off their physiques, which were like living art. There was also information about how the men developed themselves. *Strength* told me how to change and gain muscle and power, which was pretty much all I wanted in the world.

I stood there for more than an hour poring over the writing and pictures. Then I picked up another issue and gave the owner one cent—old periodicals were two for a penny—and ran home and read my magazines over and over.

Strength was put out by the Milo Barbell Company, the first maker of adjustable plate barbells in the United States. Alan Calvert founded the company in 1902, then started the magazine to tell people about the benefits of exercise and healthy living and promote progressive resistance strength training with weights. The big idea, of course, was to sell more barbells. The name Milo refers to an ancient symbol of the power of progressive training, which, put very simply, means to slowly and incrementally add more pounds to the weights you train with—as the weights get bigger, so do your muscles.

In the sixth century B.C., Milo of Crotona was the champion strong man and wrestler in all of Greece. It was said he gained his strength by lifting the same calf every day. Of course, as the calf kept getting bigger and heavier, Milo got stronger. Even after the animal was fully grown, Milo could lift it to his shoulder and carry it the length of the Olympic stadium. The story shows that the basic principals of strength training have been known for thousands of years. They only seem new.

I kept turning back to one page in my magazines. It had a picture of a young guy walking out of a little lake or pond. He looked relaxed and natural, but his muscles showed in amazing detail—abs in clean individual ridges, biceps and triceps hefty even though the picture showed the arms straight-on, not in profile, and he wasn't flexing them. The legs were something, too—slabs of quads ending in a sharp overhang above the knee, and a nice distinct bulge on the upper-calf *gastrocnemius.* Of course I couldn't name any of the muscles, but that didn't stop them from amazing me. Even more impressive was the overall balance and proportion of the body. The man's physique was just exactly right.

I saw so much of what I wanted in that picture. Artistry. Design. Beauty. Complexity. Most important, I saw manly strength. The man wasn't trying to look tough—in fact, he looked like a very nice guy—but nobody in his right mind would give him trouble.

I had a new hero.

I also had a path to follow to be like my hero. The copy next to the picture said he built his body by lifting weights.

My fixation on that particular picture shows that bodybuilding greats look great, even if you have no idea why.

I was looking at a very young John Grimek—pronounced Grimmek not Grye-meck—then in his early twenties. In those days he was a serious competitive weightlifter who became the 1936 U.S. National Champion and competed in that year's Olympics in Berlin. Unlike a lot of lifters, he also had a perfectly proportioned and defined body and a talent for posing to display it. The editor of *Strength* discovered Grimek and started using his pictures in ads, and he became the physique superstar of his time. Grimek's focus went from lifting to bodybuilding, which was still undeveloped and under the shadow of competitive lifting—where it would stay until I brought it into its own. Still, Grimek was able to advance the sport. He was amazing. In motion you saw lithe athletic power, then he'd pose and become an object of splendor. He could hit knockout poses, one after the other, for 20 minutes without repetition.

Every generation has a superstar, and there are super-superstars who span generations and still excite people. Arnold is one. Grimek another. Pictures of such guys, in magazines, have inspired millions of boys and young men, all over the world, to pick up weights and start building their muscles.

Back in 1998, I wrote these words about seeing the wonderful image of Grimek:

I was mesmerized by that picture. I stared at it for hours, and when I finally went to sleep, in dreams I continued to conjure what my eyes had recorded. Sixty-five years later that image, seared indelibly into my consciousness that night, has never left me. It started me on my journey...

Sad to say, that was part of a memorial tribute. John Grimek, born in 1910, died in 1998.

I suppose it could have been something else. But it was strength and muscles and fitness.

I don't need to write another word for bodybuilders, because they all got the call like I did, probably looking at a magazine. If they're younger than 65, chances are 95 percent it was a Weider magazine.

Actually everybody has had an experience like mine. Think back to a moment when you came across something new—a profession, a sport, an art form—and had a moment of excitement and recognition that changed your life. Whatever it was, it was you.

It makes me mad to have to stop and make explanations like this about my sport and my guys and muscle magazines. But I've had to do it all along.

Pay attention.

There is nothing the least bit weird or perverted about guys looking at images of other guys who have terrific physiques.

If a kid picked up a car magazine and got all excited about building a hot rod and bought the magazine and took it home, nobody would ever assume that the kid was going to play with himself because he wanted to have sex with cars. Would you think that? If not, why in the world would anyone think such things about a guy looking at a muscle magazine? Please, give this a little consideration.

Nowadays it's hard to believe how rare weights once were. For the next few days I ran around Montreal trying to find barbells and dumbbells with no luck whatsoever. In the city and suburbs, there were a few gyms and clubs with weights, but they were tiny and hidden away, and I had no idea they even existed. Most of the merchants I asked didn't know what I was talking about. They thought I meant bells like school bells or cow bells. People who did know told me I didn't want anything to do with weights, because I'd hurt myself, or because lifters were oddballs. I eventually met a man in a hardware store. He couldn't picture what I wanted, so I described the barbells I saw in magazines. He said he didn't know anywhere I could find such a thing for sale, but I might find something I could use in a nearby scrap yard.

The yard, along the railroad tracks, was a graveyard for locomotives and railroad cars. The foreman there seemed amused by what I wanted, and he soldered two old flywheels onto the ends of a rusty iron shaft. For this he refused to take any money.

I ran to find a buddy of mine whose father had a moving van, and we took my new barbell back to Colonial Avenue.

The real initiation isn't the image—it's the iron.

If you're born to the iron, you know it the first time you lift a weight.

I knew it.

My barbell weighed about 75 pounds. Out in the back yard I tried a few simple standing lifts that a kid would know to do—clean, overhead press, curls, rowing. I loved it, and I still love it. Iron isn't dead. It communicates and feels like many, many things.

It feels like the strength you will gain.

It feels like fellowship. Even when you lift alone, you belong to the brotherhood of iron.

It feels like cosmic power. You lift against gravity, the force that holds the universe together, which pulls down toward the core of the planet, which is made of iron.

It feels like personal sovereignty. Even if you don't own one damned thing in the world, your body is yours.

And it feels like free will. You know, because you feel it happening, that you can change your body. If you can do that, you can change yourself and your world.

I didn't dare bring my barbell inside—not when Ma was home, anyway—so I kept it in a little shed at the back of the house. In nice weather I trained in the yard and in wintertime did my lifting in the shed, wearing gloves so my skin wouldn't freeze to the iron.

There was no line between my training and my other pursuits. I read everything I could get my hands on about building strength and bigger muscles with the same skeptical attitude that I brought to the great philosophers. Back then experts peddled all sorts of training systems, some of which were really ridiculous. But I didn't accept anything until my own logic and analysis told me it made sense and—most importantly—that it worked for me.

Even as a kid I understood something that later became one of the Weider Training Principles. These principles, which have been called the foundation of modern bodybuilding, did for workouts what Einstein's relativity theory did for physics. Some of the older training systems had merit as far as they went, but they were linear and rigid like Isaac Newton's physical theories. I knew that the human body was complicated and always changing and designed a system to fit. One key, especially for advanced athletes, is the Instinctive Training Principal. Basically, it says that you should follow my rules—but only until you're ready to make rules of your own. Only you can discover your own ideal way to train, because only you know what's good for you and your body.

No kid ever did so much with one single barbell, but after a while it was like playing a piano with no black keys. The more I could do, the more that I couldn't do drove me nuts. I needed a real adjustable weight set, with barbell and dumbbells and plates I could change for various exercises and to add weight to get bigger and stronger.

The sets advertised in magazines cost around $10, and you had to pay import duty on top of that because they came from the States. I knew I'd never get that kind of money all at once and wrote a letter explaining my situation to George F. Jowett, one of the great old-time strong men and authorities on strength, who sold his writings and equipment through mail order.

I wrote to him partly because he was the best writer and made the most sense of all the muscle men of the day. Jowett, who was a former editor of *Strength,* always seemed like he cared more about truth than selling himself and peddling gimmicks. I especially admired his book *The Key To Might and Muscle,* which is still worth reading. Another reason I wrote to Jowett was that he had a home not far from Montreal in Morrisburg, Ontario. He was an Englishman who lived in Canada before he moved to the U.S. and became internationally famous, but he still spent a lot of time in Ontario and did business there, too.

That must have been some letter I sent to Morrisburg. Jowett later said that it was so earnest and appealing that he couldn't turn me down. He agreed to send me a basic 100-pound outfit on the layaway plan. I would send what I could, and he'd ship the weights when he had the entire price—$7 Canadian, if I remember, which at that time was worth more than $7 American. I paid Jowett the way Ma paid the shoe store. Once a week, on the button, I mailed 50 cents. That was a long couple of weeks after I sent the last money order. Four or five times a day I'd come by the house with my delivery wagon and yell inside, "Did my weights come yet?"

"Nein!" Ma would yell back and tell me to go do my job.

The last time she told me *"Nein!"* she was lying, but for good reason. The weights came on Friday, and Ma hid them because if I knew they were there I wouldn't come to the evening *Shabbat* meal with the family and I'd violate the Sabbath on Saturday. Even though she didn't have much religious feeling, Ma respected the old traditions.

After I finally got my weights, I lifted until every muscle in my body ached and shook and I could hardly pick up the bare bar.

George F. Jowett later wrote these words about that day, one of the best in all my life: "Such is the happiness of spontaneous, unadulterated youth when it is fired with a clean worthy ambition."

Nobody writes like that any more, do they?

I recently received a letter from a lifelong bodybuilder and reader of my magazines named Peter Kennedy who lives in Georgia. Back in 1960, when he was 14 and my publishing company was based in New Jersey, he wrote to me asking if I could send him damaged or worn copies of my weight training courses because he didn't have the money to pay full price. In the recent letter, he writes that he was amazed and delighted to receive the complete Weider System training courses and materials, all brand-new. Full price for the package was $35—equivalent to $225 today. I didn't charge him a dime, though, and to this day the guy is grateful.

Even better than his thanks were these words in his letter: "Had it not been for Joe Weider I probably would have followed the path of others with smoking, drinking, no exercise and poor diet. Instead I have followed the natural lifestyle of physical culture."

I did things like sending that kid that stuff all the time, always responding to genuine interest and need among bodybuilders whether they were champions or kids starting out. This doesn't mean I'm a saint—it means I'm a bodybuilder. Ours is a generous community, particularly to beginners who show real commitment and enthusiasm. For the same reasons Jowett couldn't say no to me, I couldn't say no to that kid.

Jowett, by the way, got more than my thanks. He also got a job as consulting editor on my first magazine where I showcased his writings and gave him ad space to sell his materials. He told his version of the story I just told you, about how I got my first weight set, in the May 1947 issue of *Your Physique* magazine.

At first my mother hated my lifting and bodybuilding. She never did get to like it, even after it made Ben and me world famous. Almost right away, though, she recognized that everything was changing for me.

Ma started saying to people, "Joe was born with a barbell in his hands."

CHAPTER TWO

RABBI JOE

Joe Weider

A few years before I got that first barbell, I had a magnifying glass. For a while I looked at bugs and leaves, but then I used the glass to focus sunlight down to a tiny point of brightness and heat. This fascinates kids more than making things look big.

The glass showed me something important about life. It made me realize that unfocused energy is weak, but concentrated on a single point it becomes a very powerful force—the smaller the point of focus, the greater the power. What was true of the sun's energy was true of mine, too. I said to myself that I would concentrate all my passion and efforts exactly where I wanted and never let anything dissipate or go to waste.

I would be like a magnifying glass.

Lifting appeals to those who are solitary by nature. Most young guys start out like I did, alone and at home. In my day there wasn't much choice, because lifters were so few and far between and there were practically no training facilities. But there's also a psychological aspect—people take up strength training for reasons that are much more personal and particular than the reasons they get into basketball or hockey or other mainstream group athletics. In his autobiography Arnold Schwarzenegger wrote that team sports didn't satisfy him because they didn't bring the individual recognition that he needed. Solo training met my inner needs, too.

Isolation explains why muscle magazines are so important in our world—more so, I think, than any other kind of publication for athletes. You don't need to read and look at pictures to get into baseball or football, because you can learn to play with your friends or at school. Fans can go to games and follow the action on TV and in the papers. But bodybuilding depends on specialty publications.

If I didn't pick up that back issue of *Strength* in the bookstore I wouldn't have dreamed that men with physiques like John Grimek's even existed. I would have had no idea that I should lift weights to build my own muscles or known where to buy weights and what to do with them. That magazine was my only window to a world that I didn't know existed. These days there's much more public awareness about strength training and the fitness lifestyle in general. But magazines still are the only clear windows on bodybuilding, which the mainstream sports press continues to look down on and ignore. If you don't read muscle magazines, you won't understand our sport.

I didn't mind training alone—just like I read and wrote alone and delivered groceries alone—because I was so focused on my thoughts. Even at home with Ma yelling and no privacy for anybody, I could wall everybody out. On the other hand, I sometimes had a burning desire to communicate. When I came across things that other people needed to know, I'd tell them. Often I think I should have been a teacher because of the way I loved to simplify and interpret important ideas so others could understand. I was good at it, too.

My younger sister Freda talks about how I'd make her sit at the dining room table and then lecture her on philosophers like Nietzsche. When an idea really took hold, maybe I was a bit of a dictator, but I didn't lecture. I explained things, that's all, so they would make sense to a young girl.

Pa gave us kids nicknames according to our individual characteristics.

Ben, a much more light-hearted kid than I was, Pa called *Benchuk*—Sweet Ben.

I was *Rabbiyoss.*

Rabbi Joe.

Some time around 1960, after the end of my first marriage I took my new wife-to-be, Betty, up to Montreal to meet my family. At the time, Ben owned a beautiful cabin cruiser, and we all went boating on the St. Lawrence River and had a wonderful time. The whole family, especially Ma, was crazy about Betty, and they all noticed that I was a changed man.

"Why Joe," Freda said, "You have teeth!"

"What do you mean?" I asked her.

"I never saw you smile before," she said.

My sister wasn't exaggerating. All the old family pictures show me looking serious and far away, like I was seeing into other places and times—which as a matter of fact I was. I never developed the habit of smiling. Why would I? Ma and Pa weren't smilers. Life was a serious business for them as it was for me as far back as I can remember.

Sigmund Freud would say that I lacked what he termed the "pleasure principle," because I lived like a grownup during the years when kids are supposed to play around and have fun. There are critical times in life for developing certain behaviors, and if you miss one of those times you can never fully develop the behavior. This is true for animals, too. If a kitten doesn't learn how to hunt and kill from his mother, he'll never be much good at it. The same goes for cats learning to fight—or, in my case, for a kid being playful and carefree. Once the critical stage passed me by, that was that.

Being serious didn't mean I was always down in the dumps. My work always brought me tremendous joy, and I saw humor in things and liked to make other people laugh. René Leger, the first champion bodybuilder I trained, still talks about how I could crack him up. And I've always sought the company of people who are full of the pleasure principle. One of the reasons I first took to Arnold was the kick I got watching the fun he had—smiling and bubbling over with enjoyment and life—just being Arnold. But fun and games were never my strong suit.

Because of my new muscles, other kids started calling me Tarzan. The bullies quit picking on me and wanted to be my pals. The girls looked at me in a new way that made me feel funny, and the grownups treated me like a young man worthy of attention and respect.

More important, though, was the change in my inner being. All along I had felt helpless, doomed by my lack of education and opportunity. But then bodybuilding changed me—body, mind, and soul—and altered my circumstances. For the first time I knew that doors could open for Joe Weider, instead of slamming in my face. I sensed that I could control my own destiny just as I controlled my body. This set me free and made the whole world look better and brighter. Nobody realized it back then, but scientists now recognize the powerful psychological effects of exercise. People can get as much out of a good workout as talking to an analyst. Iron is better than Prozac.

If you want to understand my zeal, my lifelong commitment to building muscles and fitness, you must understand the miracles these things worked for me. They changed my life—and maybe even saved my life.

Anybody who has built his body knows I'm telling the truth. Human beings, both female and male, respond in deep instinctual ways to muscles. Evolution made us that way because, for most of our history, physical power and prowess meant survival. The weak depended on strong individuals, and alpha males, who lived or died by their own strength, also needed strong allies in hunting and warfare. Up to a few hundred years ago, battles were physical contests fought with weapons that weak men couldn't even pick up. Muscle power also counted in times of peace. The strong farmer could harvest more food for his family and help the community prosper, and strong tradesmen and laborers did more productive work. We depend on machines now, but muscles still are like magnets to us.

What humans need for survival, they also perceive as beautiful. The great tradition of Western art is the depiction of powerful men. Ancient Grecian urns show athletes and muscle men in action. Greek and Roman statues celebrate strength. God and Adam on the Sistine Chapel ceiling look like they spent some time in the gym, as does Michelangelo's David. Go to Rockefeller Center in New York City and take a look at the two-ton bronze statue of Atlas holding the world. The guy's all lean muscle mass, with terrific ab definition. Atlas is a bodybuilder—he has to be or he wouldn't be strong enough to carry the world.

Word went around town about this Jewish kid from The Main who was training like crazy in back of his house. When I was 15, Harvey Hill, president of the weightlifting club at Verdun, sent Eugene Tremblay, another lifter from the club, to see what I was up to. Eugene, who became a buddy, took me back to Verdun, a town next to Montreal and maybe six miles from where I lived. At the club I amazed the guys with a military press of 145 pounds. That was five pounds more than my bodyweight, but I did it with ease. Harvey and the other lifters invited me to train with them and talked me into entering a citywide competition. I did and came in second in the lightweight division. When I was still 15, a local promoter and judge of strength asked to see what I could do, and I impressed the hell out of him by performing a two-handed Continental jerk of 225 pounds at a body weight of only 145. In Continental lifts you brought the weight to waist height, then boosted it to the shoulders, rather than making a single explosive movement like the clean or snatch. The Continental style suited old-time European lifters who were huge, big-bellied guys but also strong as bulls. And it allowed you to handle heavier weights. It's a shame the Continental style died out.

Some historic background is needed here:

Back then weightlifting was the only organized muscle sport. You could get involved at clubs like Verdun, and there were officially sanctioned competitions from local all the way up to the world championships and the Olympic Games. If you were serious about strength training and wanted to compete, lifting was what you did.

Bodybuilding as we now know it—training to create powerful, aesthetically pleasing musculature, with the opportunity to compete in physique contests sanctioned by bodybuilding's own, independent federation—did not exist. It wouldn't exist until I, with the help of my brother Ben, brought it into being.

In the 1930s, the very beginnings of the modern exercise and strength movements still were living memories. I personally knew the guys who knew the guys who planted the seeds back in the 1800s. As a boy in England, my friend George Jowett was inspired by seeing Eugen Sandow, a German who toured the world performing feats of strength and displaying his physique. Sandow had phenomenal power and, unlike most famous strong men of the day, he wasn't built like a truck. He looked like a god, and the high point of each performance was his posing, which he raised to an art form, adding music and special stage effects.

Sandow was a huge hit at the 1893 World's Fair in Chicago and in vaudeville shows, but he was more than an entertainer. He tried to educate the masses about the benefits of exercise and healthy living with pamphlets, books, and his own magazine of physical culture, an old-time word for bodybuilding. He invented and sold exercise equipment and trained pupils at the Sandow Institute of Physical Culture in London, where women could work out as well as men. And in London in 1901, Sandow staged The Great Competition, the world's first physique contest with any kind of class and showmanship. One of the judges was Sir Arthur Conan Doyle, writer of the Sherlock Holmes stories.

If you know anything at all about Joe and Ben Weider, you see a lot of threads here that we picked up. The difference is that we wove everything together and made it all last—we made it pay, too, so bodybuilding could get bigger and better and spread to every corner of the world. Most of what Sandow created died out in his lifetime. Still, we recognize and honor our debt to him. Bodybuilding's ultimate prize, given to the winner of our annual Joe Weider Mr. Olympia contest, is a replica of the beautiful little statue given to the winner of Sandow's Great Competition. It depicts Sandow in his muscular prime holding an old-time barbell with globular weights. The bodybuilders and the guys who produced the Olympia contest said the trophy ought to be a statue of me, but I wanted Sandow the Great and Immortal.

Sandow died when I was about eight years old. I wish he'd lived longer so we could have met. Some call me the Father of Bodybuilding. If it's true, Sandow was certainly the grandfather.

Others also made advances in the science of muscle building. Around 1900, Dr. Theodore Siebert in Germany and Dr. Vladislav Krajewski, physician to the czar of Russia, developed systems of progressive resistance weight training and published them. Alan Calvert's method, distributed with Milo Barbell weight sets and publicized in *Strength,* was pretty much a copy of Siebert's. This became Bob Hoffman's method after he started his own magazine, *Strength and Health* and then acquired Milo. It was the same system I began with, then revolutionized. In the classic old formula, you trained three times a week, Monday-Wednesday-Friday, with exercises to build all the muscle groups, working your way up from sets of eight repetitions. When you could do a given number of reps—usually 12 or 15—you added five or 10 pounds and started over. Siebert and Krajewski also promoted healthy living, rest, and diet as vital parts of training. It seems incredible that such simple, self-evident stuff was ever new to people, but those were really the Dark Ages in terms of exercise and health.

In 1905, Bernarr McFadden, the great American publisher and crusader for fitness and healthy living, held the first big physique contest this side of the Atlantic. McFadden put out a magazine called *Physical Culture,* and he ran his contests in New York City through the '20s. In New York in the late '40s, when he was pushing 80 and I was on my way up, McFadden sought me out. I'll never forget our meeting and the things he said to me, which I'll share later. McFadden was another visionary and pioneer, like Sandow, but his accomplishments didn't last. By the time I picked up my first barbell, his physique contests were gone. He never managed to make bodybuilding and fitness really pay, either. Though he made his name promoting exercise and health, McFadden made his fortune publishing huge general magazines like *True Story, True Detective,* and *Photoplay,* the biggest sellers of their day. He had newspapers, too. In terms of how he made his money, McFadden was more like William Randolph Hearst than Weider. We're the first, and only, to build our name and a worldwide business and sports empire on the same foundation—bodybuilding, fitness, and health.

When I was a kid getting into the iron game, all these things that others had started were lying around, mostly dormant. Bodybuilding was a sleeping giant. It needed somebody to wake it up and take it to the world. There were signs, too, of the coming fitness revolution, just like there were signs of the Russian revolution when Ma and Pa were kids in Europe. The revolution needed a leader.

The way things turned out, I guess what was needed was Joe Weider, but the personal revolution must come before the world revolution. For the first few years I wasn't thinking so much about history or destiny. I just knew that I was doing something that excited me more than anything ever had, which was changing my life. I trained my heart out, read everything I could, and got bigger, better built, and stronger. Pretty soon I was setting local lifting records for my age and size.

If you're a peace-loving sort of guy, muscles keep the peace. As I said, the neighborhood bullies laid off right away. I didn't have problems anywhere else, either. To save streetcar fare I sometimes walked to the weightlifting club in Verdun, which meant I had to go through what we called the "deaf and dumb neighborhood," one of the worst parts of town, where anything went, and some of the guys hanging around were killers. But nobody bothered me.

One time, though, trouble came to my own front door.

I was inside the house reading when the doorbell rang and I answered it. There was Ben with this mean-looking French guy.

"Joe," my brother blurted out, "He wants to fight you. I told him that you could beat him up, but he says he can lick anybody."

Later Ben explained that the guy jumped him on the street and wouldn't leave him alone. Ben, who was smaller and younger, said go away, my big brother can knock the hell out of you. And the guy said, "Okay, take me to your brother!"

This is all I need, I said to myself. I told the guy we didn't have any reason to fight, but he started shoving and getting really fresh and took a swing at me. I had no choice but to let him have it.

After I hit him, the guy fell flat on his back. He had blood on his face and didn't move a muscle. Ben and I were sure he was dead. We'd never seen anybody knocked out cold before—I'd never even punched anybody before. This was horrible! We were scared to death about what would happen because I killed somebody, but then a neighbor who saw everything laughed and got a bucketful of water and threw it on the Frenchman, who woke up and went away.

I must have packed a wallop, but it brought me no pleasure because I hated violence of any kind and found fist fighting particularly distasteful and stupid. To win you had to pulverize somebody else's face, which was a mess, and maybe you got your own face messed up, too.

Wrestling, on the other hand, was different. Wrestlers didn't beat each other bloody or try to do harm, and a match was over when one guy signaled that he gave up. This struck me as an intelligent, civilized contest of manly strength and skill, like chess or billiards but with muscles. In my late teens I got into wrestling and really loved it.

I met a younger Jewish kid from the neighborhood named Rusty Halpert, and we hit it off right away. Rusty, whose given name was Irving, read all the strength magazines and wrote away for courses. He also had a nice set of weights from Bob Hoffman's York Barbell Company in Pennsylvania. Rusty's mother, unlike Ma, didn't mind if he lifted at home, so we started training together in the kitchen of the upstairs apartment where Rusty lived. The Halperts, who were somewhat better off than the Weiders, owned their apartment building, and Mr. Halpert had a bicycle shop on St. Lawrence Boulevard.

Rusty was small and slight, but he worked like crazy and became my steady training partner. Everybody ought to have one. The companionship is fun, and you can accomplish a lot more with somebody spotting for you and yelling at you to squeeze out a few more reps. I took the leadership role, but working out with Rusty still did me a lot of good. My very first "muscle man" pictures show me flexing and posing in front of the huge coal stove in the Halperts' kitchen. In the pictures I'm still pretty light, but for a change the bumps are sticking out more than the bones. You see the start of real muscular development.

We might have kept training in Rusty's kitchen, except one day I attempted a snatch with the barbell really loaded and dropped it. What a noise that thing made. The impact actually damaged the ceiling of the apartment downstairs.

After that, Rusty's mother threw us out, and we took our weights to Halpert's Bicycles and General Repair where Rusty's father made us very welcome. He liked our training because he had been a champion athlete back in Latvia and once won a medal for swimming around an island in the St. Lawrence River. We set up in a storeroom adjoining the bike shop. Mr. Halpert made a squat rack for us by welding upright iron bars to a couple of heavy clutch plates, and we did our bench presses lying on a wooden box.

My jobs still were miserable. After I outgrew delivering groceries I found a job busing tables and helping out in the kitchen in a restaurant called Shap's. There were four Shap's, all in our part of town, and the young people loved them because they stayed open all hours and served lighter fare, sodas, and ice cream treats. Ben later worked at a different Shap's than I did, as did Vicky Uzar, my first love.

At all my jobs people liked me because I worked hard and took pride in my work and minded my own business, but I also had to put up with some real jerks. One time at Shap's, about three in the morning, I was eating the little sack lunch that Ma made me. The night manager picked up some blueberry pie that didn't sell during the day and said, "Hey Joe, how would you like a nice piece of pie for dessert?" Would I ever—I never got stuff like that. "Come here, I'll give it to you," the manager said. Then right in front of me he turned over the plate and dumped the pie into the garbage. "Help yourself," he told me.

I kept my mouth shut because I didn't want to get fired, but why would somebody do such a thing? I wouldn't treat a dog like that.

The more I look back, the more I like the kid I used to be. I worked day and night and never complained or felt sorry for myself or got into trouble. I was honest and very devoted to my family and my home. Except for 50 cents that I kept for myself, I handed my entire weekly earnings over to Ma, and I did my best to look out for my brothers and Freda. Ben, unlike me, had a healthy dose of the pleasure principle, and I didn't want him to be led astray. Once, when I heard he was with some guys in a pool hall, I went and dragged him out. I didn't want him hanging around there because in those days pool was a pastime for bums.

Even by the standards of the day, which were far more strict than now, I was a very straight-laced kid, and people made jokes about it. One time at Shap's the other guys said I had to go out on a delivery. It was one in the morning and that wasn't my job, but I said okay, and they gave me a box with donuts, cups of coffee, and a few packs of cigarettes. I went to the address I was given, and a little observation hatch in the door opened just like in old-time gangster movies.

A woman asked what I wanted, and I said I was delivering the order somebody at that address made. The door swung open, and there, just inside, a dozen girls stood wearing negligees and looking me over. Some of them weren't much older than I was.

I remember thinking to myself, "Wow, this family has a lot of daughters."

I didn't catch on to what kind of house that was until the girls took me back to the kitchen and one started pawing at me and making lewd remarks about paying me in service rather than cash. I was in shock. I never even imagined young ladies spoke and carried on like that. I was still in shock back at the restaurant, where the rest of the crew laughed themselves silly. The experience left me feeling very funny. For the rest of the shift I washed my hands over and over.

I kept that kind of innocence all through my teenage years, long after other guys my age were out raising hell.

Meanwhile, I needed more money and a better chance to get ahead. But my God, did I have a terrible time finding my next job. For weeks I walked around the city sticking my head into every single place that might need help. Stores, offices, restaurants, I didn't care what kind of business, or what kind of work. But I heard "No" a thousand times, and every "No" pushed me deeper into depression and despair.

I went around the whole city once and then started around again. Downtown on Saint Catherine Street, I went into a restaurant called Murray's, which any old-time Montrealer remembers. The partners who owned Murray's got their start feeding railroad men and lumberjacks, then came to the city and opened a restaurant famous for serving good, solid food. Everybody went there from socialites on down.

I walked into Murray's just before the lunch rush, and the guy in charge was frantic.

"Our goddam sandwich man is gone. I need somebody to take his place," he said.

I told him I was ready to start. Whatever he asked me—Was I an experienced short-order cook? Was I fast? Had I been a sandwich man before?—I said, "Yes," even though the truth was "No." This wasn't dishonesty; it was desperation.

A few minutes later I stood at my station trying to fill the orders that the waitresses brought in faster and faster. Another cook saw that I was in over my head and said, "Joe, just do what I tell you, you'll be fine." By the end of lunch, thanks to his help and my ability to pick things up fast, I looked like the experienced sandwich man I said I was. That other cook said he helped me because he recognized a brother athlete. He was a Czech immigrant and very active in the Montreal *Sokol,* a Czech nationalistic gymnastics and fitness society much like the Germans' *Turnverein.* We became very good friends, and he even encouraged me to go out with his sister, but by then my heart belonged to Vicky.

After a couple weeks, the boss called me in to fill out my application form, which I was too busy to do when I got hired. He questioned me and then filled in the blanks. When he asked me my religious affiliation I said, naturally, "Jewish," but he shook his head and said if he wrote that down I'd lose my job because Murray didn't hire Jews. He said, too, that he really wanted to keep me.

"Do you mind if I just put you down as Roman Catholic?" he asked.

I told him, "I don't care what you put down, so long as I have a job."

A waitress at Murray's once came to me with tears in her eyes, and I asked what was wrong. She said some customers bawled her out for some little mistake that wasn't her fault. Men would get abusive for any reason at all, she said, and it hurt her feelings. I felt for her, I really did. Customers sometimes gave waitresses guff just because they could get away with it, and it made me furious. The poor girls deserved better than that. They were so nice.

My friends at Murray's were mostly Irish, and I learned to appreciate their people and culture, especially the sweet songs they sang, which I'd sing too. All my life I've been been drawn to Irish people, and I still love an Irish tenor doing a number like "Kathleen":

I'll take you home again, Kathleen.
Across the ocean wild and wide…

Thinking about that old tune has me feeling sentimental.

At age 17 I won my division in the Montreal City Weightlifting Championships and then placed second in the Quebec Provincial Championships.

The trophy I took home from the city champs showed me my ultimate direction in life, my destiny. Without it you might be reading somebody else's story.

The fateful moment happened some time after the actual contest when I saw a photo shot in our backyard. In the picture stood Pa wearing his one and only good suit and holding my trophy in his hands. The trophy was just a cheap, little loving cup, but Pa held it like the most precious, wondrous object. He didn't smile in the picture but you could see an inner glow brighter than any smile. He was completely and utterly happy and full of pride—full of love, too.

The feeling I got, looking at the picture, is the feeling I still get today across all the miles and years and the boundary between life and death. Pa loved his son with every fiber of his being. Somewhere he still does. God knows I still love him.

That picture of Pa set me on fire. I knew I had to do something much greater and significant that would be truly worthy of Pa's pride and his love, something bigger than my own athletic achievement and glory. What I had done to that point had mostly been for my own benefit. What I did in the future would change the world for everyone's benefit.

"I will make the Weider name famous," I said.

For many years Pa was the only person in the world who believed me.

I knew I had a mission before I knew what form it would take. But I never doubted—not for a moment—that I was destined to spread the word about the great, transforming power of strength training, exercise, and healthy living.

I became like the Apostle Paul. Before Jesus appeared to him on the road to Damascus, he was just an ordinary businessman who would have been forgotten 2,000 years ago if he hadn't been touched by something bigger and better than himself.

Like Paul, I preached to whoever would listen.

Rusty and I mostly worked out by ourselves, but other guys came by now and again, and the storeroom of Halpert's Bicycles became the center of weight training and physical culture on The Main. Young as I was, I became the training guru. I loved to teach and inspire guys to train.

A cab driver who knew me saw a young guy shoveling snow on the street who had the most powerful arms he'd ever seen.

"There's somebody in town you need to meet," the cabbie said to the guy with the arms, who was René Leger, then about 18 years old. He and his father worked as a team clearing streets for the city, and nobody could touch them for throwing snow. Paid by the truckload, the Legers made almost a dollar a day—apiece!—a lot more than most people made, including me.

The minute he walked into the bike shop, I could see René was something special. He wasn't a great big man, but he had the foundation on which to build a wonderful physique—pleasing proportions, heavy musculature across the arms, wide shoulders, and nice taper down to a narrow waist. Without such basics, which are gifts of genetics—or God—a guy will never get from good to great. René also had a chiseled profile and a good head of hair. Strong-back work gave René a great start on conditioning, too. I forget how many pounds he lifted for me, but I remember being very impressed.

"You're strong, René, very strong," I said to him.

Then and there I started to train the first in my unbroken string of champion bodybuilders. In 1946, after he came back from the army, René won the first contest that Ben and I organized and became Mr. Canada. He also placed respectably in competition in the U.S. and was pictured in my magazines and others.

Early on, René beat me in a physique contest and cost me a title, which shows the rewards and hazards of being a teacher. If you're really good at it, your students go on to glory that may outshine yours.

In that crazy little gym in the bike shop I earned the first title I would give myself for promotional purposes—Trainer of Champions Since 1936.

Later, of course, I became the Master Blaster.

A person who didn't know better would have said that René looked great as he was, but there's a world of difference between a handsome guy with nice muscles from swinging a shovel or an axe and a trained bodybuilder in top condition. The toughest, best-built guy you know would look foolish up on stage at one of our contests. Nobody comes in off the street with a bodybuilder's head-to-toe balance and proportion and symmetry. Heavy work builds muscles in some, but not all, places. And it can't build to the limit, because it doesn't isolate muscles and work them individually to the point of exhaustion, which is what it takes for maximum growth. Only an expertly designed weight-training regimen can take a body to its ultimate size and perfection. This training is merciless and exhausting, but it's artistry, too, which begins with imagination—both the trainer and trainee must first see a body that doesn't exist. Then they must take the medium in which they work—I'm talking about muscle bulk—and chisel and shape to create a physique that's both massive and fine. Training is strategic, it's tactical, it strengthens weak points, and makes inborn strengths overwhelming. It takes hours of gym time at a stretch and rules every other hour of the day because absolutely everything that affects the body—nutrition, sleep, mental attitude—is part and parcel.

I'm crazy for training, can you tell? Even so young I loved bringing other guys to full potential as much I loved building my own power and physique.

Going into a gym still excites me. I hear the voices, the weights clanging, and I feel like I'm home, among guys I understand. If you're somewhere straining and yelling to get out one more rep, you're my kind of people.

René, by the way, is still going strong. He lives on the outskirts of Montreal where he hauls scrap wood and works on his house and landscaping. He looks great and could easily lie 15 years off his age. My old pal Rusty works out at the Y in Toronto, where he now lives. Here in California, my friend Bob Delmonteque, a lifelong devotee of bodybuilding and healthy living, has a build a 45-year-old could be proud of. I'm currently recovering from very extensive back surgery, which my doctor said I never would have survived if I weren't so damned strong. The doctor told me he's never seen anybody my age in this kind of shape. Of course I owe it all to my lifetime devotion to bodybuilding.

There can be no doubt: Bodybuilding makes for a longer, better life. Old bodybuilders are younger than their years.

When I was 18, a new gym opened in the city, and I started to train there, too. The owner was Johnny B. Young, who later became the first Canadian sent away for life for being a habitual criminal. By the time that happened, in 1950, he was linked to selling dope, gambling, every kind of corruption, and even murders. A solid-built guy about 5 foot 9, Johnny made an impression much bigger than his actual size. Only an idiot would have crossed him. In the confines of his gym, though, he didn't act tough. He was always really nice to me and proud because my wins in weightlifting reflected well on his gym. Whatever he did on the outside, Johnny and I got along because he was a true devotee of strength training and athletics.

The name of that place—Young's Studio of Physical Culture—was a lot fancier than the reality. It was in a red-light district in a seedy old part of town near the river. The hookers who saw me walking to Young's would yell from the windows, "Hey, athlete. Want to come in and have a good time?" but I paid no attention. The gym, up on the third floor, had punching bags and a ring for boxers and a mat for wrestlers as well as weights. You met all kinds up there—guys from Johnny's crowd, cops, politicians—and everybody got along fine. At Young's I got into wrestling and beat pretty much everybody, including thugs I probably should have been scared of, but I was too innocent to know the difference, and they didn't mind.

Johnny said to me one day, "Joe, how would you like to make more than a hundred bucks this week?"

I'd like it a lot—a hundred dollars was 20 times my weekly pay at Murray's!

Before I said yes, though, I wanted to know what was involved. Johnny told me I was a good strong guy who looked like I could handle myself, and he wanted me to help out some friends of his by standing near the voting booths on election day. Some of his other guys would be there, too, to make sure there was no trouble. I turned him down because the deal seemed fishy, which it was. Johnny, I later found out, provided muscle to the dirtiest politicians in the city. He sent his crew to scare people into voting the way he said and to beat up anybody who objected. Some of his guys went to the voting places carrying baseball bats.

To Johnny's credit, he never asked me to work for him again, and he didn't hold my refusal against me. I went on training with him and his gang, who always treated me with friendship and respect. You'd never have dreamed they were dangerous criminals.

About the same time I went to an art school that was looking for models. My weight was getting up around 170 pounds, all solid muscle, so I looked really good, and I thought what the heck, I can do this. I met the art teacher and stripped down to my trunks.

"I like your body, and I like you," the teacher said, "But I don't like your shorts."

"What I am supposed to wear?" I asked.

"Nothing," he said, "You pose nude, and we give you $5 for an afternoon."

I wouldn't take it because I refused to be naked in public. The teacher said he'd give me $2.50 to pose in a G-string, but I wouldn't do that either, because I was too shy and too clean-cut to be almost naked.

Even the Communists wanted me.

On a nice warm day I sat on a park bench reading *Das Kapital* by Karl Marx, the social philosopher who founded socialism and communism. As I said, I studied influential individuals on all sides. A guy handing out handbills in the park saw me reading and struck up a conversation about Marxism. He invited me to a meeting that night where he said I could hear lectures on political philosophy and join in discussions. I went because it sounded interesting and I thought I might learn something.

The session turned out to be indoctrination, not education. First we heard a talk on dialectic materialism, the foundation of Marxist political philosophy and the Communism system. Most of the people in the room were Reds and took it all in, but I questioned and challenged the lecturer, who didn't know what to do.

This caught the attention of the man in charge, who took me aside after the meeting.

The man in charge was Fred Rose, who later became the first and only member of the Communist Party to be elected to the Canadian Parliament. But then he got caught spying for the Soviet Union and thrown in prison.

Rose was a heck of a spieler, I'll give him that. He told me how brilliant and analytical I was and how good in front of a crowd and what a bright future I could have in the Party hierarchy and politics. He wanted to put me to work handing out leaflets and talking to people about the benefits of the socialist system. Then, he said, he'd sponsor me as a candidate in a local council election.

I told him I'd never work for Communism because I disagreed with it, especially the Marxist doctrine of "historical determinism." In a nutshell, the doctrine says men can't make history because history makes men. I knew from my studies and my observations of the world that certain individuals have the power to change the course of events and put the whole world on a new track. I challenged Rose to explain to me how Hitler came into power and altered everything? And Stalin? And Lenin and Alexander the Great and Jesus Christ and Napoleon and every other guy who came out of nowhere and rocked the world? I asked him if he really believed such individuals were merely products of history—not makers of history—and he couldn't answer. But my arguing made him try even harder to recruit me for the Party, which he said needed powerful thinkers like me. Finally he gave up and said if I ever changed my mind, the Party had a spot for me. By then it was three o'clock in the morning.

For me, an argument like that was recreation, like wrestling with the brain and mouth. Right before World War II people were agitated and politicized every which way, and I used to take on all comers—left-wingers, right-wingers, even Fascists and out-and-out Nazis. I could argue for anything better than the true believers and then turn around and argue against it.

And I knew all along that most of what people were yelling about was bull.

I am living proof that Marxist determinism is nonsense.

If the historic times and economic circumstances shaped me and made me—instead of vice versa—fitness and health wouldn't be multibillion-dollar industries. You wouldn't have heard of Joe Weider or Ben Weider or, for that matter, Arnold Schwarzenegger, because I wouldn't have brought him to America and coached him and set him up.

If I were lucky, I'd own a restaurant, and Arnold would own a gym in Austria.

"Joe, won't lifting make me muscle-bound, so I can't play hockey?"

"Joe, what kind of food should I eat?"

"Joe, I hate squats. Isn't there something else I can do?"

"How do I get bigger arms? Should I take vitamins? If Charles Atlas says I'll get big and strong like him with Dynamic Tension, why should I bother with weights?"

Joe, Joe, Joe...So many people came to me for advice, and I wanted to reach a public much wider than the guys I coached in person. My dream, then and always, was to tell the world about bodybuilding and fitness and good nutrition for health and well-being. At first I wanted to disseminate this vital information by putting out pamphlets and training courses and selling them mail order like Jowett and Atlas and other big names. But to do that I'd need to pay for printing and advertising in advance, which I couldn't afford. Whatever I did, my up-front costs couldn't be more than $7, the total of my cash savings. So I thought up a way to get into publishing even though I was broke.

I'd start a magazine and pay for the first issue by pre-selling subscriptions.

CHAPTER THREE

MAGAZINE MAN

Joe Weider

I really can't explain where I got the nerve to go into publishing. Maybe I was nuts. Maybe I just didn't know any better. What you don't know can't hurt you, the old saying goes. Actually, what you don't know can do you a lot of good.

I was too ignorant to know I was doing the impossible.

I went through back issues of *Strength and Health* magazine and wrote down the names and addresses of every Canadian in the Pen Pals section where guys posted contact information so other lifters and bodybuilders could get in touch. I stayed north of the border because the magazine would be for Canadians. Our population was tiny compared to the U.S., and we got very little attention in *Strength and Health*, by far the dominant North America muscle mag.

There's something funny about where I got my mailing list that I should stop and explain. *Strength and Health's* publisher was Bob Hoffman, then in his early forties. In about five years he would declare a war on Joe and Ben Weider that lasted until his death in 1985. Long before that we beat him on every front, but we never had peace.

I'd rather keep Hoffman out of my story because I don't like conflict and badmouthing people. But this would be like David not mentioning Goliath, or like leaving the Nazis out of a history of World War II. If he could have, Hoffman would have squashed me like a bug when I started to get successful and threaten his position. For years and years he did everything in his power to smear my name and tear down my reputation and discredit all that Ben and I did for the sake of bodybuilding.

Hoffman was an egomaniac, a faker, a hypocrite—this is not to mention an anti-Semitic, anti-Black, anti-foreigner bigot.

On the other hand, Bob Hoffman was a towering figure and one of the heroes of my youth. Some call him the Father of American Weightlifting. To my mind the title belongs to George Jowett, who organized the first North American lifting association, but Hoffman picked up where Jowett left off and pushed Olympic lifting as faithfully and fanatically as I would champion bodybuilding. He also became an important supporter of the U.S. weightlifting team.

In spite of claims he made, Hoffman was never much of a lifter himself. After fighting in World War I—he never quit bragging about his heroics—he started working out with weights to bulk up and build his strength. He got the bug for the iron game and set up a training center for lifters in York, Pennsylvania, where he owned a factory that made oil burners. In York he ran a club that became the core of the U.S. weightlifting team and gave athletes jobs in his company. In 1932, he began to make barbells in his factory and started *Strength and Health* magazine to tell the world about competitive lifting, strength training, and the glories of Bob Hoffman. George Jowett came over from *Strength,* which was on its last legs, to be Hoffman's editor. It finally went under in 1935 when Milo Barbell declared bankruptcy. Hoffman bought what was left of Milo and folded it into his York Barbell Company.

While the Depression wiped out other guys who might have challenged him, Hoffman became a sort of colossus, and York, Pennsylvania, became the capital of muscles and strength. There Hoffman ruled over America's best lifters, published the only muscle magazine that really mattered, and used it to promote York Barbells and his training methods, which, as I earlier indicated, were pretty much warmed-over Alan Calvert. The Depression didn't hurt Hoffman a bit because his oil burner business kept bringing in money. Even in the worst of times, people need to stay warm.

Right when I decided to go into publishing, Hoffman did something that made our future conflict pretty much inevitable. He kidnapped bodybuilding, the sport my brother and I would champion, and locked it up. He held it for ransom, actually. He did this by organizing physique contests under the U.S. national weightlifting committee, which he controlled. The committee belonged to the Amateur Athletic Union, which, back then, had most non-professional American sports under its thumb. The first AAU Mr. America contest in 1939 was an add-on to the national weightlifting championship. Its winner, Roland J. Essmaker, got the "Bob Hoffman Trophy" presented by the man himself. But then Hoffman later ignored Essmaker's win because the guy didn't belong to Hoffman's club in York.

For years to come Hoffman put major AAU bodybuilding events at the end of lifting meets, which meant the poor bodybuilders didn't compete until late at night—sometimes after midnight. This crazy arrangement worked for Hoffman because weightlifting couldn't draw flies as a spectator sport, but bodybuilding brought in the crowds. People lined up for tickets and packed the seats to get a look at the greatest physiques of the day—even when they had to wait until one in the morning to see the guys in one of Hoffman's rinky-dink productions in some Turner's Hall or high school gym.

Hoffman needed the ticket sales from bodybuilding to support weightlifting, which wouldn't have made a dime all by itself. He also wanted the guys who went into bodybuilding rather than weightlifting. He ranted and raved that we were siphoning talent that rightfully belonged to competitive weightlifting. Of course he was kidding himself. Never the twain shall meet, as the old saying goes. Bodybuilders don't want to be Olympic lifters or powerlifters. And the lifters don't want to be bodybuilders. The exceptions are so few they prove the rule. Hoffman couldn't see it, though. He believed that anybody who picked up a barbell belonged to him.

Hoffman's deal was even more unfair and backwards because he didn't like bodybuilding. He and his magazine writers would call us "boobybuilders" and claim that our guys were really weaklings with muscles that were good only for show. This is not to mention calling bodybuilders queers.

Written history, personal or otherwise, is mostly hindsight, including what I just told you. When I was a teenager and making my plans to go into publishing, I had absolutely no idea that I was on a collision course with Bob Hoffman, no more than Alexander the Great, when he stood up and took his first steps, knew he was walking toward battle with King Darius of Persia and conquest of the known world.

My seven dollars bought 600 or so one-cent postcards and covered the cost of printing the cards with an announcement of my new magazine and an invitation to subscribe—75 cents for six bimonthly issues. With Rusty Halpert's help I got the cards out and then waited for the response. I was way out on a limb there, but the thought of failure never crossed my mind. I rented a typewriter and went to work at Ma's dining room table putting together Volume 1, Issue 1, dated August 1940.

The physique you care about most, and the only one you can do anything about, is your own. Am I right? For this reason I named the magazine *Your Physique*.

I, publisher and editor, named my friend Harvey Hill, the weightlifting coach at the Verdun club, as associate editor. But in truth, I did everything. First, I wrote the editorial copy using the bylines of the guys who gave me information for the articles. I ghost-wrote like that for years, until I had other writers to do it for me, because some of the most knowledgeable and authoritative muscle men couldn't write a decent sentence—much less an article—to save their lives. On the other hand, they've got extremely valuable information, and readers like to know they're getting it straight from the champions and guys in the know. For the first issue I did an article on exercise and longevity—"I Am Young At Sixty"—under the byline of the wonderful old-time French Canadian strong man Arthur Dandurand, a true gentleman who was a friend and an inspiration to me. Johnny Young got credit for a piece on weightlifting personalities, and I ran an ad for his gym on the back cover. "Vitamins For the Bodybuilder" appeared under my byline.

Your Physique gave Ma fits.

She couldn't stand seeing the typewriter and my papers on her dining room table, so I'd wait to start work until she went to bed. I bought a little pad to go under the typewriter so it wouldn't make noise, and I covered myself up with a sheet and used a flashlight to see. Quietly as I could, I pecked away at the typewriter with one finger—I never did learn touch typing. Since Ma was practically deaf, I figured I wouldn't disturb her, but she sensed what I was doing and got up and yelled at me to go to bed. I'd say I had to do my magazine and tell her to go to bed.

How she knew I was working, I'll never know. But she did, and there we were like cats and dogs in the middle of the night.

Day and night Ma told me how silly and hopeless my ambitions were. I was poor, with no formal education and no experience. I'd never even touched a typewriter before. I was trying to get into a field dominated by a rich American industrialist who'd been putting out his magazine for years. On top of all that, money was still tight from the Great Depression, and Canada, like the rest of the British Commonwealth countries, was already at war with the Nazis. Enough with this craziness, she'd yell at me. Who do you think you are? Find solid, good-paying work like everybody else! And on and on and on.

I needed discouragement like that—in my own home, from my own mother—like I needed a hole in the head. I'd be lying if I said it didn't bother me, but Ma could not get in my way. Nobody and nothing in the world could turn me from my chosen path. I was like steel. This strength of purpose was, I think, the real reason Ma got so angry. She wanted everything under her thumb, and God knows I was not under her thumb or anybody else's. We were just too strong-minded and too much alike to get along.

I believe there was something else in the trouble between us. Ma was, in her own way, being motherly, obeying the powerful maternal instinct to protect her child and ensure his lifelong prosperity and happiness. However hard on me she was, Ma also tried to save me from poverty and failure, which she was sure I was headed for. With good reason, too. Everything she yelled at me was true. Anybody with common sense would have agreed.

Even my good friends thought I didn't have a prayer. Johnny Young turned down a chance to become my partner, with half-ownership of my magazine, for seven dollars. Rusty Halpert, who gave me hours and hours of very valuable help, wouldn't put up any of his money, either.

After a few months, when the magazine was a going concern, Johnny asked me if he still could be my partner. Sure, I said, but it would cost him $25. Johnny would drop that much on a roll of the dice or throw it away on some floozy without batting an eye. But again he wouldn't buy in. He didn't have $25 worth of confidence in me and *Your Physique*. Looking back, I should be grateful, because that was not a guy I wanted to be tied up with.

I wrote these lines for the first issue's masthead:

Dedicated to:

The Weightlifter,

The Body-Builder,

And Health Culturist.

And, in my first editorial: "You will, no doubt, think us ambitious. Well, so we are!...We do not shrink from our end of the job...Later on we shall grow bigger and we will print each month..."

Real printing cost too much, so I typed all 22 inside pages onto mimeograph stencils. By now I was up to two fingers, but the job was still laborious. With the copy in place, I hand-lettered the big display type and drew some muscle-man illustrations. The artwork isn't bad, if I do say so. Then came hours of cranking out pages on the rented Gestetner mimeograph machine. I used the cheaper, wet mimeo process so we had to spread the pages out to dry. We had paper everywhere, and the air stank from the mimeograph fluid.

You can imagine how unhappy this made Ma.

The only part of the first issue to be professionally printed on coated paper was the cover page. On the front I put a picture of Barton Horvath, a New Yorker I particularly admired who, like me, was both a serious lifter and a bodybuilder. Later Barton would go to work for me as a writer and editor. The full-length cover shot showed him in a front double biceps pose with a jet black background and dramatic shadowing on the body. I still like that image.

Proud as I was, I also felt nervous and sort of embarrassed because I knew *Your Physique* looked as much like a homemade newsletter as a real magazine. And I knew that others might not see all the bigger and more important things to come, which to me were clear as day.

One of the very first people I showed it to was Arthur Dandurand. I'll never forget that grand old guy holding Issue 1 in his great big powerful hands. He put on reading glasses and turned through the pages, taking his time and not saying anything. About when I decided he didn't like it, Arthur said this: "Joe, from such small acorns, giant trees grow."

His words rang in my head like Biblical prophecy. I really loved and admired Arthur, who was incapable of saying anything he didn't believe, even to be nice to a young friend dying for a pat on the head. He related what he said to trees because they meant something to him. He'd spent years working as a lumberjack, way up in the woods.

Besides the personal aspect, this was like being blessed by history and the land of my birth. "The Cradle of Strong Men," George Jowett called Quebec. He also declared Arthur Dandurand "The Canadian Sandow." Our province had a long tradition of turning out men of incredible power who performed amazing feats and were lionized by the people. King of them all was Louis Cyr, considered by many the strongest man in the world. Arthur, who made his living in the woods and working as a stevedore in Montreal, put on shows of strength as a sideline. He was famous for picking up a 400-pound Ford engine block, lifting it to his shoulder and walking around with it. What made the feat so amazing was the awkwardness of the engine block, a very hard thing to get hold of, much less lift and carry.

Of course the approval that meant life or death for the magazine came from guys I never met—the readers. Almost right away I knew they liked *Your Physique* because new subscription forms poured in after the issue went out. Guys in all these places I never heard of saw buddies' copies and sent in their 75 cents. And the magazine sold like crazy at Young's studio and a couple other places that offered it.

I would have been happy to sell half of the first print run and spread the rest around for free. But 80 percent went out at full price. The issues and subscriptions brought in a couple hundred dollars, more money than I'd ever seen in my life. Any other kid my age would have blown at least a little on himself, but I was never even tempted. I used every nickel I cleared to make the magazine better, a practice I followed for 60 years of publishing. Always I poured more and more money into the magazines, and the bean counters had fits.

Issue 2 went out to a real typesetter and printer. It was only 12 pages long, but, as I explained in my editorial, the word count was actually higher. "Secondly, it is more attractive," I wrote. It really was, too. Instead of my hand-drawn muscle men, I had photos on the inside pages.

The magazine was more authoritative, too. I ran a long piece on conditioning reprinted from a book by Mark H. Berry, coach of the U.S. Olympic weightlifting team, whose writings appeared in other early issues. He and I had a no-money deal that was good for both of us. I got to run his articles, which were excellent, and he got exposure in Canada, another market for the training courses and books that he sold. For years to come I would do business on the same basis with other famous writers, running their articles and providing ad space to sell their stuff. I dealt that way, too, with the best physique photographers, like Lon Hanagan in New York, who gave me shots for the cover and inside pages. Being in the magazine was good for the bodybuilders who modeled, too. As my magazines got bigger and better, a Weider magazine cover shot became like gold. It meant a guy was a superstar.

Of course the real beneficiaries of the quid pro quo deals were my readers. Right from the start, I could give them good photos of the strongest and best-built men in the world, with expert information about how to be like those men.

Not bad for 15 cents a copy.

Take a look at that old shot of Jack Gallagher on the cover of the second issue, and you'll see that somebody inked in the G-string he's wearing. It was common practice for physique photographers to shoot nude figure studies that had to be touched up for magazines. The shooters sold the untouched nudes mail order in special photo sets and art books. "Eagerly sought by artists and sculptors everywhere," read the copy in an ad I ran for photographer Al Urban. Truth was, pictures like that were mostly sought by gay men. On the other hand, the better photos really were works of art. Back then photographers produced beautiful formal compositions with the men posed like classical sculpture.

Lucky for me I thrived on work and didn't need much sleep, because for the first few issues I kept my job at Murray's. My responsibilities with the magazine didn't slow me down at the restaurant at all. The boss told me how much he admired my hard work and intelligence and offered me a position as night manager at a new Murray's opening in Ottawa. I'd make more money, and I could look forward to moving up.

I had come to a fork in the road. I could run a restaurant in another city or stay in Montreal and publish. I knew the path I'd take, but I hesitated because this was such an important decision.

Ma, of course, made it hard to think straight by yelling at me about how nuts I was to even think about saying no to Murray's for the sake of my muscle magazine. I must admit, for a few days I lost confidence and floundered.

But then I thought about the Spanish conquistador Hernan Cortez, whose story I read back when I was a delivery boy. I remembered how Cortez landed on the mainland of Mexico with just a handful of men, vastly outnumbered by the warriors of the Aztec kingdom. It would have made sense to have an escape plan, but what did Cortez do? He burned his ships, that's what, which must have seemed insane to his troops. Cortez knew what he was doing, though. If his men had a fallback they wouldn't have fought so hard, and they probably would have retreated. As it was, they had no choice but to march to Mexico City and conquer the Aztecs.

Cortez's story gave me the courage to burn my own ships, which were Murray's restaurants. Not only did I say no to the position in Ottawa, I quit my job in Montreal.

I would be a magazine man, or I would be nothing.

Pay attention, you with big dreams and ambitions. Hedging your bets, keeping a fallback position, might be smart for a little while, but then it holds you back. Pretty soon you've got to commit so there's no way to go but forward. You've got to burn your ships.

Do or die.

There's another lesson here: Men dead for hundreds or thousands of years can give you courage and wisdom and show you what to do.

It pays to study history.

Anybody who knows history might be wondering why I wasn't serving in the Canadian Armed Forces like most young guys, including my brother Ben, who was about to go into the army. I was healthy and fit, and God knows I hated the Nazis, but the government considered work like mine to be vital to the war effort because magazines boosted the national morale, so I was exempted from military service.

I did all I could for the cause with patriotic editorials and information to help keep military-age men healthy and fit. In Issue 3, I urged the men in uniform to stay away from boozing and smoking cigarettes and other vices. "The nation's strength depends on the health of its youth!" I wrote. This was more than a slogan. The military had to turn away tens of thousands of young men because they were unfit to serve. And many went into the service puny and weak. By encouraging clean living and physical fitness, I helped provide the strong and healthy recruits that the military desperately needed.

Early in the war *Strength and Health* was not available in Canada. Some have said there was a paper shortage, but I believe the Canadian government banned it for a period because Bob Hoffman had praised the training methods of the Germans and admired the accomplishments of the Nazi regime.

So, for a while, Hoffman was out of the picture, and Canada was like an incubator for my magazine.

Here in Los Angeles people have clothes closets and bathrooms a lot bigger than our old living room. It was up at the front of the house with double windows facing out on the sidewalk and street, and it connected to another room where we boys slept. It wasn't much, but Ma made it the showplace of her home. She scrimped and saved for a little suite of parlor furniture, and the centerpiece was her brown horsehair couch. I think it stood in for all the other nice things she didn't have, and the genteel life she couldn't live, because we were always so short on money. How she loved that couch.

This made what Pa did with it more incredible.

As I said, he alone believed in me and what I was doing. All along he told my brothers and sister to give me their support. "Joe will make our name famous all over the world," he said.

It bothered Pa a lot that I didn't have a decent place to work. One day a used furniture seller came by with a nice old wooden desk on his wagon. Pa knew he had to have it for his son. He didn't have a dime so he worked out a trade. The furniture man hauled away Anna Weider's most precious possession and put the desk in its place.

You better believe there was hell to pay when my mother saw that her couch was gone and her living room was now also my office. But for the first time Pa stood up to her. "We have never done a thing for Joe," he said, "Our son deserves this."

I'll never forget the gratitude and love and pride in Pa that I felt. It took some kind of guts to defy Anna Weider.

One time I came home and saw all my files stacked out front, like I was moving. Another time there were papers from my desk flying around in the breeze.

In the winter, my mother threw the inkwell on my desk out the door. What a sight to come home to—India ink splattered on the snow. It looked like a murder scene in a black-and-white movie.

Before long I had enough money coming in to move out on my own or at least rent some humble little space for an office. But I stayed home until I moved to the United States in 1947.

The reason, especially with all the conflict I'm telling you about, may surprise you.

I lived and worked at 4466 Colonial Avenue for eight years because I loved my home with all my heart. I loved living there with my family. In spite of the crowding and the fact that it was sort of a nuthouse, there was nowhere else in the world I wanted to be.

I loved Ma, too. Of course I did. And of course the relationship was very complicated. But everybody in the world, the best and worst of humanity, loves his mother.

Ma finally got off my back because of a strange and inexplicable event.

She was walking along The Main with one of her lady friends, yacking and window shopping the way women do, when her friend stopped in front of a fortune teller's parlor. She wanted them both to have their fortunes read, but Ma said stuff like that was nonsense. Her friend told her it was only for fun, and it was cheap, so Ma went in to be a good sport.

The gypsy got Ma's attention right away. "You have three living sons," she said.

She went on to say, "One son, the middle one, is tall and pale. He's very serious and ambitious and hard-working, but you do everything in your power to thwart him.

"Why do you fight him and make his life miserable like you do?" the gypsy asked. "You must stop and give him your support. He will be very famous and do great things and change the world."

There was no way in the world that woman could have found out such details about us in advance. And there's no way that Ma was just telling a story. She came home white as a sheet and shaking, and Pa wanted to know what terrible thing had happened.

Then and there Ma ended her war against me and *Your Physique*. She still didn't like what I was doing, but she kept quiet about it.

Like Ma and everybody else, I was baffled by the message from the fortune teller, which turned out to be absolutely true. But I was glad to have some peace.

I had an accident that turned out to be more good luck.

All along I stuck with my weightlifting, and I was really going places as a competitor.

Some friends asked me to come and play handball, which I'd never tried. Right after we started I took a swing at the ball and felt a muscle in my shoulder tear. I guess I didn't warm up properly and then over-reached. I went to a doctor who sent me to a hospital. In those days, medical people didn't know anything about torn muscles, so they just put heat on the injury and sent me home. Besides the pain in my shoulder, I felt like I would catch pneumonia waiting for the bus because it was the middle of winter.

That was that for my competitive lifting. A young fellow with power you wouldn't believe, who could put a 300-pound barbell up over his head, got done in by swinging at a little rubber ball. After the shoulder healed I went back to pumping iron with weights that very few guys could handle, made big gains and built a tremendous physique, but the extreme stress of lifting was out.

Later I could look back and see that the injury was for the good. With the big competitive successes I was headed for, lifting would have distracted me from my work.

But here are some numbers from early in my 19th year that show I really could have been a contender.

Stripped weight: 165 pounds

Two Hands Military Press: 224 pounds

Two Hands Snatch: 220 pounds

Two Hands Clean and Jerk: 285 pounds

Two Hands Continental Jerk: 300 pounds

The lifts are labeled "two hands" because back then guys also did one-handed lifts—with barbells! The game was for he-men in those days.

"Come on, Joe, you can't work all the time."

"Don't be a stick in the mud."

"You've got to have some fun."

"Let's go to a nightclub."

"Let's go skiing."

"Let's go skating."

The other young guys never let up trying to get me to go out with them, and I kept telling them no, no, no, no. The only time off I allowed myself was Saturday night, when I sometimes went where there was music and dancing. But I didn't drink or go wild like other young people. I had to be sharp for work in the morning, and I had to save my money. Except for a little allowance I gave myself and money I gave Ma to help out the family, every penny went back into my business.

One of the guys took me aside and said if I didn't loosen up and go out more, nobody would want to be my pal. "You won't have a single friend in the world," he said.

He could not have been more wrong. I always had friends—but they were new and different friends. And, to tell the truth, better friends. The more I advanced myself, the more I had people around who understood and shared my passions and my commitment. First I was surrounded by guys devoted to strength and bodybuilding. As my magazines got bigger, I enjoyed the company of the most famous strength experts and writers, as well as photographers and artists. I liked them all, and many of them became true friends. Ben and I are bound by blood, but we're closer than any brothers I know because of our shared mission and our business relationship. The great bodybuilders I knew and socialized with became like extended family. Arnold Schwarzenegger became like a son. I made great friends outside my field, too, because men of accomplishment are drawn to each other.

What happened back in Montreal was natural and predictable. If you've got serious ambition and commitment, you part ways with some of the companions of your youth. When they pull against you—like that guy trying to shame me into goofing off and wasting money—they're not the kind of friends you want, anyway.

To tell this next story I have to back up a little to when I was first putting together the magazine and working at Murray's.

On a Saturday night I took a break and went stag to a dance in the neighborhood. I stood there listening to the music and watching the people out on the floor when a friend of mine came up and said I ought to have a dance with the girl he brought. I said sure, why not. The girl was so cute—blonde, blue-eyed, petite—and she seemed like a nice girl, by which I mean proper and respectable. But then while we were dancing she snuggled in close and put her head on my shoulder, which shocked me deeply. I thought this was my friend's steady girl, so what was going on?

I took my friend aside and told him that his date was acting more like mine. Since they were going together, I said, I had to let him know. But the guy laughed and told me I had it all wrong. The girl was a friend, not a girlfriend, who told him she wanted to meet me.

The girl and I danced and danced, and I walked her home to a house a few blocks from mine. I asked if she'd go out with me some time, and she said yes. The girl's name was Vicky.

Only one love is your first love, and mine was Vicky. A man's first love has a special place in his heart, and that's where Vicky is—here in my heart, for all eternity. I hope I'm in hers, too.

I can't remember when I last saw her—40 years ago or even more. I don't mind because if we don't meet we can always be for each other the way we were, so young and beautiful and vibrant and strong.

The way Vicky remembers, I first caught her eye when she was a waitress at Shap's. One day I came in with some friends, and she brought everybody else's food but held mine back so I'd take notice of her. I paid no attention because I was completely wrapped up in telling about bodybuilding and my magazine. Beautiful as she was, she was not used to guys ignoring her, and she was really annoyed.

Vicky says, too, that I was rather awkward at courtship. The first time I called at her house, I took her a pie from Murray's. She would have loved flowers or a box of candy, but there I stood at her front door with a pie, and she had no idea what to do with it. I don't remember the pie, but I'm sure I was a little shy because I was so inexperienced with girls and dating.

Whatever awkwardness there was, though, true love quickly swept it away. Vicky was the woman I dreamed of—sweet, kind, supportive, soft-spoken, and ladylike, there for me when I needed her. And she made me feel so strong. She'd lean on me like I was a mighty tree.

Vicky Uzar was born in the city of Lvov, which was then in Poland but now belongs to the Ukraine. Though our ancestral homes were very close, Vicky's family and mine might as well have been from Venus and Mars, because they were Polish Catholics and we were Jews. This didn't mean so much at my house where everybody adored Vicky and she became like part of the family. And most of Vicky's family got to like me. But Vicky's father was an anti-Semite through and through—he was proud of it, too. He was proud in general because the Uzars were some sort of gentry in the old country, or so he said, and he insisted that people call him *Pan* Uzar—which in English would be something like Squire Uzar.

Vicky's father had one very strange way of showing that he didn't want me around. When I came to visit Vicky or pick her up for a date, he'd get out his worn-out old socks and darn them. He'd do it in the living room where Vicky and I sat. Vicky said he never touched his socks unless I was around, and he normally sat in the kitchen, not the living room. Obviously he intended to insult me and my people, but I had no idea what he meant. Who knows what goes on in the mind of a bigot?

Who cares?

Being nice to the man did no good whatsoever. Once I took him a beautiful leatherbound history of Poland. He looked at the cover and said, "Who is this guy who wrote it, this Horowitz? He must be Jewish. I don't want the book."

Eventually the prejudices of Old Man Uzar and the world would catch up to Vicky and me. Until they did, though, we lived in our own world where nothing mattered except our love and the happiness we gave each other.

Those years in Montreal with Vicky and my new magazine were golden. There I was, a young man just discovering my powers and talents, with not one first love but two. I loved every publication I ever put out, but I loved *Your Physique* most of all. I love that it lives on as *Muscle & Fitness,* the biggest and best magazine of its kind in history, which is published in more than a dozen languages all over the world. That's my baby, my first-born, which will always have a special place in my heart. Just like Vicky.

It's hard to judge one good time in life against another, but those were some of the happiest years in my life. Everything was new and fresh, even happiness itself, because my childhood and youth had been so miserable. And life was still so simple. My office was my home. The money coming in went right back into the magazine, and I lived a lot like I did when I was a kid, even sleeping in the same room. I still trusted people because nobody had double-crossed me—not yet. I didn't have any of the headaches that come with running giant, complicated businesses and achieving notable success.

I had everything that I wanted and nothing that I didn't want.

Who wouldn't be happy?

Today I woke up with the mopes, but then I looked through some of my old magazines, and the old excitement, the energy, came back. I ought to do this more often.

Sixty years later and 3,000 miles away, I'm like Bill C., a reader from Hamilton, Ontario, who wrote a letter to the editor in the early 1940s that I put in the magazine. He said he had to look twice at his latest copy because he couldn't believe how much bigger and better *Your Physique* was, from just one issue to the next.

Even though I'm the guy who did it, I can't believe it, either. I can't really explain how, but the kid putting out the magazine knew what he was doing and kept getting better and better. After the first couple issues you start to see Weider touches like covers with guys in new, dynamic poses and teaser lines to get the reader excited about what's inside. Most of the lines—"The Ultimate in Arm Development," "Sandow the Immortal"—would still work today. On the inside, you see me start to play around with graphics and typography. Design-wise, I went from the early- to the late-twentieth century in a matter of months. I didn't look at other magazines to see what I ought to do so much as I looked at *Your Physique* and the images in my own head.

What really sold the guys was solid, up-to-the-minute, interesting, and, above all, usable information about how to get stronger and better built. Since bodybuilding and health-building are one in the same, I put in articles on every aspect of health—diet, digestion, personal hygiene, mental health and attitude, the hazards of drinking and smoking, advice on sexuality, and even personal grooming—as well as how to make big gains in muscle and power.

A guy could still do himself a lot of good by following the advice I put out on Colonial Avenue.

However beautiful and brilliant I made my magazine, half or more of the readers weren't ever going to subscribe. Such is the nature of muscle magazines, which depend on single-copy sales more than most publications. Nowadays, as many copies of *Muscle & Fitness* are bought retail, off the magazine rack, as are mailed out to subscribers.

I knew I had to get *Your Physique* onto newsstands, and to do that I needed a distributor. King of them all was American News Co. in New York City, which pretty much controlled the North American market. As soon as I had a few issues to show I made an appointment to see Mr. Roy Hawken, manager of the local office of American News, which was downtown on de Bleury Street.

When the day came, there I was in my best dress-up clothes and holding my magazines, waiting to see the boss. His secretary said I could go on in, and I introduced myself.

"Where's your father?" Mr. Hawken asked me.

He wasn't kidding. He assumed because of my age that I was tagging along with the real Mr. Weider. After we straightened that out, I showed him *Your Physique* and started telling him about the importance of fitness and health, the thousands and thousands of guys who would buy the magazine off the stands and my plans to improve and expand. I got so carried away that I kept talking, fast as I could, even when Mr. Hawken tried to say something. Eventually he broke in and stopped me.

"Be quiet," he said, "I've been trying to tell you 'Yes' for 10 minutes," he said.

He explained that the home office would never approve Canadian, much less North American, distribution for a magazine as small and new as mine. But he wanted to give *Your Physique* a local tryout. If it did all right in Montreal, he'd send it across the country and then—maybe—into the U.S., too.

I walked out of that office on air. Starting locally didn't bother me at all, because I knew my magazine would pass whatever test the distributor wanted to give it. With the No. 1 distributor in the world, Weider Publications was on its way. I could feel it in my bones.

A while ago, on the phone, Vicky reminded me how I had to stop at every single newsstand we passed and check out the magazine's placement on the rack and maybe buy a copy. I did it even when we were out on the town, going to dinner and dances. This drove her nuts because she dressed so gorgeously and did up her hair and makeup, and I only had eyes for the magazine. Ben and I still stop to see how the Weider publications look on the rack.

The better the magazine got, the more the big names wanted me to run their stuff. George Jowett, who remembered helping me buy my first weight set, started writing for me, as did Earle Liederman, who put out extremely popular books and training courses that were mostly based on using chest expanders. To be honest, both these guys were past their primes, and Liederman was just about wiped out during the Depression, but they had very valuable information for the readers. A giant with gray hair is still a giant.

Dr. Frederick Tilney, a famous authority on diet, health, and mental well-being, who was a huge advocate of exercise, wrote for me, too. Doc, as we called him, was an Englishman who lived in Florida. He wrote dozens of books and pamphlets and had a line of natural vitamin and mineral supplements. He had very advanced ideas for the time. Later he talked me into going with him to a nudist colony. I kept my shorts on and still felt really uncomfortable, which Doc thought was hilarious. Doc was a card, in that dry, British way, but also brilliant and years ahead of his time. And he was one of the most dynamic and energetic people I ever met.

These men all wrote beautifully, but each in his own way. Jowett had old-school formality and dignity, which was how he acted in person. Doc's stuff gave off positive energy like it was electrified. And Liederman was a poet. People still admire his way with the language. All three also became editors for my magazines. Young as I was, they accepted my leadership because I knew how to showcase their talents, and they said I was going places.

To give credit where it's due, Jowett and Dr. Tilney were also gifts from Bob Hoffman. They both had worked for him, but they left and then jumped at the chance to work for somebody who treated them with respect and fairness. For years to come, terrific people crossed over to the Weider side because they couldn't stand Hoffman's abuse. This was true of bodybuilders, too. Larry Scott, one of the all-time greats who won the first Mr. Olympia contest, became a Weider man because Hoffman developed a grudge against him for no good reason. That guy was like my own personal talent scout and recruiter.

In those early days I accidentally gave Hoffman two little pieces of ammunition that he later used over and over in his magazine. Mind you, this was before I had any idea how unpleasant and crazy things would get.

First, I let Johnny Young talk me into doing a little item for *Strength and Health* that introduced me as an up-and-coming Canadian athlete who admired Hoffman and used his training methods. The point was not to flatter Hoffman, but to generate some publicity for Johnny's gym, which got prominent mention as the place where I worked out. I didn't want to do it, but Johnny kept after me until I gave in. In years to come, Hoffman trotted out that little blurb, saying I got my start as a York man and my training system was a knockoff of his. Pure nonsense, every word of it, but that didn't stop him from putting it in his magazine.

And then Doc Tilney told me I needed a middle initial to dress up my name and add to my dignity and stature. Since I never had a middle name, we could pick any letter. Doc thought "E" had the right ring to it, so I became Joseph E. Weider, "E" for Edwin. It never occurred to Doc that he gave me the initials J.E.W., which Hoffman beat to death. He used anti-Semitic slurs against me, too. The guy's taunts never bothered me—I knew what I was and who I was, and I was proud of it—but it shows how low Hoffman would go.

Doc Tilney had another connection that shows what a fantastic writer he was. Back before he worked for Hoffman he created the Charles Atlas exercise courses that sold by the millions for years and years, which you can still buy today. I have to credit Doc's writing and the famous "97-pound weakling" ads because Atlas' system, Dynamic Tension, was a con.

There was nothing phony about the guy's body. Atlas, whose real last name was Siciliano, won two of Bernarr McFadden's "Most Perfectly Developed Man" contests back in the 1920s and then did a strong man act on stage. He built his physique and strength the only possible way, by lifting weights. But in his courses he told men they could get big and strong with no weights or apparatus of any kind just by pushing muscles against each other—like building the biceps by flexing one arm upward while you hold it down with the other. Atlas said he invented his system after he saw the great cats flexing and stretching at the zoo. He claimed that lions and tigers got their power doing Dynamic Tension, just like he taught. In truth, stretching does not build muscles—for animals or for human beings.

On the other hand, Dynamic Tension was a fantastic racket. Once I met Atlas in a gym in New York City, and he said to me, "You know, Joe, you're no businessman." I asked him what he meant, and he said selling weights mail order, the way I was doing by then, was crazy because I had so much tied-up in inventory and the stuff was heavy and expensive to ship.

"Do what I do," Atlas said. "Just run off sheets of paper and some pictures and charge the same amount of money."

I wasn't rude to the guy, but I don't believe in doing that kind of business. I don't like taking advantage of people, and I don't like telling them anything but the truth, plain and simple, which is this:

If you want to build your body, you've got to lift weights.

Since I advocated weight training, I had to provide the guys with what they needed.

It took a couple years to get to the point where I could set up a deal with a local foundry and go into the weight business. First I started a mail-order bookstore, with ads and order blanks in the magazine, so the readers could buy literature and courses by the experts who wrote for me. Then I sold some small equipment like chest expanders. And then I had weight sets made and sold them. I pretty much had to, to satisfy the readers, who wrote in asking me what I had asked back when I was a kid: "I know I need barbells and dumbbells—so where do I get them?"

And I went into the mail-order equipment business to satisfy the readers in another sense—by making the magazine bigger and better every issue, as fast as possible. Magazine sales brought in enough money to survive and a small surplus, but I needed more. If I was really going to spread the word about strength and fitness and health all over the world, I needed to put more into the magazine and create something truly worthy of the world's attention. Where, I kept asking myself, can I get more money?

All magazine publishers face this same problem. No matter how many subscriptions and newsstand copies the readers buy, sales revenues alone can't keep you in business. And the readers wouldn't buy a magazine they, and nobody else, paid for, because it would look too cheap. To make a high-quality, attractive publication, you need money coming in from somewhere else. For most magazines, it comes from selling ads. A lot of publishers pretty much give away their magazines to pump up circulation so they can sell more ads for higher prices. This explains why you can buy all these big, fat, beautiful magazines for 10 or 12 bucks a year. The advertisers are kicking in a lot more money than the readers.

I couldn't get money from ad sales, though, because there weren't any. The few little companies that sold strength-related stuff couldn't pay much of anything for their ads, which I ran mostly for the sake of the readers. And other advertisers didn't want anything to do with a muscle magazine. Major brand names, like car companies, soft drink makers, men's toiletries, and so on, treated us like lepers for 60 years. Only in the last few years have big brand-name advertisers started to buy significant space in *Muscle & Fitness.* It's about time they wised up. All along we had the young, athletic, intelligent, male readers they're dying to reach. This shows you the power of the prejudice against bodybuilding, which I fought all my life.

But the point, in this story, is that I was all on my own. If I needed more money for *Your Physique,* I had to make it myself.

So now, instead of pumping iron in the shed out back, I put together sets of Weider-brand iron for other guys to pump. The foundry dropped off weights over at Halpert's bike shop, too, but it's working behind the house that I remember. In the wintertime I wore gloves with the fingertips cut off so I could turn the little screws on the collars that hold weight plates onto the bars. I blew on my fingers and put them inside my coat, but they still turned blue and numb.

Look at it one way: I became my own major advertiser. Or another way, *Your Physique* was a mail-order catalog for Weider-brand products, but with excellent editorial content and pictures.

Either way, the business now stood on two legs, publishing and equipment. Later, when we introduced food supplements, it would be three-sided, like a triangle. Everything was good for everything else. The magazine sold weights, which meant I had to develop the Weider System of training and write a course to send with the weights. But then the guys with weights turned back to the magazine to keep up with the latest developments and refinements in the system and learn about the champions and their techniques, as well as the newest information about health. Every product created a demand for something else. Guys getting bigger with weights wanted chest expanders and cable devices to work on muscle definition, and then benches and racks. Readers who really delved into the magazine wanted more in-depth material, so I wrote books, advanced and specialized courses, and on and on.

This didn't happen because I was some kind of business genius—it happened because I was a bodybuilder, and I anticipated others' needs. They loved what I had to offer because I loved bodybuilding as much as they did.

No, I loved it more. I still do.

How did I know how to do all these things, with no business education, no training, nobody to show me the ropes?

I knew the same way a one-year-old knows to stand up and put one foot in front of another. A human being is born to walk. When we're ready, we figure out how to do it and practice until we're good at it, all on our own. Well, I just stood up and took one step and the next and started a publishing empire and a couple major industries and changed the way the whole world thinks about exercise, health, and the human body.

I did it because I was born to do it.

I believe my brother Ben was born to do what he did, too. Our sport was a laughingstock until he organized it under its own international federation, which he led, and he made the world take it seriously. Ben had no more schooling than I did, but he did better than trained diplomats with degrees from the finest universities. All over the world, he looked kings and presidents and sports ministers straight in the eye and talked them into recognizing and supporting the International Federation of

Bodybuilders (IFBB). After 52 years he won provisional Olympic recognition for bodybuilding, which even I had decided was impossible. At one point I told him to give up because I didn't want him to break his heart. I don't know who else could have done what Ben did. He always knew the next step to take the same way I did. He used his eyes and his ears and his brains and his heart, and he just knew.

Millions of men are born as brothers and it doesn't mean a thing. But Ben and I were born to be a team.

This stuff might seem crazy, but if you're doing what you were born to do, you know it's absolutely true.

I was 5 foot 11 and about 175 pounds, muscular and strong, good hair and features, and most girls liked me. Joe "Barrymore Profile" Weider, a woman reporter called me in a personality piece. She meant John Barrymore, a movie star the women went nuts over. Looking back, I think maybe the reporter had a thing for me. But I was pretty much oblivious.

One of the women I knew from the restaurant offered to proofread magazine copy for me and fix spelling and grammatical errors. She was from Scotland and in her mid-twenties. Everything went fine for a couple issues, but on the third one she said to me, "You know, I left the copy at home by mistake." We went to her place and we talked for a while about this and that until she said, "Excuse me for a few minutes and let me freshen myself up." She came out dressed in a long negligee you could almost see through, but I didn't pay any attention. We finished our work, and I went home without making a pass at her. When I brought the next issue I got the brush-off. "I'm too busy now," she said.

She wasn't the only one who wanted to be my girlfriend. Some of my buddies' girls practically threw themselves at me, which was very awkward and embarrassing. Mothers got into the act, too, telling me I ought to go out with their daughters. This happened even at Hungarian and Polish neighborhood dances. Many of those people despised Jews, but the mothers would say to me, "With you it doesn't matter, you're such a good-looking, nice, young man."

A different kind of guy would have been a Lothario and had his way with all those girls. Not me, though. I had my Vicky. And even if I didn't have a girl, I was not the type to take advantage.

I have to thank Ma for keeping me on the straight and narrow.

Over and over she told me, "You only have one woman and one God." And she said if I went with a girl, I should never ruin her, by which she meant having sex. If I did that, I would bring shame to her and her family and diminish her chance of making a good marriage. For my selfish pleasure, everybody would get hurt.

Don't you dare do such a thing, Ma said. And I listened and took what she said to heart. All my life I have revered and respected womanhood.

Somehow I caught the eye of a daughter of the Bronfmans, the richest Jews in Montreal and all of Canada. She was dying for me to ask her out and she spread the word so I'd hear. In our world, this was like a beautiful royal princess summoning a commoner, but I didn't call her.

The owner of the factory where my father worked got into the act, too. One day he called my father and offered him a promotion from pants-presser to supervisor if he could persuade me to go out with his daughter.

Pa said forget it. He'd never make such a deal because his family's honor and feelings were not for sale, not for any price. And he'd never interfere with his son's personal life.

Think about what he was turning down, how much nicer his life would have been if he supervised people instead of slaving away at his horrible, hot pressing machine. He would have made more money, too. He hated his job like death, and he hated being poor, but he loved me too much to ask me to compromise my feelings for Vicky, whom he adored.

People used to call Pa a saint, but he was a man, too. That gentle little guy had the backbone of a giant.

I wanted him to have money of his own—instead of the pittance Ma let him have—but he wouldn't take it. I tried slipping folded money into his pockets when he was sleeping, but then I'd find it under my pillow and in my pockets.

Even though Ben and I could have set him up so he didn't have to work there any more, he slaved away at the factory all his life.

He liked it when I did things for the family like giving Freda money to fix her teeth and buying her singing lessons, but he didn't want anything for himself. After all he had done for me, he never let me do a thing for him.

I could make him proud, though, and make him smile. One of our happiest moments together came when Pa made good on a promise to me. Back when I didn't have two nickels to rub together, he said that when I made my first $10,000, he'd celebrate by drinking a shot of schnapps. This was a big deal because he didn't like alcoholic beverages at all, even to taste or sip, but he'd drink to toast my success. He never saw more than $500 in his life, so maybe he thought he wouldn't have to take the drink for a long time. But then success came faster than either of us expected. In only a couple years I built up a $10,000 cash reserve for my businesses. I showed him the bank book, handed him a glass and said, "Well, Pa, here's your schnapps." Seeing him so proud and happy was better than $10 million in the bank. Pa lifted the glass to me. I think he just touched his lips to the liquor and poured it out when I wasn't looking.

God bless my father, wherever he is. I hope I'll see him again.

CHAPTER FOUR

OPENING SHOTS

Ben Weider

Linked Destinies

I had every confidence that Joe's great dreams for bodybuilding and fitness would be realized. I did not know, however, that my brother's destiny had anything to do with mine, and it didn't until after World War II, some six years after Joe launched *Your Physique*. Then at Joe's invitation, I joined forces with him.

In our more than 60 years of working together, Joe and I never had a difference of opinion degenerate into an argument. Nor have we exchanged harsh words. Our relationship absolutely amazes businessmen and attorneys experienced with family-owned ventures, which often come to grief because conflicts, usually over money, escalate and become bitter and personal. Such a thing happening to Joe and me is unimaginable. We never focused on gaining wealth, so we had no issues about money. We had no conflicts about who was in charge because we served causes much greater than ourselves. We fought the same fight with the mutual trust and love that true brothers possess. In our rare disagreements, we didn't butt heads. No, we put our heads together and worked things out. Our heads, it seems, were specially made to fit together.

To drastically simplify our roles and personalities: Joe, the creative one, concentrates on his visions and thoughts; I, the diplomat, look outward, understanding and adjusting to the world. Anywhere in the world, whatever the customs and cultures, I can understand people's sensitivities and adapt to them. I've done so in visits to more than 110 nations on behalf of my sport of bodybuilding, as founding president of our sport's governing body, the IFBB. I have the ability to set my feelings completely aside. As I like to say, I can be friends, even with my enemies. Joe is more emotional, and his feelings lie closer to the surface. This is why our family dynamics had more of an effect on him than on me. Some things that bother Joe to this day pretty much rolled off my back.

A Different Kind of Kid

I was born on February 1, 1923, a day when the temperature went from minus 11 Fahrenheit to plus 23, not bad for winter in Montreal. I love the cold here, as I love most everything about Canada and my city. For all the millions of air miles I've logged, I also stayed very close to home. It might take 45 minutes to walk from my office in the Weider Building on Bates Road to our old house at 4466 Colonial Avenue, which is only about five miles from where I live today. Every so often I drive through the old neighborhood, full of struggling blue-collar immigrants when I knew it and now called The Plateau and quite fashionable among young people in arts and entertainment. But I can blink away the years and see the past. I can see it wherever I am, actually, and every day something takes me back for a moment or two.

That said, there's no need to go into detail about my boyhood. If you read the story of Joe's early years, you have pretty much read mine. The major difference is that we were different kids. You could say only one of us ever was a kid. When Joe was 10 years old he had the brains and temperament of a 20-year-old, and a serious 20-year-old at that. But the world didn't weigh so heavily on me. As Joe would say, I had more of the "pleasure principle". I played more readily and ran around with pals as a boy and later loved to go out on the town and dance to the big bands. Though I worked long and hard, I had the ability to cut loose and have some fun from time to time.

Joe could have used some of my *joie de vivre.* He also could have used my ability to speak the French language, which he never really picked up. Even as a boy I spoke so well that other kids called me Frenchy, a nickname that stuck for years. Later, my ability to converse like a true French Canadian opened some important doors for Joe and me.

Planting a Seed

Like Joe, I said goodbye to teachers and classrooms after the seventh grade and thereafter educated myself. I make no apologies for being an autodidact. In my view, they don't hand out brains in colleges and universities. On my wall are four honorary doctorate degrees awarded for advancing the knowledge of physical fitness and Napoleonic history, my other life's work.

One bit of self-education in my boyhood led to my avocation as a historian.

It happened about the time I left school. I was in the front room of our home reading a history book that dealt with Emperor Napoleon Bonaparte, who rose from obscurity to lead the French army to amazing victories against the reactionary kings of Europe, and become ruler of France. He was the first to aspire toward a United Europe, which has since become a reality under the European Union. Most English-language histories took a highly prejudiced view and depicted Napoleon as a brutal conqueror and dictator.

My father sat nearby, and I remarked that this Bonaparte must have been a terrible person.

"That isn't really true," Pa said. "Napoleon treated the Jews and other religious minorities with great fairness and respect."

Pa explained that Emperor Napoleon was the first ruler of France, a Catholic country, to extend to Jews and Protestants the same legal protections as Catholics and make the followers of minority faiths equal in the eyes of the law.

I listened and went back to my reading. At the time I felt nothing momentous, but that little exchange planted a seed that would grow into a lifetime passion for Napoleonic history and a burning desire to set the record straight. The more I read, the more I realized that Emperor Napoleon was a towering figure, a man 200 years ahead of his time who brought a spirit of fraternity, liberty, and justice where people had known only oppression. Napoleon became a personal hero, and the study of his life became my second career. I wanted desperately to correct all the calumnies directed against him, which were first put forth by his enemies and later believed by historians who presented them as fact.

The Seed Takes Root

It was actually my first career, bodybuilding, that led me to my special focus in Napoleonic research, which would reveal a terrible crime 185 years old, alter our understanding of the past, and change a crucial part of Napoleonic history.

A knowledge of human health gained from work in fitness and nutrition led me to doubt the accepted opinion about Emperor Napoleon's death. Historians claimed that he succumbed to stomach cancer while he was held captive by the British on tiny, remote St. Helena Island, where he spent the last five years of his life. Napoleon was sent into exile after his final defeat by the combined armies of England and the reactionary kings of Europe at the Battle of Waterloo in 1815.

Though historians pronounced their verdict on the French Emperor's death as if there could be no doubt, the symptoms reported by witnesses were nothing at all like cancer or any natural illness. The more I read first-hand accounts, the more suspicious and sinister the circumstances seemed. I learned of another investigator, Sten Forshufvud, a Swedish dentist and noted expert on toxicology, who was convinced that someone murdered Napoleon by slipping him doses of the deadly poison arsenic. In the 1960s, Sten had a strand of Napoleon's hair analyzed with a then-brand-new laboratory technique, which showed that he died with very high levels of arsenic in his body. We began to correspond, and when I met Sten in 1974 we decided to work together to prove to the world that Emperor Napoleon was, indeed, poisoned.

Thus began my campaign to establish the truth and rewrite the history of Emperor Napoleon's death. While Sten pursued scientific work, I negotiated permission to get more of Napoleon's hair for scientific study and searched the historical record for clues about this long-hidden crime. I also publicized the results of our research.

The year 1978 saw the publication of a scholarly book I co-authored with Sten Forshufvud, *Assassination at St. Helena: The Poisoning of Napoleon,* which recounts Napoleon's death as it really occurred, as revealed by our scientific and historic detective work. It also unmasks the murderer, a French nobleman who went into exile with Napoleon. A few years later, I collaborated with writer David Hapgood on a popular historic version of the story. *The Murder of Napoleon,* first published in 1982, became one of the most successful history books of all time with 44 foreign editions in languages from Czech to Urdu. The 45th edition, due out this year, will be published in Mongolia.

Though the book set the record straight, it brought down the wrath of scholars and historians. Particularly in France, I was attacked in print and from the podium, jeered at, and dismissed as an ignorant amateur historian whose ideas were not worth considering. Meanwhile, technology improved, and new laboratory tests strengthened the case for poisoning. Roger Martz, chief of chemistry and toxicology for the U.S. Federal Bureau of Investigation, analyzed a hair sample taken from Napoleon at the time of his death and issued a letter stating: "The amount of arsenic present in the submitted hairs is consistent with arsenic poisoning." I then asked that criminal investigators at London's famous Scotland Yard review the results of my research and answer this question: Would Scotland Yard investigate the case as murder if everything happened today, and they were presented with the same evidence? Detective superintendent Suzanne Williams wrote that her unit would, indeed, investigate and take the case to the Crown Prosecution Service.

At first, such expert opinion only made the intellectual establishment more intransigent. But, as is said, the truth will come out. Recent molecular analysis at a laboratory near Strasbourg in France provided incontrovertible proof of crime. It showed that Napoleon ingested the most toxic form of mineral arsenic, then used only in the manufacture of rat poison. In a press conference following the release of this new scientific study, Dr. Pascal Kintz, president of the Société Française de Toxicologie Analytique, said that the only explanation for the findings was that Napoleon was deliberately poisoned.

Case closed.

Truth goes through three stages: First, it is ridiculed; second, it is virulently and violently attacked; third, the world finally accepts it as self-evident, as if everyone knew it all along.

I am gratified to say that after many years of study and scientific research we have finally arrived at stage three. I was officially honored in France where my research on Napoleon's death and bringing out the truth about his life has been widely recognized and accepted. In the year 2000, by decree of the French government, I received the Legion of Honor, the country's highest award, established by Emperor Napoleon himself in 1802. I have on my desk a letter I received not long ago from French Prime Minister M. Dominique de Villepin praising me for shedding new light and deepening the understanding of a great and significant Frenchman.

The story of my adventures as a Napoleonic researcher and historical detective belongs in another book, not this one, where the subject is what Joe and I accomplished together. But you should know that while I fought for the international recognition of bodybuilding, a great but badly misunderstood branch of athletics, I also led a fight for a great but badly misunderstood historical figure. In both cases I began facing odds that seemed impossible, with the laughter of the established authorities ringing in my ears.

I must love long, uphill battles because I fought two of them simultaneously for many, many years. To solve the Napoleonic crime took 40 years. It took me 52 years to get bodybuilding the place of honor I sought for it, which was recognition from the International Olympic Committee.

Thwarted Ambitions

After finishing the seventh grade, I dropped out of school and went to work full-time to help my struggling family get by. I worked as a helper in a pajama factory and then got a job at a Shap's restaurant where I made ice cream sundaes, a task I made more interesting by creating my own assembly-line system and becoming the fastest sundae maker in Montreal.

Late in my teens, I applied to join the Royal Canadian Mounted Police. Since boyhood I had dreamed of becoming a Mountie, a career that seemed to combine high adventure with preserving law and order.

I went down to the recruiting office with Gerard Lauzon, a French Canadian who was my best friend. We met separately with the recruitment officer, a proper, spit-and-polish type who was English Canadian, as most Mounties were at the time.

Toward the end of our interview, the officer told me I was Mountie material, which I was thrilled to hear, but then the other shoe dropped. "Unfortunately," he said, "our current quota for new recruits has been met. We will, however, contact you in the near future."

I went home full of hope and excitement and waited for a call. Sixty-some years later I'm still waiting.

What the officer really told me, in a polite, English fashion was "no Jews allowed."

Gerard, meanwhile, got in. The Mounties had just begun to take on a small, token contingent of French Canadians. I can't tell you how many times my friend, who retired as an RCMP sergeant after 25 years of service, has told me how lucky I was that the Mounties never called. Think of all I might have missed—seeing the world, advancing the cause of our sport and international understanding, helping to solve a crime of great historical importance, writing books, my honorary degrees and special recognitions and awards, and so on.

Of course I couldn't see the future, and I felt let down. However, at no time was I angry. Blatant anti-Semitism was a fact of life in those days, and resentment would get me absolutely nowhere.

I didn't have time to brood, anyway, because a higher duty called. Canada, as part of the British Commonwealth, went to war with Nazi Germany. At age 18, I joined the Canadian Army.

I'm very proud of my service, and I think my wartime experiences laid the groundwork for some of my work as IFBB president. While organizing and promoting competitive bodybuilding, I always used our federation and our sport to promote understanding and friendship among the nations and peoples of the world. These efforts would earn me, much to my surprise, a nomination for the Nobel Peace Prize in the 1980s.

Before being demobilized from the Canadian Army at the war's end, I became keenly interested in architecture. After I got out of uniform I came home, bunked down with Joe in our tiny bedroom, and looked for an apprentice-level position in an architectural firm. For weeks I combed want ads and knocked on doors before I walked into a well-known downtown company that had an opening.

I met with the head architect, a striking man in the prime of life. He wore a beautiful tweed suit, and, like practically all of Montreal's educated elite back then, was of English extraction. At the end of our talk he asked if I could start on Monday and then put his hand on my shoulder and walked me to the elevator, a courtesy that seemed like a sure sign that I had a job.

While we waited for the elevator the architect asked me what faith I followed.

"Hebrew," I replied.

"I see. That's fine."

By the look of him, it was perfectly fine. He thought another moment and said, "It just occurred to me, Ben, we need to evaluate a few more little details. Don't come in Monday. Sit tight, and we'll call you on Tuesday."

I'm still waiting to hear from him.

Much as I hated discrimination, I didn't let this rebuff get to me. Time and energy are much too precious to waste on anger. And it didn't take me long to see that the architect actually did me a favor. I owe him my thanks for giving me a push toward bodybuilding.

Joining Joe

Here's one of the morals of our story: The best opportunities are the opportunities you make for yourself.

If somebody shuts the door on you, don't stand there pounding on it. Get moving and find yourself another door. Better still, make your own door.

My brother Joe was a master door-maker. Together he and I worked to open new fields of opportunity where none previously existed, where nobody even imagined there could be opportunities.

But first I stepped through the door that Joe held open for me. When I was demobilized at the end of World War II in 1945, *Your Physique* and Joe's mail-order business were progressing splendidly. So great was the demand for information about bodybuilding, fitness, and nutrition, that Joe launched another magazine, *Muscle Power,* which was edited by Earle Liederman, a famous American muscle man who also was a wonderful writer. Earle worked in Los Angeles much of the time.

With two magazines and more and more orders for Weider products, my brother was up to his ears in work. Naturally I pitched in. When I wasn't out job hunting, I did whatever came to hand, taking care of product orders, going through correspondence, and so forth. Joe didn't act like he was the boss. He trusted me to figure out what needed doing and not screw up. To this very day, our work is based on deep, largely unspoken mutual trust.

Shortly after the director of the architecture firm turned me down, Joe and I formed our alliance. We sealed the deal in less than 30 seconds, a half-minute that changed our lives.

Here's the gist of the conversation:

"You know, Ben, I've got a lot more work than I can handle here. I need your help, and I'd really like for you to come in with me for good. What do you say?"

"Sounds fine to me, Joe."

Having said what needed to be said, we went back to work.

Toujours de L'Audace

We had Joe's magazines to spread the word about Weider-style bodybuilding and the benefits it brought, and we had equipment and instructional materials that bodybuilders required. What we didn't have was a public event that did bodybuilding justice. All the competitions, such as they were, were organized in the United States under control of the AAU and under the thumb of Bob Hoffman. Early in 1946, Joe and I decided to mount a competition in Montreal to showcase Canadian bodybuilding talent and thrill the growing number of enthusiasts. Because of the pressures on Joe, it made sense for me to assume responsibility for the event.

For our contest, where we would select Mr. Montreal 1946, we needed a venue. The easy solution was a neighborhood arena or school auditorium, the sort of place Hoffman used for his events. But I fixed my sights on the Monument National Theater on lower St. Lawrence Boulevard. This elegant hall was built in 1898 for French Canadian plays and cultural events.

A sporting event had never been organized in the theater, which explains the shock and incredulity of theater manager Monsieur LaPointe when I first approached him. I don't recall his first name because I never addressed him as anything but "Monsieur." He was an energetic, high-strung character no more than 5 feet, 2 inches tall.

Had I spoken English, I'm sure the manager would have turned me down the instant I told him why I wished to rent his theater. But he appreciated the fact that I did business in French. Still, Monsieur LaPointe ridiculed the notion of bringing something as bizarre as a physique contest into his august cultural landmark. The very idea!

As I would do thousands of times and still do, I patiently explained the merits of bodybuilding as a lifestyle and sport and spectator event to a person with no knowledge, but a great deal of prejudice.

"You'll never sell enough tickets to pay the rent," the manager said.

I told him that the bodybuilding public was bigger than most people imagined, using numbers from our businesses to prove the point.

He said to me, "Even if I were willing to rent this theater to you for such an enterprise—and I'm not saying I will—it's going to cost you $200. Have you got that much money?"

"No," I said.

"How much do you have now, to put down on deposit?" he asked.

"None," I said.

"Bah!" the little man exploded. "You're wasting my time!" He stood to show me the door, but I very gently took his arm and asked him to reconsider.

After a moment of shock, he softened and smiled and said, *"Vous avez de l'audace,"* meaning, "You've got a lot of guts." Then, sighing as if to say "I must be crazy to do this," Monsieur LaPointe told me he had one available Saturday night in October that he would hold for me for two weeks, at which time I had to put down a deposit of $50. Failing that, I could forget about renting his theater.

Likely this was a ploy to get me to go away. For me it was victory. Instead of saying "No!" as he clearly meant to, the theater manager presented me with a challenge I had every intention of meeting.

I quoted Monsieur LaPointe in French because his words bring to mind Napoleon's famous saying about what a military leader needs most: *"De l'audace, de l'audace, toujours de l'audace."* Literally, "Audacity, audacity, always audacity." As Napoleon showed many times on the battlefield, a smaller army, outmanned and outgunned, can defeat a more powerful force by doing things bold and unexpected. The principle applies in all areas of life. I marched into M. LaPointe's office with no money, no experience, no backing, no credentials, trying to get space for an event he was sure did not belong in his theater. All I had was *l'audace,* and that's all I needed.

Impresario

Immediately I spent the few dollars I had on a rush order for 1,500 tickets, the Monument National's capacity. Prices ranged from $1.50 for prime seating close to the stage to 75 cents for seats in the balcony. The next day, tickets in hand, I made the rounds of clubs and gyms where Joe had been a well-known figure for years. I talked up the contest and left blocks of tickets with the owners to whom I offered an incentive: For every dozen tickets sold, the seller got one free. I figured I could count on at least 12 sales per gym so the owners could get their free seats.

I'll never forget Mr. LaPointe's reaction when I presented him with $50 after only a week. His eyes grew wide and his jaw dropped, and then he smiled and said to me, "I had a hunch you might succeed. You're a gutsy young man, and you are going to go far."

With a venue and a date and a promising start on ticket sales, we needed to finalize official sanction from the AAU, which in those days also controlled amateur bodybuilding in Canada. Because of Bob Hoffman, that organization treated our sport as a stepchild of weightlifting. The men to talk to were the AAU representatives in Montreal who were in charge of weightlifting, Harvey Hill and Charlie Walker, who happened to be old friends of Joe. As Joe wrote, Harvey helped him get started in competitive lifting. Joe's friends had already said they would look favorably on our contest if we agreed to pay a percentage of our profit to the AAU. After things got rolling, they assured us that we had our sanction, no problem.

If you're wondering why official sanction was—and is—so important to a contest producer, here's a two-word answer: top talent. Crowds pay to see the best athletes, but those athletes stay away from non-sanctioned events because they don't want to risk being penalized by the sport's governing body. A bodybuilder who went outside the system could be barred from the AAU-sanctioned competitions in the U.S., which back then were the only route to the top. Hoffman, in short, held the keys to the kingdom, and nobody wanted to get locked out. With our sanction, though, we had no worries.

I did whatever I could do to generate excitement and sell tickets, providing it cost little or nothing. I made my own flyers, typing and drawing a muscle man on a mimeograph stencil, then cranking copies off by the hundreds. I put them up all over town. I called on all the newspapers, telling sports editors about the contest and asking for coverage. The reception was mixed, to say the least. One editor tore up the typed press release I gave him and roared, "Bodybuilding? In my newspaper? You must be out of your mind!"

To add star power to the event we booked, as guest poser, Alan Stephan, the newly crowned AAU Mr. America. Under the rules of the day we couldn't pay him, but we took care of his expenses, one of the biggest items in our meager budget. This was a sound investment, though, because some fans would buy tickets just to see such a great star in the flesh. To this day contest promoters bring in big-name champions to help fill seats and add special excitement. The arrangement is good for the stars, too, because it gives them valuable exposure and publicity.

I hired musicians, worked out staging, lined up stagehands and ushers and security men, and had a program printed. On contest night I'd be the director and also the emcee, an honor I earned because I could address the crowd in both English and French. I joked that I was ready to go out and sell popcorn and soft drinks, too.

Fans quickly bought up tickets until we sold out. Alan Stephan arrived the day before the contest and bowled us all over. He was blond, tall, handsome, and in great shape. I knew his physique would absolutely astound the crowd and that his personality would please, too. Alan was well-spoken and personable and a genuinely nice fellow.

On contest night I saw to last-minute details in a sort of frenzy. Every muscle man of note in our area came to compete. The turnout amazed even Joe and me. Upwards of 80 bodybuilders stretched, paced, or simply waited backstage as show time approached. Joe deserves credit here. His close association with the event gave it stature and credibility among men who had known and admired him for years. His name still remains the ultimate stamp of approval in our world. The top professional contest, which Joe started in 1965, officially bears the name Joe Weider's Mr. Olympia.

While the musicians arrived and began to tune up, I assembled the competitors and told them how the contest would proceed and gave instructions for lining up and taking their turns onstage. I couldn't resist dashing outside to watch the crowd gathering. Hundreds of excited fans stood in the crisp fall night. A few hundred people without tickets milled around trying to find somebody with extras to sell. It bothered me to disappoint them and bothered me even more to think of the lost revenue. If we had more seating we could have brought in another $400 or $500 or even more. My pang of regret didn't last long, though, because duty called from backstage.

Surprise Attack

Minutes before the contest time, Harvey Hill and Charlie Walker of the AAU, both grim-faced, came backstage and motioned for the bodybuilders to gather around. Harvey pulled a letter from an envelope and began reading. Joe and I went to see what was up.

The first words we heard were Charlie Walker's. "This is not an officially sanctioned contest," he told the bodybuilders. "If you participate, you'll lose your amateur status. We strongly suggest that you leave now."

"What the hell is this?" Joe exploded.

His friends told us our sanction had been withdrawn, and I asked on whose authority.

Harvey showed us his letter, saying, "This is from Dietrich Workman. We're supposed to inform the bodybuilders."

Dietrich Workman headed the AAU weightlifting committee in the U.S., which meant the order came from the highest levels.

I asked if there was any way to redeem the situation, but Harvey and Charlie shook their heads and said it was too late.

"It's a deliberate stab in the back!" said Joe.

Harvey said, "Joe, it's not us."

"You guys are hypocrites and liars," Joe shot back. "If you cared about bodybuilding or your friends, you'd never be part of this."

The bodybuilders stood open-mouthed, wondering if their big night was over before it even started. I was so angry that I called over a pair of policemen working security and asked them to show Harvey and Charlie the door. The two left willingly, undoubtedly on their way to report to their superiors that our contest was over. Joe asked the bodybuilders not to leave until he and I had a chance to speak privately.

Joe fumed and said to me, "Those jerks are not going to shut us down."

I replied, "To hell with the AAU and Bob Hoffman. Joe, we don't need them."

We knew we had to do something fast because we could hear the audience growing restive. People began shouting for the contest to begin. In an instant, as if with a single mind, we came to a decision to form our own sports federation that would be of, for, by, and about bodybuilding. Though this was a bold move with no prior planning, it made perfect sense. Didn't our sport deserve an organization all its own? And why should we subject ourselves to a petty tyrant in Pennsylvania and his national committee? The immediate problem was our Canadian contest, but we saw beyond that. Our federation would be international and serve all the world's bodybuilders.

I just wrote more words than we spoke, but we understood everything and even named our new creation on the spot. Joe turned to speak to the bodybuilders, who were understandably anxious. He said, "We're putting on this competition, and you don't have to worry about sanctioning. As of this moment, we have our own governing body. We're calling it the International Federation of Bodybuilders, and it's going to make bodybuilding bigger and better than ever."

The fellows stood, mute, and Joe went on, "If you want to withdraw from the competition, we will not hold it against you."

Not one man left.

"Okay, gentlemen, let's go," I said.

The contest went off without a hitch, the crowd cheering for their favorites and roaring their approval for Alan Stephan, who fulfilled his commitment like the gentleman he was. Excitement went up as I announced the judges' picks for category awards, such as best arms, best chest, most muscular, best poser, and the runners-up and winners in height divisions. The biggest trophy and the title of Mr. Montreal 1946 went to René Leger, the powerhouse bodybuilder discovered and trained by Joe when they both were teenagers.

Clearly the contest was a hit with the crowd, and it received some surprisingly good newspaper write-ups. I'm sure most of the reporters who showed up expected to ridicule all they saw, but they left favorably impressed and the coverage showed it. We managed to clear a couple hundred dollars, which we earmarked for our next contest.

The Olympic Dream

Like the contest, the federation would be my responsibility. I became founding president, a position I still hold thanks to the continuing support of voting delegates at our international congresses. Joe was always available to provide advice or even financial support for federation activities. However, my position put some needed distance between our sport's governing body and my brother and his work, which brought him into constant contact with individual bodybuilders as trainer and advisor and sponsor as well as publisher of the magazines that elevated bodybuilders to stardom.

Even at that tense backstage moment when we founded the IFBB, I sensed great things to come and made a vow to myself to take the federation and bodybuilding to the top in organized athletics. Somewhat later I saw with great clarity what the top looked like: recognition by the International Olympic Committee leading to participation in the Olympic Games. In sport you can go no higher, and that's where we would go, whatever it took, however long it took.

I would have been shocked to learn that we were 52 years away from reaching the goal of IOC recognition and staggered to know the millions upon millions of dollars that would be spent and the endless effort on my part and that of scores of dedicated individuals. But such knowledge would not have deterred me a bit.

Why did this quest assume such great personal importance? Why, for that matter, did I ever get such a crazy idea to begin with? One answer might seem strange, but it's true nevertheless. I would strive for Olympic recognition for the same reason I became the fastest sundae maker in Montreal back at Shap's Restaurant. For me, good enough never is good enough, and if there's a top, I aim for it. This is my nature, just as it's Joe's nature to be driven from deep within by his own brilliant ideas.

And bodybuilding truly deserves a place in the pantheon of Olympic sports. It dates to the original Olympic Games of the ancient Greeks, which inspired the modern Olympics. Between competitive events, the ancients put on impromptu physique shows for the public by going about nude with their bodies oiled to accentuate musculature. Like modern bodybuilders, the ancients used weights for conditioning and to improve their appearance. As for the modern games, if you look past prejudice and ignorance about bodybuilding, our sport differs very little from other Olympic sports that are judged subjectively, such as diving or figure skating. As in those sports, winners must show both athleticism and beauty. The more you know about amateur competitive bodybuilding, the harder it becomes to deny it a place alongside other Olympic sports.

Greater ideals also called me to the Olympics. The IOC and the games are about much more than sport. Pierre de Coubertin, the French aristocrat who founded the IOC and revived the Olympics in 1894, promoted athletics for the good of the world's young people and to bring them together in a spirit of friendly, clean, sportsmanlike competition. The games were meant to encourage peace, mutual respect, and understanding. The same Olympic spirit reigns within the IFBB. Our constitution bars our members from bringing politics, international strife and prejudice of any kind into bodybuilding. Such things cannot even be discussed in our proceedings.

You can read this credo on the letterhead of official IFBB correspondence: "In sport, there are no limitations, no barriers of race, religion, politics or culture. In sport we are in touch with each other."

Over the years, Joe wholeheartedly supported my quest for IOC recognition, and he understood that it would do a great deal of good for bodybuilding. But the Olympics was never one of his big dreams, which all had to with advancing the cause of bodybuilding to make people stronger, healthier, and happier. The Olympics was my dream and nobody else's. I could not have given my life to somebody else's dream. Here's something else that has made Joe and me such a good team. We pursued our own dreams in our own ways, but like so much in our lives, these dreams were a perfect fit. I like to say we walk parallel paths, always headed for the same place.

The Olympic quest, the focus of my professional life, will also be the focus of my portion of this book. Other stories could be told, but this is the most significant. My signal contribution to our work was to take Joe's great ideas and visions to the world, promoting our sport and organizing IFBB affiliates, country by country, region by region, continent by continent.

Self-Inflicted Wound

In his surprise attack on Mr. Montreal 1946, Hoffman fired one of the opening shots in what would become a long, hard-fought war for control of bodybuilding. In a way, the double-cross flattered us because it meant that Hoffman saw our nascent efforts as a threat to his own supremacy in publishing and organizing bodybuilding contests.

A wiser man than Hoffman would have put on a friendly face. As the Chinese general Sun Tzu wrote in *The Art of War,* "Keep your friends close, and your enemies closer." Precisely because he saw us as dangerous rivals, Hoffman should have said, "Welcome to the club, boys," and kept us in the AAU fold where he could watch us closely and exercise some control. At that early date, we would have stayed in the fold, and it would not have occurred to us to form our own bodybuilding federation. But Hoffman's treachery created one of the instruments of his own destruction. As my story will show, his faction eventually lost control of American bodybuilding, and the IFBB overcame the criticism and resistance that Hoffman fomented, largely because of our federation's size and prestige outside the U.S. Not only did Hoffman create an enemy when he didn't need to, he created an enemy that would grow and gain strength in places he couldn't reach—all around the world.

Hoffman's move was a textbook case of bad planning born out of arrogance. He underestimated the Weider brothers and overestimated his own power over the situation. Then he struck a blow that backfired because it wasn't decisive and didn't put us out of action. In the final analysis he did us more good than harm, while helping to ensure his own defeat.

Here's a lesson to be learned from Mr. Hoffman: If you're going to be rotten, be smart about it.

The World Calls

While we made arrangements to sell Joe's magazines throughout the English-speaking world, we discovered we already had a growing international readership. Enthusiasts here in North America sent foreign friends copies of *Your Physique* and *Muscle Power,* and travelers took copies overseas. We were amazed to get fan mail, letters to the editor, and subscription requests from the far corners of the planet. The letters showed what we already knew in our hearts, that there was a worldwide hunger to learn about bodybuilding both as a lifestyle and an organized sport.

Strangely, a disproportionate number of letters came from South Africa, some from knowledgeable bodybuilders. Stranger still, most letters came from farms and remote villages in the South African hinterland, not from major cities such as Capetown, Johannesburg, or Pretoria. I had a good sense of the geographical distribution because I made it a policy to respond to each person who wrote in regardless of who they were or where they lived. I always included back issues of our magazines. The international postage could be quite costly, and most people who wrote in weren't in a position to buy anything, but the point was to promote bodybuilding, not sales.

Shortly after the Mr. Montreal contest I received a letter postmarked "Cape Town" from a fellow named Jack Lunz who loved our magazines and wanted to become our South African distributor. He also wanted to organize an affiliated federation in his country and open an office of the IFBB in Cape Town. I could tell from the tone of the letter that this was a serious contact from a responsible person. He went so far as to offer to pay for my plane fare as well as to put me up in his home.

I said yes to the invitation, but turned down the offer of a plane ticket. Pride would not allow me to accept, and I had other misgivings. Taking a gift so valuable would weaken my position in business dealings, and I didn't want to feel beholden. On the other hand, there was nothing wrong with staying in Lunz's home, which could promote good relations by establishing a personal bond.

The response from Lunz showed that my insistence on paying for the plane ticket made a very favorable impression. Obviously he assumed we had considerable financial resources. What the gesture really meant was that I hadn't priced the airfare. What a shock that was, discovering that round-trip flights cost more than $1,000, the equivalent of almost $10,000 today! On many days I would have been hard-pressed to come up with 1,000 cents, much less dollars, but I could not swallow my pride and ask for the ticket I had already turned down. I went to a travel agency and negotiated a credit arrangement whereby I would get the ticket up front and then pay for it in installments.

Chalk up another win for *l'audace*.

I laid plans to exploit all the possibilities of the trip. In those pre-jet days, such a long journey involved a good many stops for refueling and making connections. At some of the stops, like Paris and Cairo, were people I very much wanted to meet to advance the cause of bodybuilding and the IFBB. So I sent out a flurry of letters and cables to set up face-to-face meetings and finalized an itinerary that gave me more time where I needed it. Meanwhile, I had to obtain the proper visas, get the required inoculations, and secure accommodations. Making arrangements took two full months, from early January 1947 to March 3, when I left Montreal.

To anybody else, the trip would have looked like absolute, unalloyed, extravagant madness. I was 23 years old, strapped for cash, still sleeping with my brother in our old bedroom, with no formal schooling, and no experience in sports governance or international commerce. The only long-distance trips I had ever taken were courtesy of the Canadian Army. As a business proposition, the trip was beyond crazy. We couldn't hope to recoup the costs for years, if ever.

The one person who understood and supported me was the only one who mattered: Joe. The trip, like all our undertakings, was not for money or any kind of immediate benefit. It was for bodybuilding. We couldn't rely solely on the magazines to spread the word about bodybuilding and fitness and health. If we wanted to take the message to the world, we had to go out and meet the world in person.

South Africa was on the far side of the world, but so what? It looked like a promising place to start.

The Journey Begins and Almost Ends

On March 3, 1947, I boarded a Delaware Hudson Railway train bound for New York City. My family and a few friends came to the station to see me off. I knew Ma and Pa were full of trepidation, but the glowing pride on their faces masked any worry and fear. To people who struggled so hard just to keep us sheltered and fed, it must have been a wonder to see how far their sons' work had come.

At 11 o'clock the following night I sat in a window seat of a Trans World Airlines Constellation, a four-engine propeller aircraft that was then the ultimate airliner. I peered out the window at the lights of New York's La Guardia airport and listened to the engines sputter and roar into life. Never had I felt such excitement. I knew I was starting the adventure of my young life. In truth, the adventure would be lifelong and more challenging and thrilling than I dreamed. It goes on yet, after more than 60 years and more than a million miles of travel all around the globe.

A few hours after we left New York I got out and stretched my legs at an airfield on the island of Newfoundland while the plane refueled before the flight across the Atlantic Ocean. After takeoff others settled in and dozed, and I read a book. But then suddenly I was gasping for breath with a horrible pain in my ears. The plane went into a nosedive, and passengers who weren't wearing seatbelts were thrown against the ceiling while people's belongings caromed around the cabin. Temporarily deaf, I could see but not hear people shouting and crying. Death seemed imminent, but somehow my thoughts remained quite calm. My only emotion was disappointment. I remember thinking what a shame it was that all my preparations were for naught and nothing would come of this trip.

But then the plane pulled out of the dive, and my ears popped and equalized so I could hear the crew reassuring us that we were perfectly safe and would land at the Earnest Harmon Air Force Base in Newfoundland. The whole story of what happened emerged back on solid ground. The early model Constellations had Plexiglas domes called astrodomes where the navigator could look out and steer by the stars. At an altitude of 20,000 feet the astrodome on our plane blew off, causing an explosive loss of cabin pressure, and our navigator was sucked out into the void. We all might have died from lack of oxygen except the captain made an emergency descent to 8,000 feet where the air was breathable. On the ground we cheered the captain's heroics, which had scared people out of their wits. But there was sadness, too, for the navigator. The poor fellow's body was never found.

After overnighting at Harmon, we had a smooth and uneventful flight to Shannon, Ireland, where I was to catch a flight to Paris. Two things made an impression during the brief layover in Ireland. We heard details of a horrific accident the week before in which a plane like ours attempted a landing in heavy fog and crashed into the Shannon River, killing everybody on board. The story didn't affect me. I always reasoned when my number was up, it was up, and in the meantime, why worry? Far more interesting, to my young eyes, were the local ladies. As I wrote in a personal account of my travels just after the trip, "I found the Irish maidens most pretty."

You're only young once.

French Resistance

On that first trip I established practices that I follow to this day. One was to study the countries I planned to visit and learn as much as I could about the history, culture, and customs. I'd also study the individuals I would meet to gain some insight into their priorities and thought processes. It's much, much easier to get people to see things your way if you first see things their way.

It didn't take much digging to learn about the first person I was to meet in Paris. Edmond Desbonnet, then 80 years old, was famous worldwide and a national icon in France where he was known as the Father of Physical Culture. Much like Bernarr McFadden in the U.S., he was an influential publisher, author, and advocate of fitness and healthy living. During the Belle Epoque, the period around 1900 when decadence and love of pleasure ruled, Desbonnet was one of the very few calling for exercise and disciplined, clean living. Some of today's bodybuilding basics we owe to him. Among other things, he promoted adjustable plate-type weights, and he also helped to modernize weightlifting techniques. He introduced mirrored walls in the exercise studios he established, and he made photography an important part of studying and appreciating muscular development, displaying his photos in his magazine *La Culture Physique*.

In 1947, Monsieur Desbonnet greeted me at the door of his home on the Rue de Varenne and we hit it off immediately. He was an intent, serious individual about 5 feet, 5 inches tall, with a short, snow-white beard, wearing a black French beret, large loose sweater, and baggy pants. We talked through lunch and for some hours afterward. He was familiar with *Your Physique* and gave me his complete attention as I outlined my plans for building the IFBB into a worldwide federation. Though I never lost sight of the ultimate Olympic goal, I didn't emphasize it in early meetings like this one. My immediate plans were plenty of grist for the conversational mill.

In a gracious way, Desbonnet let it be known that I could not hope to succeed with the French, who had a much different conception of ideal muscular development than North Americans. While our champions were big, rugged, massively muscled men, Desbonnet's countrymen preferred physiques that were more elegant and symmetrical. The two incompatible types couldn't properly compete, and it would be wrong to try to mix them in one organization.

"I regret to say your efforts here will come to nothing," Desbonnet concluded.

We talked on about training and physical conditioning, before bidding each other a fond *adieu*.

The next morning I set out toward Boulevard Raspail in Paris and the home of another eminent Frenchman, Arax, who was at the time the most famous physique photographer in the world. Arax made me welcome and asked me to join him for breakfast. His two young children ate with us before leaving for school, and his wife amazed me by serving wine to all of us, including the children, with our breakfast. For the rest of my stay, Arax was wonderfully helpful, introducing me to top bodybuilders and leaders of *la culture physique.*

For all of his hospitality, Arax, too, said the IFBB had no future in France, where the American type of physique would never, ever find acceptance.

I heard the same thing from Juan Ferrero, a Spanish bodybuilder living and training in Paris. Strikingly handsome, warm, and friendly, Ferrero was one of Europe's rising stars. His physique actually bridged the transatlantic gap, too big for French aesthetic standards and not quite big enough to win competitions in America. He later had some success in European competitions and might have risen much higher but, sad to say, he died in a car crash.

I met two more star athletes, Andre Drapp and Robert Duranton, who made names for themselves in both bodybuilding and professional wrestling, and they told me the IFBB didn't have a prayer in their country.

Even in casual contacts with the fair sex, I talked up the benefits of strength training and fitness. You don't have to be a bodybuilder, just work out and you'll feel better and look better, I told a number of lovely Parisiennes, but they laughed like I was some sort of lunatic. All they wanted in the world were stylish clothes, jewelry, perfume, lavish meals, and champagne. Exercise and health were the farthest things from their minds.

My last full day in France was much like my first. Once again I sat down with a famous figure who told me to give up on France. At the seaport of Marseilles in the South of France, I met with Marcel Rouet, a bodybuilder who became a notable authority on fitness and iconic figure in France and all of Europe. He published his own magazine on physical culture.

"Bodybuilding as you conceive of it will never succeed in this country," he said, then wished me good luck and *bon voyage.*

To be sure, I met with resistance, but I left France full of hope as bright as the luminous blue Mediterranean Ocean beneath my plane. Never did I expect instant, easy results. My goal was to make contacts and plant a seed, and then in the coming years do what I could to help the seed take root and grow.

The seed in France would, it turned out, burst forth and bloom. Later we formed a large, well-run national federation. In 1971, the first Mr. Olympia contest held outside New York City took place in Paris, where Arnold Schwarzenegger created a sensation. Several years ago a survey showed bodybuilding to be the most popular physical activity for both French men and for women.

Welcome to Egypt

For more than a year I had been corresponding with El Sayed Mohammed Nosseir, an Egyptian weightlifter who was a well-known figure worldwide and a national hero in his own country. Nosseir, who set records for lifts in the light heavyweight class, was a former world champion and gold medalist at the 1928 Olympic Games. After he left competition he developed an Egyptian team that won an incredible five medals at the 1936 Olympics, including gold medals won by Khadr Sayed El Touni and Anwar Mohammed Mesbah. At the time of my trip, Egypt was famous for its competitive lifting, with two rising stars, Mahmoud Fayad and Ibrahim Hassanien Shams, who would win gold medals at the upcoming 1948 Olympics.

After learning I had a stopover in Cairo on the way to South Africa, Nosseir wrote back insisting that I spend several days in Egypt as his personal guest. How could I refuse such an offer? Not only was I eager to spend time with this great athlete and leader in international sport, I wanted to see the ancient splendors of Egypt, a land that had attracted my attention ever since I was a young boy.

I expected a quiet, anonymous arrival at Cairo's airport, but a greeting party stood outside my plane. It was easy to pick out Nosseir, because he was a big bear of a man, 6 feet tall and weighing more than 200 pounds. On his head he wore a Turkish *tarbush* or *fez,* like a flower pot made of bright red felt and sporting a black tassel, and though he hadn't competed for numerous years, he radiated physical power and vitality. As I came down the steps from the plane he rushed up and took my hand in his. To this day I can feel that immensely powerful grip. But even more vividly, I can see Nosseir's gentle smile as he said, "Welcome, my friend. Welcome to Egypt. You are my brother. You are a member of my family." Like many of the giants of strength, he had a tender, true heart under the hard muscle, and I knew we were friends for life.

Inside the terminal building a couple hundred miserable-looking travelers stood waiting to clear customs.

"How many hours is this going to take?" I whispered to Nosseir.

He smiled and said, "I estimate we will be out of here in a few minutes. Come!"

He led me past the crowd to a special area where uniformed officials saluted us and waved us through. This was my first taste of VIP treatment, and more was to come. A limousine took me to Shepherds Hotel, now long gone, which was then one of the most famous hotels in all of the Middle East. Nosseir told me to rest because he had arranged a party for me that evening. My suite at Shepherds, decorated in traditional Egyptian style, was the most opulent hotel room I had ever seen. Here I was, fresh from The Main in Montreal and barely a year out of the army, in Egypt enjoying the royal treatment. That night, Nosseir threw a fantastic party where the guests included the country's most famous strongmen. It was a marvelous evening of brotherhood, friendship, Egyptian music, and dance.

The next day, Nosseir took me to lunch at Cairo's most famous restaurant, Groppi's. On my own I could have walked from my hotel to Groppi's in 10 minutes, but it took an hour for us to get there. Every few steps Nosseir stopped to speak to a group of admirers. I'm absolutely convinced that after the country's ruler King Farouk, Nosseir was the most popular person in Egypt.

Discussions

Had I come purely for pleasure I could not have had a more wonderful time in Egypt, but Nosseir and I accomplished a great deal. For hours at a time we talked about matters related to strength training and our respective sports. When I asked Nosseir how he produced so many champion lifters, he told me of two key techniques: Number one, he trained his athletes as bodybuilders before narrowing their focus to the Olympic lifts. Nosseir explained that balanced, all-around muscular development was the most solid foundation on which to build championship technique and power. His appreciation of bodybuilding surprised me. After all, the American weightlifting guru Bob Hoffman had nothing but contempt for bodybuilding. Nosseir avidly read Joe's magazines and studied the new training techniques that Joe developed. Indeed, some of what Nosseir taught the Egyptian team he lifted straight from the pages of *Your Physique* and *Muscle Power.*

I couldn't wait to tell my brother that he, the Trainer of Champions, had helped to train Egypt's world champion weightlifters.

The other reason for Egypt's great competitive success, according to Nosseir, was his innovation in lifting technique called the Camel Method. He got the idea watching a camel rise from a kneeling position while loaded with heavy burdens. First the animal straightened its back legs, then the front legs, and then stood erect. Nosseir adapted the same motions to lift a heavy barbell from the floor to an overhead position in a single motion, a move called the "snatch" in competitive weightlifting. He tried bending down as low as possible, then moving the weight upward while lunging forward on one foot and continuing the lift in one uninterrupted motion, until he stood fully upright with the weight overhead. He also developed a Camel Method "clean," another move in competitive lifting wherein the weight is brought to shoulder level.

I was fascinated and asked Nosseir to write a series of articles about his techniques for Joe's magazines, which he was happy to do. The articles were very well received, especially by lifters and coaches who wanted to duplicate the Egyptians' great successes.

One day Nosseir asked me, "How do you feel about Bob Hoffman?"

I hesitated before answering. After all, Hoffman was a very powerful figure in the International Weightlifting Federation (IWF) and had done great things for his sport in the U.S. Thinking that Nosseir might hold Hoffman in high esteem, I spoke carefully but honestly. I said that although I greatly admired Hoffman's work with weightlifting, I did not appreciate his treatment of bodybuilding.

"I have cut off all contact with that man," said Nosseir, showing terrible anger.

My friend went on to say he was deeply upset by turmoil Hoffman caused within the IWF. Hoffman, according to Nosseir, was a menace to his own sport. Nosseir didn't say much more, but clearly there was a history of bad experiences and bad blood between him and the man from York, Pennsylvania.

My friend had really surprised me. Obviously, my brother and I were on the outs with Hoffman, but I had no idea that he had made bitter enemies within international weightlifting. In Egypt, things looked much, much different than they did back home. Here, there was no rift between weightlifting and bodybuilding. Nor was there any dislike of the Weiders on the part of the lifters—far from it. This great Egyptian champion and coach made bodybuilding a foundation of his training regimen, and he read our magazines and used Joe's techniques.

I asked Nosseir if he would support the organization of an IFBB affiliate in Egypt. He said he would do all he could to help me and my federation. Thus Egypt became the No. 3 IFBB nation, after Canada and the U.S.A.

It was slow going at first because of the Egyptian passion for weightlifting, but our sport flourished on the banks of the Nile. Credit must be given to the efforts of men such as the great bodybuilding champion Abdel Hamid El-Guindy, who later won the Mr. Universe and Mr. World championships and went on to become president of the Egyptian Bodybuilding Federation. Today, under the leadership of EBBF president Dr. Eng. Adel Fahim El Sayed, Egyptian athletes win numerous medals at our competitions year after year.

Egyptian Magic

If I found out I could take one more trip, and only one, I might go back to Egypt. Of all the lands I visited, this one made the deepest, most lasting impression. The ancient past is so vivid and close at hand, as if you could turn a corner and walk into another time. And I fell in love with Egypt's present, as well. Everywhere I went there were sounds, smells, and sights I'd never known. At the time, Cairo was very cosmopolitan, with enclaves of Greeks,

French, Egyptian Christians, and Jews. It was the most exciting, colorful city I'd ever been to.

Nosseir gave me one last Egyptian dream, a farewell party in a tent at the base of the pyramids. I tried to beg off because I didn't want to miss my plane, which was due to take off at 10 that night, but Nosseir said, "Don't worry, my friend. I have everything worked out." Festivities started about seven, and at nine I began to fidget. I told Nosseir we had to leave right away, but he acted like we had all the time in the world and told me to relax and have fun. I couldn't relax, but I couldn't leave, either, because I depended on Nosseir for transportation. At 10:30, sure that I had missed the plane, I couldn't hide my extreme frustration, but Nosseir kept smiling and saying I shouldn't worry. I was absolutely bewildered when we left for the airport at a quarter past eleven. With the plane gone for more than an hour, what was the point?

"All is well, my friend," said Nosseir.

At the airport, our car went straight out onto the tarmac, where, amazingly, my plane sat. Nosseir explained that engine trouble had delayed departure, but repairs were now complete. I accepted his words at face value, but then, as I took my seat on the plane, everybody stared and I heard somebody say, "Is that the man they held the plane for? Who is he? He must be a very important person."

I realized that Nosseir used his influence to ground my flight until I arrived. While I flew through the night I let all my wonderful experiences soak in. I left a small part of my heart in Egypt.

Cape Town

My flights hopscotched southward. Next stop was Khartoum, capital of what was then called the Anglo-Egyptian Sudan and the hottest place I ever visited. In temperatures well over 120 degrees I saw what I thought were dead camels and donkeys in the streets, but the animals weren't dead, they just didn't want to move. After that I had stops at Nairobi in British East Africa (now Kenya); Salisbury (now Harare), Rhodesia; Zimbabwe, then Johannesburg in South Africa and finally Cape Town, the southernmost city on the African continent.

Jack Lunz, the man who instigated the entire trip, met me at the airport and drove me to his house in Sea Point, a lovely suburb with a spectacular view of the ocean. Jack, who wore glasses, was a slim fellow who stood about 5 foot 5. I took a liking to him instantly, as I'm sure everybody did because he was so easy to be around. I settled into a wonderful, airy room at his house, and we began our conversations about bringing the IFBB and Weider publications to South Africa.

Jack, who wasn't much of an athlete, focused more on the commercial side of bodybuilding. He was in the sporting goods business, which gave him good connections at gyms and clubs all over his country, and he believed that by building the sport, he'd increase bodybuilding-related business. For us, he proposed to put on two hats, as IFBB representative and organizer and also as a rep and distributor for Weider products, primarily Joe's magazines. In the early days we had to build from the ground up, and we needed people who knew something about bodybuilding. Believe me, they were few and far between.

There aren't many stories to tell about my time in Cape Town. I met no resistance, because Jack approached us, not vice versa, and things were generally quiet and pleasant. In terms of my mission, the visit was a complete success. We gained a new national affiliate for our bodybuilding federation and the first foreign Weider agency on the far side of the world. Not long after my visit, a small store selling Weider-brand equipment opened at Number 138 Plain Street, Cape Town. That was our first retail outlet outside Montreal, where we had also opened a small store. Circulation of our magazines would later increase to the point that we sold more copies in South Africa than in Canada.

Only one thing cast a shadow over my visit to South Africa, and that was the government's system of apartheid, which separated the races and kept the white minority on top. In my post-trip account I wrote that the discrimination against non-whites was shocking and wrong. In 1975, at the height of apartheid, I would confront South African authorities in order to assure that black athletes got the same treatment as whites at a major international competition and federation congress that we held in South Africa. However, I'll tell that story later.

The day before I left for home, the King and Queen of England and their two young daughters arrived at Cape Town for an official visit to South Africa. They arrived on a huge British battleship, the HMS *Vanguard* and Jack and I went down to the waterfront to watch the arrival and tumultuous welcome by the people of Cape Town, who turned out in droves.

Big Decision

There I was, back in Montreal in our cramped little living room/office at 4466 Colonial Avenue.

"Tell me how it went in South Africa," my brother said.

I gave him the high points of the entire trip:

1) Instead of two IFBB member nations on one continent, we now had four on two continents;

2) In Egypt we had a powerful friend and ally in El Sayed Nosseir, who also was an admirer of Joe's work;

3) Jack Lunz in Cape Town, who wrote the letter to me that started our international ventures, was a go-getter who would advance the cause of bodybuilding and help us grow; and

4) I also met some great Frenchmen who wanted to help, but it would take time and effort before we had a French federation.

Joe and I spent the evening analyzing the trip and making plans to follow up.

About the same time we sat down together and had a lengthy, detailed back-and-forth discussion about a decision that faced us—our most important decision to date and maybe the most important ever. That talk was our one and only business meeting that a regular businessman would recognize as such.

Joe and I had come to the proverbial fork in the road. The Weider enterprises, in particular Joe's magazines, had outgrown Canada, which at that time had a population of only about 12.5 million. My brother now had his magazines printed in New York City because our printer in Montreal couldn't handle the growing press runs. This arrangement cost time and money that my brother didn't have to spare because he was obligated to carry the plates for the issues to be printed from Montreal to New York. Not only was the trip inconvenient, crossing the border was a problem because of holdups at customs. And there was more to our dilemma. To grow the way we wanted to grow we had to go where the growth potential was, the United States, which had 10 times the population of Canada and immense wealth.

On the other hand, Canada had distinct advantages for us. As a member of the British Commonwealth, business could be done more easily and cheaply with other Commonwealth countries as well as countries where Britain still had some type of colonial authority. All told, this meant preferential trading with about 50 countries that comprised almost the entire English-speaking world. There were advantages for the IFBB, too. A federation based in the U.S. would be seen as American, with an American outlook and agenda, which could create a barrier to certain potential member nations. Canada, on the other hand, was more inviting because it seemed like neutral ground.

After weighing our options, Joe and I decided to have it both ways. He'd move south to the U.S., taking Weider Publications with him and running all our businesses in America, where we had great growth potential. I, however, would stay put and operate the Weider business in Canada and the rest of the world. I also had responsibilities for the French-Canadian edition of *Muscle Power* that I named *Sante et Force*. And, of course, I had the IFBB and our contests.

I was sorry to see Joe go to the U.S.A., but I understood why it had to be. At the same time I was immensely gratified and proud. Less than two years after we teamed up, Joe entrusted me with a big part of the enterprises built on his ideas and vision and hard work. And he trusted me to expand bodybuilding as an organized sport and take it to the world, an impossible challenge that I accepted with great relish. I really can't express what this meant to me, and how much I owe to my brother. If it weren't for his honesty, integrity, his generosity and the respect and trust he showed me, I would never have succeeded as I did. I would not have known such great challenges or met so many interesting and exciting people. Don't misunderstand me here—over the years I did more than my part. I played key roles in making our business grow and developing our sport on the international level. Along the way, I was happy to solve a lot of problems for Joe, as he did for me. This was teamwork at its best. But when you get down to the basic facts, I owe my major accomplishments in life to what Joe started. He was my mentor and my leader. He could have set things up in any number of ways, but when he went to the U.S.A., he said to me, "This is all yours," making it clear that I had freedom to do what I had to do. Never did he second-guess me, argue about a decision, or give me any headaches of any kind—never, never, never.

Imagine having a brother like Joe. This is a blessing only God could provide.

CHAPTER FIVE

JERSEY JOE

Joe Weider

Breathes there the man, with soul so dead,
Who never to himself hath said,
"This is my own, my native land!"

These lines always moved me. I've known them by heart since I was a kid. The rest of the poem, by Sir Walter Scott, says you're no good if you don't love where you come from.

It hurt to leave Canada, it really did. That's where my family was, my girl, my old friends, all that was familiar and dear to my heart. But the U.S. was the only country big and rich and wide-open enough for my growing magazines and my dreams for bodybuilding.

In February 1947, I flew down to Miami. Doc Tilney and his wife had been working on me to set up shop near their home in Coral Gables. This made some sense because Florida was a center of health-consciousness and exercise, and we could have outdoor photo shoots all year on the beaches and in other beautiful settings. I pictured making Florida a world bodybuilding mecca, much like Southern California later became.

Like every other Northerner who goes to where the palm trees grow in the middle of winter, I fell for Florida. Immediately I wrote back to Vicky: "It's a paradise—nicer than shown in the movies. It's heaven on earth. The flowers, scenery, are more colorful than any rainbow ever seen. Already have a tan. The weather is grand."

Later I wrote that I was working out two hours every day and had built up to 187 pounds. Doc showed me all the sights, and we went out on a sailboat and to the races at Hialeah where I won $18. To a guy who never did anything but work and lift weights, this was a revelation, my first taste of what people did with leisure time in beautiful places. In truth, I never learned to relax and really enjoy myself on vacations, but thanks to Doc I had an experience to remember.

I saw, however, that Florida would not work for me. If I wanted to do big things in publishing, I had to be in or around New York City, where the big things happened.

At that time, New York ruled the roost in bodybuilding, too. Sig Klein's Physical Culture Studio on Seventh Avenue at Forty-Eighth Street was the most renowned bodybuilding center of the day, and there were other great gyms around town where top guys trained and champs passing through took workouts. Through the 1950s and into the '60s I'd send my stars over to train in New York, like I later sent them to Gold's and other gyms in Los Angeles. New York is where I would revolutionize bodybuilding. The city gyms became like laboratories where I could observe the top guys' training techniques and experiment with my own. There I formulated the famous Weider Principles, the basis of my Weider Bodybuilding System and the source of much of what people think and say about strength training today. Go to a gym and you'll hear people using words and concepts—supersets, drop sets, pyramids, split workouts, double splits, intensity, flushing, and more—that I thought out and put on paper within sight of Manhattan. Bodybuilding contests as we now know them, full of drama and excitement and beautiful stage production, came out of the city, too. The year after I came down from Montreal, Ben began to put on our biggest events in New York.

Even if I could have afforded it, paying Manhattan prices for workspace was nuts. I set up shop just across the Hudson River in Jersey City where costs were much cheaper, but I was just as close to the action and the wonderful resources and talent—photographers, writers, artists—that I needed. The location worked so well that I never moved my offices more than a mile for 25 years.

I'm sorry to say that I made the smart move to New Jersey simultaneously with the stupidest move of my life. My first wife lived in Jersey City, and I'm sorry that I met her and married her. What a mistake. What a mistake, too, letting Vicky go.

Try to understand my position, though. By then it was clear to me that prejudice would make it impossible for Vicky and me to live a normal life. Being young and in love was one thing. Making a home with healthy and harmonious family relations was another. It wasn't in the cards, not with Old Man Uzar and his kind making trouble.

When I took my new wife up to Montreal to meet the family, Ma said to me, "How dare you bring an immoral woman like that into my house!" Ma said she looked like some gangster's moll. Nobody fooled Anna Weider.

Just a few weeks after the wedding, I knew the marriage was a mistake. I think my wife knew it, too. But our misery went on for years and years.

The Book of Proverbs says you're better off living in the wilderness than with a nasty woman, whose company is like the drip-drip-drip of rain that never ends. The rain stopped when we finally split up at the end of the 1950s, but to this day a black cloud hangs over those years in my head. Even though I accomplished many amazing things, the memories don't seem as brilliant and bright to me as they ought to.

Maybe it's a combination of events that casts a shadow. This era of my life began and ended with disasters. The marriage ended at more or less the same time I took the worst financial hit in my life, through none of my own doing, which put me millions of dollars in the hole so I had to start over from scratch.

Just before I moved to New Jersey and got married, some business trouble came to a head—nothing even close to the late-1950s catastrophe, but still a pain in the rear end. I wanted to leave out this episode because I don't harbor hard feelings or hold malice in my heart. No one should, because it saps the energy and wounds the spirit. But the trouble shows that I was still a babe in the woods who had to learn, the hard way, to watch my back in case somebody I trusted might stick in a knife.

Honest people are always susceptible to shady characters.

I first got involved with Dan Lurie because I needed somebody to make Weider-brand weight sets in the U.S. American readers demanded them, but import duties drove my costs up, and shipping cost too much and took too long. Lurie, who lived in Brooklyn, seemed like a good pick to become my American agent. He was a bodybuilder himself and his dad owned a trucking company. So I set Lurie up with a manufacturing operation. Our deal was that he made the weights and shipped them to U.S. buyers, and I sent my Weider weight training courses direct to the customers from Montreal. I used the number of courses I sent to keep track of how many weight sets should be shipped and the expected sales revenues. But right away the numbers didn't add up, and I wasn't collecting as much from U.S. sales as I should have. Then a customer in the States sent in a really bad copy of my training course, which led me to believe somebody was counterfeiting my courses and selling weights without making proper records.

On top of that, clients started complaining to the U.S. Postal Service about non-delivery of orders, and I had to make good to the tune of thousands of dollars. With problems of that nature arising, I should have dropped the barbell deal in Brooklyn like a hot rock. Instead, I gave Lurie the benefit of the doubt and wasted a couple years trying to straighten out the books and find an innocent reason for the discrepancies.

In the meantime, Lurie did something that cost me more than money.

He was a powerful guy with a pretty good physique who once was named "Most Muscular Man" at an AAU Mr. America contest. In those days, judges gave out side awards for best arms, chest, back, and so on, in addition to the first-place "Mr." Title.

Lurie's title damaged the cause of weight training after a reporter found out the military rejected him for wartime service for having a heart murmur. The press went wild with stories presenting new "proof" that using weights damaged the body, and anti-exercise doctors had another excuse to kick around their tired old garbage about "athlete's heart." To be fair, none of that was Lurie's doing. What happened next was, though. That contest title went to Lurie's head to the point that he publicly challenged John Grimek, rightly known as the world's most muscular man, to go one on one in front of physique judges to prove who was most muscular.

This could have been just a bad joke, but Lurie did it in my magazine!

Some have said that I engineered everything to stir up controversy with York. Grimek, after all, was Bob Hoffman's superstar. Give me a break! Never, ever, would I do such a thing; Grimek was my idol. My writers praised him to the skies, and I had just put him on the cover.

The way it really happened, Lurie put his challenge into an issue just closing while I was out of town. I came home, saw the challenge, and had a fit, but it was too late to pull the thing out of the magazine.

This killed me—and still kills me—because right then, Grimek wanted to come to work with me. We had started talking about him making the switch when I bumped into him at Tony Sansone's gym in New York City and he told me he was sick of working for Hoffman. But then that stupid challenge spoiled everything. No way would Grimek cross over to the Weider camp if Lurie was part of it. Insults started flying in Hoffman's *Strength and Health,* and I felt I had to back up Lurie because he appeared in my magazine. Of course I should have washed my hands of the guy, disavowed the challenge, and tried to patch things up with Grimek. But I took the wrong side out of loyalty.

It kills me, it really does. Think about the opportunity missed—Joe Weider and John Grimek, as a team!

After I moved to New Jersey, we decided to go to court to straighten out the trouble with the barbell business. Over and over my guy trying to serve legal papers went to a little gym Lurie had in New York, but the server could never find him. Finally I said, "I'll go with you." The gym manager tried to stop us at the door, but I pushed past him because I saw Lurie, who ran to the toilet and locked himself in. For the longest time the server and I waited outside the toilet. I called through the door, "Look, Dan, you can't stay in there forever. But we can sit here very comfortably with food and whatever we need." While I spoke, Lurie charged out like a bull. He meant to take me by surprise and escape, but I threw a headlock on him and twisted him around and made him take the papers like a gentleman.

That guy was like gum on my shoe.

Read and learn:

The moral of the story is to stay away from troublesome individuals because they can't do anything but make trouble. Give them the benefit of the doubt and they'll just cause difficulties and drag you down and hurt your dealings with decent people. The Books of Proverbs and Ecclesiastes say the same thing in so many words.

I rented a place on Ocean Avenue in Jersey City for my offices. It was a dump, but I wasn't trying to impress anybody with the address and decor. I'm still not what you'd call office-proud even though I've got a huge corner suite at Weider headquarters that's full of wonderful antique furniture and artwork. I happen to appreciate things of beauty and love collecting, but material things are beside the point. An office is beautiful because you do beautiful work in it. In that sense, the dump in Jersey was a palace. The magazines got better and better.

One day on Ocean Avenue, I answered the phone. "This is Bernarr McFadden," the voice on the line said. "Meet me at the New York Athletic Club tomorrow at noon." He hung up before I had a chance to say yes or no—as if I'd say no to the father of the American fitness and health movements and one of the greatest magazine publishers of all time. By then he was way past his prime, his businesses mostly in serious decline or gone. His great wealth was mostly gone, too. Still, time with him would be like sitting at the feet of a giant. I'd swim to Manhattan for such a privilege.

The New York Athletic Club on Central Park South has great training and sports facilities—including a weight room—but you'd never dream guys grunted and sweated under the same roof as the dining room where I met Bernarr McFadden.

I had time to take in the elegant surroundings because I got there first. The dining room, up on the 11th floor, had deep-toned wood paneling, thick, dark carpeting and the most beautiful table settings. The place made me want to conduct myself with great dignity and speak in a hush.

But here comes this wiry old guy walking up and yelling, "You are the smartest sonofabitch I ever met!" Out on the street you might have thought McFadden was a nut case or a bum. He wore a summer suit that was all rumpled and disheveled-looking. His hair stuck out messy and wild, and his toes poked out of his sandals. I tried to say how deeply honored I was to make his acquaintance, but he went on talking. "Imagine how stupid I feel!" he said, "All those years I put out my magazines and my newspapers, and I never thought of doing what you do—using the publications to sell my own products! People pay you to buy a magazine that's also a mail-order catalog, and they pay you more money to buy the stuff you promote. Young man, you are absolutely incredible."

While we ate, McFadden told me about himself. He was 80 years old, give or take, but he had more energy than men 50 years younger, and he still looked very fit. About that time he married his fourth wife who was half his age. As we said goodbye, he told me: "I predict that one day you will become one of the most famous publishers in America."

To a man not yet 30, in my position with my ambitions and dreams, the words were electrifying. I felt like God anointed me in the New York Athletic Club.

About 10 years later, after my marriage fell apart and I needed someplace to stay, I rented a room and lived in the New York Athletic Club.

People who don't believe you can build a fantastic body without spending a fortune or—I hate to say it—taking dangerous drugs, should pick up my magazines from the 1940s and '50s. You see some mighty, mighty men on the covers and inside pages. The drugs those men took were great big, heavy iron pills. They didn't swallow them; they loaded them up on Olympic bars and dumbbells and lifted them using tricks that Joe Weider taught them. They bulked up eating steak and hard-boiled eggs and drinking enough milk to suck whole dairy farms dry. They didn't have any of the scientific foods and supplements and specialized knowledge and equipment available today—mostly because I made it all available—but look at what they did.

Look. And be inspired. Those iron men inspired me when I worked with them. Looking at the old pictures, I'm inspired all over again.

I was glad to have Earle Liederman, editor of *Muscle Power,* out in Hollywood, because big things were happening up and down the West Coast. The Bay Area, specifically the city of Oakland, produced some great immortals back to back. Jack LaLanne, who's over 90 now and still in good shape and spirits, already had his health studio in Oakland, one of the first of its kind, and he was about to go on national TV with his famous exercise show. I can't tell you how important that program was in spreading the message about healthy living and exercise decades before such things were generally accepted. Millions upon millions of people got their first exposure to working out and the benefits of fitness in their own front rooms watching Jack. His shows still air on classic TV and people buy his videos. Jack started the way we all did—pumping iron as a kid to get bigger and stronger. You can see some of his writing in my old magazines.

Clancy Ross, another Oakland guy, won an AAU Mr. America title and became a star contributor to my muscle magazines. Clancy was one tough customer, also one of the first champions to train using multiple sets, a basic principle in the Weider Training System. For you non-bodybuilders, this means doing so many repetitions, or "reps," of a certain exercise—10 barbell curls, say—and then resting for a moment and doing them again, and then again, for a total of at least three, but often many more sets. Clancy pumped out six sets at a shot. This quickly became standard practice, but back then many bodybuilders did very few sets or sometimes just one, and that was that for the workout. Guys didn't pile on sets like they do now for fear of overtraining.

Adding sets generally means lifting lighter. But it's on record that Clancy did sets of flat-bench and incline presses with two 140-pound dumbbells—amazing in those days.

Clancy became a major spokesman for the Weider System in articles about how he utilized various principles—cheating, muscle flushing, and so on. I helped him get what he wanted to express down on paper, but Clancy did the lifting and gaining, as the articles and pictures documented. If I never ran one word from him in print, his pictures would have proved to the world that the Weider System worked wonders. His pecs would bring down the house even today. For years, I used his image in ads for my products.

Clancy was handsome enough in a rugged way, like his face was chipped out of stone, and he did a little bit of movie work. But he didn't care about Hollywood. What he loved was building great big muscles. Clancy was a bodybuilder's bodybuilder. If you're not a fan of the old-time champs, you've probably never heard of him.

The next great from Oakland, straight out of Ed Yarick's gym who came a couple years after Clancy, was a face and a name familiar to millions of people who wouldn't know their triceps from their big toe. This was Steve Reeves, famed as the star of the Hercules films of the late 1950s. Until Arnold came along, Steve was by far the biggest Hollywood star to come out of bodybuilding. Probably more people now remember him as Hercules than the great champion he was before he went into the movies.

Like Clancy, Steve won the AAU Mr. America title and had more big wins, including the Mr. Universe contest in London. That was the most prestigious world event until we started the Mr. Olympia contest, now officially called Joe Weider's Mr. Olympia. Like Clancy, Steve had a long relationship with me and my publications. I named him an associate editor, and he was a major presence in articles, pictures, and ads for Weider products for years.

For all the parallels, those two guys out of Oakland were apples and oranges, physically as different as a sculpture by Rodin, say, and a Renaissance statuary. What you saw looking at Clancy, was pure, elemental, manly muscle power. Steve was taller—6 foot 1—and more finely put together. You'd know him a mile away by the incredible V-shaped torso, tapering from wide shoulders down to a tiny wasp waist almost like my wife Betty's. Up close, you saw the handsomest bodybuilder of all time, hands down. Of all the champs, Steve Reeves alone fulfilled the ideal for masculine beauty of the Ancient Greeks, who said that the head and face had to be as perfect as the body. It's hard to describe his features because you were pretty much blinded by perfection. I'll never forget the mobs of people stopping and staring when he and I walked up Broadway. They didn't know who they were looking at because he wasn't a celebrity yet, but he absolutely dazzled them. He made a bigger sensation on the beach in California because his physique was out in plain view. Steve mesmerized women. With him around, other guys felt invisible.

Comparing Clancy and Steve side by side shows something very important about bodybuilding: Greatness defines itself. It comes in all different sizes and shapes.

Take a look at our Mr. Olympia titleholders. You go from a big, tall guy like Arnold Schwarzenegger, over 6 feet with his highest competition weight above 230 pounds, to Franco Columbu, who's almost a foot shorter. You see lighter, fine-chiseled men like Frank Zane, who competed at around 180 pounds, and big muscle-mass bruisers. All-time king of mass is the reigning Mr. Olympia, Ronnie Coleman, who last competed at over 300 pounds! Ronnie has built the most muscular body of all time. Nobody in the history of bodybuilding—or the history of mankind—has ever been so huge, but also so lean and cut-up. But sooner or later, somebody else will come along and wow us all in an entirely different way.

Steve Reeves shows something else important in bodybuilding and life in general.

I've known it since I was a kid. Anybody who pays the least bit of attention to the people around him ought to know it, too.

Heredity is destiny. Not all of destiny, but too much of it to pretend it doesn't matter. To soar like an eagle, you've got to have a certain amount of eagle genes. Of course you've also got to know what to do with them and work like crazy to get off the ground. But genes make it easier for some guys—harder or even impossible for others.

The arguments I had over this, for hours and hours, even with medical doctors who had the evidence in front of their faces every day. But I never doubted the truth because I saw it all around. Back in Montreal, I spent time in gyms like Young's and clubs where boxers trained. Some of them worked hard for years, but then somebody would show up, train for a few months and knock everybody else on their behinds. Why? Because he was a natural-born fighter.

Well, Steve was a natural-born physique star. He could get more, out of less, than anybody I knew. He'd go to the gym and make phenomenal gains with shorter workouts than the other guys, lifting only medium heavy, and beat fellows who lifted huge and trained until they fell over. To his credit, Steve trained very efficiently with no down time and no wasted motion. And he worked out smart. He knew exactly the results he wanted and what he had to do to get them, and he did just that and knocked off. But whatever he did or didn't do, Steve Reeves had the winning edge, because God was so good to him.

Sometimes I thought that God might have been a little too good, and I wanted Steve to push himself harder and see what his ultimate limits were. On the other hand, I never knew a nicer, more honest, more likable guy. His good looks, his fame, never went to his head. He was courageous, too. Before he competed, he fought as a soldier during World War II. Maybe he had the ground so solidly under his feet because he was a genuine man of the American West. Steve spent his boyhood years in Montana before moving down to the city. As soon as he made some money he bought a beautiful ranch in California.

I really liked that guy. When he died back in 2000, I spoke a few words at his funeral and got all choked up.

Why would stars like Steve Reeves and others work with me in those early days when I was an upstart and an underdog? Hoffman, who put out about 60,000 copies of *Strength and Health* a month, had me beat in magazine sales three- or four-to-one. And he had a stranglehold on AAU-sanctioned bodybuilding, which gave him the clout to influence certain competitions and shaft guys he didn't like.

I'll tell you why bodybuilders became Weider men instead of York men back when you had to be one or the other. It's simple, really—I knew what bodybuilders wanted, and I gave it to them. In my magazines, bodybuilding was the main event, never a sideshow. Champs came my way because I knew how to showcase them. I knew how to create stars, and I knew what to do with them so their stardom lasted.

Back then I printed a letter from R.E. Hunt, a reader from Los Angeles, who wrote, "Through your efforts, [you] have made possible the careers and fame of many deserving young fellows. This cannot be said of certain of your competitors..."

Mr. Hunt was right about Hoffman. He couldn't stand to have anybody—not even the immortal John Grimek—outshine him.

Early in 1950, I moved the offices to 16 Hopkins Avenue in Jersey City, a three-story structure painted some off-color—bluish, if I remember—on a side street in a neighborhood that had mostly changed from Irish to African-American. I put the mail-order operation down at street level. The editorial offices went on the second floor, and upstairs we had storage and weights that guys who worked there—including the editor-in-chief and publisher—lifted whenever we got a chance. The place was nothing fancy, but perfectly functional and a step up from the dump.

After the move, I ran a 273-word item in *Your Physique* that is the most important and famous thing I ever wrote. This book opens with a reproduction of my words as they actually appeared in the magazine, but I'll save you the trouble of turning back:

1. I PREDICT that civilization will speed up in every phase, and that the stresses and strains on mankind will continue to increase.

2. I PREDICT that the resulting increase in mental and physical illness will force the world to recognize the importance of systematic exercise and physical activities.

3. I PREDICT that bodybuilding will become the chief form of systematic exercise and physical activity, and that it will come to be looked upon as one of the greatest forces in the field of preventive medicine.

4. I PREDICT that a full realization of the importance of muscular development will sweep the world, and the sport of bodybuilding will grow by leaps and bounds.

5. I PREDICT that the basics of good bodybuilding—which include a balanced diet, adequate sleep, plenty of fresh air, ample sunshine, and regular workouts—will become basics of living.

6. I PREDICT that bodybuilding will become the stepping-stone to every other sport and physical activity.

7. I PREDICT that the art of relaxation, one of the fundamentals in bodybuilding, will become more and more important as tensions increase, and that relaxation will be universally taught and advocated.

8. I PREDICT that bodybuilding will spread to every corner of the world and that it will one day be recognized as the king of all sports and physical activities.

9. I PREDICT that those who practice bodybuilding will live healthier, happier and more useful lives.

10. I PREDICT that bodybuilding will one day become one of the greatest forces in existence, and that it may be hailed as the activity that actually saved civilization from itself.

"I PREDICT" expressed what I thought and felt and lived for and still live for. It was a personal testament of faith in the power of bodybuilding—by which I meant exercise with weights or resistance apparatus for improved musculature and strength—and exercise and healthy living in general.

In the "Ten Predictions," I told how modern civilization, by increasing mental stress and doing away with muscular exertion in day-to-day living, brought mankind to a health crisis both physical and psychological. And the predictions foretold that bodybuilding would someday redeem us and restore us, as it is already doing for millions of people all around the world.

I want to emphasize that in the predictions I used the word "bodybuilding" in the broadest sense—doing resistance exercises, usually with weights, to tone and shape the body and build strength for fitness and health and to get more out of life. In this sense, hundreds of millions of people the world over are bodybuilders. Chances are you're one of them.

In other places "bodybuilding" refers to our sport and the hardcore strength training pursued by serious, hardcore muscle-builders, both men and women. In my life's work, I pushed bodybuilding at every level from the general public to the top pro champs.

The Ten Predictions were simultaneously my prophecy, my hope, and my plan for the future. I wasn't like Nostradamus, having visions of the future and writing them down. I, and my brother Ben, had to make everything come true.

We did, too.

Back in 1999, the editors of *Muscle & Fitness* put out a special edition marking the 60th anniversary of Weider Publications that included an article showing point by point that each prediction is now reality.

I'm not going to do that again here. As Abraham Lincoln said, these truths are self-evident. Exercise and its benefits are part of the collective consciousness. People who don't work out know they ought to. Doctors prescribe exercise, especially weight or resistance training, as a treatment or preventative for everything from depression to osteoporosis. Coaches and athletes in every conceivable sport make weightlifting, to build up strength and musculature, part of the training regimen. Race-car drivers, tennis players, sprinters, train with weights, and their muscles help them win and stay competitive into their thirties and forties and even older in some sports—unheard-of before strength training became part of every athlete's life. Even movie stars and models build their bodies because beauty and strength now are one in the same. People considered attractive are people who work out.

My brother's part of this book is all about the No. 4 prediction, that the sport of bodybuilding would gain respect and grow huge all over the world. It happened, but only because he made it happen.

Maybe the most amazing thing here is that I had the nerve to make the predictions in the first place, at a time when there was no chance the world would take me seriously.

This was some kind of guts for a 29-year-old running a couple of muscle magazines.

Unless you were there, you would never believe how ignorance reigned. I've got a book from that era, *You Don't Have To Exercise,* telling men 40 and older to give up athletics and strenuous exertion. The author actually calls exercise poison. In another book, he claims lifting weights interferes with circulation and could kill older men. An MD—a cardiologist!—wrote that. And people still worried about "athlete's heart," an imaginary condition where exercise blew the heart up like a balloon and made it weak and susceptible to failure. Scientists knew better, but BS is hard to kill. Athletic coaches had their own myth that weightlifting made guys muscle-bound so they were clumsy and weakened and not worth a damn in competition. Coaches would actually throw guys off sports teams for lifting—now, 50 years later, they get rid of the kids who won't lift!

The state of public awareness about exercise and health, then and now, would be another whole book. The point here is that I came out of an age of darkness and I saw the light and then let it shine on the world.

And all along I had Hoffman and his writers taking shots at me and bodybuilders, saying that we were just "mirror athletes" and sissies and wimps compared to the York gang.

I was fighting on all fronts. Believe it.

In the same period that I made the predictions, I put out a series of features called "Secrets of the Champions." Each story in the series, which ran for years, explained one of the Weider Training System Principles in great detail. Pictures of the most famous muscle men spoke just as loud, or louder, than the words. I always included exciting images of guys who showed the results of effective, Weider-style training, and told their success stories. Sometimes the champs also told, in their own words, how they benefited from the Weider System. Readers loved getting the goods straight from their heroes.

I based the Weider Principles on discoveries I made in my own training and things I saw and heard watching top guys work out. People have made cracks about how I stole techniques and concepts from my bodybuilders, but this is wrong. A lot of the time, the guys had no idea what they were doing until I observed, analyzed, and documented it.

Here's an example:

Not too long after we met, I visited Clancy Ross at the gym he owned in Oakland. We talked while he did some curls with a pretty heavy barbell, but then he stopped and told a pupil of his, also curling a barbell, that he was doing it all wrong. He made the guy stand straight and hold his elbows into his sides, keeping them stationary during the exercise. The strict, rigid form he taught came straight out of nineteenth-century Europeans, Calvert and Hoffman.

I laughed and said to Clancy, "If you're supposed to curl the way you told that kid, why don't you do it yourself?" Clancy asked me what I meant, and I pointed out that he gave himself a boost by leaning back and letting his elbows come back to get the weight moving upward. He didn't observe textbook form at all. Most guys training hard with heavy weights didn't.

No, they cheated.

Don't be misled by what it means to cheat in other situations, like cheating on a test in school or cheating on taxes. Dishonest and weak individuals do such things because doing right is too tough for them.

The Weider Cheating Principle is 180 degrees opposite. I taught bodybuilders to cheat to make things tougher, not easier.

Put very simply, cheating helps guys get past weak points in exercises that would limit how much they could do if they stuck to strict, old-time form. In curls, for instance, the weak point comes at the beginning where the barbell must begin moving upward. But the payoff part of the exercise comes up high where the biceps take all the strain. These big muscles, which the exercise targets and builds, can move more iron than you can bringing the weight from its low-point to mid-point, where the muscles are handicapped by the arm's built-in mechanical disadvantage. Cheating a little bit, like Clancy, lets you get past that to work harder and make more gains. That's the whole point, isn't it?

Cheating works the same way in all sorts of exercises. Guys can handle more weight in pullovers if they raise their hips a bit. In pull-ups, which serious bodybuilders do with huge weights hanging from waist belts, the weak part of the movement is the beginning. Halfway up to the chinning bar, the major muscles you're working to build take over. Therefore, it pays off to do partial reps starting half-way up to the bar after you can't do any more full reps. I devised a sort of super pull-up, loading up guys with huge weights, more than they ever could handle unaided, then starting them at the bar and having them lower themselves very slowly. This takes help from others, but the load on the muscles—and the benefit—is incredible. In barbell flyes, I taught guys to bend their elbows a little instead of locking their arms out straight, but this isn't cheating any more, because it's accepted form.

There's principle behind the cheating principle. Simply put, the Weider System set bodybuilders free from old rules that held them back and gave them new ways to do more, better, faster, and to better comprehend what they were doing. I gave my principles and techniques exciting new names that stuck in the mind, so they were easy to teach and talk about. And I organized everything in a system that was easy to understand and use.

Here's another area where I could write another whole book, and I already have, more than once. Instructional videos have been made, also, that show the Weider System and how it works. If you want to know more, find some of these materials. If you want to see me introducing the system back when it was brand-new, look into my magazines from more than 50 years ago.

Don't be surprised that nobody previously had thought to take his eyes off a bunch of obsolete rules and pay attention to the way things really work.

Think about Galileo dropping a big lead sphere and a little one off the leaning Tower of Pisa. The weights hit the ground at exactly the same moment, proving that gravity makes everything, heavy or light, fall at the same rate. That happened around the year 1600 after who knows how many thousands of years of people believing that heavy things fell faster. Galileo also looked through a telescope and saw that our planet travels around the sun. Other people said the same thing, but Galileo said it too loudly for the Pope and the Catholic Church, which taught that the earth stood still at the center of the universe. Galileo could have been burned at the stake, but the church let him off if he agreed to keep his mouth shut.

All the poor guy did was look around and tell people what he saw, and it almost got him killed.

Pope Bob Hoffman over in Pennsylvania would have loved to burn me at the stake or at least shut me up so he could go on unchallenged, telling everybody that York was the center of the universe and he was infallible.

Since he couldn't shut me up, he tried to discredit me. Hoffman and his writers attacked my Weider System like wild dogs. They went on and on about the supposed dangers of overtraining if you worked out as often and intensively as my system allowed. The old-time schedule they defended, Monday-Wednesday-Friday like the days were carved in stone, was nowhere near enough for an intermediate-level bodybuilder, much less an advanced one, or a competitor in training. With the Weider Split-System Training Principle and Double-Split Principle, guys could train on consecutive days or even twice a day by concentrating on different areas of the body from one workout to the next. You could work an area like crazy, but still give muscles the proper 48-hour rest and recovery. The York gang didn't get it, or they didn't want to get it. They also misled readers about the cheating principle, making cracks about how Weider men were muscle-bound weaklings who had to "cheat" to lift heavy weights. And they absolutely hated bench pressing, calling us "boobybuilders" because we worked so hard to develop big pecs. He'd slam me and my system and then, in the next breath, say I learned everything from him. Go figure!

Newspaper guys have a colorful term for this sort of endless, unresolved hostility and trading of insults. They call it a pissing match.

I believe Hoffman and I had the longest, craziest pissing match in the history of magazine publishing, also in organized sports. Imagine the editor of *Newsweek* publishing a challenge to the editor of *Time* to get into the ring and box bare-knuckled—while accusing him of being a Communist sympathizer, corrupting youth, turning men into "pansies," and encouraging people to do themselves terrible physical injury. Hoffman wrote that I had my offices in a horrible slum, in a building so dilapidated it was about to fall over—a very strange claim since the place on Hopkins Avenue is still in use. Hoffman published a satire that depicted Doc Tilney, a nutrition fanatic, loading up on pizza and beer. His writer and cartoonist Harry Paschall—a talented guy, actually—did a comic strip about the York hero Bosco, a big, old-time strongman with a handlebar moustache, who always showed up Weedie Man, sometimes called Latissimus Superpex. That was, of course, me. Nothing was off limits. Nothing.

Hoffman once called me a kike—in print!

Here's the actual quote, from *Strength and Health,* September 1957, page 49: "Apparently you can take a kike out of the slums, but you can never take the slums out of the kike."

Imagine if somebody did such a thing today.

The fight behind it all—lifting versus bodybuilding—made no more sense than the crazy insults. Think about other sports that are related. Baseball doesn't dump on softball. Speed skaters don't run down figure skaters because their sport involves artistry, and because judges, not race results, determine the outcome. And nobody in his right mind would insist that figure skating also include races so the competitors could prove they really were athletes. But Hoffman did just that by making tests of strength obligatory at bodybuilding contests he controlled.

There should have been room in the world for him and me because, in truth, we did different things for different people. I trained my guys to get bigger and stronger and look fantastic, head to toe. If that's what you wanted, Weider was the way to go. It's true that Hoffman had guys who could beat my guys in the snatch and clean and jerk, but the York gang had competitors on the U.S. weightlifting team. Some of them looked pretty good. Grimek looked fantastic, but he didn't peak as a bodybuilder until after he quit competitive lifting, which is not the road to developing a body beautiful. Watch an Olympic lifting event and you'll see what I mean. Who wants to look like one of the monsters in the super-heavyweight class instead of Arnold Schwarzenegger in his prime?

Nobody, that's who.

Some of the readers who got caught up in this stuff took it much more seriously than I did. To me it was a lot of noise, and once in a while pretty entertaining—like the time Hoffman put out some nonsense saying physique stars who posed nude or near-nude were homosexuals or at least leaned that way. My editors and I came back with a very funny piece entitled "People Who Live In Glass Houses," illustrated with photos of York guys bare-ass or close to it. We ran a shot of Hoffman himself when he was younger, posing in a jock strap with his behind stuck up in the air.

Most of the time I let Hoffman take his shots and just sat back and smiled.

I had good reason to smile, too, because Hoffman created a lot of curiosity about me and caused thousands of guys who wouldn't have bought my publications to look into them and see what the ranting and raving was all about. What they saw, of course, was a better muscle magazine, and I got more readers.

Somebody smarter would have ignored a new competitor, like he was beneath notice. Or if he took a shot, he would aim very carefully. Lucky for me, my competition kept shooting himself through his own great big foot, and he did me a lot more good than harm.

I should have sent that guy a check every month. An enemy like the one I had is as good as a friend.

I worked at least 10, usually more like 12, hours a day, seven days a week. But I also stayed in good shape. A couple times I stood in front of impartial judges and proved to the world that I was a bonafide muscle man and strength athlete. I wanted to show that I practiced what I preached, and the results were there for all to see.

The first time I put myself on the spot was sort of a fluke, and I wasn't prepared. It happened because of my close relationship with Reg Park, a young Englishman who was the first big Weider star from overseas.

Reg was good enough to give Steve Reeves a run for his money in the first Mr. Universe. Like Steve, Reg stood above 6 feet, but he was bigger and more rugged looking. After our agent in London told me about this up-and-comer, Reg came over to train and do pictures and articles for my magazines. Like Europeans to this day, Reg's physique needed some polishing. First thing, I told him to quit overtraining. Reg lifted way too heavy. He couldn't help himself, I guess, because he was so powerful. When I met him, he trained doing multiple sets of 400-pound squats and later became the first man in Europe to bench 500 pounds. I also helped Reg improve his diet. For years after World War II, people in England ate too much starch and fat because good, fresh food was scarce.

I don't know why, but people lean on me. And instinctively I play a paternal role.

Age-wise, I was more like Reg's big brother, but he found me a very soothing and steadying presence, so much so that he asked me to be with him at the upcoming Mr. Universe contest in London. Reg was already back home in England training for the contest, and I decided to make the trip to join him on the very famous British ocean liner, the *Queen Mary*.

We sailed in very nice weather, but then it turned horrible. As I reported afterward in *Muscle Builder,* the ship rolled so badly that 35 passengers got hurt. Nobody could sleep, and practically everybody got seasick. I avoided sickness by following an old sailor's advice to keep the food down by eating more food. The dishes slid all over the table, but I sat down and packed in three big meals a day. The calories stuck with me because I couldn't work out.

When the *Queen Mary* finally docked, 18 of the injured went straight to the hospital, and I felt bloated and weak. In the five days before the contest, I worked out twice at a friend's house—in the kitchen, actually, just like back in Montreal with Rusty Halpert. I could barely manage 10-rep sets of bench presses with 235 pounds—30 or 40 pounds less than my usual.

Right before the contest Reg shocked me by demanding that I join him onstage as a competitor. He gave me an ultimatum, actually—no Joe in the contest, no Reg. This was nuts, but I couldn't let him miss his shot at the Mr. Universe title, which I figured was his for the taking. So I went to the contest venue, a theater called the Scala that's been gone for years, and signed up as a last-minute surprise entrant. Looking at the other contestants, I saw that the Europeans had gained a lot of ground. Reg, as I expected, looked unbeatable. I didn't kid myself that I'd finish anywhere but last.

By rights I should have fallen flat, but I made a respectable showing. After struggling just a bit I performed the onstage demonstrations of strength that the rules required and then, after the posing, came in fifth out of six in the tall man's class.

No surprises at the top—Reg won and brought down the house. The crowd loved seeing a 23-year-old Englishman clean up.

A few years later a kid in a tank town in Austria would discover my magazines. He couldn't read a word of English, but the pictures spoke loud and clear, especially the pictures of one great big, powerful international champion.

The kid later wrote, "I became obsessed with Reg Park; he was the image in front of me from the moment I started training."

The kid was Arnold Schwarzenegger. What John Grimek was to me—a boyhood idol, lifelong inspiration, and hero—Reg was to Arnold.

I recently saw some shots taken at the 1951 Mr. Universe. I don't look so bad onstage in posing trunks, if I do say so, especially considering what I had just gone through.

In one picture I'm lined up with other contestants wearing their trunks, but I'm in my suit pants and street shoes. I was half-dressed because I thought I was done onstage and went back to change, but then somebody ran back and told me I had to go out again.

An English anti-Weiderite kept that picture in a desk drawer for years and years and showed it to people to try to embarrass me. He claimed I competed in long pants because I didn't want anybody to see my entire physique. He knew better than that because he had competed in that same contest. This guy, Oscar Heidenstam, who headed the National Amateur Body Building Association in England, which sanctioned the Mr. Universe, became sort of a Junior Bob Hoffman. In years to come, he would deliver tirades against me and my brother Ben at his contests like that was part of the show. He took shots at us, too, in print. Ben held out the olive branch more than once, offering Heidenstam the chance to cooperate with the IFBB, which would have been terrific for him and NABBA. But he wouldn't see reason.

I bring this up to show how truth didn't matter to certain individuals in those days, if bending the truth could make me or my brother Ben look bad. Some of the people who went on the warpath acted like they lost their senses—even when we tried to do them a favor!

My heart and soul went into my muscle magazines, cover to cover. Much of the content I wrote under my own name or rewrote to fix somebody else's work. I kept my staff plenty busy but still worked hands-on more than any top magazine boss I've heard of, assigning and editing stories, writing and designing the ads, going out on photo shoots with photographers and picking the right shots to use, directing the illustrators who did inside art and covers, and working on layout, headlines and subheads, and teaser lines on the cover. As publisher I dealt with the distributor American News, the printer, suppliers, watching the finances and so forth. I ran the mail-order business, too. And all the while I devoted myself to bodybuilding—training my guys, perfecting my system, visiting gym owners and other contacts all over the country, keeping an eye out for future champs. As the Mr. Universe contest showed, I also managed to stay in decent shape.

But my responsibilities did not end with the muscle magazines and bodybuilding. After 1952, Weider magazines started multiplying like rabbits, and the bosses at American News pushed me to put out still more.

"Joe," they kept telling me, "you've got the touch."

CHAPTER SIX

THE RISE, FALL, AND RE-RISE OF WEIDER PUBLISHING

Joe Weider

I have a picture taken in the office on Hopkins Avenue that shows me making a phone call at my desk. I'm wearing a white dress shirt with the collar open and sleeves rolled-up, looking like somebody with way too much to do. The other three guys in the shot are goofing around, not a care in the world.

I used this picture as a sort of joke, telling people, "Look, the boss is the only one who does any work. Here's the proof."

In truth, I wanted my people to stay loose and have a few laughs. Creative individuals especially have to feel free in order to do their best.

In Jersey, a girl from the shipping department told me how much she loved to come into the office. It was like a trip to some enchanted island, she said. All the girls felt that way, and the guys did too, and they'd gladly work until six or seven instead of five o'clock when they were supposed to go home. It pays to run a happy shop.

In the old picture you see a young artist and illustrator named Tom Beecham leaning back in a chair next to my desk. Tom, who became a good family friend, had a farm in upstate New York and came down to the city so we could go over his assignments. Later he became a very famous painter specializing in nature and wildlife, and I commissioned him to do a portrait of my father and life-sized paintings of some of my most famous champions that now hang in the foyer of our company headquarters.

You'd never know it, seeing him older and wearing business attire, but the guy mid-frame in the picture, laughing out loud, is Barton Horvath, the muscle man on the cover of my very first *Your Physique*. The other guy, facing away from the photographer so you only see these big shoulders stuffed into a suit jacket and the back of a balding head, is Charlie Smith.

By Tom's and Barton's expressions, I'd say that Charlie just made a joke. Knowing him, it was off-color. Charlie, one of those burly, bulldog-looking Englishmen, constantly came out with dirty sayings and ditties. One line from a rhyme of his sticks in my head—"and he hit her in the titty with a hard-boiled egg." I never liked such vulgarity, but that was Charlie. He picked up his salty talk as a sailor on British Royal Navy warships, which first brought him to the U.S.

Charlie and Barton held various senior editorial positions and wrote many of the articles. In another company, guys with such responsibilities would have years of publishing experience, but neither of them worked on magazines before I hired them. I can't recall what Barton did previously. Charlie had some kind of job at a bank. Both guys lived and breathed the muscle game, though. Barton had been a lifter and bodybuilder. Charlie grew up around the game back home in England. When I hired him he was serving on an AAU weightlifting committee. He also loved bodybuilding and was very knowledgeable.

Those two were typical of the people I hired for my muscle magazines. It takes fanatics to put out a publication for fanatics, and you can't make fanatics out of people who aren't already that way. On the other hand, you can train a fanatic to do editorial work. Even if he's lousy at it, but is a bodybuilding star or a notable strength expert, you can still use him because somebody else can whip his stuff into shape. For these reasons I made muscle men and muscle heads into magazine men, rather than vice versa.

The same principle applies to any sort of specialized enthusiasts' publication. Gun magazines have gun nuts in their editorial departments, for example. If they didn't, gun nuts wouldn't read them.

Because of the staff's inexperience I kept my hand in all aspects of editorial work and production, more than anybody else running a publishing company that I ever heard of. I had to go over every little thing to make sure the issues came out correct and professional looking. Things wouldn't change until the 1980s, when we started to get college-educated guys who were knowledgeable about bodybuilding, which, by then, was much more respectable and mainstream. Some of this new breed had studied exercise and sports medicine—fields that previously didn't exist—and also had the polish and skills for big-time publishing.

Charlie and Barton, though, had something else in common besides their devotion to muscles and strength: Each, in his own individual way, could be a pain in the neck.

Barton was a terrible know-it-all, the world's greatest authority on pretty much everything, who sometimes acted like the rest of us should feel lucky to have him around. Charlie wrestled with inner demons. Just like that, he'd go from joking to gloomy and sullen. He was insecure and bitter, I think, because he grew up a poor orphan boy in London. But feeling for him didn't make dealing with his difficult side any easier.

I'm not singling these guys out for criticism—I loved them as brothers and truly valued their work. The point is that in my position, I had to get along with and keep things smooth around people with rough edges. Skills, talent, and expertise come in all sorts of packages, especially in creative endeavors like putting out magazines—also in bodybuilding where the egos can be bigger than the muscles and a lot more fragile. Since I had bodybuilders doing creative work, I got it both ways. I never minded, though. Whatever their personal problems, I never had problems with my people, and I tried to make sure they didn't make problems for each other.

I first branched out from bodybuilding with *Boxing and Wrestling.*

After word got out about the new title, a guy walked in and said he wanted to be my boxing editor. His name was Eddie Borden, and what a prize he turned out to be. What muscles and exercise were to Joe Weider, the fight game was to Eddie, a bona fide New York legend. He boxed some when he was young and became a trainer and promoter as well as a boxing writer and a recognized, all-around authority. I swear he knew every single person involved with the fights, honest and crooked.

He also gambled like nobody I ever knew. Eddie, who at one time was a bookie, put down money on fights and absolutely everything else you could bet on. The old stories of guys betting on rain drops running down the window and which fly crawling around would take off first aren't just stories. I witnessed such things. Eddie and his pals could have stepped out of a story by Damon Runyon, who wrote wonderful, funny tales of gamblers and hustlers in New York. Rent the movie version of the musical *Guys and Dolls,* based on Runyon's stories, and you'll see the kind of characters I met through Eddie.

Even though I put out a boxing magazine I never got to like the fights in person. The sound of the punches landing and sweat and blood flying made me a little queasy. On the other hand, I loved the history and lore of boxing and put stories and photographs of the old-time greats and their immortal battles in every issue.

Boxing had tremendous visual drama. I remember assigning an artist to do an oil painting for a magazine cover. I wanted an intimate study of the face of Rocky Marciano, then the heavyweight champion of the world. As I explained to the artist, Marciano was more of a slugger than a great boxer. Some fighters could fend off opponents, but Marciano, who had short arms, just took the shots until he could get inside. He had a cast-iron head and jaw, and he packed such power he knocked out practically all his opponents. The artist rendered his features in a way that emphasized the scars of battle, while the eyes and facial expression showed inner power and determination. That cover told the whole story of what made Marciano a champion.

The wrestling editor I found in-house. Charlie Smith was steeped in the sport just like he was steeped in the iron game. The two aren't so far apart, actually. Whatever you think about pro wrestling—whether it's for real or a circus act—the guys in the ring are strength athletes. How else could they pick up other guys and throw them around, night after night? Wrestlers are physique stars, too, because the fans want them to look big and powerful. It makes sense they were among the first athletes to openly train in gyms with weights.

After *Boxing and Wrestling* came *Inside Baseball,* then *Inside Sports.* I farmed out much of the new work to freelancers and stringers in New York. Some of the full-timers like Eddie Borden worked away from the office, too, so the home-office crew stayed pretty much the same.

I hired an eager-beaver kid named Jimmy Breslin to cover baseball part-time, thereby giving a legendary New York writer his start. Jimmy went on to become an internationally known columnist and author. He remains a beloved figure and voice of the city, sort of a Damon Runyon of his day. Even though he was a kid, I knew Jimmy was going places as a journalist and I might not have him around for long.

A few years back he came to California to cover Arnold's first gubernatorial campaign and we got together. Afterward he did a funny piece about how things were on Hopkins Avenue: "Joe kept the barbells up on the third floor. Every time somebody dropped a barbell upstairs, my hands flew to my head."

Jimmy also wrote about Eddie Borden naming a notorious gangster as "Manager of the Year" and trying to teach me to box.

"Eddie set up the heavy bag for Weider and supervised his work on it.

"Here is a cover conference for *Boxing and Wrestling* magazine: 'Same hand to the body, same hand to the head, Joe.'"

Jimmy took some liberties to be funny like claiming guys had to come in and wrestle me for their paychecks. But every other great humorist did the same thing. As Mark Twain said, never let a little truth get in the way of a good story. On the other hand, Jimmy didn't bend the truth much. People really did jump when somebody dropped a weight upstairs, and we did have a heavy punching bag. And unforgettable, colorful characters came and went all the time.

When Jimmy Breslin heard I was working on my life story, he said this:

"The book ought to make people smile."

I can't speak for anybody else, but I'm smiling right now, remembering Hopkins Avenue. For so long, this time in my life lay dead and buried, but now it's coming back with all those great people—muscle men, kids, artists, fast-talkers and shady characters from New York, the sweet, sweet girls from the office.

Nobody ever had a publishing company like mine.

And nobody ever began with absolutely nothing and rose so fast.

I ran into another bright kid at Abe Goldberg's gym on Manhattan's Lower East Side. Some great bodybuilders, many of them Jews, trained there—Abe himself, who was terrific, Art Zeller, who later became one of my star physique photographers, and Marvin Eder, considered to be the world's strongest youth. I sent some of my top guys like Reg Park and Dave Draper over to train at Abe's.

The bright kid in question, Mel Sokolsky, was only about 16, but already he had to support his family. He developed a new kind of stretchy posing trunks that he adapted, believe it or not, from factory seconds ladies' girdles. I liked the trunks so much I got a pair of my own and gave Mel ad space in my magazines. Mel then came out with a line of T-shirts specially cut to fit bodybuilders, and I gave him space for more ads. In them, Mel used his own photographs, which showed some real talent, so I encouraged him to keep shooting and ran some of his shots in my magazines. Mel had found his calling. Pretty soon he rented a little studio and got too busy with commercial and fashion work to shoot muscle men for me. I could see this coming, because I saw the kid's genius. Mel has shot for *Vanity Fair, Vogue,* and all the elite publications. His best work is fine art, and he's received photography's highest honors and awards. One of his pictures just sold for $30,000 at a show in Paris.

Last time I saw Mel and his wife, he still talked about how I took him seriously and dealt with him man to man, as an equal, even though he was just a kid off the street.

Why would I talk down to him or anybody else? I always had great respect for people with ambition and talent and tried to help them. I'd go out of my way for a struggling kid like Mel, a teenager with nothing in the world going for him but brains and guts and hustle and heart. I was once in his shoes, wasn't I?

You can't do what I did without a special eye for talent. I looked for it all the time, high and low. Where I didn't look very much was on pieces of paper like college degrees and resumes. Such things deserve consideration, but too many guys who look good on paper let you down. And if you focus on paper instead of people you miss the diamonds in the rough, the real human treasures.

I should mention that I financed Abe Goldberg's gym and became partners with him, but the deal fell apart in a dispute over getting my fair share of the money. Years later I'd try to get into the gym business again, this time under my own name, with the idea of establishing a national chain. But I had the same sort of bookkeeping problems, as well as complaints about mismanagement that tarnished the Weider name and image. I said no more running gyms, once and for all. With all of our business interests, they were too tough to control. Unless you're looking over every manager and franchisee's shoulder, every minute, you don't know if you're getting robbed or if the guy is screwing up and damaging your good name.

I started looking into men's action adventure. "Pulps," people called the he-man magazines of the 1950s, because the inside pages were uncoated pulp paper. They were full of harrowing tales of combat, crime, the Communist peril, the Wild West, fights to the death with headhunters, Amazon women, animals, and who knows what. Sensationalizing aside, the pulps had some quality writing and reporting. They had a few photos of sexy women, but the pics were pretty tame, and sex did not predominate as it did in later girly magazines. Mostly the women were in some sort of terrible danger so he-men could charge in and save them.

As I branched out, I said goodbye to the oldest and dearest title of all. It was time to retire the name *Your Physique,* which was too French-sounding and soft for U.S. readers. I thought it was time to remake the magazine, too. I folded it into a new launch called *Mr. America,* my own original mix of a muscle magazine and men's adventure. The combination seemed to make sense, because young men bought both kinds of magazines, and guys who read tough stuff would want to build their bodies to get tough. It didn't work, though, because the two genres had different readerships. And even guys who bought both kinds of magazines didn't want them together. Magazines, in this respect, are like food. A guy who eats eggs in the morning and pie at lunch doesn't want them on the same plate.

After a few months, I put out a reborn version of *Your Physique* called *Muscle Builder* and tried a pure he-man book called *Mr. America.* The action-adventure name that would stick, after another try or two, was Fury. I still liked the look and sound of *Mr. America* and put it on ice until 1958 when I re-titled *Muscle Power.* All told, *Mr. America* would survive in various forms for more than 20 years.

The Weider enterprises did millions in business annually, but the magazines and mail-order products were the millionaires, not me, because the money went right back into them. I still lived modestly, as Ben did back in Montreal. Even if I were so inclined, I couldn't wallow in luxury, because the hours and minutes went where the money went—into the businesses. I put in 14 or more hours a day, seven days a week. Sometimes I slept in the office on a cot.

One night I got out and saw a new movie version of *The Student Prince,* an operetta from the 1920s. It moved me so much that I saw it three more times.

The plot involves a lonely German prince, who goes to the great university at Heidelberg incognito so he can fit in and enjoy the carefree college life. He has a great time with his fellow students and, at their favorite tavern, he meets and falls for the owner's beautiful daughter. They have a wonderful romance, but then part because the heir to a throne and a commoner have no future together. Their hearts break, but they must accept their fate.

It made me so happy to watch the students sing and have fun and feel like I was one of the crowd. But the movie also took me back to my own youth. Everything that was so great to watch onscreen, I never had. In Montreal, poverty and working day and night cut me off from others, just like the prince in his castle. But he could break out of his isolation and find manly camaraderie and happiness. I couldn't escape, and what I missed, I would miss forever—the joys of youth are only for youth. The movie made me even more melancholy because the romance of the prince and the beautiful, pure Kathie took me back to my own first love. The prince would never forget his girl, and his heart would always ache for her.

The Student Prince touched me so deeply.

A few too many times Bob Hoffman claimed that Joe Weider was fat and weak and ignorant about strength training, so I proved, one more time, what kind of man I was. I went to Sig Klein's gym in Manhattan and presented myself to be measured and to demonstrate my strength. I had the deepest respect and fondness for Sig, considered to be the foremost expert in taking measurements. He was like bodybuilding's gold standard, and all the top guys went to him. I also went to Sig because he was friends with Bob Hoffman and had written for *Strength and Health* for years. Had I gone to somebody in my own camp, people would have been suspicious of the results.

My measurements, as reported by Sig Klein in *Muscle Builder:* normal chest, 51 inches; neck, 17.5 inches; waist (relaxed), 34.5 inches; upper arm, 17.3 inches; thigh, 25.2 inches; calf, 16.8 inches; and bodyweight 206 pounds.

Sig reported some of my heavy lifts: 355-pound bench press; 245-pound standing Olympic press; one-arm snatch, 145 pounds with the left arm and 150 pounds with the right; two-arm snatch, between 220 and 240 pounds; clean and jerk, between 280 and 305 pounds.

About my style of training, Sig wrote: "I find that he enjoys heavy workouts, trains on the average five times a week for about an hour at a time. By using heavy weights, he feels that he is forced to concentrate on his training, while lighter weights would permit his mind to wander, possibly to business matters, which he wants to forget during his training."

What could Hoffman say? He couldn't very well call his own trusted writer a liar, could he?

I launched a few more action/adventure titles like *Animal Life, Safari,* and *Outdoor Adventures.* Big-game hunting and fights to the death with dangerous wildlife were not my cup of tea. I've never had the slightest desire to harm one of God's creatures, especially not the great cats, the cousins of my very favorite animal, the house cat, of which Betty and I now have five. But my feelings didn't stop me from running hunting stories or ordering up a cover depicting a tiger as a vicious, evil creature going after an adventurer who looked like Gregory Peck. And I didn't mind showing two men fighting for their lives against a giant octopus, knowing full well that the giant octopus is actually a shy, inoffensive animal. I called the story "Diving With Sea Killers."

The readers paid for excitement, not factual accuracy, so we gave them a little reality wrapped up in thrilling myths—just like Homer and Shakespeare.

In some respects, a magazine is a magazine is a magazine, whatever the subject matter. And my hands-on touch, which pulled in readers for my muscle magazines, worked in every genre I got into.

It didn't really matter whether I put out one magazine or two or more than a dozen, as I did in New Jersey, because I had a very fast touch. I still do.

Indecision is a disease, and I thank God I'm immune to it. It's sickening to think about the millions of man-hours and dollars going down the drain from people yakking and second-guessing about a decision that somebody should just make.

In business, I've never had time for useless talk of any kind. I remember asking one of my ad guys in New Jersey about his meeting with a prospective client. He started telling me this and that about what went on, and I stopped him cold.

"You mean you didn't get the sale," I said. "That's all I want to know."

If I wanted a story, I'd hire a writer.

All the New Jersey magazines had this in common—the majority of readers bought them one copy at a time rather than by subscription. This meant they lived or died in the time it took a guy at a newsstand to look at the cover and decide whether to pick it up.

A few seconds, that's all I had to hook them or lose them. A cover picture had to pop up off the page and move. I don't mean simply catching people in action—although I liked that, too. Somehow the picture had to tell a story, so people saw a whole chain of events that they wanted to be part of.

In muscle magazines, the cover had to tell a story about how great it was to be like the champs and rising stars I showcased. Often I'd show the guys with pretty girls, relaxed and smiling, which told readers that muscle men got all the dates they wanted and generally had more fun. The backgrounds pulled people in, too, which is why we shot so much at beautiful beaches and spectacular settings in California. Who doesn't want to have fun at the seashore, under the palm trees, with a physique that stops traffic? A champ striking a heroic pose, high on a rocky pinnacle, is an embodiment of manly power, soaring and triumphant over the world. Such an image made guys want to feel the same sensations.

I like to go out to personally supervise the photo shoots. With the action/adventure covers, which were original paintings, I'd very carefully go over preliminary sketches with the artist. We had to depict the exact moment at which a story inside the magazine turned, so thrilling and action-packed that people absolutely had to know what happened. Usually this involved the hero of the story in a life-or-death situation, facing some terrible menace. Such covers asked two big, burning questions: How did this guy get into such a terrible situation? How in the world will he get out?

For years everybody scoffed, but people have rediscovered the old he-man magazine covers and recognize their artistry. The original illustrations go for thousands of dollars.

Everything had to pop, every single thing. I had the name *Fury* printed in bright red, mottled a bit with a background color so the letters jumped out like flames or blood, and the mottling looked like battle damage. I reverse-printed the title of *Outdoor Adventures,* so the white letters jumped out from a deep-colored background. All the magazines' covers had boxes and circles for the lines teasing the stories inside. Those, too, had to be boldly colored.

The cover lines had to grab people, too: "White Queen of the Comanches," "Vice on the Waterfront," "Is Your Doctor Robbing You?" When we ran reprints of stories by literary giants like William Faulkner, Somerset Maugham, or John Steinbeck, the cover lines said so.

Inside, I had to keep things popping so somebody turning through the pages at the newsstand wanted to buy the magazine. Each story had its own cover, so to speak, with the opening spread of pictures and heads and subheads. Everything, cover to cover, had to be hyped—but it couldn't be empty hype or people would feel gypped and never come back. Each story had to be good enough so people read to the end and also read the other stories and looked forward to next month's issue.

The contents had to be more than just good, actually. They had to be mixed just right so there was variety, pacing, ups and downs, laughs—and always lots to look at. The entire magazine had to fit together and function as a whole. I always saw it as a whole before we started putting it together.

What I really did was put on a show. When I had 13 magazines, I put on 13 shows a month, each one with its own purpose and audience.

Often I think of a movie mogul running a great big studio, putting out films the way I put out magazines. Hollywood kingpins like Louis B. Mayer and Darryl F. Zanuck knew how to keep dozens of creative projects on track, how to create stars and make the public crazy for them, how to put stories and spectacles on screen so people couldn't resist. Nobody sent those giants to entertainment school. They just naturally knew what they needed to know. But you can't light a fire in those who lack it. The other side of the coin is that people who don't have a flair for getting people excited, for entertaining them, don't. Whatever they do, such people fall flat in front of the public. Just like I had an eye for talent, I could recognize the people who couldn't punch up a story or a picture spread if their lives depended on it. However hard they tried, their work would just lie there on the page. Such people could be fine, dependable employees—but I kept them away from creative work in the editorial and art departments.

Later, 1981, I would launch a new fitness magazine for women called *Shape,* which was a fantastic hit. People hailed it as revolutionary, and competitors came out with imitations.

To me, though, *Shape* wasn't revolutionary at all. In 1956, I brought out two magazines, *Figure & Beauty* and *American Beauty,* that promoted exercise and health for women. In them, I ran ads for my line of light, pink-colored weights called Beauti-Bells, with a Beauti-Bench for prone and incline lifting in four decorator colors. Articles showed women how to put the equipment to best use. I also ran traditional women's magazine fashion spreads and grooming tips, but the emphasis on weights and the overall message were absolutely brand new. Nobody before had equated femininity with muscle tone and strength. And I told women exactly what I told the guys—you can build yourself a brand-new body to look better and feel better. I was so far ahead of the times that it took 25 years for the times to catch up.

For every new title I put out—like *True Strange,* featuring tales of the bizarre and supernatural—I thought up others. And American News pushed me to launch more, more, more, offering to advance money for new publications of every kind. This wasn't generosity, but a sure thing—if the new title flopped I had to pay back the advance, and if I succeeded, the distributor got its advance, plus its piece of my new sales. The bigger the sales, the more it got.

To understand why I needed advances from the distributor to grow, you must grasp one of the basics of the magazine business: A publisher pays to put out each issue at least three months before he sees a nickel from sales. Because of production time, you're always working two or more issues ahead. Then, after an issue hits the stands, it takes time for the retailers to settle with the distributor, which in turn gets its cut before anything comes to you. The distributor and printer and others actually made more on the magazines than I did. Usually only about 30 percent of the sales got back to me. And believe me, the money took its own sweet time to come home.

An established company would have had the resources to put out a new title. But even with business booming, I was too strapped for cash to absorb the cost of a new launch. So, American News had to front me the money. On the way up, it was win-win for everybody.

After Hugh Hefner's *Playboy* hit big, American News wanted me to come out with knockoffs. I didn't really want to, but for the sake of the business relationship I started *Jem* and *Monsieur.* Like Hefner's book, they combined high-tone writing, racy humor, and shots of nude women showing their breasts. I had no hang-ups about nudity or sexuality, which my muscle mags and mail-order books dealt with openly and frankly as part of healthy living. But my heart was never in *Jem* and *Monsieur,* which took off like rockets anyway.

About the same time, one of my editors, who was also a good friend, got the idea of publishing picture magazines with artistic physique shots of men. He had no resources of his own and asked if he could bring out his magazines under Weider Publishing. I really liked the guy, who happened to be gay, but I had no hang-ups in that direction, either. I've never understood why guys get all shook up about homosexuality. Maybe they think it rubs off. Maybe they feel threatened because they're not so sure about themselves. But I had no problems with my friend or his concept, because the best physique studies really were art, and I didn't mind going out of my way to help. So, I published another couple of magazines I never would have put out on my own.

I should have thought a little longer and harder and told my friend "No." *Adonis* and *Body Beautiful* became an embarrassment that I didn't need. The magazines, which were actually pretty tasteful, naturally sold big to gays and gave Bob Hoffman a new excuse to smear me.

People later put out nonsense about me playing both ends against the middle by pandering to both homosexuals and heterosexuals, as if I had some sort of grand scheme. But those magazines were other peoples' ideas, not mine, and I had almost nothing to do with them.

The above story shows something that caused me trouble all my life. I hate turning anybody down and agree to things even when I know I probably shouldn't.

My sister Freda tells people that if I were a girl I'd get pregnant every nine months because I don't know how to say "No."

When Mel Sokolsky heard about Freda's remark, he said I'd figure out a faster way to make babies and get pregnant every two months.

Funny guy.

In January 1957, the guys loaded one last moving van and then I locked the doors forever on Hopkins Avenue. About a mile north of there we celebrated the opening of a brand-new headquarters at 801 Palisade Avenue, Union City, New Jersey. Finally I had a building custom-designed for my businesses with the name Weider on the deed. It was a single-story, red brick structure with big metal letters over the entrance that read "Weider Enterprises." After Hopkins Avenue, the place was a palace but still pretty modest and simple. I picked up the lot for a song from the Union City municipal government, which had recently acquired it for one dollar. I might have put about $80,000 into it—a substantial amount in

1957, but not so much for a company headquarters that became a legendary locale to muscle men and muscle kids the whole world over.

Early in 1957, an article in American News' in-house magazine for its clients made it clear why I needed growing room. Headlined, "There's a Million Dollars in These Powerful Sellers," it told about my rapid rise to success. My magazines then had combined print runs of more than two million copies a month. Annually, 25 million copies of Weider magazines went out. With cover prices ranging from 35 cents to 50 cents, each issue in the line was worth more than $1 million—$1,082,500 to be exact, in the U.S. and Canada. The real totals were even higher because we had foreign-language editions overseas.

The article said more and more of the best creative people in Manhattan worked for me in secret. I especially liked this part about a hotshot guy from the city:

A well-known writer recently returned from an expedition to Union City, and looking back on his few electric minutes with Weider, explained that he's never had a publisher or an editor look at him just like that. "It wasn't that he said everything," mused this writer, "but he looked to me as if to say 'Don't just stand there—write something!'"

Weider smiles disarmingly at the growing list of such stories. "The Hudson River's getting narrower every year," says he.

The more I did, the more I wanted to do, and the more fun I had doing it. I planned to expand into distribution in a year or two, but kept it under my hat because I didn't want the distributor to know that I might become a competitor.

So I was still American News' golden boy.

Fat lot of good it did me.

In the Middle Ages, people believed that fortune was like a wheel turning round and round. It took you up and up, and then at the highest point started down. Good or evil, proud or humble, the wheel of fortune turned for everybody, and there wasn't a thing you could do about it.

The wheel I was tied to was none other than American News, my first and only distributor since I started. Even though I saw horrible trouble coming, I couldn't save myself.

The head accountant at American News, who was a friend, actually went out on a limb to try to save me. One day I went over to the company's headquarters in Manhattan on business. As I always did, I stopped in my friend's office to chat. Usually we kidded around, but he told me to close the door and sit down because he had something very serious to say.

"Joe," he said, "American News is going to close down operations. I'm supposed to keep my mouth shut, but we're friends and I had to tell you."

What he said sounded absolutely crazy. American News controlled half the distribution business. Nobody else came close in volume, and nobody was as old and established and highly regarded. But, as my friend explained to me, trouble was on its way. Taking advantage of a slump in the company's share prices, some financiers had bought up stock and engineered a takeover. Everybody knew about this, but nobody in publishing was too concerned. The new top guys assured everybody that the distribution business would continue, uninterrupted. In fact, this was a condition of the takeover.

My friend revealed to me that this was all a lie. In a few months management would close down the distribution business, as they intended to do all along. They bought up American News because it had real estate holdings worth far more than the company's book value. Since the 1800s, the distributor had put up its own warehouses in cities all over the country, and that property now was incredibly valuable. On the other hand, distribution brought in pretty low profits. So the plan was to pull the plug on the business and make an instant fortune selling the real estate. Never mind that hundreds of guys like me would suffer, the owners were going for the fast buck.

The was, of course, supposed to be a deep, dark secret. But, God bless him, my friend the head accountant didn't want to see me get hurt. He told me to find another distributor right away and make a good deal. Run, don't walk, he said. After word got out there'd be a stampede, and guys with no distributor would get screwed.

I wish it had been that simple.

The company that did my printing, Neo Gravure, had Weider Publishing under a very tight contract that said the printer did its work on credit and collected its money from sales before any came to Weider. The money came down the pipeline from the distributor, which the contract stipulated had to be American News, and nobody else. I got tied up like that because my company came up so fast, out of nowhere, and Neo Gravure didn't want to get stuck if I got in trouble. The printer figured Weider would be less of a risk if I stuck with American News. I had no objections, because I had no intention of leaving the biggest and best distributor.

After the distributor's head accountant tipped me off, I set up an emergency meeting with a couple bosses at the printer. In light of my inside information, I was sure they'd let me make new arrangements. I thought they'd probably insist on it.

Boy, did I have it wrong. The guys at the printing company just laughed and said that everything I told them was ridiculous. In a hundred years, American News never, not once, failed to fulfill its obligations—how in the world could I think that a company like that would go out of business? I kept trying to explain the inside information I had, but they wouldn't listen. I thought I had a chance with one guy, but the other, the head accountant, scoffed and brushed me off like I was a child or a simpleton. The arrogant bean counter—did he think my friend at American News was pulling my leg? Did he think I made it all up? I didn't matter what he thought, because he laughed in my face and held me to the contract.

In a matter of months everything predicted by my friend, the distributor's head accountant, came true. Word got out about American News, and publishers ran like rats from a sinking ship to other wholesalers. Just remembering makes me crazy. It's like one of those dreams where something horrible chases you but you can't run away because your legs won't move, or you need to scream but no sound comes out of your mouth. I knew what was coming before anybody else, and I got hurt worse than anybody else.

The timing of the shutdown at American News was absolutely devastating. I got caught just when one month's issues were about to go out, and the next month's were being printed. So I had two months' print runs—more than two million magazines—sitting in boxes in warehouses. I owed money on those issues, but past the publication date they had no value except to guys who bought paper by the ton.

In the meantime, other publishers made adjustments and moved on. Bob Hoffman, who also worked with American News, put a little note in *Strength and Health,* skipped an issue to get going with a new distributor, and that was that. I was thrown into a bottomless pit.

I'll never know the exact total of my losses, which went into the millions. I had to quit publishing all the magazines I had added with encouragement from American News. But I would not give up my muscle magazines, not as long as I lived and breathed. Somehow I managed to keep those magazines alive.

My brother Ben advised me to get out from under my load of debt by declaring bankruptcy and wiping the slate clean. Everybody agreed, but I ignored the advice, which I knew was well-meaning and sensible. I couldn't just walk away from my obligations. Rather than simply erasing my debts, I made settlements with the people I owed. So many people did right by me, how could I not do right by them, or at least try? I did this, too, because of the example set by Ma, who always paid off the grocer, the shoe store, and everybody else she owed, even in the depths of the Great Depression. She did it because she was too proud not to. For all the strife between us, I owe her for showing me what strength and pride looked like. Because I was Anna Weider's son, I, too, settled my debts, even though it took years and it hurt like crazy.

While I struggled, American News and the printer launched court proceedings to collect money they claimed was owed to them from my unsold issues. The case dragged on for years. Can you imagine the nerve? The same people who put me in the hole in the first place, wanted to put me in deeper.

Somewhere during this period, Barton Horvath walked up to my desk, slapped down a muscle magazine called *Muscle Sculpture* and told me I had new competition. That was his way of saying that he was leaving to start a magazine of his own. Since he put together Issue 1 while working for me, I had a good idea where his pictures and material came from. Still, I didn't get mad. I didn't worry much about the competition, either. I wished Barton luck, knowing that he had absolutely no idea how tough it would be to survive.

In my business you can't take comings and goings too personally. Some magazine people are like rabbits, hopping around just because that's their nature. Some are like kids, too. No matter how much you pamper them, they still get resentful and leave. Charlie Smith was already gone before the financial catastrophe, nursing a grudge I never understood. Probably he didn't, either.

I should add that Barton was not the first or last to come down with a bad case of Joe Weider disease. Most people are immune, but a few guys who spend time around me decide they can do what I do—put out a muscle magazine, bring along champs, sell products. Maybe it's my fault for making things look so easy. But it isn't easy. Barton's magazine, *Muscle Sculpture,* was history in 1960, three years after he launched it.

During this same period, I suffered a breach of personal trust that I couldn't shake off or forgive, and I moved from our family apartment in New Jersey to a room at the New York Athletic Club. It would take a few years to get a final divorce decree and settlement, but my marriage was finished, over and done with. Once broken, some things can never be fixed, and it still hurts to tell about it.

This period seems worse in the telling than it did when it happened. It really wasn't so bad. Every day I went over to Palisade Avenue and put my head down and worked. Good hard work, which I loved, made life worth living. And it kept me alive financially while I fought to save the only part of my businesses that really mattered to me.

People say that home is where the heart is. All along, no matter what, my heart stayed where it always was—in my two muscle magazines and in bodybuilding. If I had those things, I had a home to go to, where nothing in the world could get to me.

There's a lesson here, I think, for everybody. Your work is your best friend. Believe in it and stick to it, and you cannot doubt yourself. Work saves you. It protects you. You should never run away from your work. If you do, you're running into deep, deep trouble.

Not long ago a friend of mine said that the American News disaster might have been for the best, because if I added more magazines and started wholesaling, my true interests might have suffered because my attention would have been divided. As it happened, though, I went back to square one where I had nothing but bodybuilding, and I made it explode. My friend was wrong. No matter how high I rose in general publishing, I never would have neglected my muscle magazines and bodybuilding. Nothing would have come between me and my passion and purpose in life. Nothing. One good thing came out of the American News catastrophe. I said to myself that I would never, ever allow someone else to control my destiny, and I didn't.

Now that I'm thinking about it, I see my real diamond in the muck. While I was still flat on my back, financially speaking, I made friends with Betty Brosmer, a blue-eyed California blonde in her early twenties who was a top model and cover girl and one of the most beautiful women in the world. To me, she was more of a friend than a dazzling beauty, maybe because I needed friendship just then more than anything. We stayed friends for months before it ever occurred to either of us that there might be deeper feelings.

If it took all that horrible business and personal trouble to clear the way for my Betty, it was worth it. She's been my wife for 45 years, and she'll be my angel forever.

I liked one thing about Betty long before we met—her pictures sold magazines like crazy. Back in 1956, I bought stock shots of her and put them on the covers of a couple he-man magazines, and they went flying off the shelf.

That same year I put a photo spread of Betty posing in a gym with weights into one of the ladies' muscle magazines. Unlike most women of the time, Betty actually knew what barbells and dumbbells were for. As a kid in California, she bought a weight set and training course from Joe Bonomo, a famous Hollywood muscle man who had a mail-order business. Betty was exceptional for even knowing about strength training, because female muscular development was not only taboo but unheard-of. Guys wanted girls who jiggled. Betty once posed for a hosiery ad hanging from an overhead bar to take the weight off her legs so they wouldn't show any signs of muscle definition. It took years and years—and a lot of work on the part of the Weiders, Betty included—for good tone and definition to become part of beauty.

Betty stood apart in ways other than appreciating exercise. She was the first supermodel to receive residuals for her work. She made a deal with top Hollywood glamour photographer Keith Bernard, who did all her pin-up shots, which gave her a third of all photo sales. Since some of her shots resold many times all over the world, she collected money for years after girls who got paid by the session cashed their checks. Betty was careful with her money, too, so she hung on to what she made. And she protected her precious personal assets. Nobody had a chest like Betty's, but she refused to bare her breasts for any amount of money, even when *Playboy* offered her a photo spread. Showing herself went against Betty's personal principles, and she thought ahead to how nude pictures would affect her loved ones. Other models didn't think about principles or the future. Some of those poor girls didn't think, period, and they ended up broke or worse.

The first time Betty heard about me, she was back home in California. I liked her work so much I decided to put her on the cover of a muscle magazine, so I set up an outdoor shoot with Dick Dubois, a terrific bodybuilder training in Los Angeles. The location was down in Newport Beach, a couple hours' drive south of town, and Betty and Dick sat together in the backseat and passed the time talking about Zen Buddhism, philosophy, and psychology. Betty studied such things on her own and in college, and Dick, who later became a minister, also had deep spiritual interests.

Bob Delmonteque, one of the photographers who drove down with the models, said, "Betty, I know a man in New York City who would fall madly in love with you."

Betty asked him why, and he said, "Because you two are exactly alike, always talking about heavy stuff like philosophy, politics, religion, and history."

The New York guy was, of course, Joe Weider. Even though she worked for me that day, my name didn't ring a bell because Betty got modeling jobs through her agency. But what Bob said kind of stuck in her mind. As a model, she was front and center in my mind because the issue with her on the cover—*Muscle Builder,* December 1957—broke all previous sales records.

Meanwhile, as my finances went down the tubes, I saw in the papers that Betty was back in New York. She had a part in a big Broadway play called *Starward Ark.* Because her cover was such a success, I wanted to sign her on for more photos and left word at Betty's modeling agency asking her to come over to my office and meet.

When Betty got my message, she started to say forget about it. At the time she was a top model who could pick and choose her work in Manhattan. And successful, glamorous New Yorkers stayed away from New Jersey like they'd catch a disease if they crossed the river. Eventually we set up a meeting in Manhattan, and Betty signed a contract to do a series of cover shots and pose for photo illustrations for women's exercise courses. Afterward, it came to Betty that I was the guy who was supposed to fall madly in love with her.

That same day, Betty got a contract offer from a much bigger publisher who had magazines similar to mine. Betty turned him down because, she said, she just signed a contract with a competitor. When she told him about her arrangement with me, the publisher laughed.

"A check from Joe Weider isn't worth the paper it's printed on," he said.

Betty asked why he would say such a thing, and he told her the story of American News and my financial troubles. Instead of scaring Betty away, what he said intrigued her. She sympathized with my plight.

Betty would sometimes get carried away with psychoanalyzing me. But the way she remembers, I was kind of a mess—overweight, not paying attention to my appearance, ink under my fingernails, and way down in the dumps. She thought my world of muscle men was really strange, too. But she also thought I was a sincere, nice guy.

I liked her because she had such a good head on her shoulders. After a shoot we'd go out for something to eat with the photographers and art directors and editors, and Betty and I would get into long conversations about philosophy and the human mind and pretty much everything under the sun. Sometimes we'd go over photos and discuss page layouts and design issues. We were never alone, but that didn't matter. The more time I spent with Betty, the more I appreciated her good qualities and enjoyed her company. She was compassionate, a good listener, and the first woman I could really talk with. The better I knew her, the more she reminded me of my father.

It must have been a relief for her, being with a man who wasn't head over heels or trying to put the make on her. Being a regular guy with dirt under my fingernails didn't do me any harm, either. I think Betty was drawn to me because I reminded her of her father, Andy Brosmer, who wasn't too proud to get dirt on his hands. In fact, he loved the soil. He had a business in Central California buying produce from farmers and selling to big food companies, and he was an avid gardener. He also was sports reporter on the radio. I never met a guy who could spout sports facts and figures like Andy. His interests went far beyond sports, and he could converse knowledgeably on many subjects. A walking encyclopedia, I called him. What a fascinating guy—and what a great guy. I really believe our resemblance appealed to Betty.

It might have been three or four years after I first put her picture in a magazine, and I don't know how many months after we met and started talking, but finally my heart got out in front of my head.

It happened at a Spanish restaurant in Greenwich Village called Granada. One night we worked really late and went out for paella, which was wonderful at Granada. Instead of the usual crew, only one person went with us. That was Bud Parker, who worked with me on the magazines and also promoted and emceed at contests. Bud didn't stay to eat, though.

For the first time, after almost a year, we were alone at the table late at night like a couple on a date. The lights were low, and we drank our wine and looked in each other's eyes, and I reached across the table and took Betty's hand.

I didn't plan to make a move, it just happened. I always tell people somebody spiked my wine, but that's just a joke. It didn't take anything in the wine to make Betty desirable. She was smart, well read, hard-working, frugal, and more moral and chaste than any girl I'd known. For all the millions of guys drooling over her pictures, you would have been amazed at how straight-laced Betty really was. Away from her work, she hid her womanly curves under prim, extremely conservative clothes. She wore glasses, mostly to hide her beautiful face. To me, an old-fashioned person, this meant a lot. Besides all those inner qualities, Betty was beautiful beyond belief. She still is.

The mystery is what took me so long to fall for her. No, there's a bigger mystery: Why in the world would she fall for me? Even if I wasn't the wreck she says, I was not a prize catch compared to other men she could have had. Before I met her, a top executive at a TV network courted her, taking her to glittering affairs where she met the biggest stars in entertainment. His mother flipped for Betty, too. The son of the governor of a big Midwestern state—Betty doesn't want me to tell which one—fell hard for her, and so did his family. Three separate times Howard Hughes made approaches through intermediaries. Last time around he offered to get her a screen test, but she just refused. She could have hooked up with the cream of the crop—Harvard men, Yale men, attorneys, doctors, heirs of great fortunes. Such men showered her with expensive gifts, but she sent their stuff back and kept them at arm's length—until she met this guy putting out bodybuilding magazines in New Jersey.

The human heart is the one muscle in the body that's a complete mystery to me.

Why, I can't say, because we were estranged, living apart, and legally separated, and we couldn't stand each other, but my wife made ending our marriage as difficult and nasty as possible. Divorce back then was hard enough to begin with. New York State law required that one party prove adultery. I had more than enough evidence to make my case, so I served divorce papers. But then I got counter-sued for doing the other party wrong, which was ridiculous. The lawyers made a fortune, and the New York tabloids had a picnic. Worst of all, Betty's name got dragged though the mud because of her connection with me, which was still just professional, not personal. Instead of driving her away or angering her, it deepened our relationship. She felt for me and stuck by my side, as she has ever since.

All the trouble and humiliation got me absolutely nowhere. The judge ruled both sides not guilty of the other's charges, so we were still stuck with each other. Rather than go through such an ordeal again, I moved to Las Vegas for six months to establish legal residency and get a divorce there.

Relieved as I was to end my first marriage, it also brought terrible pain. We had a little daughter in her toddler years, and my ex-wife cut off contact completely. I provided support through our attorneys, but to me, my ex-wife and daughter dropped off the map. For years I had no idea where she was.

In Vegas I rented a little apartment off the Strip. The side street I lived on, which wasn't even paved, is now Convention Center Drive. Though I came strictly to finalize the divorce, Vegas cast a spell on me. I loved the desert—the clean, stark beauty, the clarity of the light, the pure air—and love it to this day. Las Vegas has always been a special place for Betty and me. We bought our first getaway home there. Our latest is a penthouse on 38th floor of a brand-new condominium tower, not two blocks from where the little apartment I rented in 1960 stood. Of course everything has changed beyond recognition. When I looked east from my little apartment I saw nothing but open desert. Now there's development as far as the eye can see.

I think maybe I got to Vegas at the perfect moment in time. It still felt like a dusty little desert town. People were so friendly, and they knew my name at the one big grocery store that was the closest thing to a supermarket. On the other hand, the casinos showcased the biggest stars of the day. For \$6 or \$7 dollars, you could eat prime rib at a front-row table watching Frank Sinatra. I was somewhat short on money, but I could have fantastic meals for practically nothing in the big casinos, which were classier establishments in those days. Then, as now, I didn't gamble and didn't drink, so I got the best of Vegas and avoided the pitfalls. I'm still energized by the place and love all the activity and excitement going on day and night.

My feelings about Las Vegas are summed up by what I once told Betty when we first discussed buying a place in the desert. Being a Californian, she wanted to go to Palm Springs. I told her no, Palm Springs is where you go to die. Vegas is where you go to live.

In Vegas, I did what I always did—I worked. I ran the magazines back in Jersey by phone, and I created new courses to sell mail order. Among other things, I wrote and designed one of my most powerful and dramatic best-sellers—*Destructive Self-Defense.*

The weekly lessons came in a folder, everything illustrated with fantastic art of guys engaged in every sort of fighting, all in red and black. Inside the cover I wrote a private and confidential message to the buyer:

Welcome to the ever-growing army of Weider Terror Fighters:

You have stepped into a daring new world. Because in just 12 short weeks, you are going to be one of the greatest, most destructive fighters of our time. You will fear no man ... whether he outweighs you by 100 pounds ... whether he be armed with switchblade, gun or brass knuckles! You will be the most feared man in your neighborhood...an invincible fighting machine.

I signed that opening message as "Your Friend and Instructor, Joe Weider." By that point, the guy reading felt like I really was his friend. This gives you some idea how I could touch somebody personally and make him crazy to learn what I had to teach.

In light of the misery I had escaped, it might seem surprising I was so eager to remarry. But I guess I'm the marrying kind. Betty and I were wed on April 24, 1961, in a simple ceremony at the Little Church of the West, a replica of a mining town church that was then on the property of the old Last Frontier Hotel and Casino. It was moved a number of times, but the chapel still stands, and people still get married in it.

Ma told me what kind of wife I had.

When I first took Betty up to Montreal, she made a big hit with Ma, who said this: "Betty will love you. She will kiss you always and love you always."

Once again my mother was right on the money. She called Betty a *mensch,* a Yiddish way of saying a solid, reliable, upright person. My guardian angel, I called Betty, because of how she hovered and watched over me. I always felt she saved my life.

Betty says she civilized me.

For a famous beauty goddess, our first year of marriage must have seemed like a step down. I was still trying to get on my feet, working day and night to keep the magazines going and pay off what I owed. Because of work pressures and the need to economize, we put off our honeymoon and moved into a room with a kitchenette in the Middletown Hotel on 48th Street just off Lexington Avenue.

You can see how things were business-wise by looking at copies of *Muscle Builder* and *Mr. America* from that period. Since they stood on their own, I had to earn every nickel I could from the magazines. So I introduced new equipment and products like crazy, including vitamins and nutritional supplements, with more stuff constantly coming out. With staffing cut back I was like a publishing one-man band, doing practically everything cover to cover. I wrote and designed all the ads and wrote a lot of the articles under various bylines. Sometimes I posed for pictures, too. I put Betty's pictures everywhere—sometimes with dark-colored wigs and disguises so the readers wouldn't know she was the same model they just saw a few pages back.

After a year we flew to Paris for a belated honeymoon in the world's most romantic city. Immediately I got word that I had to appear before a judge back in New York. The court had suddenly settled the old, unfinished business with American News and Neo Gravure. I tried to get a continuance, but the judge didn't care that I was overseas on my honeymoon. So after two days I had to cut the trip short and fly home.

What a homecoming I had, too. Five years after it happened, I had to interrupt my honeymoon and pay $250,000 to the companies that almost put me out of business.

The good thing was, I could say goodbye to the American News catastrophe, once and for all. Goodbye, and good riddance.

It didn't take long after that to get back on my feet. The page count of the magazines went up, and mail-order sales were better than ever. In 1962, a new Weider Enterprises office opened in London. The next year we planted the flag on the West Coast with a little store and office in Santa Monica, on Fifth Street off Wilshire. Bodybuilders ran both offices, and Santa Monica was also a family affair. Betty's Aunt Annie, who had raised Betty like a daughter, worked as our office manager. She was in her seventies and retired, and the bodybuilders loved her. Arnold still talks about how he misses her, even though she gave him holy hell now and again. We all miss Annie, who was sharp and on the ball until a few months before her death, just short of her 108th birthday.

The business comeback meant that Betty and I could move out of the hotel. We happened to catch a slump in the New York rental market and got fantastic concessions—two months' free rent every year—on a lease for a two-bedroom apartment in a building called York River House just off the East River at 63rd Street. Dr. Joyce Brothers and the British and Cuban U.N. Ambassadors lived in the building. Our place was pretty small, but you could not improve on the incredible view of the East River. We didn't move until we came to California.

I loved living in New York. There was so much life just out the door. Every day I worked out in the gym at the Shelton Hotel. And I could walk over to Madison Avenue and look around the best antique and art galleries in America.

Once I was back in the chips, I started my serious collecting, a lifetime interest that I owe to Betty. She told me that before we met, her favorite pastime in New York was to attend auctions at major houses like Park-Bernet, now Sotheby's, and haunt the finest art galleries and antique stores and dealers of old books. She started when she was just 15 years old. Without buying, she observed and studied and became very knowledgeable, then passed on the bug to me.

It took Betty a while to get used to the idea that she could have the things she used to dream about. I'll never forget one of my first major buys—how could I forget? It was a very fine Louis XVI folding table, and I paid, if I remember, more than $4,000, which was very reasonable for such a piece. I was absolutely thrilled, but when I told Betty what I spent, she was so upset she felt ill. "That's a down payment on a house!" she said. From then on I'd understate what I paid for things so she wouldn't get upset.

One night, two executives from my new distributor, Kable News, wined and dined Betty and me at a very high-priced restaurant. They started saying how they were going to help me become, once again, the biggest sensation in publishing. The sky was the limit, they said, and told me about all the new, non-bodybuilding publications they wanted me to launch—celebrity gossip and scandal, sports, crime, sob stories, and on and on. Kable would advance me all the start-up funds I needed, they said.

I listened and then told them my own ideas for new magazines devoted to healthy living, diet, and exercise for everybody—different titles for women and men, younger and older people. But my words fell on deaf ears, and they went back to pushing their own ideas.

Ten years earlier I might have been more gullible, but they were talking to a different Joe Weider, who knew the score. They didn't care a bit about my beliefs and plans—they just wanted a piece of whatever they could talk me into publishing. All that sweet talk was about them cashing in on my golden touch.

It was American News all over again.

And I said forget it.

True to my vow to myself, I would not put my destiny into somebody else's hands or deviate from my own passions and beliefs and my mission in life.

CHAPTER SEVEN

MAN IN MOTION

Ben Weider

Too Good

I can't think of anybody but my brother Joe who would have carried personal integrity to such amazing lengths as he did in the wake of the American News disaster. I was very upset and disturbed when Joe decided to pay his debts rather than follow my advice to declare bankruptcy. I could not understand why Joe felt the need to meet obligations that were created by other people's dishonesty. It hurt to see what he went through, but at the same time I felt admiration and pride. I always looked up to my brother for doing what he believed was right even when it cost so dearly.

1948: A Very Expensive Lunch

A year after our first competition, we were back at the Monument National Theatre staging a national-level contest, Mr. Canada. René Leger, our first Mr. Montreal in 1946, won the title Mr. Canada 1947. The event was such a smashing success that I was emboldened to mount the IFBB's first international competition at which the top Canadians and top Americans would vie for the Mr. Eastern North America title. This grand event would take place in New York City at the Brooklyn Academy of Music, an elegant old opera house with about 2,100 seats. The Academy became our venue of choice in New York for more than 20 years.

On a late May morning in 1948, Canada's best bodybuilders and I set out for New York City in two rented cars, one of which I drove. The group included the photographer Tony Lanza and the very best of Canadian muscle men, among them René Leger, Joffre L'Heureux, Leo Robert, and Al Paivio. Joffre was police chief of a small town in Quebec. Al developed a superb physique and his intellect as well, becoming a distinguished professor on the faculty of the University of Western Ontario. Leo Robert was one of the most popular bodybuilders of French Canada who became a gym owner, teacher, and trainer. Another member of the team was Ed Theriault, who stood only 5 feet, 4 inches tall, but had an incomparable physique and a talent for acrobatics. Ed was also our first full-time employee and worked at Weider headquarters in Montreal until he retired.

Were automobiles powered by human energy, we left Montreal with enough excitement to take us coast to coast. Bodybuilders back then were a jolly and fraternal bunch, even before a contest. This time the camaraderie went even deeper because the fellows were off to win trophies for the honor of their country. In New York, such outstanding Americans as Clarence Ross, Alan Stephan, and Abe Goldberg awaited, each with followings who could be relied on to come to the contest and raise the roof.

After a few hours on the road I pulled up to a modest-looking restaurant on the outskirts of Albany, New York.

As everybody got out and stretched, I announced, "Lunch is on me, boys."

For that I got a rousing cheer, followed in short order by a terrible shock. Instead of having hamburger plates or lunch specials as I expected, the fellows had full-course dinners. If it was on the menu somebody wanted it, never mind the price. The waitresses loaded up the table with steak, chicken, any number of side dishes and desserts. Nowadays competitors would eat light and extremely carefully, if they ate at all, immediately before a competition. But those bodybuilders had a lunch that would have stuffed twice as many lumberjacks.

I kept smiling even though I felt very uneasy about what it all might cost. When the check came I looked at it once and then looked again in the hopes I misread the total. No such luck. With the tip, it came to about $50, more than three times what I had counted on spending. I was extremely concerned because my funds totaled only about $150. I'd just wiped out a third of my liquid assets, and we were only halfway to New York!

After lunch, the bodybuilders, full to bursting, happily got back into the cars for the balance of the trip.

"Something you ate didn't agree with you, Ben? What's wrong?" asked Tony Lanza.

"Not a thing is wrong," I said, "Let's get this show on the road!"

Apparently I allowed the expression on my face to betray the horrible sinking sensation I felt, facing the very real possibility of running out of money before the contest even started. I still had to buy gas and pick up incidental expenses in New York and then get us back to Montreal.

In New York I made it my first order of business to seek out a close friend named Joe Plaia who lent me enough money to stay afloat. The next evening we all went to the Brooklyn Academy of Music for what turned out to be a spectacular and historic evening. The sellout crowd of New Yorkers, always bodybuilding's most vociferous fans, greeted every pose with raucous cheers. The crowd's favorite Canadian turned out to be Ed Theriault, who won his height class to thunderous applause. The crowd got even louder when New York's own Abe Goldberg became the first to earn the title Mr. Eastern North America.

We had another success, our greatest yet, and Joe and I felt happy, but also shaken because we failed to break even. The New York contest was like the lunch at Albany, involving shocking new expenses that we didn't anticipate. Our losses weren't catastrophic, just a couple hundred dollars, but winding up in the red was a jolt because we had no money in reserve.

Joe and I sat down for a solemn postmortem.

"We can't let this happen again," Joe said.

I replied, "You're absolutely right. No more flying by the seat of our pants!"

We resolved to manage all our future contests in a much more businesslike manner. A couple successes had blinded us to the harsh realities of producing big events. You can pack the house to the rafters, thrill the audience, please the press, and still lose money if you don't budget and plan with the utmost forethought and care. Joe and I agreed that every event we put on had to pay for itself, at least. This was not the profit motive, but a necessity if we wanted our federation to grow. We could not afford unanticipated losses, which robbed us of resources to put back into bodybuilding, our federation, and our business.

Early Wins

A wise man said that an error becomes a mistake only when you repeat it. Our error did not become a mistake, and we never got blindsided like that again. Into the 1950s, we produced a run of highly successful competitions in Canada and New York. Our home base remained Montreal's Monument National Theater, where the formerly doubtful Monsieur Lapointe became our biggest supporter.

"I was right to take a chance on you. I knew it," he said to me, seeming to take a special personal pride in our successes.

We spared no expense to bring in the most famous muscle men of the day to guest pose. At one of our Montreal contests we showcased the British superstar Reg Park, at another the incomparable Steve Reeves, later to become bodybuilding's first Hollywood movie star. As Joe wrote, Steve was as handsome as a Greek god but also a very modest, pleasant fellow. Clancy Ross was another sensation. Greats such as these helped pack the theater with fans and also brought us press notice and the attention of the general public.

My work started months before a competition. Planning was everything, and if I neglected one area I jeopardized everything else. Say I lined up the very best competitors and the most distinguished panel of judges and a guest poser who was out of this world with great incidental acts and fine musicians. None of that mattered if nobody bought tickets because I failed to publicize and promote the event. Preparation involved myriad details, from making up a program to booking rooms and setting up meals for the bodybuilders, who, as I just made clear, had unusual dietary requirements. And I had to watch every penny.

Contest night brought a new set of challenges. Having packed the hall with fans, I had to keep them on the edges of their seats. This meant building an entire evening's entertainment around the competition. I have a program from the 1950 Mr. Montreal contest that lists 16 onstage events, among them bench press and wrist-wrestling contests, acrobatics, a pair of illusionists from France, and "Rhythm in Motion" by an American performer named Art Dion. Doing posing routines we had three Canadian stars and our special guest—the one and only Reg Park. I had to see to it that every participant remained comfortable and content, while making sure they followed instructions so things went smoothly on schedule. Directing a contest requires patience, understanding, and great skill. The bodybuilders could be very nice, but some of them required a great deal of attention. Most of them came to win, which meant each fellow believed in his heart that he was the best of the competitors, and not all, but a few, wanted star treatment. I on the other hand had to ensure that everybody got equal treatment and that judging and scoring went according to protocol. I also emceed in both French and English.

Always there was much more at stake than the event in progress. Running a great contest was the best way to attract the fans and top athletes at the next one. A flop would do damage very difficult to repair.

When I call our early contests smash hits, I don't mean we reaped fabulous profits. Even with sellout crowds we were satisfied to clear enough to get the next event going. Joe and I never considered contests as business in the same sense as the magazines and mail-order sales and, later, sports nutrition. The secret of the bodybuilding contest business is that it's not such a great business.

On the other hand, Joe and I couldn't advance the cause and fulfill our personal missions without contests. You can't have champions without holding championships, which are the only reason athletes undertake championship-level training and push the limits of the sport. You can't have a growing fan base without giving the fans first-class, well-organized sporting events. Try to imagine baseball without a league of its own and scheduled games, playoffs, and the World Series. That was pretty much our situation at the outset, and it was up to us to fill the gaps. The contests brought other benefits, too. The champions and cadre of hardcore fans gave us a base on which to build a general interest in strength training and spread the word about exercise and healthy living. Contests helped drive our business, too, but that was never our primary motive.

In truth, we put on contests because we loved doing it for the sake of our sport. It was as simple as that. As Joe explained earlier, Bob Hoffman undermined our sport by relegating it to a sideshow status at his weightlifting events. Under that system, the sport could never have come into its own and gained worldwide respect and recognition. My own dream of Olympic recognition would have been an absolute impossibility.

In years to come, after I got the IFBB contests up and running, others would take over production.

Back Roads of Quebec

In my home province of Quebec, outside of Montreal, people knew virtually nothing about strength training and bodybuilding, a situation I found paradoxical because French Canadians were revered throughout the U.S. and Canada as strong men. Louis Cyr, the 19th Century prodigy of strength from Quebec, was a folk hero whose feats were legendary, much like the mythical giant lumberjack Paul Bunyan in the U.S. I was something of a Cyr buff myself. I first heard tales of him as a boy on summer holidays in rural Quebec, and the first history book I wrote was a life story of Louis Cyr based on material his family provided to me. My book *Louis Cyr: L'Homme Le Plus Fort De Tous Les Temps* came out in English as *Louis Cyr: The Strongest Man in History.*

To raise awareness of bodybuilding in Quebec, I organized bodybuilding contests and exhibitions along with lectures dealing with physical education, sports, and fitness. The difficulty in small towns was to find a site for the event. But then a friend pointed out that life in every Quebec village and town revolved around the Roman Catholic Church and that the best places to hold events were the church parish halls.

So my first contact in a given place was the priest. I would ask to rent the parish hall and explain what we were about and why a presentation on physical culture and strength training was a good use of church property. This wasn't a hard sell, actually, because we, like the Church, promoted discipline and clean living while discouraging vices like smoking and drinking alcohol. And we showed kids and young men a way to prove their masculinity and blow off steam without causing trouble. I sweetened the deal by offering to donate half the receipts from ticket sales to the parish. The money involved was very modest as I charged low admissions just to cover expenses and the hall rental. Some priests took more persuasion, some less, but I can't remember ever being turned away.

In a little village I'd go with one or two bodybuilders, give a brief talk and then have the fellows amaze the audience with their physiques and demonstrate training techniques. In bigger towns I sometimes organized contests so local muscle men could get into the act. I also lectured at schools.

A talk I gave at a school in the town of St. Hyacinthe made a tremendous impression on one certain youth. I found this out approximately 25 years later in a surprising manner.

At an official function, Claude Wagner, minister of justice for the Province of Quebec, approached me and offered his hand.

"You know, Mr. Weider," he said, "I admire you very much."

"Thank you," I said, wondering what about me he admired. So far as I knew we'd never met before.

"You changed my life," the minister said and explained that my words so long ago moved him to quit smoking cigarettes and take up exercise and healthy living.

Hearing that distinguished gentleman's words gratified me, as does re-reading an old letter from a priest thanking me at great length for bringing bodybuilding to the young people in his flock.

How many thousands of miles I put on the old cars I drove back then, I'll never know. I went to some very remote places in Quebec, deep in the woods, and had great fun with the fellows I took with me.

Foe in London

By 1950, I had visited 27 countries on behalf of the IFBB, focusing mainly on Western Europe and Africa. In terms of awareness of bodybuilding and exercise, Europe was less of a foreign territory than rural Canada. However, as my experience in France showed, an acquaintance with bodybuilding didn't mean people were ready to welcome the IFBB with open arms.

In Great Britain I ran into a wall of resistance from the London-based National Amateur Bodybuilding Association (NABBA). Britain's leading muscle magazine, *Health and Strength,* organized the NABBA in 1950. That was two years after the magazine mounted the first London Mr. Universe, held in conjunction with the 1948 Olympic Games in London, the first postwar Olympics. The well-known English bodybuilder, Oscar Heidenstam, who was affiliated with the magazine, assumed control of the NABBA.

In that same period, I made visits to Britain, canvassing gyms and clubs to make friendly contacts and look for openings for the IFBB. It quickly became apparent that the NABBA had a lock on bodybuilding on its own home ground that would be very difficult to break. I wanted very much to meet the man in charge of this organization to see what sort of fellow he was and establish a personal relationship. I also had an idea that we might be able to work together to our mutual benefit.

When I first spoke with Heidenstam, I mentioned the possibility that we might find ways to cooperate. In the most pleasant and polite way, he said he had no interest in working with us under any circumstances. He had the NABBA, which controlled the London Mr. Universe and had *Health and Strength* magazine behind it, so what use could I possibly be? He wasn't at all rude, but I saw that behind the smile there lurked a new enemy of the IFBB.

Thus began the conflict between the NABBA and our federation. Eventually we, of course, would prevail, in spite of the fact that Oscar Heidenstam did virtually everything he could to keep us out and then later became openly hostile. Had he kept the peace and cooperated, he and his organization and the sport would have been much better off.

The conflict went far beyond Britain, because the NABBA was a sort of bodybuilding extension of the British Empire, which in the early 1950s was still intact. In fact, wherever the British flag flew, over dozens of countries, colonies, and protectorates, bodybuilders took their cues from London-based NABBA. Through the 1950s, I would feel the long arm of Oscar Heidenstam and run into the NABBA wall in such farflung places as Malaya (now Malaysia), Thailand, Singapore, and British-controlled Caribbean Islands.

As the old saying went, the sun never set on the British Empire. Nor did it set on the NABBA. Not, at any rate, for a few years more. But then, one by one, starting later in the '50s, the British colonies gained their independence, and sports officials and athletes didn't want to bow to London any more. I determined that the NABBA's great weakness was that they organized their Mr. Universe in London without exception. This upset many of their national federation members. The IFBB had a totally opposing view of promoting bodybuilding worldwide, and the venue sites for our world championships changed every year. When the political bonds with Britain were broken, the sun began to rise on the IFBB in the former British colonies.

Friends

In London I also met a man who would become the best friend our federation and our sport ever had as well as my own dearest and best friend—Oscar State, secretary of the British Amateur Weightlifting Association (BAWLA), who had organized weightlifting events in conjunction with the London Olympics.

His contests were such a success that the International Weightlifting Federation asked him to help set up its world championships. Eventually he would become the most powerful IWF official and one of the most respected administrators in all of organized sports. Oscar also liked and supported bodybuilding. He had a hand in the formation of the NABBA and emceed at the early Mr. Universe contests. Unlike Heidenstam, though, he was not anti-Weider. This I could sense when I first called on him.

Oscar, balding and very lean, was a schoolteacher by profession. He was about 10 years older than I, with an air of authority and gravity that made the age difference seem greater. I felt an instant respect and admiration, and Oscar showed great interest in me and my work. Our mutual respect was the foundation on which we would build our friendship. But Oscar was a rather cool, reserved individual, as I am, and our relationship took a long time to ripen. After we met I had no idea that Oscar would be the best friend I ever had, outside my family, but I knew I had met an admirable and forthright and hard-working man and that I liked him very, very much.

In pages to come, you will read a great deal more about Oscar. Without him there would be less of a story to tell.

I returned to Europe repeatedly, making contacts and doing the spadework that would one day allow the IFBB to grow. It's a good thing I didn't expect instant results because I didn't get them, but my enthusiasm and optimism never flagged. Ironically, the most determined opposition I met came from within bodybuilding—in France from the leaders of physical culture with their supposedly incompatible physical ideals, and in Britain from the NABBA. I got a much warmer reception from the weightlifting world, beginning in Egypt with El Sayed Nosseir, followed by Oscar State. And then my first big breakthrough in Europe came with the help of another leading figure in weightlifting.

In terms of his prominence in his country and the roles he played, Borje Franzen was a sort of Swedish Bob Hoffman. He was editor-in-chief of *Kraftsport* magazine, then devoted more to strength than bodybuilding, much like Hoffman's *Strength and Health,* and he was very involved with the national weightlifting federation. Borje was no Hoffman, though. He was wonderfully warm and welcoming when I met him, and he immediately decided to throw his support behind bodybuilding. Much to the irritation of some in the weightlifting community who resented sharing the spotlight, he expanded coverage of bodybuilding in his magazine, which would be renamed *Kraftsport & Bodybuilding.* The Swedish Weightlifting Federation became the Swedish Weightlifting and Bodybuilding Federation. And Borje and I joined forces to produce the biggest bodybuilding competition Sweden had ever seen at the Stockholm Music Hall. A few years later, in 1955, an IFBB affiliate was organized in Sweden.

With Sweden, our federation now had five members on three continents.

Important Invitation

At that time, an enormous part of the world lived under brutal Communist dictatorships, including Eastern European countries under the military occupation and political domination of the Soviet Union, and Communist China. Winston Churchill memorably named the impenetrable barrier between the Soviet controlled countries and the West the Iron Curtain, and others spoke of a Bamboo Curtain sealing off Communist China. For ordinary people in Communist countries, contact with the outside world was forbidden, sometimes on pain of death. Distrust and paranoia ran both ways. Western countries made it very difficult to travel to the East. Newspapers and radio broadcasts in the U.S. and Canada were full of anti-Communist rhetoric as both sides went into the long, dangerous armed standoff known as the Cold War. All-out nuclear war seemed to be an imminent possibility.

Given the tense situation, I was surprised to see letters asking for training tips and other information from young bodybuilders in Eastern Europe and the Soviet Union. As I later learned, Soviet sailors went out of their way to buy Joe's magazines in non-Communist port cities, then smuggled the magazines into their homeland where they were pored over by fellows just as eager to build their muscles as their counterparts in the West. Their interest was actually illegal and potentially dangerous because authorities condemned bodybuilding as a bourgeois activity promoted by decadent, narcissistic Americans. Still, a tiny bodybuilding underground sprang up. To me, a reader was a reader, and a bodybuilder a bodybuilder, and I answered each letter from the Communist Bloc, always enclosing issues of our magazines. Joe also sent magazines behind the Iron Curtain in response to interest from trainers and sports officials.

You would have been hard put to dream up a challenge more impossible than taking bodybuilding into the Communist World in the 1950s. This, however, is exactly what I decided to do: A) because there were many millions of people behind the Iron Curtain and I knew, from the correspondence, that many of them were eager for what we had to offer; and B) because people thought I was nuts to even think of such a thing. When I broached the idea to Europeans, they practically fell over laughing. North Americans considered my ideas crazy or subversive, as if I supported Communism.

One and only one person looked toward Communist countries and saw the same sort of opportunities as I did. That was, of course, Joe, who gave me his moral support and offered to back me all the way.

"I know you, Ben," Joe said. "If anybody can make a hole in the Iron Curtain, it's you."

In 1953, I made the acquaintance of Vladlen Katchanov, an assistant charge d'affaires at the Soviet Embassy at Ottawa. Vladen, who handled public relations at the embassy, supplied me with all the information available, which wasn't much, about developments in his country concerning bodybuilding. Though our sport, *per se,* was officially forbidden, there was growing interest in strength training with weights as part of conditioning for other sports. At that time, the Soviets made a huge push to dominate international athletics, and Vladlen liked to brag that the Soviets had the greatest sports programs in the world.

"He's a spy, you know." If I heard this once, I heard it a dozen times, and for all I knew the people may have been right about Vladlen. Embassies, especially Soviet embassies, were full of secret agents posing as diplomats and civil servants. If he was spying, though, he got nothing from me because we talked mainly about sports. And he seemed to agree with me more often than not. He told me that he approved of bodybuilding, and when I mentioned that I would love to visit his country to see its sports programs for myself, he said nothing encouraging, but I knew from his smile and the twinkle in his eye that he'd do his best to help me. I grew to like him and consider him a friend. He was a warm, expansive character, always joking and laughing, and yet very serious about his profession, and he genuinely liked Canada and Canadians. All my instincts, which I trusted, said this man was not an enemy. We still keep in touch.

My government, however, was not so sure.

I'll never forget taking Vladlen out on the St. Lawrence River in my cabin cruiser, an indulgence I allowed myself after our business got going. My boat was really rather modest, but to Vladlen owning a pleasure boat of any kind, with the freedom to go anywhere in it, was unimaginable luxury and freedom.

"Ah Ben, this is the life!" he said to me as he lolled on deck.

I happened to look astern and see two men in a runabout that was matching my course and speed. Wherever my boat went it followed. I made a couple turns to confirm my suspicions that the little boat was following us.

Not wanting to spoil Vladen's fun, I didn't say anything, but when I returned to Montreal I went to the local headquarters of the Royal Canadian Mounted Police, which handles domestic intelligence much like the Federal Bureau of Investigation in the U.S. I met with the head of security, superintendent N.W. Brakefield-Moore, who was a trim, rather dashing fellow.

"Sir," I said, "I have reason to believe I'm being followed. I can save you the trouble if you let me explain my relationship with Vladlen Katchanov of the Soviet Embassy."

"I am listening," said the superintendent.

I laid out my professional interest in keeping abreast of developments in Soviet strength training and told about my ultimate desire, to spread the word about bodybuilding behind the Iron Curtain.

The security officer smiled and said, "I appreciate your taking the time to come in. I think you have cleared things up to our satisfaction."

In the friendliest manner, Superintendent Brakefield-Moore said there would be no more surveillance if I informed him in advance whenever I was meeting with Vladen, and he wished me the best of luck.

Some months later, Vladlen paid me an unexpected visit at my office in Montreal.

"This document arrived from Moscow, and I have orders to present it to you personally," he said, handing me an envelope.

"What is it?" I asked.

"I am not authorized to know such things," he said with a smile on his face. Then he beamed as I opened the envelope and pulled out a special invitation from the Soviet minister of sport Nicolai Romanov to visit him and tour Soviet training facilities. This was an unheard-of invitation at a time when the Soviet Union tried very hard to keep visitors out.

Instead of sharing my joy, a lot of my friends found the invitation alarming. They warned me against going, lest I be labeled a Communist, which in those days was more than an insult. Suspicion of disloyalty or merely Communist sympathies ruined many reputations and careers. I decided to pre-empt suspicions by getting a clear go-ahead from the Canadian government. In Montreal, I went to the RCMP office and met, once again, with Superintendent Brakefield-Moore. He smiled and made me feel at ease as I told him of my invitation from the Soviets.

"If I go, how will it affect the government's perception of me?" I asked him.

"As far as we are concerned, your reputation with us is excellent," said Superintendent Brakefield-Moore.

I also contacted the Department of External Affairs in Ottawa, equivalent to the U.S. State Department. Robert A.D. Ford, head of the department's European Division, understood the nature of my trip and encouraged me to accept.

With the blessing of my own government, I felt much more confident about accepting Minister Romanov's invitation. As with all my travels, I made plans to get the most out of the trip by making stops along the way. I set up visits to Czechoslovakia and Poland, both under the control of the Soviet Union, on the way to Moscow.

The Workers' Paradise

Communism made a very poor first impression on me. Because I had two cameras (as I usually did when I traveled), I was presumed to be a spy by the inspectors and guards at the airport security at Prague, capital of Czechoslovakia, now the Czech Republic. I explained that one camera had black-and-white film to take photos for publication while the other had color film for my own use. Who knows how long I would have been held up if I hadn't thought to show the chief inspector my invitation from the sports minister in Moscow. The great doubts about me and my cameras were swept away, and the chief security officer was happy to clear me in a matter of minutes.

A small contingent of Czech sports officials met me at the airport and accompanied me on the drive into town. Everything I read about Prague before the trip made me eager to see this storied "Golden City" as it was called before the Second World War because of the gold leaf adorning many of its buildings. I rechristened it the "Dirty City." Soot blanketed buildings that would have been lovely were they fixed up and cleaned, but all was dreariness and decay.

An official from the Sports Ministry accompanied me to my room in the Esplanade Hotel. When we were alone in the room I asked for news about the current political situation so I could act and respond to questions intelligently. He placed his finger to his lips, signaling that I should not speak, and then pulled a pencil and paper from his pocket and scribbled a note: "Please do not discuss politics. There are hidden microphones in the room." From then onward we spoke of serious or political subjects only outdoors. Later I searched the room and, sure enough, I found a small listening device in an air duct.

A tramway ran past my hotel, and one morning I decided to sit out and watch the locals go to work. At a newsstand I picked up the only English language publication available, *The Daily Worker.* Published in London, it was an official organ of the Communist Party. The paper happened to have an article extolling the happiness and prosperity of Czechs in their Communist worker's paradise. I looked up from the paper and saw crowds of people in clothes that Westerners would never think of wearing. The faces were weary, empty, unsmiling. I wondered what fool could have written the lies in that paper, and who could possibly believe them.

That first exposure to life in a police state was truly an eye-opener. I'll never forget a night on the town with my hosts from the Sports Ministry that began with a dinner of stringy chicken and a gray potato and ended at a nightclub where liquor was in plentiful supply. The house lights went down and a nattily dressed master of ceremonies stepped into the spotlight. Someone in our group translated for me as he spoke.

"Ladies and gentlemen," the emcee proclaimed, "I have been authorized to introduce this evening's entertainment."

At that I laughed out loud. My companions asked what was so funny, and I tried to explain that I'd never heard a floorshow introduced in such a strange manner. They still didn't understand, because for them it was perfectly natural that any public activity, of any kind, be introduced with official authorization.

The rule of the authorities over every aspect of life, including sports, explains the character of my work in Communist and other totalitarian nations. In such places, all business was government business, and my trips to promote bodybuilding and our federation were like official state visits, with the formalities of international diplomacy. Since visitors from the West were so rare, I was sometimes perceived as a sort of representative and spokesman for Canada and the entire Free World. This was a marked contrast to Western countries where sports were run by sportspeople whose governments couldn't care less if they took up bodybuilding, joined the IFBB, or wanted to buy Weider magazines and products.

In Prague, it was crystal clear to me the Communist overlords in Moscow were not about to smile on bodybuilding. On the other hand, people I met, most of whom were connected with the Czech weightlifting federation, had a keen interest. Some dared to speak, rather wistfully, of holding contests in their country. I had absolutely no doubt it would happen. With more freedom and less fear in the land, I knew Czechs would embrace our sport. And they did. As early as 1966, Czechs held bodybuilding competitions, and Czechoslovakia became the first national Communist IFBB member.

Poland

My arrival in the Polish capital Warsaw happened to coincide with a Communist youth festival, which drew young people from dozens of countries to participate in cultural and athletic events. Oscar State, who helped to organize the festival's weightlifting events, met me at the airport along with a representative of Poland's weightlifting federation.

Oscar took me under his wing and introduced me to a Who's Who of influential people in sports in Communist countries, including China. One highlight was getting VIP treatment at a weightlifting match between Poland and China. The event was exciting, but even more so was meeting and befriending Chinese sports officials who helped clear the way for me to visit their country a few years later.

Oscar introduced me to another notable, destined to become a lifelong friend and colleague. Malih Alaywan, who coached the Lebanese weightlifting team at the festival, was keenly interested in bodybuilding. After forming a Lebanese bodybuilding federation, he would help organize in other Middle Eastern countries, earning the title, "The Father of Bodybuilding in the Arabic Countries." My dear friend for more than 50 years, Malih became the IFBB's vice president for the Middle East.

I was shocked by the devastation in Warsaw, scene of bloody fighting during World War II. More than 10 years later, half the city was still in ruins, and the new buildings followed the grim, ugly Soviet pattern. The populace looked even more weary and bedraggled than the Czechs. By far the most beautiful sight I beheld was a gorgeous young lady who came to my hotel and informed me that she was to be my guide and hostess for the duration of my stay. This Polish girl displayed impeccable manners and dressed in the most stylish clothes, with perfect makeup and hair. Honestly, she would have stopped traffic in Paris or New York. In Warsaw, she was a dream.

After I gained her confidence, I asked her how in the world she could afford to be so gorgeously turned out. She confided that the clothes and shoes and cosmetics were on loan from the government, and she'd have to give everything back when I left. To me that was Poland in 1955.

Though I made many friends and contacts that would later prove fruitful, my attempts to promote bodybuilding as a sport in Poland were much like they were in Czechoslovakia. Athletes were keenly interested, but the government, which controlled everything connected to sports and took its cues from Moscow, stood in our way and refused to work with the sport of bodybuilding.

Unofficial Diplomacy

As I indicated, I sometimes represented more than our sport and our federation.

My trip to Poland came about two years after the end of the Korean War, fought between Communist North Korean forces backed up by the Chinese and a coalition of non-Communist nations led by the U.S. Though the shooting was over, people in Communist countries were very agitated over allegations that the U.S. had used germ warfare in Korea. This was pure fabrication, but it came up repeatedly in conversations in Poland. Always I defended the United States. The more I had to do it, the more emphatic my defense became. One day some Russian and Polish weightlifters brought up the germ warfare business.

"You can't possibly believe this nonsense. It's pure propaganda," I said.

The athletes asked me how I could be so sure.

"Use your heads," I said. "The U.S. is big and wealthy and powerful, isn't it?"

They young men agreed to this obvious truth, as they did when I pointed out that the U.S. was a mighty military power that defeated Japan virtually without assistance and was very instrumental in defeating Nazi Germany.

"Didn't it arm its allies, including the Soviets, and doesn't it now have weapons of unimaginable power?"

Yes, they said.

"So why would the U.S. have to employ germ warfare to defeat a poor little country like North Korea and risk worldwide condemnation?"

My companions didn't have an answer.

Afterward I thought I might have spoken too forcefully, particularly after I got an important-looking government notice that I feared was an expulsion order. Since I couldn't read Polish, I took it to Jean-Louis Delisle, charge d'affaires at the Canadian Legation in Warsaw. At that time Canada didn't have an embassy in Poland, and Mr. Delisle was our top-ranking diplomat in Warsaw. The letter contained amazing news. It was a personal invitation to a private meeting with Poland's prime minister, Jozef Cyrankiewicz, the country's head of state.

When I arrived at his office the prime minister stood to introduce himself. He was a short man, slim, with an intense gaze, but also relaxed and pleasant. We sat in chairs with a little table between us that had on it some Polish wine and fruit. After a few pleasantries, he came to the point. His government was asking for the return of Polish art treasures that had been sent out of Poland at the start of World War II for safekeeping, which were now stored in a Catholic church in Quebec. The Church refused to return the treasures because, as church leaders said, they belonged to the Polish people and not the Communist regime.

Knowing I was from Quebec, the prime minister had called me in to see if I could shed some light on the situation. He couldn't understand why the Canadian government didn't just remove the treasures from the church and return them to Poland where they belonged. I explained that the Canadian authorities really were powerless to intervene. Of all the Canadian provinces, Quebec was the most overwhelmingly Roman Catholic. Seizing the Polish treasures would have been political suicide for the national government. If leaders did such a thing they would forfeit the political support of Quebec and thus lose the next election.

What I said didn't please the prime minister, but he seemed to understand.

As we were about to say goodbye, I brought up an issue that Mr. Delisle had asked me to clarify. He and other Western diplomats had gotten worrisome reports that the Roman Catholic primate cardinal of Poland, Stefan Wyszynski, had been jailed.

"Mr. Prime Minister, as I mentioned, I am from a Catholic province, and the people of Quebec are very concerned about a rumor that Cardinal Wyszynski has been arrested and is now in jail. Can you please let me know if this is true or not?" I said.

The prime minister's face changed and became very serious. He replied that the cardinal was, in fact, arrested and charged with illegal activities involving the black market and dealing in foreign currency. However, he said, because of the sympathetic understanding of the government, he was confined to his small native village.

"I assure you that he is not in jail," the prime minister said to me.

Mr. Delisle was most grateful to receive this news and pass it on to the officials in Ottawa who were very concerned about this subject.

My spirited defense of the U.S. over the germ warfare allegations must have caused a stir, because Mr. Delisle heard about that, too. I know this because after I left Poland, the charge d'affaires mentioned it in a letter to Robert A.D. Ford, the head of the European Division at External Affairs back in Ottawa. Mr. Ford sent me a note quoting from some of Mr. Delisle's letter:

I soon realized he [Ben] was an intelligent observer and also a keen defender among his communistic acquaintances here of western viewpoints and standards. He may have told you for instance that he took up Polish and Russian weightlifters on the question of germ warfare in Korea. I think his direct, simple, and forceful way of arguing must have impressed his entourage...and certainly people like him should be encouraged to pay visits behind the Iron Curtain.

The Abyss

During my meeting with the Polish prime minister, I noticed numbers tattooed onto his forearm, a telltale sign that he had been imprisoned in a Nazi concentration camp during World War II. When I asked him if this were so, he said he had been held in both the notorious Auschwitz and Mauthausen camps.

This gave me an opening to repeat a request for permission to visit Auschwitz. Lower level officials had already said, "No," telling me I had no right to go because I was only a sports official. The prime minister, learning of my interest, coupled with the fact that my parents' birthplace and ancestral home was in Poland, said he personally would authorize my trip to Auschwitz. He told me a car would pick me up in the morning.

Although we were authorized only to follow the most direct route to and from the concentration camp, I persuaded the driver to make a side trip to Kurov, the town my mother and father came from. I recognized certain landmarks from my parents' descriptions, but I felt very little emotional connection with the town. Perhaps it would have been different if any of my relations or their friends and acquaintances were there. But the entire Jewish community had been wiped out. Kurov, to my eyes, was just another small Polish town. The few people on the streets were obviously frightened to have strangers in their midst in a car that could only belong to the government. We had an unpleasant scene with the town commissar, or political officer, who placed me under arrest and threatened to have me locked up for making an unauthorized visit. In turn, I amazed him by threatening to report him for interfering with a visitor who traveled with the personal blessing of the prime minister. He then reluctantly let me go.

Auschwitz had an impact on my mind and my heart that remains to this day. Of course I knew the horrors that transpired under the Nazis. And I knew that my own extended family was obliterated. But such knowledge did not prepare me for what I saw there, where more than a million and a half innocent people were killed. The deaths were worse than murder because the Nazis built death factories, reducing killing to an industrial process with no mercy whatsoever. Never will I forget a building full of hair shaved from the heads of doomed people. In my mind it's like I was there yesterday, and remembering brings back the feeling in the pit of my stomach and the anger and sadness. Here was intolerance taken to its most horrible extreme. Experiencing intolerance, in a small way, had already motivated me to work for equality, brotherhood, and individual liberty through the medium of international sports. After seeing the death factory in Poland, I rededicated myself to fighting intolerance in my own life's work.

Moscow

Normally I stay healthy all year, but on that trip I picked up a cold that had me in absolute misery as I took off for Moscow. In other circumstances I would have postponed my meetings, but I didn't dare put off a special invitation from the Soviet sports minister Nicolai Romanov. The man was simply too important and our scheduled meetings much too precious to jeopardize. In the realm of sports his word was the law for millions upon millions of people in the Soviet Union and its satellite nations. He had considerable political power, too, with a position equivalent to a Cabinet-level post in the West. I felt lucky to get an invitation from Romanov in the first place, and there was no way in the world I'd risk offending him or losing my appointment.

I got the VIP treatment from the moment I stepped off the plane, breezing through customs and riding in a deluxe sedan to the Metropole Hotel in Moscow's historic Kitai Gorod District not far from Red Square. Next day I met with Minister Romanov, whose disarming smile instantly made me feel welcome. He stood about 5 foot 10 and was very smartly dressed in a suit that flattered his burly, muscular frame.

Try as I might, I couldn't stop coughing or hide how wretched I felt.

"You are not well?" the minister asked.

"A little cold, that's all," I said. "It's nothing."

"Nonsense!" he said. "I will send you to a villa in Sochi, and you will come back a new man."

Sochi, it turned out, was a resort city far to the south on the Black Sea. Romanov said I would be put up in a hotel normally reserved for leading Communist officials and their families.

The plane for Sochi, a very decrepit-looking DC-3 that was no doubt a gift from the U.S. during the Second World War, did not instill confidence. The engines started reluctantly, sputtering like old cars on a winter morning, and the whole plane shook during takeoff, but then it flew without mishap southward across the vast Russian steppes. Sochi was lovely, like a Russian version of the French Riviera. Built during czarist times as a warm weather retreat for the rich, it was now a playground for political bigwigs and workers who earned special privileges. My hotel, built before the Communist takeover, was elegant and well appointed. After a few days of fresh food, rest, and hot mineral baths, I was ready to go back to work.

In Moscow, Nicolai Romanov beamed and greeted me like an old friend, asking about my stay in Sochi and expressing delight to see me fully recovered. He introduced me to several Soviet sports scientists, and we got down to substantive discussions.

I quickly understood why this high official pulled out all the stops on my behalf. He firmly opposed bodybuilding as a sport in itself, but he saw tremendous value in bodybuilding as the basis of conditioning for all sports. And he and the Soviet sports scientists at our meeting recognized that Joe's Weider training system had revolutionized the techniques for development of strength and muscularity for everybody. Mr. Romanov and his associates had the highest respect for Joe's work and repeatedly reminded me to thank Joe for sending his magazines free of charge. To them, Joe was the top guru of bodybuilding, and they referred to his numerous contributions to the sport.

The sports minister set up meetings for me at the Soviet Academy of Medical Science and Institute of Nutrition, where athletic training and performance was the subject of rigorous scientific study. I attended a breakfast meeting with researchers and coaches and then adjourned to their main planning room where they worked out training regimens for athletes. Much to my amazement, I saw Joe's muscle magazines spread across a table. The Soviet experts used them as sources of state-of-the-art information for instructing coaches and also to train top world-level competitors. I assured them we would continue to provide them with magazines and all our latest training materials.

The old saying goes that a prophet is not honored in his own land. Well, Joe was certainly respected in his own land, the U.S.A., but he was revered and treated as an iconic figure in the Soviet Union. And the name Weider never lost its luster, even to this day. Arnold Schwarzenegger tells about fans clustered around him in Red Square, asking excitedly if he knew Joe Weider. That was in the mid-1980s. Joe's friend and colleague Dr. Leroy Perry saw archived copies of Joe's old magazines at the prestigious Leningrad Research Institute of Physical Culture. Dr. Perry worked with Communist countries' athletes as a trainer and served as physician for the last Olympic track and field team fielded by the Soviet Union before it broke up into smaller republics after the Communist regime fell. Dr. Perry says that once word got out that he knew Joe well, people wanted to hear all about the great philosopher of athletics, as they called my brother.

I quickly realized I was one of many foreigners brought to the Soviet Union to contribute to their astonishing effort to turn out world-class athletes. Top athletes and experts of all kinds were invited to give demonstrations and lectures to Soviet coaches and competitors. At a school for coaches I watched Joaquin Capilla Perez, a champion diver from Mexico, lecture on his winning techniques, then give a demonstration in the pool. Not only did the Soviets watch, they filmed the Mexican star, who won four medals, one of them gold, at three summer Olympic Games and placed first in both springboard and platform diving at two consecutive Pan American Games. The Soviets analyzed the films and used them as the basis for their national training programs. The strategy was simple, but highly effective. To catch up to the rest of the world in sports, the Soviets invited the world's best athletes and sports experts and then used them as teachers and models for training their own competitors.

That sort of systematic approach on a national level was something new in athletics. So was the Soviets' emphasis on conditioning, including strength conditioning, as fundamental to training in all sports. At that time, workouts in the West focused on sports-specific drills and practice matches, with much less attention given to aerobic conditioning and little or no attention to strength training. As Joe wrote, many coaches in North America outright forbid weight training, repeating the old nonsense about getting "muscle bound" and the dangers of "athlete's heart." The Soviets were light years ahead of the West here, which is why they saw the value of Joe's work. At that time his techniques were in wider use behind the Iron Curtain than in the U.S.A. I found it ironic that this great Communist power, which forbid bodybuilding, trained thousands of their athletes to be bodybuilders.

There was nothing in the West even remotely like the great sports machine the Soviets had built. The more I saw of it, the more I was amazed, and the more I recognized that the West was about to get a rude awakening. Very soon, the Communist countries would field world champions and challenge the U.S. in medal counts at the Olympic Games. The way I saw it, the whole Western sports establishment was about to have an experience like that of a West German soccer team that I watched in a match in Moscow.

Facing the Germans was the leading Soviet soccer club called Dynamo. For the first half of the game, the Germans outplayed the Dynamo club, jumping to a three-goal lead. Then, in the second half, the Germans faded while the Soviets stayed fast and strong and erased their deficit, goal by goal, then went ahead to win. The Germans had greater skill, no doubt about it, but it didn't matter because they ran out of steam, and stamina and strength carried the day. Dynamo came out the winner because of superior conditioning, which would help turn Soviet athletes of all kinds into world-beaters.

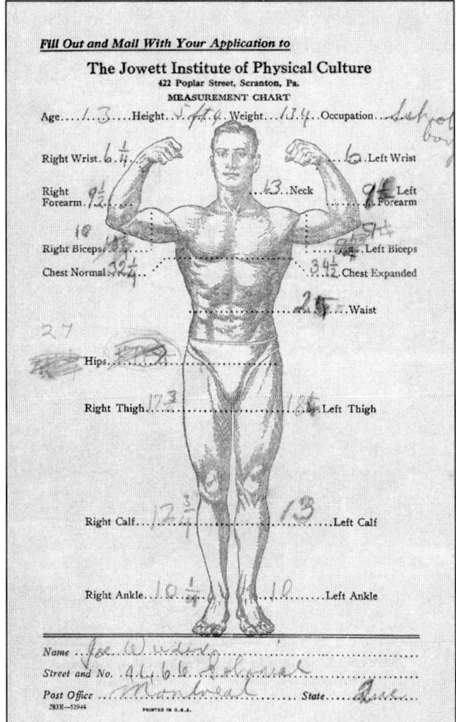

Fill Out and Mail With Your Application to

The Jowett Institute of Physical Culture
422 Poplar Street, Scranton, Pa.
MEASUREMENT CHART

Age 13 Height 5 ft 4 Weight 134 Occupation School boy

Right Wrist 6 1/4 — 6 Left Wrist

Right Forearm 9 1/2 — 13 Neck — Left Forearm

Right Biceps — Left Biceps

Chest Normal 32 1/4 — 34 1/2 Chest Expanded

Waist

Hips

Right Thigh — Left Thigh

Right Calf 12 3/4 — 13 Left Calf

Right Ankle 10 1/4 — 10 Left Ankle

Name Joe Weider

Street and No. 4466 Colonial

Post Office Montreal State Que.

283E—51944 PRINTED IN U.S.A.

Planting a Seed—In 1934, 13-year-old Joe filled out this application at the start of a weight training course by George Jowett, who sold Joe his first real weight set on the layaway plan.

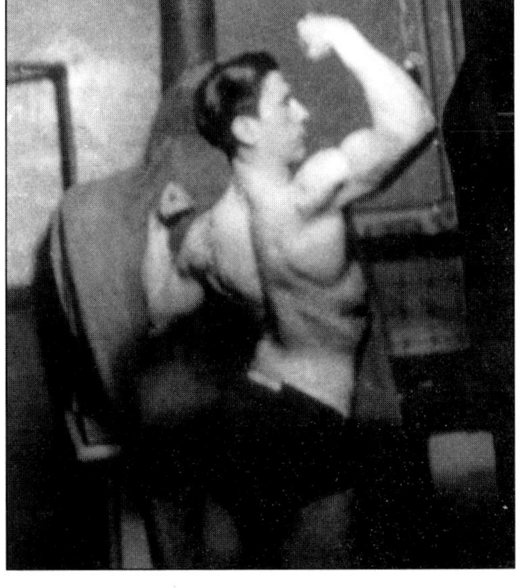

Kitchen Gym—Teenage Joe flexes in the kitchen of his first training partner Irving "Rusty" Halpert. This is Joe's first known physique photo.
Photo by Irving Halpert

Proud Papa—Louis Weider holds a first-place trophy won by Joe at the 1938 Montreal weightlifting championships. Seeing this photo, and his father's evident happiness and pride, inspired Joe to take his message about bodybuilding, health, and fitness to the world.

Combat Ready—Ben in the Canadian Army in 1942 at the age of 18.

Golden Gloves—Ben, age 13, had boxing aspirations.

Cover Worthy—Joe's classical outdoor pose was used on the cover of a 1944 issue of *Your Physique. Photo by Forbes*

Balancing Act—Joe (right) supports the weight of two friends at a park in Montreal. Bodybuilder Ed Theriault, also the Weiders' first employee, is balancing on top.

The Stage is Set—Ben and the contestants wait backstage at Mr. Montreal 1946, the first bodybuilding contest produced by the Weiders, where the IFBB was born.

Paradise Found—While visiting Mr. and Mrs. Frederick "Doc" Tilney, 26-year-old Joe (left) was encouraged to move the Weider operations to sunny Florida. Joe chose New York City instead.

Grand Tour—Ben's first overseas trip on behalf of the IFBB took him to the Paris home of professor Edmond Desbonnet, father of *la culture physique* in France (top), the Eiffel Tower (middle), the Egyptian pyramids (bottom), and many other locales.

Heavy Workload—In the front room of the family home on Colonial Avenue in Montreal, Ben smiles up at Joe, holding a stack of magazines.
Photo by Jock Carroll

Iconic Joe—*Your Physique* art editor George Quaintance rendered this image of Joe from a photo by Lon Hanagan and it ran on the November 1947 cover.

Ironmen and Hardware—Onstage at the 1949 Mr. North America contest in New York City, Joe is flanked by (from far left) Armand Tanny (fourth place), Alan Stephan (second place), Clarence "Clancy" Ross (first place), and Floyd Page (third place).

Pumped Up—Joe's "most muscular man" pose was often used as his picture byline in magazines.
Photo by Frank Giardina

Learning From the Master—Joe and his boyhood hero and mentor, George Jowett, relax in Joe's home.

It's an Honor—Ben presents the IFBB's silver plaque to Soviet sports minister Nicolai Romanov in Moscow in 1955.

Beauty Meets Fitness—Betty demonstrates her proficiency in the gym for the 1956 photo story "Meet Betty Brosmer" in Joe's women's magazine *Beauty and Figure.*

"The Only One Working"—This favorite photo of Joe's, taken in the Weider office at 16 Hopkins Avenue, Jersey City, shows Charlie Smith (with his back to the camera), sharing a laugh with Barton Horvath (center), and painter/illustrator Thomas Beecham (right) while Joe is hard at work.

Bon Voyage—Proud parents Louis and Anna Weider see Ben, their globetrotting son, off at the airport in Montreal.

Taxi Ride, Chinese-Style—During his rare and historic trip to the People's Republic of China in 1958, Ben travels by rickshaw.

Surrounded—At Ben's desk in the Montreal office, Joe is surrounded by bodybuilders, mostly Canadian. *Photo by Jimmy Caruso*

Tying the Knot—Joe and Betty's wedding portrait was taken following the nuptials in Las Vegas on April 24, 1961.

Beloved Mother—Ben and Joe pose with their mother Anna Weider in Montreal.

The Newlywed Game—Joe and Betty embark on a long-delayed honeymoon aboard the Cunard ocean liner RMS *Queen Mary.*

Making History—At the historic first Mr. Olympia contest at New York's Brooklyn Academy of Music in 1965, Ben (far left) and Joe (far right) present the awards to winner Larry Scott (second from right) and runner-up Harold Poole.

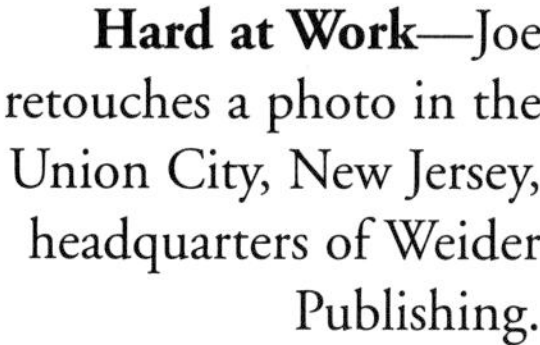

Hard at Work—Joe retouches a photo in the Union City, New Jersey, headquarters of Weider Publishing.

Contest Night—In 1968, Ben presents trophies to Chuck Sipes (left), crowned the new IFBB Mr. World and Frank Zane (right), named Mr. America.

Desire—Backstage with Joe at the 1968 IFBB Mr. Universe contest in Miami, a young Arnold Schwarzenegger looks with longing at the first-place trophy, which he would not win. *Photo by Jimmy Caruso*

A Great Team—The morning after losing the 1968 IFBB Mr. Universe competition to Zane, Arnold meets with his new mentor and sponsor, Joe Weider. *Photo by Jimmy Caruso*

It's a Tough Job—Shooting on Santa Monica Beach, Joe positions the models for photographs with Dave Draper.

Gallery of Stars—Promoting Weider products in a 1969 print campaign are (standing in the middle row, from left) Arnold, Draper, Betty, and Zane. *Photo by Art Zeller*

I'll Be Back—Joe presents winner Sergio Oliva with the 1969 Mr. Olympia title in front of a bemused-looking Arnold, who had just won the Mr. Universe contest, challenged Oliva for Mr. Olympia, and lost.

Mr. Olympia—Joe and Ben congratulate Arnold onstage at the Brooklyn Academy of Music in New York, after he captured the 1970 Mr. Olympia title. *Photo by Jimmy Caruso*

Meeting of the Minds—Joe and Arnold strategize over lunch.
Photo by Albert Busek

Trainer of Champions—Joe with Arnold, his favorite champion, at Gold's Gym in Venice Beach, California. *Photo by Art Zeller*

Great Minds Think Alike—Ben (right) and his best friend Oscar State, OBE, pause for a moment in their quest to promote bodybuilding.

Surprise!—During a visit to Warsaw in 1971, Ben (right) learns from Polish sports minister Dr. Wlodzimierez Reczek (at the head of the table) of his country's official acceptance of bodybuilding and the IFBB.

A Great Honor—Ben (left) receives the Order of Canada in 1975, his nation's highest honor.

Equality for All—Ben meets with South African president John Vorster (left) and sports minister Dr. Piet Koornhof (right), outlining the IFBB's mandate for racial equality among its bodybuilders.

Ambassador of Bodybuilding—Ben sits in the audience with Philippine president Ferdinand Marcos (right) during the 1980 IFBB World Amateur Bodybuilding Championships in Manila.

Guest Lecturer—Ben delivers a lecture on the Weider Triangle of Peak Performance, with translator Zeng Weiqi, to students at the Beijing Institute of Physical Culture in 1985.

Still Going Strong—This photo of a muscular Joe at age 62 unmistakably shows the lifelong benefits of body-building.

Two Generations of Leadership—This oil portrait of Joe (left), Ben's son, Eric (center), and Ben was painted by Robert Bruce Williams.

African Adventure—During a vacation to Kenya in 1989, Ben (left), his wife Huguette (center), and their three sons Eric (second from left), Louis (second from right), and Mark (right) take time out for a family photo on the savannah.

All You Need is Love—Joe and Betty celebrate their 35th wedding anniversary in Sedona, Arizona.

At the 1995 Mr. Olympia contest, Joe was joined onstage by all the Mr. Olympias past and present (from left): Larry Scott (1965-66), Sergio Oliva (1967-69), Chris Dickerson (kneeling, 1982) Arnold Schwarzenegger (1970-75, 1980), Samir Bannout (kneeling, 1983), Joe Weider, Franco Columbu (1976, 1981), Frank Zane (1977-79), Lee Haney (1984-91), and Dorian Yates (1992-97). *Photo by Robert Reiff*

Mid-East Tour—Ben sits with Palestinian president Yasar Arafat during his trip to Gaza City, Palestinian Territory, in 1999.

Champion for Napoleon—In recognition of his Napoleonic work, Ben receives the Legion of Honor from the French ambassador to Canada, His Excellency Denis Bauchard. Looking on is Ben's friend, Prince Charles Napoleon (left).

An Important Ally—Ben and his executive assistant Rafael Santonja (left) present then-president of the International Olympic Committee, Juan Antonio Samaranch (center), with the IFBB Gold Medal in Lausanne, Switzerland, in 2000.

Next Generation—Ben (left) and Joe (right) pose with 2002 Mr. Olympia winner Ronnie Coleman backstage in Las Vegas. *Photo Robert Reiff*

Conversation With Nicolai Romanov

In one of my final talks with Nicolai Romanov, he thanked me for providing sporting materials and information his people found so helpful. I, on behalf of the IFBB, presented him with a special silver plaque given only to those who made great contributions to the sport of bodybuilding.

The sports minister was touched but also somewhat confused.

"I don't understand," he said. "Since I am entirely opposed to bodybuilding, why am I receiving this award?"

I replied, "We consider you a great friend and supporter because you make bodybuilding a foundation of training for all your athletes."

He smiled and thanked me.

By that time we were quite friendly, and I felt comfortable asking him the ultimate question. I asked the minister if he would consider allowing Soviet bodybuilders to form their own sports federation and to affiliate with the IFBB. Doing so, I said, would allow them to communicate with other bodybuilding federations and to organize competitions from time to time in their homeland. We would provide information and support to the group.

"Although I appreciate the importance of bodybuilding as critical to developing elite athletes, we cannot allow it to become recognized because it is a bourgeois activity and American and therefore unacceptable in a Communist society."

I said, "Bodybuilding is not a sport of the bourgeoisie. It is a sport of the people. All it requires are barbells and dumbbells."

I also pointed out that bodybuilding was rapidly gaining acceptance in the developing world, and our philosophy of disciplined living and abstinence from drugs, alcohol, and tobacco was entirely consistent with Communist doctrine.

Romanov's one-word response was *nyet,* Russian for "no." He said he respected me and appreciated my work and wished me well.

Clearly that was supposed to be the last word on bodybuilding, but I wasn't finished. I said, "Mr. Minister, bodybuilding is a sport that can benefit every young man and woman in Russia. It can help them feel better and look better, improve their health, give them greater self-confidence."

Firmly but politely, he said, "Mr. Weider, I appreciate your opinion, but you must also appreciate mine. Bodybuilding has no future here. None."

At that I looked him straight in the eye and said, "Mr. Minister, no amount of government control or interference will prevent bodybuilding from becoming popular in the years to come. This is what young people want, and they will get it."

Having said our pieces, we went back to being friendly as ever. I got the idea that Nicolai Romanov actually liked me more for voicing my beliefs, which were born out by later events.

In 1987, before its governmental collapse and breakup, the Soviet Union recognized the sport of bodybuilding and allowed the organization of its own federation, which officially joined the IFBB in 1988. At the same time, I was awarded a medal for my contributions to sports in the Soviet Union. As far as I am aware, no other foreigner was ever so honored. Four of Joe's magazines, *Muscle & Fitness, Flex, Shape,* and *Natural Health* now are published in Russia and in the Ukraine and have substantial readerships. In 2004, our Amateur World Championships and the IFBB International Congress were held in Moscow. And athletes from Russian and other former Soviet states are winning competitions, both professional and amateur. Were he alive today, Nicolai Romanov surely would revise his opinion of bodybuilding.

Homeward

Before leaving the Soviet Union, I visited the capital of the Ukraine, Kiev, where I met Yakov Kutsenko, a weightlifting champion who had carried the Soviet flag at the 1952 Olympic Games and bore the title "Honored Master of Sports," the highest official honor bestowed on athletes. Yakov was 250 pounds of solid muscle with a heart of gold. He entertained me at home, which at that time was strictly forbidden. People had gone to prison camps for less, but such was the prestige of Yakov's position that he never gave it a thought. Replete with a magnificent Ukrainian dinner and warmed with a few glasses of vodka, Yakov confided to me that he, like others in his sport, disliked and resented Bob Hoffman because of the man's pushy, abrasive nature. We went on to speak of my plans to organize a bodybuilding federation in the Soviet Union. He said he'd assist me in any way possible, but he didn't think that a bodybuilding federation would ever be accepted. True to his word, Yakov unofficially encouraged bodybuilding, and I sent films, magazines, and instructional courses for him to distribute.

I also flew to Tiflis, the capital of what is now the Republic of Georgia, where I was received by the mayor of the city and sports officials. When the mayor asked me if I was enjoying my visit, I answered, "Yes, with one exception." I told him that I missed eating fresh fruits and vegetables, which had not been available during all the time I was in the Soviet Union. The next day he took me to a nearby collective farm where I was served a magnificent luncheon of chicken, fresh vegetables and all the fruit I wanted. After the meal, someone brought out a bottle of locally produced champagne and asked me to pass judgment on its quality.

I was completely at a loss about what to do, because before that trip I had never touched a drop of alcohol. However, I remembered that I once saw a French movie where fine wine was served. The host first swished his wine, then sipped and swallowed very slowly. I did the same, then spent a moment in deep thought and said, "Ladies and gentleman, I must admit this is the best I have ever tasted. It is far superior to the best French champagne."

For that I received thunderous applause and cases of both champagne and local wine, all of which I gave away.

In the plane flying homeward I took stock of my experiences, feeling encouraged in spite of the adamantly anti-bodybuilding reaction of the Communist authorities. Under the extant system, our federation would not be welcome, but things could change, as indeed they did. I felt confident about the future because I had seen people's desire to take up bodybuilding. I knew that time was on our side and that our message, promoting strong bodies, strong minds, self-improvement, and self-reliance, was universal and would eventually be accepted in Communist countries even if governments were opposed.

Back in Canada I wrote articles about my experiences that appeared in Canadian newspapers, both English and French. I reported that the Soviets saw competitive athletics as part of their ideological warfare against the West. To that end, a huge push was on to develop young athletes and perfect training techniques to produce new champions and show the superiority of the Communist system. Not only were the Soviets and their satellites about to catch up to the West in sports, they were going to move ahead and dominate the Olympic Games in the near future.

That turned out to be true, but in 1955, very few people understood the situation. One of them was Robert A.D. Ford, head of the European division at External Affairs in Ottawa, who wrote this in a letter to me:

[Your articles] constitute the most complete report on the Soviet sports program that I have seen, and we shall certainly find them a valuable addition to our knowledge of the Soviet Union. My impressions while I was in the Soviet Union were much the same as yours—the concerted Soviet efforts in the athletic field may soon result in their domination of amateur sports, thereby enhancing Soviet prestige abroad.

Other people saw my observations as disloyal, among them Myrtle Cook, an Olympic champion sprinter and very prominent figure in Canadian athletics. She accused me in the press of being a Communist, to which I replied: "I am not and never was a Communist, but I am trying very hard to become a Capitalist." That was the end of our exchange.

The Bamboo Curtain

Some people are doubtful when I say that Joe and I never worked in pursuit of wealth or power or self-aggrandizement. But I believe my forays into the Communist world in the 1950s prove the point. In terms of monetary gain, the work behind the Iron Curtain was an absolute bust. I have no idea what it cost us, but it wasn't cheap. At one point we provided so much free material that Soviet officials asked me to sign a statement declaring I would not charge for what we sent. In terms of my own ultimate ambition, Olympic recognition, there was no payoff in sight, either. Teaching bodybuilding to Communists didn't strengthen the IFBB or our Olympic bid because our sport was barred by their governments. The only reward of planting the seeds, in the early days in those places, was planting the seeds, but that was reward enough for me and for my brother Joe who never questioned the money and time and effort we put into my work overseas.

In 1957, I received an invitation to visit Communist China from Chang Lien Hua, who headed the All-China Athletic Federation. The invitation included assurances that I'd have the freedom to go where I wished. Before I went to China in 1958 I sought, and got, my own government's blessing, from both Superintendent Brakefield-Moore at the RCMP and officials of the Department of External Affairs, and I informed the U.S. Consul General of my trip and its purpose. I also secured an assignment to write about my experiences for a French language paper, *Le Petit Journal*. The editor was delighted to get an exclusive first-hand account of conditions in China, a nation even more isolated and mysterious than the Soviet Union. Very, very few Westerners had set foot in the country since the Communists, under party chairman Mao Tse-tung, took power.

Within minutes of my arrival in China, I realized this was a nation committed to exercise. As I deplaned and entered the airport at Beijing, all work ceased while all employees had a 15-minute exercise session under the direction of an announcer piped in on the PA system. Meanwhile, passengers stood and waited for our baggage. I was fascinated because I'd never seen anything like this anywhere in the world. I saw such scenes repeated for the rest of my stay, and on later visits I made to China. Twice a day, government radio broadcast an exercise program, which everybody dutifully followed. People in the streets lay down their parcels and began performing the moves called out by the announcers. I also noticed that workers at offices and factories exercised before reporting for their shifts. The routines were a sort of light calisthenics with lots of stretching and moves to enhance flexibility.

At the airport I was greeted by Chang Lien Hua, a man of medium height and build. I was struck by the brightness of the man's eyes, which seemed literally to dance. Ha welcomed me with the warmth and enthusiasm of a lifelong friend, always in motion, full of life and good cheer.

My first clue that the Chinese visit would be a true adventure came in my hotel in Beijing. By other standards, it was a modest sort of place, rating at most two stars, but, as I found out, there was nothing better in China in those days. On the hotel elevator I encountered a Western woman dressed up and wearing makeup and perfume. I can still smell her.

"Your first time here?" she asked me.

I said it was, and she asked if I was going outside the city.

When I said yes, she told me I was in for a surprise.

"I've been out in the countryside," she said, "and I just had a bath for the first time in two weeks."

Baths weren't the only thing in short supply in China. At times I felt like I had stepped back a thousand years. The country was in the midst of massive building projects, but without the benefit of modern machinery. Jobs done in another nations with bulldozers, cranes, giant trucks were accomplished by swarms of workers wielding primitive hand tools. In rural areas, many people acted as if they'd never seen a Westerner before. At one remote collective farm, everyone followed me, applauding continuously as if everything I did was amazing.

The Chinese government, like the Soviets, wanted to make sports an important national priority. But China was starting from much farther behind, in athletics and in general. As I reported in *Le Petit Journal,* athletes often had to build their own facilities, from scratch, using hand tools. And then many had to build their training schedule around a full day of compulsory work. Producing winners in such circumstances was pretty much impossible. But I didn't doubt that some day China would become an athletic superpower.

In one way, the Chinese were ahead of the world. Their training techniques included lifting weights to build strength and muscularity. I saw athletes using weights in urban training centers and even saw athletes using barbells of a primitive sort at a collective farm.

Like the Soviets, the Chinese invited foreign guests to share their expertise, and they opened special schools for coaches. I was invited to speak to approximately 200 coaching students at Peking University, a lecture that set a precedent for subsequent visits. With no access to state-run media, and absolutely no prospects of distributing our magazines and materials direct to individual citizens, I found a great solution that I called, "leverage." I set up lectures at educational institutions for teachers who would spread the word to hundreds of students. Before long, the majority of schools and universities in China were teaching the Weider methods.

One of my favorite old photos shows me teaching a class at the Shanghai Institute of Physical Education and Sport. I'm at the chalkboard, drawing the Weider Triangle of Peak Performance, our simple but very powerful formula for athletic excellence. One side of the triangle represents sport-specific skills, another side conditioning, including bodybuilding, and the third good nutrition. To win, you need all three sides. Nowadays this seems self-evident, but it was radical new thinking when we first came out with it. The Weider Triangle became a fundamental of China's training programs.

Toward the end of my 1958 visit, Chang Lien Hua presented me with a medal designating me "Master of Sport." I also met a super athlete who was living proof of the value of bodybuilding in sports. It happened in the dining room of a hotel in Shanghai where I was staying. When dinner was served, I asked the waiter for a knife and fork, but they were not available. I therefore tried without success to feed myself with chopsticks. After watching me fumble with the strange implements for several minutes, a European approached my table.

"Allow me to demonstrate. It really isn't so difficult," he said.

The helpful stranger turned out to be Emil Zapotek, a Czech distance runner who had won multiple gold medals, including an incredible "triple crown"—gold in the 5,000 meters, 10,000 meters, and marathon at the 1952 Olympics in Helsinki.

After teaching me the fundamentals of using chopsticks, Emil sat down at my table and we talked. It was the beginning of a friendship that would last many years. We hit it off right away partly because he was a true believer in bodybuilding, one of the first world champions in any sport to systematically make weight training part of his regular regimen. Nowadays, of course, all runners spend time in the weight room, but in the 1950s this was unheard of. Emil was well aware of the Weider System and training principles, which he learned while training in the Soviet Union.

All told, I logged 12,000 miles of travel within China on that first trip. As in the Soviet Union, my hosts had no interest in bodybuilding as an end in itself, but that didn't concern me. So long as people wanted to learn about bodybuilding as the basis for sports conditioning, I didn't worry about the short-term prospects. Greater things would come, I firmly believed, and they did. In 1980, China recognized bodybuilding as a sport and officially joined the IFBB in 1985. In 1994, our IFBB World Amateur Bodybuilding Championships and International Congress were held in Shanghai for the first time, and then in 2005, Shanghai again hosted these IFBB events. Our international delegates found Shanghai most enjoyable. China has its own national edition of *Muscle & Fitness* magazine, and a certificated Weider Training Course is offered for coaches and athletes in five major cities.

Love Walks In

The day after I got home from my trip to China, I met the woman who would become my wife.

Huguette Drouin was an employee of *La Presse,* French Canada's largest newspaper, but she wanted extra income and was looking for part-time employment. She saw a notice I had placed in *La Presse* advertising an opening for an evening physical culture instructress at a gym operated by Billy Hill, a former Mr. Canada, and myself.

The ad ran just as my China trip ended, and Huguette happened to be the first candidate I saw. I was stunned. She looked a great deal like Grace Kelly, one of the most famous beauties of the day, and she had the poise and bearing of a star or princess. I was so taken with her that I couldn't bring myself to talk about the job. Instead I told her all about my trip to China, which at that time was extremely unusual, and before she left I asked if she'd like to attend a performance of Puccini's opera *Madame Butterfly* with me. She said yes.

We never did get around to discussing the job.

When I met Huguette, she was unable to speak any English, but she quickly mastered the language; so well, in fact, that you'd think she spoke it all her life. She came from a respectable French Canadian family. Her father was a police sergeant in charge of a district station. The fact that I was Jewish did not bother her parents at all, and we were married. Huguette has been at my side for almost 50 years—a great companion and friend to me and a perfect mother for our sons, Louis, Eric, and Mark. Since Eric is president and CEO of Weider Health and Fitness, you'll read more about him later.

CHAPTER EIGHT

JOE AND ARNOLD

Joe Weider

As anybody who knows Arnold Schwarzenegger can tell you, the guy is absolutely hilarious. He loves laughs more than anybody in the world, and he knows how to get them. If you could hear his imitation of me, for instance, you'd howl. Everybody who knows me tries to mimic my manner of speaking, which has been described as Yiddish-inflected Canadian Californian. In my opinion, Arnold's is the funniest, maybe because he does me on top of his own Austrian accent.

But there's something else about Arnold's sense of humor. The guy has a little bit of Don Rickles in him, and the laughs come at another person's expense. When he starts telling a joke, you know somebody's going to take it in the shorts, and maybe this time it's you.

So you can imagine how I felt at my 80th birthday party, when Arnold announced that he was going to reveal something about Joe Weider that nobody else knew, and the room got very quiet.

"The shocking secret," Arnold told my family and friends, "is that Joe and I once slept together!"

Oh no, I thought, what kind of nonsense is this, but Arnold kept talking, and it came back to me—one night we did sleep back to back in my apartment on the East Side, not in any weird way, but like guys who were tired and needed a place to sack out.

It happened late in 1970, in the days after Arnold first won our Mr. Olympia contest, which we held in New York City. Arnold would successfully defend his title for the next five years, giving him six wins in a row, and then later he'd come out of retirement and win Mr. Olympia one last time. But in many ways, 1970 was the biggest win because it put him on top of the entire bodybuilding world for the first time. It was a big deal for me, too, because I recognized that Arnold, as bodybuilding's ultimate champ, would do great things for the sport. Arnold stayed on in New York after the show to go over business with me and do some magazine work. On the day he was supposed to fly back to California, he came over to my apartment on the East Side and we got so wrapped up in talking, he missed his flight. I said I'd call for a car to take him to a hotel.

"Joe," Arnold said, "I'm already in your home, and I'm comfortable, so why waste your money on a room? I'll just stay here..."

Betty happened to be in California visiting her Aunt Annie. Arnold offered to sleep on the floor, but I ruled that out because it seemed rude on my part. We had a couch, but no way in the world would I let him sleep on that. It was a valuable antique, and I had already found out the hard way that Arnold and antiques didn't mix. One day he sat down hard on a little eighteenth-century chair that was one of my prized possessions and it broke into pieces.

The only accommodation I had to offer was half of our bed, which fortunately was king-sized. Fine, no problem, Arnold said, and there we were. He was still too excited to fall asleep, and he talked and talked about his future plans and dreams. He told me how he wanted to help advance our sport and promote exercise and healthy living for everybody. And he talked about his plans to break into movies and become a great star and then use his stardom to reach people and improve their lives. For hours he dreamed out loud about his future achievements and accomplishments.

At the time, I was in my late forties, and Arnold was in his early twenties, but that didn't matter. We were like Tom Sawyer and Huck Finn on their raft, looking up at the stars and drifting into the future.

Next day, I took Arnold to my favorite galleries and gave him his first look at fine art and antiques. The stuff fascinated him, and he wanted to know about everything we saw. He especially admired one little English table. I got hold of the gallery owner to find out the price and then asked Arnold how much he thought the table cost. After a minute, he said $800 in a way that showed he considered such an amount astronomical. He about fell over when I told him the asking price was in the thousands. The kid had no idea in the world that a little piece of furniture could cost so much—how could he, coming from a hick town in Austria?

Over the years, I've had some wonderful times with Arnold, who has been my pupil, my protégé, my business partner, my friend, and ultimately—Arnold says so, too—my surrogate son. But that night and day in New York was one of the best. We were just two guys enjoying each other's company and knocking around town.

Even from the little bit I've told you, you can see some of the strengths that would make Arnold such a great success. First off, he was very careful with other people's resources. This showed in the way he saved on hotel expenses. At that time, I'd been paying his way so he could train full-time for two years, and I never knew him to waste a dime. He didn't waste opportunities to learn, either. I never met anybody with such a hungry mind, so observant, asking so many questions, who could soak up information like a sponge and then know exactly how to put it to good use. He's so funny onstage because he sent himself to comedy school, so to speak. When he moved from bodybuilding into showbiz, Arnold went to top comics like Milton Berle to learn all about delivery and timing. His interest in art and objects of beauty, which started that day with me in New York, grew into a passion for collecting that still gives him great pleasure. Arnold was like the president of his own university. If you knew something that would do him the least bit of good, you were the professor.

It was in bodybuilding, though, where you really saw the guy's hunger to expand his knowledge and improve. If he hadn't been such a great learner he wouldn't have won Mr. Olympia once, much less seven times. Believe me, there were things he had to learn when he first came over to the States that nobody but Joe Weider could teach. But what really made Arnold a champion, and then a movie star, and then governor of California—what made Arnold Arnold—was the guy's will. All the dreams and plans he talked about up in my apartment would have been hot air coming from somebody else. I doubted not one word, because I knew what this guy could do. If he said he would achieve something, he did it—whatever sacrifice and effort it took. Never before or since have I encountered a will to win so powerful, so indomitable, so steely.

Except my own, of course.

When the student is ready, the teacher appears.

When Arnold Schwarzenegger was ready, Joe Weider appeared.

And when bodybuilding was ready, Arnold appeared.

The moment was right because I had made it right.

To explain how and why I did it, we need to back up a few years. In truth, the why goes back to the first time I picked up a barbell. If you want to know why I did what I did at any stage, there's one answer—I did it because I loved bodybuilding and bodybuilders and everybody who trained with weights. I loved them as one of their number. Understand that, and you understand my story and my life.

You cannot imagine the mess that was competitive bodybuilding in the early 1960s. It was like the Biblical Tower of Babel. In a given year, two or three or more guys won titles with the same name. There were two Mr. America contests—one sanctioned by the AAU physique committee, which Bob Hoffman controlled, and one by the IFBB. For a brief period, there would be three Mr. Americas and who knows how many Mr. Worlds. In England, there were two contests called Mr. Universe and sometimes another Mr. Universe in France. The London contest, sanctioned by NABBA, was the closest thing to a recognized world bodybuilding championship. But NABBA was really only an English organization, and, as I said earlier, its leaders were as anti-Weider as Bob Hoffman. After we got fed up with the hostile attitude, Ben and I started a Mr. Universe sanctioned by the IFBB, which really was international. Under Ben's leadership, the federation had grown to more than 60 member countries in the mid-1960s.

To add to the confusion, each of the bodybuilding organizations had its own rules and eligibility standards. Hoffman's AAU Mr. America was supposedly for amateurs, but mostly he used the rules to shaft guys he didn't like and challenge the legitimacy of IFBB guys' titles. Every year NABBA awarded two Mr. Universe titles, one pro and one amateur. This all would have been bad enough if we were friendly rivals, but hostility poisoned the atmosphere. Civil war is the cruelest kind of conflict, and that's exactly what we had, bodybuilder against bodybuilder. Considering how small our sport was, the situation was ridiculous. We should have united and pulled together.

With such disarray, how could anybody outside the sport take us seriously? The situation made it much more difficult for champs to make any money, because it cheapened their accomplishments. Nobody would want to pay big for an endorsement from the 1962 Mr. America when the competition could get a guy with the same title. And all the sanctioning bodies—IFBB included—had a policy that was very hard on the champs. The top contests in North America could be won once and only once. Win a Mr. America, say, or our Mr. Universe, and you couldn't enter that contest again. The idea, I think, was to spread the glory around, but the system hurt the best guys because it cut their careers short. It cheated the fans, too. They never got to see champions defend their titles against up-and-comers, and with the top guys forced out, the fans could only argue about who could beat who.

What really bothered me personally, was that the system held back bodybuilding itself. I wanted to push muscular development to the limits, to see what years and years of scientific training and nutrition could accomplish. But the best of the best quit in their twenties when they were nowhere near peak form.

I also wanted to help the guys make more money from bodybuilding, both for their good and the good of the sport. All along I did what I could; over the years I've paid bodybuilders under contract something like $50 million, in total. But I couldn't bankroll everybody, and competitors lived hand to mouth. Even the champions had to hold down jobs so they could support themselves while they trained.

Everything finally came to a head because of a great champion named Larry Scott, bodybuilding's original golden boy.

Larry had blond hair and a great smile and that sort of all-American, nice-guy appeal. He was a Mormon from Idaho who trained in Los Angeles, building up a wonderful physique in spite of problems that could have held him back. Larry stood only about 5 foot 7, with a light frame and narrow shoulders, but he overcame his deficiencies by working the hell out of his deltoids, the muscles that cap the shoulders, which gave him more width, and he built up arms like nobody else's. To this day, people talk about Larry's "guns"—our slang for biceps. He stood as proof that you could build a great physique even if God was a little skimpy with you. I promoted Larry like crazy in my magazines and was glad to do it because I liked him.

On one of our California visits, Betty and I had dinner with Larry at the old El Matador, a Spanish restaurant on Pico Boulevard in Los Angeles. Larry was coming off a big win at the IFBB Mr. Universe. A couple years earlier, he had won our Mr. America. Larry should have been on top of the world, but he was down in the dumps.

"Joe," he said to me, "where can I go from here? I've won everything there is to win, and I'm really afraid that I have to get out of bodybuilding."

We all agreed that this was a terrible shame, and Betty started talking to Larry about an idea she'd been pushing for years, that we should establish a new professional world championship open to all major title holders. Like other championships—boxing, say, or golf—the same guy could win year after year until somebody beat him or he quit. And there'd be cash prizes worth competing for. Larry got excited about Betty's idea, and I knew the time had come. For the likes of him and the future of bodybuilding, there would be a new champion's championship. I announced my decision, and we started talking about what to call the new super-contest.

Very, very rarely do I drink beer. Betty says she's seen me have a beer maybe a dozen times in all the years we've been together, and then only with food. I had a beer that night because it went just right with paella.

While Betty and Larry kicked around names, none of which I liked, I looked at the bottle of beer in front of me—Olympia beer, from Olympia, Washington.

That was my "Eureka!" moment. I think maybe the gods intervened to put the perfect, majestic word for the new contest in front of me.

Larry, whose religion forbid drinking alcohol said, "What, you're going to name this contest I want to win after a beer?"

But of course the name had nothing to do with the beverage. It brought to mind Olympus, the mythic mountain home of the Greek gods and goddesses. Our contest, too, would be a high peak where only immortals could go.

The connection with a brewery came up again later, after the Olympic Committee tried to make us give up the contest's name because it sounded too much like the Olympics. I pointed out that Olympia was already in use all over, including the brand of beer.

By the time the Olympic people came after me, we'd been putting on the Mr. Olympia contest for 20 years. I think they waited for the Weider companies to get big and rich.

The Brooklyn Academy of Music, September 18, 1965—long before the doors opened, a sellout crowd stood outside, everybody all excited. For the price of admission they got four major events—the Miss Americana beauty pageant, followed by the IFBB Mr. America, Mr. Universe, and finally Mr. Olympia. All told, we had 150 top muscle men from all over the world. A live orchestra provided music.

I felt a little let down that only three guys competed in the Olympia—Earl Maynard, a West Indian who won Mr. Universe that night and made a last-minute entry; Harold Poole, a very popular African-American; and Larry Scott. And I was sorry that we couldn't follow through on plans to surprise the winner with a $1,000 cash prize, but expenses ate up every dime the show brought in. The crowd was not a bit disappointed, though. Harold Poole, the first black Mr. America and a favorite of the New Yorkers, got the loudest reception in the history of bodybuilding. I'd never heard anything like it. Then the crowd got even louder when Larry Scott came onstage and started hitting his poses. The guy was tan, perfectly conditioned, and smooth as silk. After the contest, the fans poured out into the street and wouldn't leave. Finally, at two in the morning, some cops helped me get Larry out to my car so we could escape.

Olympia was an absolute sensation. The world had never seen anything like it. In 1966, we had more competitors, and again the audience went wild, so much so that Ben and I started thinking about adding prejudging to the Olympia. Our other contests already had pre-show rounds where judges could study and rate the guys in quiet surroundings, but in the early years, the judges scored the Olympia contenders only according to what they saw onstage at the big event.

In '66, Larry won again and collected $1,000, a record prize and a very proud moment for me and Ben and all of bodybuilding. But then later Larry stunned us all by announcing that he was retiring. He explained he had to give up the temptations of the bodybuilding lifestyle and get back to being a good Mormon. I suspect he also looked over his shoulder and saw Sergio Oliva coming up behind him, which would shake up anybody. "The Myth," people called Sergio, because you couldn't believe he was real. Before he defected to America and took up bodybuilding, Sergio had been the heavyweight weightlifting champion of Cuba. Guys who worked out at his home gym in Chicago said that he threw around weights that would win powerlifting meets. His arms, shoulders, and chest were huge, but the upper body tapered down to the tiniest waist. Sergio posed rough, but with that build of his it didn't seem to matter.

Sergio won the Olympia in 1967. In '68 nobody wanted to take him on, and he put on a one-man performance like a Roman triumph for the man who conquered bodybuilding. Every pose Sergio hit brought a roar. No one had ever seen a build like Sergio's. When he turned around to spread his lats, he waggled his behind. Nowadays guys do goofy stuff like that all the time, but Sergio's little stunt was a first, and people loved it.

Suddenly Sergio got serious and announced that he wanted to say something important. Oh no, I thought, he's retiring like Larry. Actually, Sergio wanted to set the record straight on the subject of nutritional supplements. He said he used Weider protein products and nothing but, and they helped him make his amazing gains. Sergio then told the people that somebody had tricked him into endorsing stuff he never used. He had posed for a picture and signed his name thinking he was dealing with Weider people.

By this time Sergio looked very angry, and the hall went still.

A shout came from the audience—"That's a lie!" Sergio challenged whoever shouted those words to come forward.

Who should stand up but Dan Lurie? At that time he had a little muscle magazine and his own equipment and protein products, which he now claimed that Sergio used and officially endorsed.

"Not true!" said Sergio from the stage, in his very thick Cuban accent, "You know I no read-a English. You con me! You fool me!"

Of course Lurie was really challenging me, but I didn't have to say a word because Mr. Olympia made Lurie look so foolish in front of thousands of bodybuilders. He already looked that way from challenging me to a physique contest in his magazine. I didn't bother to respond then, either, but one of my writers went after Lurie in a column that recalled the ridiculous challenge to John Grimek way back when. Of course, my problems with Lurie started even before that.

Imagine...almost 25 years after our barbell deal went sour and I tackled him outside the bathroom of his gym, Dan Lurie tried to stir up trouble with me just to try to get a little attention. The poor guy had developed the worst case of Joe Weider fever of all time. Besides the magazine and products, he put on shows like

Ben and me. Nothing lasted, but to this day he calls himself "The Trainer of Champions," just like me. I'm surprised he doesn't declare himself "The Master Blaster," too.

And that's the last you'll read about him.

And this is almost the last of Bob Hoffman in my story. Since he couldn't beat the Weiders his way, he turned to imitation. Not long before the first Mr. Olympia, he started a new bodybuilding magazine called *Muscular Development.* He also allied more closely with his English buddies and sent his Mr. America to the NABBA Mr. Universe every year. Hoffman's magazine was a bad knockoff and dull, dull, dull, like *Strength and Health.* Whatever touch Hoffman once had, it was long gone by the late 1960s when we pulled ahead of his publications for good and drove him back on every front.

As usual, our foe was our best friend. Hoffman could have had my first two Mr. Olympias on the AAU side, training in York, winning his contests, filling the pages of his magazines and pushing his products. Larry Scott originally wanted to go to the AAU Mr. America, except Hoffman gave him the cold shoulder. Once was enough for Larry, but Sergio beat his head against the wall for a few years trying to rise in the AAU ranks. He, too, aimed for the AAU Mr. America, but he couldn't win Mr. Chicago! Sergio's biggest problem was the color of his skin. Not once, in almost 20 years of Hoffman's Mr. Americas, had a black man won. I'm sure Sergio's weightlifting background didn't do him any good, either. Hoffman would have hated to see a lifter with such ability cross over to bodybuilding.

You'd think he would have learned something, but Hoffman turned around and threw away a solid gold opportunity to work with a great big kid from a tank town in Austria who became bodybuilding's star of stars.

Other versions of the Arnold Schwarzenegger story go straight to the part where I bring him to America for the first time and start training and grooming him and putting him all over my magazines. The truth is a little more complicated. In terms of U.S. magazine coverage and recognition, Hoffman beat me to Arnold by a year. Arnold's first U.S. cover shot was on *Muscular Development,* and a month later he was featured in a story under the byline of John Grimek. Then there were a couple of how-to articles credited to Arnold himself.

Arnold had been a fan of the Weider publications and my training system since he was a boy in Austria, when he first opened up a copy of *Muscle Power* and saw his destiny in bodybuilding. Still, though, it makes sense that Arnold's first American contacts were with Hoffman, not me. He'd never been over here, and the top of his competitive world was the NABBA Mr. Universe, where the guys in charge had nothing good to say about Joe Weider. After hearing their nonsense, Arnold naturally would have wanted to go to York, Pennsylvania, for his first American training experience. I think he might have done just that, except he never got the opportunity.

Word was, Hoffman turned Arnold away because he had no use for a full-time bodybuilder. What a genius.

I was actually looking for Arnold before I found him. I don't mean him particularly, but somebody who could be a champion of such stature and talent and personality that the whole world, not just the bodybuilding world, would pay attention. All sports make big leaps forward in general acceptance when they have a superstar who appeals to everybody—Joe Namath in football, Michael Jordan in basketball, Tiger Woods in golf, the Earnhardts in NASCAR racing. Now that the IFBB had a worldwide reach and Mr. Olympia was up and running, bodybuilding was ready for its own superstar.

Please don't get me wrong, all my champs were great athletes and great guys and did a lot for bodybuilding, but always there was some final, missing element—charisma, drive, ambition, something. It was like looking at picture puzzles with one little piece gone.

Lud Shusterich, our agent in London, convinced me I had to get a look at this great big youngster from Austria, who had all of Europe in an uproar. Lud was bowled over seeing Arnold at the London Mr. Universe, and our correspondent in London, Rick Wayne, became a huge fan of Arnold and a friend of his, too. What I heard and saw in pictures impressed me enough to put a shot of Arnold on the cover of *Muscle Builder/Power* in the summer of 1968 and run a story the next month. I also invited Arnold to come and compete in one of our contests. I paid for his flight, but he almost didn't make it because he didn't have a visa. Fortunately Lud had a friend at the American Embassy who got Arnold his papers overnight.

Arnold got off the plane in Miami the day before the 1968 IFBB Mr. Universe. The previous weekend he had won the professional NABBA Mr. Universe in London, where he took the amateur title the year before. Arnold happened to win his pro Universe the same day Sergio had his one-man Mr. Olympia in New York.

In fact, Arnold was lucky to win in London, because he competed over his ideal weight. Still, the Europeans went nuts because they were sure they had a world-beater. Arnold came to Florida thinking the same thing. In sheer size, nobody was close. Nobody had risen so fast in competition. At age 21, winning was what he knew and what he expected.

I was not so overwhelmed, though, not at first sight. Arnold stood tall, pushing 6 foot 2, which gave him a grandeur that could appeal to people in or out of bodybuilding. And he did have phenomenal size in his upper body. As my magazine reported, he had 21-inch arms and a 56-inch chest—spectacular on anybody and out of this world on someone his age. What he had in size, though, he lacked in definition and overall proportion. Arnold showed up looking heavy and smooth, underdeveloped in the legs, no abs, no delts, and white as a ghost, so the cuts he had didn't show. He didn't know how to carry himself, either. I could tell he would need help with his posing like every other European.

I saw the stuff that made our people overseas so excited, but nothing jumped out at me. To be blunt, I thought Arnold was overrated.

Then I thought again.

Lightning struck on contest day—Saturday, September 28, 1968. Hours before the doors opened at the Miami Auditorium I walked by the place backstage where we set out the contest trophies and saw the darndest thing. Arnold sat there gazing at the Mr. Universe trophy. I went over and he kept looking, in a trance, and his eyes lit up with desire like I'd never seen. Pure longing filled every cell in his body—I could feel it as much as see it. He could have been a knight of old seeing the Grail or a saint having a vision of the Kingdom of God.

At that moment I perceived an inner power that impressed me a lot more than the great big muscles. I saw, too, that Arnold was a fellow true believer—a man who worshipped a trophy so must deeply love the sport it represented.

One of my own powers is the ability to size somebody up the first time I get a good look at him and know what his capabilities and limits might be. In Arnold I saw no limits. Nothing in the world would keep him from grasping what he wanted. By that time I'd seen enough of his physique to know that nothing would hold him back, physically speaking. He had the genes to be the best in the world, no question. But the spirit, not the body, set him apart.

Thinking this could finally be the one, the champ I was looking for, I called over a photographer. You should turn to the photos pages and take a look at the picture. Here's a big bruiser with a baby face and a goofy haircut, reaching his hand toward a trophy and trying to eat the thing up with his eyes. And here's Joe Weider with his eyes on the kid, smiling like he just found something terrific.

I think I got what I wanted—a future king of bodybuilding ready to listen and work with me—because Arnold did not get what he wanted. In fact, he wouldn't get a first-place trophy in the U.S. for another year, and he wouldn't get the top title for two years. In Miami, he lost to Frank Zane, winner of our Mr. America the week before in New York. Frank stood much shorter and maybe 60 pounds lighter than Arnold, but his physique was true perfection. A mathematics teacher by profession, Frank built his body with such care and precision that every muscle had cuts and facets like gemstones, and his symmetry was flawless. Arnold wowed everybody with his size and came in second, but he was like a beer keg competing against the Hope Diamond. Then Sergio came out and guest-posed. The crowd went completely wild, and Arnold got to see what a Weider world champion really looked like.

If he'd won, Arnold probably would have gone home and told everybody how he kicked the Americans' asses, just like he bragged he would before he got on the plane. It's clear he didn't plan on a long visit, because he came over with only a little gym bag and the clothes on his back. Instead of a win, though, he got the shock of his young life. Arnold says he cried all night in his hotel room. The day after the contest, I sat working at a table out by the hotel pool, and he came to me and said, "Joe, what went wrong? What happened? Why didn't I win?"

Others have written that Arnold came to me humbled, but that he was not. Arnold Schwarzenegger doesn't have a humble bone in his body. What he was, was ready. Ready to stay in the U.S. and learn everything he needed to know to beat the guys who showed him up. Suddenly he hungered for improvement and knowledge the way he hungered for the trophy that Frank Zane took home.

I invited him to stay on in Miami with me for a couple of days so we could get acquainted and set up a deal for working together. Basically, I wanted to get him started the Weider way, arrange to do a few things with him on the East Coast, and then send him out to California where he could train alongside some of the top champs. I'd pay all his expenses, and in return he'd appear in the magazines and contribute training information and endorse products.

California gave Arnold stars in his eyes. Like practically everybody else in bodybuilding—everybody, period—he dreamed the California dream. California meant even more to him because he already wanted to be a movie star. He must have been seeing the Hollywood sign floating over Gold's Gym and Muscle Beach. All that enthusiasm rubbed off. It was great to be with somebody so young and full of promise and charged up.

People have an idea about taking advice that is 100 percent dead wrong. They think it's a sign of weakness, like you're leaning on somebody instead of standing on your own like a man. In truth, it shows strength, and Arnold Schwarzenegger proves the point. The strongest bodybuilder I ever met, in terms of inner strength, was the most eager for my advice and the most willing to follow it.

Weaker individuals run into problems here. Sooner or later they resist because they feel threatened by a person who knows more than they do, and they feel small. Arnold, who believed in himself fanatically, took what he needed from me with pride, and it made him still stronger.

Pay attention, because this is important.

The story I'm telling about Arnold and me is really dozens of stories about me and more bodybuilders than I could name.

What I did with Arnold, I did with other guys going back to before he was born—and up to recent years, long after Arnold got out of bodybuilding. From early on, I helped support guys by paying for product endorsements and information for articles, providing free space to advertise their own products, giving them exposure and fame like bodybuilders never had. In Jersey I gave full-time jobs to guys like Leroy Colbert, a great star from Harlem who started at Hopkins Avenue in Jersey right out of high school. Leroy was the man who first developed 21-inch biceps, breaking through a barrier that to us was like the four-minute mile. In Jersey Dave Draper, IFBB Mr. America and Mr. Universe, came to me as a teenager and schlepped merchandise on Palisade Avenue before I sent him to work for us and train in California. Up in Montreal, our very first employee was Ed Theriault, one of our first Canadian champions, who worked with us until he retired.

Don't get me wrong, I did business, not philanthropy, and the champs I helped, helped the Weiders by promoting the magazines and products and pulling the fans in at contests. It was a give-and-take relationship, but I liked the helping part more than cashing in, and I always wanted to do more. If this seems like BS, ask the bean-counter guys in our companies. Ask Ben, who always said that the return on investment in individual bodybuilders was lousy, and that I'd give everything away if he and others didn't stop me. For me, though, the investments were always worthwhile. I think my greatest reward was just being among bodybuilders, my own kind, my people. I loved working with guys in person, helping them make the most of the bodies that God gave them. I gave personal attention and advice to gym rats nobody heard of, as well as the stars. I helped whoever I could. In my magazines and courses, I really tried to reach out and train the entire world.

If I did more for Arnold than anybody else, it's because he was a dream pupil. He was always eager to learn and appreciative and put what I taught him to work. Everything I gave him went to good use, and nothing, not a thing, went to waste with that guy. Seeing him accomplish so much would do more for me than a million thanks and any amount of return on investment—believe me, too, Arnold turned out to be a terrific investment. A farmer must feel like I did, putting seeds in bare ground and seeing bounty come forth. Or an artist, starting with some canvas and color and creating beauty for all time.

Look at some of the first pictures taken of Arnold in Florida and you'll see areas we worked on right away. The earliest shots don't flatter him at all because he stands straight-on to the shooter head to toe. Such a position makes the waist look thick. I showed Arnold a little trick to make his midsection look more slender by standing with the upper body and lower body facing slightly different directions. You keep the legs and hips in the same plane, chest and shoulders in another, with a little twist in the body in-between. Twist a rolled-up towel, and you can see how this works.

I taught Arnold other such tricks and explained how, if he wanted to be a champion over here, he had to show himself to best advantage all the time. Presidents and kings and top executives dress and carry themselves so others will look up to them and follow their lead. Physique stars must do the same thing, except their clothes are muscles.

But our greatest challenge was to build the guy a better body to show off. We had to sculpt, actually, more than build. Arnold's body was like a roughed-out marble figure. We could see, inside, a thing of fantastic power and beauty, but Arnold needed his own Michelangelo to bring it to light. He also needed a diet. We had to wean him off schnitzel and potatoes and the other heavy, greasy Germanic stuff he grew up on and introduce him to lean protein, fresh produce, and Weider supplements.

After Florida, we worked together a bit in Jersey, and I sent Arnold up to Montreal for photo sessions with the great physique photographer Jimmy Caruso. Then Arnold flew out to Los Angeles where he was met by two of my guys, the West Coast correspondent and columnist Dick Tyler and the photographer Art Zeller. I already mentioned Art as one of the notable muscle men to come out of Abe Goldberg's gym in New York.

I set Arnold up to train for the first few months at Vince Gironda's gym in North Hollywood up in the San Fernando Valley. In a column, Dick Tyler quoted Vince, calling Arnold "a vast untapped reservoir of unused tissue." There's a funnier version that I could not put in my magazines. First time at the gym, Arnold walked in and announced Mr. Universe had arrived, like everybody should be impressed, and Vince said, "To me, you look like a fat f**k." Arnold could, in fact, come off pretty cocky, and Vince would swear and fling insults at the drop of a hat. Eventually he and I got on each other's nerves, but Vince was a highly regarded trainer with absolutely no mercy for sloppiness or laziness. He helped Larry Scott build his physique, and he had a big following with Hollywood stars like Clint Eastwood and James Garner.

Arnold wanted to train closer to the Weider offices in Santa Monica, so he began working out at a little gym in Venice Beach that eclipsed Vince's place and every other gym in the world. The old, original Gold's Gym is long gone, but will be a legend forever, like bodybuilding's Camelot. Sad to say, its owner, Joe Gold, is gone, too. At his memorial service California governor Arnold Schwarzenegger recalled how Joe made him welcome and took him under his wing. "Arnold, anything you want, it's yours," Joe said. "You're just a stupid farmer from Austria and you got a balloon belly. It will take us a year to work on that!" Like Vince, Joe was a tough sonofabitch who didn't mince words, but he had a more gentle spirit. I loved that guy, a true believer in bodybuilding, iron-game immortal, and dear friend.

By the time Arnold arrived, Gold's had more of the big-name bodybuilders than any other gym in the world. Never, before or since, has there been such a gathering of champions. Bodybuilding was still a small fraternity back then, and Gold's was the fraternity house where everybody welcomed Arnold like a brother. The top Gold's guys trained using Weider techniques, and I figured Arnold would learn faster from their example than only working one on one with me back East. And I knew the special camaraderie and competitive spirit would do him good. While each guy at Gold's supported the others, he also tried to outdo them, which drove the level of training up and up.

Even with 3,000 miles between us, I monitored Arnold's progress very closely. We talked on the phone, and Dick Tyler, the writer who worked in the Santa Monica office, and Art Zeller kept me up to date. I had Art constantly photograph Arnold so I could study his physique, and every couple months I saw him in person when I went to look in on my West Coast guys and see to business at the Santa Monica office.

Back in Europe, Arnold's training had been all about power moves, lifting really heavy to build big mass. It was time to add some finesse. Together we visualized the masterpiece of living art that we wanted to create, and then I gave Arnold the artist's tools. I refer, of course, to the famous Weider Training Principles.

It's easier to understand the sort of things we did if you try a little of it yourself. Non-exercisers should do their best to imagine what's going on.

Pick up a dumbbell that feels light for doing biceps curls. If you normally do sets with 30 pounds, say, go down to 15 or so. Whatever your personal poundages, you want a weight where you still feel resistance, but doing a few curls seems too easy.

Now work one arm with some concentration curls or just regular curls. Do them slowly through the entire range of motion, starting with the arm hanging straight down—no cheating allowed. And do the movement more like you're making a muscle than just moving a weight, so the biceps constantly stays tensed. At the top of the curl, where the weight is up by the shoulder and resistance would normally let up, you want to tense especially hard and pop up the biceps. Feel what's happening, focus on it in your mind, and watch. You'll be amazed at the fatigue and burn from moving a weight that felt like almost nothing when you first picked it up.

Curling this way employs my Weider Peak-Contraction Training Principle, which works in other exercises, too. The idea is to keep the working muscle tensed when it's fully contracted at the end of the range of motion. The payoff is new shape and detail. With the curls I just described you get a biceps that comes to a peak like a little mountain and shows more striations.

You just learned, in very simple form, something that Joe Weider once taught to Arnold Schwarzenegger.

Remember that heavy and light are relative. Most guys can't pick up the weights that Arnold would have called light. Don't be misled, either, by what was said about Arnold being overweight. Unless you're a world-level athlete, you're much fatter than Arnold was when we started trimming him down. "Fat" in bodybuilding is a matter of tiny amounts of excess that make muscles look smooth.

A person reading very carefully might think I just contradicted myself by telling you not to cheat in the arm exercises. Many pages back I stated the opposite in an explanation of the Weider Cheating Principle, which says that it's okay to break form to move more weight and work the muscles harder. The principles don't contradict at all—they apply to different ends of a spectrum that a bodybuilder in training must cover. A person lifts heavy for mass, cheating if necessary to handle more weight and squeeze out a few more reps. Then for refinement he must isolate an individual muscle and work it with precision. So he lightens the weight, slows down, and takes great care with his anatomical position. There's never just one way to do an exercise. You lift heavy, light, and in-between and make all kinds of position changes. Where an average guy at a fitness center might do only a couple exercises to work a given area, like the upper arm, a champ like Arnold would do dozens.

My system ties this all together. The Holistic Training Principle says to vary the weight in exercises, high to low, and the Eclectic Training Principle says you should always mix things up and work the same muscles and muscle groups with many different exercises.

If you can't relate to resistance training, think about other endeavors. Athletes who need to run go long distances for endurance and do sprints, too. A pianist practices playing loud and soft, slow and fast, and does all sorts of technical exercises. He has to, because music demands so much.

One more little lesson related to displaying the physique:

Again make a muscle, this time without a weight, upper arm horizontal, forearm squeezing in while you tense the biceps. Flex as hard as you can to make the muscle as big as you can.

Right now, in a small way, you're a bodybuilder, hitting a pose to show what you've got. Undoubtedly you flexed hard, all at once, and then tried to hold it. The better way—the Weider way—is to go up in stages.

Try again. First make a muscle flexing hard. Then harder. Then really hard. And harder yet. Then two more times for a total of six, and you reach a level you could not get to in a single shot. You feel it and see it, am I right? Practice flexing like this, and you learn muscle control that Arnold had to master to show his physique to the best possible advantage.

I told Arnold his upper body was out of balance, and we needed to work on his forearms, his waist, and his lower back. He walked around on his worst problems, his legs, especially the puny calves. Arnold didn't mind straight talk about his deficiencies at all. He took every problem as a challenge that he accepted in front of everybody. Rather than hiding his calves while he built them up he wore pants cut off so they always showed.

I wish one of those idiots calling us wimps and mirror athletes could see what Arnold or any other competitive bodybuilder puts himself through. No athlete in the world trains longer or harder. In a day of routine workouts, Arnold lifted 40 tons. Attacking his leg problems, he would get on the calf machine and do toe raises with 1,000 pounds of weight, hundreds of reps at a crack. Every rep, every set, was an all-out assault and a contest. If somebody lifted more, he'd kill himself to out-do the guy. Sometimes he hit the weights so hard he'd actually faint and then wake up and go on like nothing happened. The time he had a car accident and the gearshift stabbed through his thigh he got stitched up and did his leg routines right on schedule. A regular person would have stayed at home for a week.

Laughing at us for using mirrors is as nonsensical as laughing at runners for using stopwatches. We win or lose by what other people see, so how could we train *without* looking at ourselves? Mirrors show progress or lack thereof. While you work out, they show if you're using proper form in the exercises. You need them to work on poses for competition. Most of all, for a guy like Arnold, a mirror is a tool for self-criticism. Looking at himself, a serious bodybuilder isn't admiring, he's looking for trouble. And he sees trouble, every time.

Whatever Arnold saw, the rest of us saw more and more of the body that would take our sport by storm. In that first year in California, he gained hard muscle in his back, his forearms, triceps, thighs. All over he showed cuts and striations that surprised even Arnold himself, because he used to think only lightweights could be so cut-up. And his calves got so good his bodybuilder buddies admired them like they admired his arms and pecs. People even spread rumors that he had surgical implants. That wasn't plastic—it was sweat, grueling work, pain, patience, belief, courage, character.

The muscles were the man—they always are.

Arnold made working together such a joy. If I wanted him to try something different in training or asked him to pose for hours using some piece of equipment for an ad or had a writer interview him for training tips, he did his best, no trouble, no BS, no anything. It didn't take long to start liking Arnold in his own right. Hard as he worked, he was also fun to be around, so energetic and upbeat, full of life and so pleased about just being himself. Day and night the guy wore a smile. For other people he was like some kind of human sunshine that lit up everything and made things happen. Just walking down the street with him was like following a one-man parade or going to some big party. That appealed to me, personally, because I lacked the gift of having such fun. Arnold was like some kind of vitamin I couldn't produce on my own.

I wasn't alone in my appreciation. Art Zeller and Joe Gold and others around town became so devoted that they called themselves the Arnia. The other bodybuilders liked him and looked up to him as a leader even though he was younger and a foreigner with a funny accent and a terrible threat to their own hopes. All that mattered around Arnold was Arnold, and everything bent to fit him. Whatever outrageous things he said or did, nobody got mad because he came off like some kind of great big, cute kid. Honest to God, he could charm the birds out of the trees.

Arnold had a powerful effect on people who never met him. His first cover shot was a huge hit, and the more readers saw of him, the more they wanted to see. The muscles were part of the attraction, of course, but the real power came from within. He liked the camera, and it liked him, and looking at a picture you couldn't help but like him, too. That special attractiveness—which Arnold had like no other bodybuilder—is a very valuable asset to a guy selling magazines. Betty, too, had it in spades and still does. She built a modeling career on her incredible ability to fascinate men looking at her pictures, which explains why she was on more than 300 magazine covers, all over the world. After we got married, she went on working her magic for my magazines. When she and Arnold posed together for a cover shot, the issue set a new high for newsstand sales. Once again, Betty on the cover broke records.

In time, Arnold and I formed a special bond that's as strong now as it ever was. Stronger, maybe. As Arnold says, we're like father and son, and if over the years we had our little aggravations and ups and downs, they were mostly the troubles that come up between fathers and sons. I did grow to love Arnold like a son, with a love never blind to things that I didn't like or that hurt my feelings, but which always went beyond them. Our troubles never amounted to much, anyway. A father knows his son must fight for distance to become a man, but he knows that some day the son will return to him.

Arnold has been back now for years. Last year, when I was flat on my back after major surgery at the Cleveland Clinic in Ohio, suffering setbacks in recovery that almost killed me, he came to my side. That was right before the presidential elections in 2004, and Arnold made time for me on a trip to campaign with President Bush in Ohio. All through the weeks before I came home Arnold kept in touch and called for updates from the doctors who must have been amazed at such concern from the governor of the State of California. There are sons who would have done much less. Back when Arnold ran for governor and won, he wanted me around for triumphant moments. At his big victory party on election night he called me up to the stage so I could stand next to him. "You know," he said, "if it wasn't for you, I wouldn't be here. I don't know what I'd be doing back in Austria." He also wrote a note to me that said, "I will make you proud." After all the years, he didn't have to do a thing to earn my pride, but a son strives forever to make the father-figure proud.

In my opinion, the key to understanding Arnold is that he had a father he could never make proud, no matter what he did to be worthy of pride. Gustav Schwarzenegger was a tyrant who favored Arnold's older brother to the point that, to him, Arnold did not exist. When Gustav died, I saw no sorrow in Arnold, who didn't even go home for the funeral. Still, though, he went on hungering for his father's approval, and I think that hunger, which could never be satisfied, drove him to strive so hard to reach such amazing heights. I think, too, that I stood in for the real father who let him down.

I still laugh about the snow job Arnold pulled about six months after he got to California.

One day he said to me, "I feel so lonely." I asked him why, and he said he had a buddy over in Germany who was his training partner and constant companion, and he missed him like crazy. The Americans were fine, Arnold said, but only a fellow European could truly understand him.

"Joe, you should bring him over," Arnold said, and started telling me all about his pal, another big tall bruiser with a fantastic build. This sounded a lot like Arnold himself, and I agreed to bring the guy over. What the heck, I thought, I could make Arnold happy and get a look at this new European colossus.

The colossus turned out to be 5 feet, 4 inches tall. After I got over my surprise at how short he was, and how Arnold fooled me, I saw the great possibilities in Franco Columbu. Franco, who came from a place on the island of Sardinia even more in the middle of nowhere than Arnold's home town, was a former Italian boxing champ who became a world champion powerlifter before Arnold talked him into focusing on bodybuilding. The one thing Arnold did not exaggerate was his friend's muscle power. Pound for pound, Franco was the strongest bodybuilder ever, and he had the makings of a great physique star, too. Franco would win Mr. Olympia twice. He also became another reader magnet for my magazines. People were drawn to his pictures, which showed his warmth and vivacity. Like Arnold, he would advance himself outside bodybuilding. Franco later put himself through school and became a chiropractor.

So Arnold's snow job turned out to be a great Weider champ and a great guy, too. He made Arnold happier right off. The two of them got an apartment in Santa Monica a few blocks from our offices. If walls could talk—those two should have had a revolving door for all the beautiful girls coming and going. Most of the guys ran a little wild back then when things were free and easy, especially by the beach in California. On the other hand, nothing interfered with training. Every day, Arnold and Franco went to the gym and drove each other to work out with intensity like nobody I ever saw.

Once in a while I dropped in and made things more intense. All I had to do was walk through the door, and the energy level shot up and everybody started loading on more weight.

"Oh no, here comes the Master Blaster," Arnold would say. In a magazine interview he recalled how I pushed him to lift heavier to build up his thighs. I told him if he wanted to accomplish something he ought to squat with 700 pounds, and he said not even the strongest bodybuilder in the world could handle such weight. I looked him straight in the eye and said, "Why can't you be the first?" He didn't have an answer, because there was no reason in the world he couldn't add weight, so he did.

Once I walked into the gym, and Arnold said, "Joe, watch this." He wanted me to see his friend Franco deadlifting more than 650 pounds, which at that time was getting up toward world-record territory. Franco really impressed me, but instead of making a fuss I said, "You know, Franco, that's a good lift. But it doesn't come close to what you can do with the power you have. You can do better." Franco could, too. He set a powerlifting record with a deadlift of 750 pounds and benched more than 500 pounds.

Never did I allow anybody to rest on his laurels. I pushed and pushed, never satisfied, and the guys loved it. Athletes in training appreciate a friendly kick in the ass more than praise.

I remember one time I encouraged Arnold and Franco by example without actually meaning to. It happened when they came to New York and I took them to work out at my regular gym in the Shelton Hotel. I started doing sets of incline dumbbell curls, not thinking about anything but my own workout, and Franco yelled, "Arnold, look at Joe! He's curling 70 pounds!" In that same session those two did their incline curls with 45 pounds. After Franco pointed out the difference in weights, I said they ought to outlift me.

"Joe, I can't do more than 70 pounds," Arnold said.

I told him, "If I can do it, you can do it. I'm double your age, and you're bigger and heavier." And I shamed him and Franco into lifting more. Arnold did all right with 80 pounds, but he had trouble with 90. I did fine, which impressed the guys and pleased me to no end.

We held our 1969 Mr. Universe in New York City, the same night as Mr. Olympia. A year with The Master Blaster had done wonders for Arnold, who was down from about 250 pounds to 230, cut and finished and with a wonderful California suntan. No surprise that he took the title and the trophy that Frank Zane denied him the year before. Then Arnold reached for the brass ring, the Mr. Olympia, which immediately followed the Mr. Universe.

The way Arnold later told it, he entered the Olympia because Sergio Oliva played a cat-and-mouse game before contest night by staying out of sight. This made Arnold mad, so he decided to face Sergio and beat him right then and there. Even without such drama, it made sense for a winner to advance to the next level right away, especially if he was sure, like Arnold, he had the goods to win.

Sergio really had been making himself scarce. At the last minute he showed up backstage in the great big overalls he liked to wear. He stripped down to his trunks, revealing a body like Arnold had never seen. Nobody had. In tiptop form, Sergio was fabulous, just fabulous. An eyeful of The Myth knocked the fight out of Arnold, who says he lost before he competed. The judge's scoring turned out to be close, but nobody argued with the outcome. Arnold gave Sergio the warmest congratulations I ever saw, hugging the guy and giving him a kiss.

After the contests in New York, Arnold went to London and won another NABBA Pro Mr. Universe. He dominated the competition, but the win meant a lot less than losing the Olympia. Over in London, Arnold said he was going to beat everybody in the game, whatever it took.

That Mr. Olympia contest was, by the way, the one and only time I saw somebody rattle Arnold's nerves and shake his confidence. He later became known as bodybuilding's all-time master of psychological warfare. People still talk about some of the little tricks he pulled to screw up other guys' morale, always while looking like the nicest guy in the world.

Boy, did I want to see Arnold and Sergio face off again.

Our triumphs contain the seeds of our defeat. I've told people this hundreds of times. And defeats can contain the seeds of triumph. Not always—real losers just keep on losing—but the right kind of person learns from a loss and uses it to strengthen and motivate himself. He uses it to win.

It's hard to think of a historic or mythical hero who didn't get kicked around for a while. Think about the Bible. God could have gone easy on Moses, who was born a Jew, but was brought up as a prince of Egypt. Instead, God knocked out all the princely stuffing, making Moses flee Egypt and endure suffering for years and years. Coming straight out of Pharaoh's palace, Moses would have felt privileged and special, but his ordeal made him humble before God and a man of his people. It was 40 years before Moses finally led his people to the Promised Land. Had things gone easier, Moses might have been less of a man, and the Jewish people's faith might have been weakened. But out of the suffering came undying strength.

I could go on and on with stories like this. You're reading one right now. I wandered in the desert of my childhood and youth, which were miserable but necessary, because I grew strong and developed a will of iron. Hardship made me the man I am, which is why I give my early life in Montreal so much attention in this book. Had things been easier, I'd be some other man who might have done different things.

So a couple defeats didn't hurt Arnold, who came over here like a prince of bodybuilding. Losing a little helped him be a greater champion and a winner in all he has done, to this day.

However hard he trained for the 1970 competitions, Arnold still couldn't count on beating Sergio physique versus physique. So we zeroed in on Sergio's greatest weakness, his posing. It seemed like he never gave it much effort, maybe because he figured he didn't have to with such a build.

Arnold, a natural-born entertainer, had no trouble getting the crowd on his side, but he wasn't such a hot poser himself, not at first. When I met him he'd do dumb, head-on European-style muscle shots and tense and scrunch up like he wanted to shrink himself to the size of his buddy Franco.

"Come on, Arnold," I said, "You're a giant. You're taller than everybody else, so don't pose like the other guys. Stand up straight. Reach upward, outward."

I told Arnold to move and hold himself as a man of immense stature, towering above the others and making them look small.

Be like a mythic hero, I said. Be Hercules.

Sometimes I wish we had a better word for displaying the physique. "Posing," I think, can give outsiders the wrong idea, because it sounds like somebody's faking it, not doing anything real. In bodybuilding, posing is as real as can be. It's a big part of winning, which is a two-step process:

1) You build the best body; and

2) You convince the judges and the crowd that you've got the best body.

Part two itself is two-part, actually, part technical and part showmanship and artistry. Before the final event onstage, judges make detailed assessments of each contestant's physique, looking at them alone, in groups, in side-by-side comparisons, and they do required poses to display the physique, zone by zone. Then, on contest night, the finalists do individual routines choreographed to music and then try to outdo each other in a free-for-all "pose-down." It's a terrific show, and the judges get caught up in audience reaction and the spectacle and individual personal charisma. The deal really isn't all that different from other sports that involve performance—the floor program in gymnastics, say, or figure skating. To win you show what you've got as an athlete, but with flair and dramatic impact.

There's nothing in the world like a posing routine done right. You see a man turn into a demigod, the embodiment of pure physical power and perfection, then back into a man. In the span of a couple minutes, it happens over and over and over. Between poses the man reveals his personality. Maybe he smiles, clowns a bit, gestures for louder applause. Then bam! he wipes the smile off his face and hits his next pose. I've always told my guys that it's fine to have fun, but the poses must be serious to show the seriousness of commitment to bodybuilding. A competitor should look like he's working hard, straining, grunting, to reflect the effort that it took to build his muscles.

This last part, showing effort, isn't playacting, because posing takes tremendous effort. As I showed a few pages back, you put skill and real exertion into flexing properly, and a bodybuilder onstage has to flex every muscle that shows. Even doing nothing—in the so-called "stand relaxed" position—a bodybuilder tenses head to toe. Think about doing isometric exercises as hard as you can with your entire body, for hours, and you get some idea of the physical strain of competing. Guys come offstage absolutely worn out, sweaty, shaking like leaves.

The same year I helped Arnold pose like Hercules, I helped him land his first movie role, which also happened to be Hercules. I got a call from a producer making a low-budget movie where Hercules, bastard son of Zeus, gets thrown out of Olympus and lands in modern-day New York. This was supposed to be a send-up of 1950s movies, in which both Steve Reeves and Arnold's hero, Reg Park, had starred as Hercules. The producer wanted to know if I had a bodybuilder who could play the hero, and I told him about Arnold.

"Sounds great, but can he act?" he asked.

"Are you kidding me?" I told him. "He was a famous Shakespearean actor in Vienna!"

Arnold appeared under the name Arnold Strong, and the filmmaker dubbed in the voice of an American actor. A masterpiece that movie is not, but people still watch it to see Arnold's first movie appearance.

By fall 1970, Arnold looked better than ever, and once again he went to London and won the NABBA Pro Mr. Universe. A day later he competed at an

AAU Pro Mr. World in Columbus, Ohio. Arnold made it to the contest only because the promoter, Jim Lorimer, had him picked up by private plane the instant he got off the jet from overseas in New York. Arnold went, I think, because ABC's *Wide World of Sports* would cover Mr. World, which was part of the World Weightlifting Championships. I didn't go, but I heard that Arnold's arrival surprised Sergio Oliva, who didn't expect Arnold to be there. Arnold claimed to be surprised, too, because he didn't expect Sergio.

Then came the biggest surprise—Arnold won. Word was, Sergio put on so much oil that it flowed onto his posing trunks and made his body shine like a mirror. Under the TV lights, his definition could barely be seen. In all likelihood, though, the oil didn't cost him the contest—Arnold did. He looked fantastic, flawless, and Sergio was a bit heavy.

A story went around that Arnold did his best to put some more pounds on Sergio before our Mr. Olympia contest, which was only two weeks away. After Mr. World they ate together, and Arnold remarked, like he was giving friendly advice, that he never would have won if Sergio had been 15 or 20 pounds heavier.

All the bodybuilding public could talk about was the upcoming Battle of the Century, the 1970 IFBB Mr. Olympia.

My God, though, the headaches that contest gave us. First, after years of making the IFBB events more than welcome, the Brooklyn Academy of Music turned us away. We ran all over the city looking for a venue that wasn't booked up and found an opening at the last minute at the Music Hall on West Forty-Second Street. A very nice place, actually, but the deal came with some catches. We couldn't get in until just before contest time, and we couldn't hold our prejudging here. Tom Minichiello solved the prejudging crisis by inviting us to use his Mid-City Gym, which had become a landmark like the Gold's of New York.

The jinx continued into the contest itself. Sergio, who just got his citizenship papers and joined the Chicago police, felt a sudden need to become Mr. America and demanded to enter the contest. But if Sergio entered it wouldn't be a contest. He'd win hands down and deny the title to some deserving guy on his way up. Bud Parker, the promoter, finally satisfied Sergio by agreeing to name him honorary Mr. America and giving him a duplicate trophy. He also got honorary wins and trophies for his bodyweight class and all the body parts awards like best arms, best back, and so on. This nonsense took some of the excitement out of the Mr. America contest, but at least we could get going with the events that built up to Mr. Olympia.

Backstage at contests, there's an area with weights so guys can exercise to enlarge their muscles. "Pumping up," we call this. An hour before the Olympia, Sergio started to pump up like a man possessed. Arnold wanted to do likewise, but I told him to take it easy, explaining that Sergio was doing too much, too soon, and if he kept it up his muscles would begin to deflate before he posed. I advised Arnold to skip pumping up and bring himself to peak form with the muscle control I had taught him.

Before their individual posing routines, Sergio and Arnold argued about who should go out first. Arnold suggested a coin toss, but Sergio insisted that he, as the reigning Mr. Olympia, should go last. This was one more tactical error. More time backstage meant he'd be more past peak, and Sergio gave Arnold a chance to stake a claim on the title.

Arnold absolutely electrified the New York crowd. I found it hard to believe this was the same bruiser kid I met just two years earlier. The whole physique had come together with harmony and balance. Terrific triceps now matched the 21-inch biceps. The calves stood out like somebody molded them out of clay, with splits and striations all over. The guy moved from pose to pose like a great cat, like poetry.

The crowd, which favored Sergio, went berserk when he came onstage. I think they shouted more about how much they loved him, not what they saw. Sergio had the stuff, all right, but he still didn't know how to show it, and that night he carried 15 excess pounds—maybe Arnold really had bamboozled him into gaining more weight. The more the crowd looked, the more the heart went out of the cheering. Sergio's fans, like all bodybuilding fans, were extremely knowledgeable, and they knew their man could be in trouble.

However, the contest was still too close for a quick decision. The judges made close-up comparisons of Arnold and Sergio backstage and made them match each other pose for pose. Then the judges brought to the stage the three Mr. Olympia contenders—the third was Reg Lewis, a veteran competitor who had appeared in another schlock Hercules movie and also toured with Mae West. Then the judges dismissed Lewis. The crowd went insane while the two top guys tried to show each other up. This went on for some time while people yelled their heads off. They were still yelling when Sergio walked offstage and left Arnold all by himself. People booed, thinking Sergio had thrown in the towel. It seemed maybe he had after Bud Parker declared Arnold Mr. Olympia. By then everybody, Oliva fans and all, was cheering for Arnold.

It turned out that Sergio never conceded that contest. He walked offstage because of what Arnold later said was a simple misunderstanding. As Arnold explained it, he saw that Sergio looked really tired, so Arnold said he'd had it, too, and they should both quit posing. That sounded good to Sergio, and Arnold said to him, "Go on. I'll follow you." Arnold said he had every intention of doing so, but the booing stopped him.

You decide whether it was all so innocent or if Arnold played a trick—I'll stay out of it. I will say, though, that Arnold would have won—and should have won—if nobody walked off stage. So the trick, or whatever it was, didn't change the outcome, except to make Sergio more of a loser. That's how it was, though. If Arnold beat you, you knew it, and everybody knew it. Most of the time he started to beat you long before the contest and went on winning afterward.

You better believe I was glad to see Arnold win. I liked him and had a big personal investment in him, and I knew how good he would be for our sport. That does not, however, mean I would have been sad to see Sergio win. I always wanted to see the best man become champion regardless of my own personal feelings about him.

Sooner or later I had to bring this up. Now seems like a good time because I've always had favorites—and never made any bones about it—and Arnold was my favorite favorite. And people have said that we Weiders use our power to make sure our favorites win—leaning on judges, loading the panel, putting the fix in some other way. Supposedly we do this to sell more magazines and Weider products. It's BS, but people say it anyway. Usually the ones who say it loudest are bodybuilders who didn't win and their fans, who dream up reasons why everything was rigged. As I always say, after a contest with 15 guys in it, I've got one friend and 14 enemies. I've been called anti-black by blacks, anti-gay by gays, anti-gay black by a gay black. And over and over people called me anti-everybody-but-Arnold, because I was always in his corner.

I remember one time somebody interviewed me on network TV. The guy was relentless, telling me people claimed our shows were fakes, that we picked winners beforehand, and what did I have to say? I didn't want to dignify that with an answer, so I turned the tables. I asked the interviewer to pretend to be me, somebody who's worked 35 years—that was 30 years ago—building a personal dream and a business and a good name and reputation. And I asked, would you be dumb enough to risk your life's work and your heart and your soul for one lousy contest? And if you did tell judges what to do, wouldn't some of them ignore you? And wouldn't somebody get mad and go public and squeal on you?

The interviewer didn't have an answer. Nobody does. With the enemies Ben and I had, dying to publish articles exposing us as crooks, sooner or later somebody with inside information that hurt us would talk. Nobody ever did—ever—because there was no damaging information. Think about it. Over the years we've had hundreds and hundreds of judges at our events, and never was there a peep about anything improper. Think about how impossible it would be to keep so many people quiet. A few years back there was a terrible judging scandal in figure skating. You cannot hide such things. The truth comes to light. For all these years the truth about the Weiders has been out in the light.

Some of the time I liked the final results and agreed with them, but plenty of times I strongly disagreed. At least once I got so mad I stood up and walked out. Two of the Mr. Olympias that made me maddest happened in 1980 and '81. In both cases, my personal favorite and the biggest-name Weider star won. Arnold came out of retirement and took the title in '80. The following year, his buddy Franco staged a similar comeback and won. Those two guys were—and still are—my closest friends in all of competitive bodybuilding, but in those particular contests I felt other men showed them up. The fact that Arnold and Franco were my buddies did not cloud my bodybuilding judgment. And my judgment didn't cloud my feelings of friendship. Not one bit. The two were entirely separate. They still are.

Make no mistake, though—Arnold Schwarzenegger was the best at the first Mr. Olympia he won in 1970. And at the next five Olympias he got better.

CHAPTER NINE

GOLDEN AGE IN THE GOLDEN STATE

Joe Weider

Looking back on the Golden Age of Bodybuilding, I see it's really a lot like other Golden Ages in history—classical Greece, say, or the Italian Renaissance.

Always somebody laid the groundwork so the great things could happen. In the Italian Renaissance, this was mostly the Medici, the richest family in Italy and the rulers of the city of Florence. Lorenzo di Medici became a patron of Leonardo da Vinci, Michelangelo, and other artistic and intellectual giants. He bankrolled the greatest gathering of creative geniuses of his time and made Florence the cultural capital of the world.

I bring this up because the Weiders are the Medici of bodybuilding. I've been thinking about this a lot lately. What Lorenzo did, I did along with Ben. We brought to our world prosperity, stability, and safety from tyrants who wanted to oppress bodybuilders. We spread the word about bodybuilding around the world and promoted our own special paradise where the best physique stars congregated and trained side by side. And bodybuilding grew and flourished like never before.

To explain what happened, I have to re-cover some historical ground and go back to our first Mr. Olympia in 1965. Though our Golden Age reached its height in the early 1970s, it really began with the Mr. Olympia, which gave bodybuilding critical mass and started a chain reaction that built and built. Fans had never witnessed anything like the great battles between Arnold Schwarzenegger and Sergio Oliva and classic '70s contests packed with the likes of Frank Zane, Franco Columbu, Lou Ferrigno, Boyer Coe, Mike Mentzer, Ed Corney, Roy

Callender, greats from outside the U.S. like Serge Nubret, Albert Beckles, and on and on. If I'm leaving anybody out, it's only because the list of stars of the '70s runs too long. Never had such men come together in one competitive event. Nowadays, the crowds expect to see the contest stage loaded with talent. At the Mr. Olympia, they see 14 or 15 or more titans with builds that nobody in Arnold's era could even have imagined. The excitement that began more than 40 years ago has never let up, and bodybuilding continues to advance.

The first Mr. Olympia gave everybody something else to get excited about—Southern California, which would be to our Golden Age what Florence was to the Renaissance.

Larry Scott trained in Los Angeles. So did the other sensation of the Mr. Olympia premier night, Dave Draper, who competed in the Mr. America. He was the first Weider star-in-the-making I had ever sent from the East to the West Coast. "The Blond Bomber," I nicknamed Dave, who was handsome and fair like some kind of Norse god. When he left New Jersey, he had enormous muscles but no definition, and before the big event the New York crowd pretty much wrote him off as a contender. One smartass who worked for me called him the "Great White Whale."

But then Dave knocked everybody's eyes out.

Dick Tyler, our West Coast columnist, wrote this about beholding Dave before he went onstage: "I have personally never seen such a combination of raw power sculptured on such bronzed, separated and defined muscles in my life."

Until that moment Dick thought Dave didn't have a prayer. All year he had wondered why I pushed Dave as a new Weider star. Well, now he knew.

The crowd went nuts for Dave, the new Mr. America. At the show's finale Larry became our first Mr. Olympia. Those two golden guys were our ambassadors from paradise. They looked like California sunshine and healthful living distilled into men with fantastic muscles. Dave especially was like a billboard announcing that the West Coast was the place to make yourself into a brand-new man.

Of course, bodybuilding in California was not front-page news. All along, great champs came out of the Golden State, and for years Los Angeles had been a center of muscle men, many in the movies, who got together and did acrobatics and feats of strength at the famed Muscle Beach. During World War II, guys on their way overseas stopped in California and saw Muscle Beach, an outdoor exhibition area and open-air gym that was then right next to the Santa Monica Pier. The sight of powerful men showing their stuff and pretty girls admiring them planted a seed in the minds of thousands of GIs. Whether they saw Muscle Beach or not, ex-servicemen gave Weider publications and products a big boost back in the 1940s and '50s. They wanted exactly what we had to offer—more muscle power and a great build to attract the ladies. What they didn't care about was Bob Hoffman's competitive weightlifting.

So California wasn't new. Its complete dominance over other places was new, though. So was Joe Weider pushing it as bodybuilding's Promised Land.

I made Dave Draper a big part of my push. Big and blond and outdoorsy-looking, he was like the world's best-built beach boy and the perfect California icon. You'd swear he was born and brought up in the warmth and sunshine instead of New Jersey. We ran shot after shot of him out by the ocean. The locale became a co-star in the pictures, and guys drooled over the beach in California as much as the great big muscles and the bikini girls I threw in for sex appeal.

A picture in one of my magazines was never just a picture—it was a dream. Always I provided the readers with thrilling, beautiful dreams about having a body as fantastic as a Weider star and the pleasures that would bring.

Now California was part of the dream.

It's hard to think of it that way now, but back then, for most people in most walks of life, California was a dream and nothing more. A working man in the East or the Midwest was lucky if he got to the West Coast once in his lifetime. Many never got there at all. This added to the allure, I think, and all kinds of people felt the California magic. Car nuts wanted to go there because it was the center of hot rodding. Kids who never saw the ocean wanted to go out and become surfers. I didn't like the hippies a bit, but they too flocked to the West Coast.

It took two Joes, actually, to lay the groundwork for the Golden Age of Bodybuilding. The other was Joe Gold, who built the gym by the beach that became our mecca.

God knows a gym was needed. By the 1960s, the myth of Muscle Beach was better than the reality. The City of Santa Monica had shut the original down in 1959 after some lifters got caught fooling around with underage girls. A couple miles away at Venice Beach the City of Los Angeles put up an outdoor weight-training area—the "Pen," bodybuilders called it—and Venice laid claim to the name Muscle Beach. Now most people think it was always there, but the old Muscle Beach, in spirit at least, actually stayed in Santa Monica. After the closing, the regulars carried weights and stuff they had at the beach to the basement of a decrepit hotel building at Fourth and Broadway. Guys called it the "Dungeon," a name it earned. What a hole that was, directly under the hotel's taproom where old guys got drunk. The poor bodybuilders had to get by with junky old weights and makeshift gear like milk crates and splintery homemade benches.

Elsewhere, Los Angeles had perfectly good gyms like Vince Gironda's in North Hollywood. But the Valley had no magic, and magic was needed for our Golden Age. We needed a shrine built on holy ground like the Temple Mount in Jerusalem or the church that stands where Jesus was born. We needed something close to the ocean, partaking of the aura of Muscle Beach.

Then along came Joe Gold. Like me, Joe got the call to the iron when he was a kid and made his first weights out of scrap metal. He worked out his first design for a gym in high school. Joe suffered serious wounds fighting at sea during World War II, but afterward he hit the weights, rebuilt his physique, and became one of the Muscle Beach stars. For a while he toured with Mae West, a comedienne famous for her big boobs and sexy talk, who had muscle men in her act. Joe also sailed on ships in the merchant marine. In 1964, in his forties, he put up a gym in Venice Beach. He designed it for serious bodybuilders and built a lot of the equipment himself. Joe was a great trainer, and he inculcated the guys in his gym with the Weider principles and techniques. Joe also had a heart like his name—solid gold. He made his place a welcoming home to bodybuilders and looked out for them.

A few pages back I stated that the Golden Age started because the Mr. Olympia gave bodybuilding critical mass. Well, Gold's created its own critical mass. Dave Draper started training at Gold's, which was full of talent by the time I sent Arnold to the West Coast, followed by Franco. Frank Zane moved to Los Angeles from Florida and worked out at Gold's. The more top guys trained there, the more others wanted to come.

If you're picturing the last great big Gold's Gym you were in, forget it. The original was small, built of cinderblocks and strictly a bare-bones operation.

You can get a look at it in the documentary movie *Pumping Iron,* starring Arnold. Most of the workout scenes were filmed in Gold's.

You get an even better feel for the place looking at candid shots taken by our photographer Art Zeller. I had Art shoot the guys in the gym all the time, whatever they did—training, resting, goofing around. Gold's might have been the first gym in the world with enough sunshine coming in for shooting without a flash. Natural light gave a natural feel to the pictures, and Art had a special gift for mingling with the guys and putting them at ease. They loved him as one of their own. Since he had been a bodybuilder himself, he understood what went on in a gym. He had a job at the post office he never gave up, and technically speaking, Art was more of a gifted amateur than a polished pro. But his rapport with the guys and his deep understanding made his pictures something special. In Art's best shots, you see bodybuilding through a bodybuilder's eyes.

You also see how packed with stars Gold's was. Art shot a classic series in 1970 before the fall competition season. You see, training together and being buddies, the soon-to-be winners of the Mr. Olympia—Arnold; Mr. America—Mike Katz; Mr. World—Dave Draper; and NABBA Mr. Universe—Frank Zane. Frank later became a three-time winner at Mr. Olympia, won twice by Franco Columbu, also in many of Art's shots taken at Gold's Gym.

I should explain what became of that gym. After only a few years, Joe sold it and its name, and it grew into the international Gold's Gym chain. About five years later, Joe opened a new gym not far from his old one. He named it World Gym because he couldn't call it Gold's. That gym he kept, and it, too, grew into a big chain. For a while, Arnold had a stake in it. Between them, Gold's and World have something like 1,000 gyms all over the world. Think of it: 1,000 fancy workout clubs starting with one guy and two little hard-iron gyms. And there are thousands of other gyms with many millions of members.

Think of this, too: The gym business wouldn't have exploded without Joe Weider pushing strength training in his magazines.

So now both coasts pulled at me. As a bodybuilder, editor, writer, and the world's biggest bodybuilding fan, I wanted to be out where the action was. On the other hand, Joe Weider the publisher wanted to stay in New York City where the publishing action was. And I still liked living in New York. Sooner or later the West Coast would have won out. I moved to the Golden State sooner, I think, because of my golden girl Betty.

After years of loving New York, she'd had it with the city, and California was calling her home. Betty made more and more trips to stay with her mother-figure Aunt Annie and see her father, who was ailing. Back in our apartment, she was miserable. She was sick of gray skies and cold, and she hated how the dirt and soot got into the apartment and settled on everything, no matter what she did to seal the windows. Before my eyes she wilted like a flower, and I felt terrible.

Another woman might have whined and worked on my sympathies to get her way. Not my Betty. She explained in a clear-headed manner all the reasons why the Weider headquarters ought to be on the West Coast. She also did something nobody's wife ever did to get her husband to relocate. Betty hired an architect and a contractor and put up a building just right for the Weider enterprises and invited me to sign a lease.

Can you imagine?

Betty had an interest in real estate investment that she picked up from Aunt Annie, who made her living buying and selling property and renting out apartments in buildings she owned. With getting me to move in mind, Betty looked around for commercial property and put together a deal for a land parcel and construction in the new Warner Center business park in Woodland Hills, way west in the San Fernando Valley. The development was formerly a ranch owned by Harry Warner, one of the movie-mogul Warner Brothers, who happened to be Canadian Polish Jews just like the Weider Brothers.

So a bright, new, two-story structure went up out in the country. Betty lined up a triple-A tenant who wanted in—so I had to decide, yes or no, in a hurry. Of course I said "yes." Whether I moved in or not, Betty made a smart investment, because Warner Center turned out to be very hot commercial property. These days, looking at all the big businesses and high-rise office towers, you can't believe it used to be farmland.

Winston Churchill said that history is written by the victors. In marriages, it's written by the wife. To hear Betty tell it, I'd still be in Jersey if she didn't make me get off the dime. As you surely know by now, nobody makes me do anything. Betty could have put up the Taj Mahal and I wouldn't have moved if I didn't know for sure it was the right thing to do.

The builders fell behind schedule, and I landed in California with no place to set up shop. I desperately needed a whole new staff, top to bottom, but I had to get by on my own because there was no place to put new employees. My West Coast accountant took pity on me and let me use a desk in his place. Besides that I had only our small office in Santa Monica. Once again, I was a one-man band—laying out pages, editing, writing, doing ads—just like after the American News fiasco. This time was crazier, actually, because I had more business to attend to. I worked until I couldn't keep my eyes open, but the magazines came out late, and unfilled product orders piled up. That was one of the few times in my life I felt completely overwhelmed.

Finally, on June 15, 1972, three months after the scheduled move-in, the Weider companies had new headquarters and I had someplace to put a new staff.

Our operation was still so small that we needed only a quarter of the building and rented out the rest to other companies. But this new headquarters was a dream. After things settled down, I could fully appreciate it. Betty had it designed to resemble the Los Angeles Music Hall, which we both love. It was glassy and both classic and ultra-modern, with a portico supported by thin columns. Later, I'd bulk up the facade to give the building more weight and power and add a Greco-Roman-style frieze depicting muscle men. The changes made it more like a mighty temple to bodybuilding, which it was and still is. From the beginning, though, our building made a worthy home for our businesses. I couldn't believe the space, the light, everything gleaming and up-to-the-minute.

This was a long, long way from the desk in Ma's front room on Colonial Avenue. The dreams were still the same, though, except now they seemed much closer to coming true. I wrote the following in an editorial about the move to the West Coast:

Our future looks bright. We have a fantastic headquarters from which to direct our worldwide operation.... Our personnel are tops. Our nutrition line and equipment are the best and we are about to make Weider a household word around the world. We want to work to make the IFBB even stronger. We want to get the message of fitness across to the millions of Americans that are not interested in heavy weight training. We want to do something for the women who are interested in exercise. We have so much we want to do, but we feel that our plans are realistic and that we are well on our way to accomplishing many of these dreams.

Everything we wanted to do, we would do in pretty short order.

In the mind's eye, I see the first few years in California in a wonderful happy glow—Joe Weider's own private Golden Age. In many ways it was a throwback to the years in Montreal after I started *Your Physique*. I had everything I wanted—my work, Betty, family, the guys—and not one thing I didn't want.

Once again, home life was very simple. Betty and I put most of our stuff in storage and moved into a little one-bedroom apartment in a fourplex that Aunt Annie owned and lived in. The units stepped up a sloping lot to ours, the farthest back and highest. Our patio became my office away from the main office and my favorite place to work. There were plants and flowers all around, and the scent of jasmine and other blossoms filled the air. After all those years in places with miserable weather, California felt like getting out of prison, and I never went indoors unless I had to. I used to tell people I wouldn't mind living in a tent, and I meant it. In this house, where we moved from Annie's apartment, Betty made me a wonderful home office, but I never used it. I worked at a big glass table under an acacia tree. These days I favor a second-story patio overlooking the back yard, which we filled with wonderful plants.

I did all my work on this book outside.

It was a good thing I loved fresh air, because we barely had room to turn around in our place on Beverly Glen. Invite in a couple of bruisers like Arnold, and we had wall-to-wall people. Nobody minded, though, and I never missed the things we didn't have, including floorspace.

We really dwell in the brain and in the heart, and the more you put in them, the bigger they grow. And without a mind fully engaged and energy and purpose and without a full heart, the biggest mansion and all the world's riches are less than nothing.

You can quote me.

On Beverly Glen, my favorite people in the world came and went all the time. Right down the steps we had Aunt Annie. She came from the State of Maine and was somewhat reserved and careful with money in the New England manner. Annie spoke her mind and took nonsense from nobody, but to us she was so generous. She wouldn't take rent for the apartment and didn't want a salary for working at the Santa Monica office. The one time she accepted some of my money, I didn't give her any choice. It happened right before we moved. Annie, then a widow more than 70 years old, looked great for her age and always dressed like a lady, conservatively but very fashionably. For some reason, though, she paid no attention to her hair. One day Russ Warner, another of our great West Coast physique photographers, who worked in our office, called up and yelled, "Joe, you've got to tell Annie to do something about her hair. It looks like she combs it with an eggbeater!"

Something did have to be done, because Annie met the public as a receptionist. I had somebody set up an appointment for her at a beauty salon and insisted that she go once a week on company time and at my expense. Those hairdos cost all of $5 or $6 apiece, but every week she griped about wasting my money. That was Annie. She stayed sharp until shortly before she died, just a few months short of her 108th birthday. Speaking at her memorial service, I said she was more of a mother to me than my own mother.

Every day I also saw Betty's father, Andy, who had an apartment in a building next door to ours. He lived in Los Angeles so Betty could help him recover from a stroke he suffered at his home in San Jose. Andy loved to see me after I got home and hear all about what happened that day. I always wanted to hear from him about the events of the world, which he followed very closely. What Andy really wanted, I think, was to exercise his intellect, and I was his workout buddy. We shared interests in politics, history, philosophy, religion. We'd talk and talk and, whatever the subject, he had something intelligent to say. On only two subjects did our interests diverge—sports and horticulture. Andy was an absolute expert in both, but I never had the luxury of leisure time for such outside pursuits.

And on Beverly Glen we saw more and more of Betty's niece Thresa, who was only about 10 years old when we came to Los Angeles. The poor little girl, who lived in San Jose, had a rotten home life. It broke her heart when Andy moved south because he had watched out for her and gave her love and stability. On school breaks and vacations, she came down to be with her grandfather and with Betty, who has a wonderful way with kids. She did goofy girl stuff with Thresa all day long. I'd come home from the office, head full of pressing business like I was carrying the weight of the world, and there they'd be, having an imaginary tea party or some crazy thing. One time they had our Siamese cat Tiger wearing a little dress and a hat.

"Betty, what in the world are you doing with my cat?" I yelled, but then I laughed all night about Betty and the kid and Tiger.

History really does repeat itself. Betty did for her niece Thresa exactly what Aunt Annie once did for Betty. She took the place of a mother incapable of mothering.

Thresa says I wasn't so good with younger children—my brother Ben's three sons would say the same thing. But as Thresa grew up, she came to appreciate how I pushed her to use her mind to the fullest and question and challenge every idea she came across. Betty must have provided what the girl needed from a mother figure, because Thresa became a terrific mother herself and an intelligent and beautiful person, so full of warmth. "Snagglepuss," she calls me, and always pets me and makes a fuss.

I love it.

After we bought our home, Annie moved in, although she kept her apartment to the end of her life to preserve her feeling of independence. Later, when she was in her teens, Thresa would move in with us, too. We had meant for Andy to live with us—in fact we bought this house with him in mind—but the poor guy died just before we moved from the apartment.

Never will I forget looking up from my table on the patio and seeing Arnold coming to see me—first head, then shoulders, then the whole man in view as he climbed the steps. He and the other guys came around all the time. We always had some kind of business, and the bodybuilders wanted to be part of the family feeling and hominess. They were, after all, still young and thousands of miles from their own homes and their people.

Run into one of those muscle men in an alley and you'd be scared out of your mind, but at our place they were perfect gentlemen. Dave Draper was a gentle soul, so quiet and mild mannered. Franco Columbu overflowed with Italian warmth. You couldn't help but love the guy, and he and Arnold went together like coffee and cream, forever playing tricks and making jokes. They're still best buddies. Just the other day they stayed up till two o'clock in the morning playing chess. A few hours later Arnold was up and sharp as a tack for important government meetings.

What was golden about the Golden Age? Everything, I'd have to say. The people. The place. The time. Things came together at just the right moment in the history of bodybuilding. The sport, thanks mostly to Joe and Ben Weider, had emerged from the shadows, gaining respectability and growing and bringing in more money so the top guys could earn a few bucks to support themselves. The money still was pretty small potatoes, though. If you got into the game, you did so because you loved it and believed in it. Everybody was a true believer—the guys, my photographers, my writers. God knows I believed, maybe more than anybody. Belief bound us all together. The bodybuilders were more like teammates than competitors going after the same titles and prizes. Arnold captained the team, and I was the owner/manager. But even though I signed the checks, devotion to bodybuilding equalized us. We were a band of brothers.

And our band was merry and carefree. There was something very special about that group in California. Not one bad apple in the bunch, and we got such a kick out of being together. We'd all eat at a deli called Zucky's on Wilshire Boulevard, a few doors from our Santa Monica office, and we socialized at each other's homes.

Arnold began a tradition of hosting a birthday party for himself, Franco, Betty, and a few of the bodybuilders, all born in the month of August. Leo parties, Arnold called them, because that was everybody's astrological birth sign. He'd buy all the food himself and lay out wonderful spreads of cold cuts. Those parties went on for years and years. Maybe they'll start up again when Arnold comes home from Sacramento. I know he hasn't forgotten. On Betty's most recent birthday he said he'd come over, but then his aides kept calling to push back his arrival time because he was tied up in meetings with the public employee union and he was running late. Finally he called Betty himself and said we should go on to the restaurant, he'd meet us there. We went and Betty told the maitre d' to have an extra place at the table.

"Come on, Betty, it's late," I said, "He isn't going to make it."

But he did make it. He had to be on a plane before dawn to fly to Boston and make a speech, but he acted like he had all the time in the world. He and Betty talked and talked about the birthday parties of years past. He even got a little teary-eyed.

My God, the fun we used to have.

Even work was like a party. For photo shoots we'd go out for breakfast, then pile into cars to take off for the beach or some pinnacle up in the mountains by Malibu. That was serious business—my magazines lived or died by the quality and impact of pictures—but the laughter never stopped. I just looked at an old shot of Art Zeller kneeling on a big rock and salaaming. Supposedly he was praying to the sun god to make the clouds go away—we needed sun to make shadows and display the guys' muscle definition.

The sun did burn through that day. Whatever we needed, California provided—good light, year-round warmth, every kind of scenery you could think of, and beautiful people. I'll never forget one shoot we had at the beach. Betty was there, and we were supposed to have two other models, but they went to the wrong spot. I thought they didn't show up for the job and got madder and madder while we stood around. Finally I said, "That's it. Let's go."

"Joe, wait," Arnold said.

"Wait for what? The girls aren't coming," I said.

"Just tell me what you need," he said.

What I needed, obviously, was a couple of fabulous-looking, sexy girls who knew how to pose for pictures.

"Don't go anywhere," Arnold said and took off down the beach.

Pretty soon up he walked with a blonde on one arm, a brunette on the other. The girls were gorgeous and good in front of the camera. Where else but California could a guy find such people in a few minutes' time? And who else but Arnold could talk them into coming along and working with absolute strangers?

Arnold didn't always play the hero. On one of his first shoots on the beach he showed up without posing trunks. I asked him how the hell we were supposed to work if he didn't have anything to wear and sent him to downtown Santa

Monica to buy something. I think he actually ran home for his own trunks. He never made that mistake again.

I pushed the people on photo shoots the way I pushed guys in the gym, always wanting more, more, faster, faster. One day we were out on the beach doing a cover. Art shot, and one or more of the guys—I forget who—modeled. Betty was also modeling that day. Art went through roll after roll of film while I directed. Things looked pretty good, but not great, until suddenly I saw exactly what I wanted. The light, the background, people's positions, their expressions, were perfect.

I waved my arms and yelled, "That's it! Take the picture, Art!"

Art didn't do anything.

"Art, come on," I said. "Take the goddam picture!"

"Joe," he said, "there's no film in the camera"

"I don't care," I yelled. "Take the picture anyway."

I loved everything I did in my businesses, but I think I loved photo shoots best. That's where everything I lived and worked for came together. I could turn loose the artist inside me, creating images as beautiful and powerful as those I saw in my head. Living art, that's what I created, and the photographer recorded it for all time. There was nothing in the world like seeing before my eyes an image of human strength, health, beauty, and happiness—and knowing that my readers would see the same thing and be inspired.

Now and again, Betty gave me grief for directing all those photo shoots. She asked me if I thought the guy who ran *Time* or *Life* or any other big magazine went out with the troops taking pictures. Of course they didn't, but so what?

I did more than direct, actually. Often at shoots I'd rub on the guys' body oil, which had to be done just right so coverage was perfectly even and not too heavy or light. I guarantee that no other guy in my position would do such a thing.

Besides having a patron and protector, a perfect locale and moment in history, our Golden Age had a heroic figure who embodied its spirit—our prince, our knight in shining armor, you might say. I refer, of course, to Arnold Schwarzenegger, the champion who made the age more golden.

Arnold, to his credit, never got complacent through his six back-to-back Mr. Olympia victories. Every year he got stronger and better. In '72, Sergio Oliva returned to the contest in fantastic shape, better than when he beat Arnold three years before. But Arnold, too, had improved. That contest was pretty much the end for The Myth. Then came a string of terrific bodybuilders who couldn't get past Arnold. By contest day, he always had what military people call overwhelming superiority. Never have I known a bodybuilder who prepared himself like Arnold did. He always showed up with what he needed, physique-wise, and he knew how to wow everybody with what he had. But he went way beyond that, making winning a science. Arnold studied the other guys until he knew their strong points and weak points better than they did. He could do their routines, move by move, and he knew how to get under their skin and mess up their self-confidence.

Truth be told, Arnold's wins were pretty predictable, but he never made them seem that way. He had a knack for introducing some kind of drama and suspense to keep the fans stirred up. Maybe he'd talk up a rivalry or create doubt that he'd be in good shape. Always he managed to put on a show and keep the attention on himself.

Arnold didn't need anybody to teach him to be competitive. He's that way by nature, more than anybody I know. I think, though, that he learned a lot from me about studying his opponents top to bottom. The more you observe, and stack up the other guy's strengths and weaknesses against your own, the more keys to victory are in your hand—that was my lesson for Arnold.

As an illustration I told him about my wrestling at Johnnie Young's gym back in Montreal. I didn't even have to see a guy wrestle to develop a winning strategy. I just looked at his physique and put my knowledge of the human body to work. To give a very simple example: A guy with huge upper-body musculature might have been stronger than me, but he was also vulnerable to low-level attack because he was top-heavy. So I'd go for the legs to take him down.

Like any ambitious guy who starts out broke, Arnold wanted to establish himself financially. For that he needed more than the basics I provided—housing, car, and walking-around money. I helped him create his own training booklets and sell them mail order. One of my editors put the words on paper for him, and he got free ad space in the magazines. At the outset, however, Arnold needed more than free ads and a ghost writer. He needed a crash course in how to communicate.

You would not believe the stuff he wanted to put out. That guy, the most exciting bodybuilder of the century, who could cause an uproar just by walking out on stage, turned out copy with no personality at all. Such-and-such an exercise promotes growth in such-and-such a muscle, blah blah blah...

"Come on, Arnold," I said. "The guys want a friend, not a schoolteacher. Talk to them. Tell them what you do and how it benefits you."

Then and there I instructed Arnold in the Weider Principles of Communication.

Nobody gets worked up about generalities, however true.

If you want a guy to pay attention and do what you're telling him, the message has to be personal and specific.

Me to you.

Using the communication techniques that I taught Arnold Schwarzenegger, I became a publishing magnate and built huge allied companies. I never would have done a tenth as much if I went around spouting general truths instead of singling out individual guys, one guy at a time, and telling each one how to get something he wanted.

It all comes down to human nature. The reader of a muscle magazine or training book—or anybody else reading or listening or watching any kind of how-to—is selfish. I don't mean this in a derogatory way. I mean that people expect a fair return on investment. Nobody will spend his money—not more than once, anyway—and devote time and attention if you don't answer this question: What's in it for me?

In my branch of publishing, there's another question: Who are you, that I should pay attention and follow your advice?

Our guys want the voice of authority and experience. They want to sit at the feet of their heroes, the big-name muscle men. The bigger the name and fame, the more guys credit the information and follow it. Guys were dying for Arnold's how-to stuff because they wanted to be like Arnold.

The exact same information credited to some skinny writer wouldn't have meant a thing.

As always, Arnold listened and learned. He still communicates the way he was taught, with great flair. To become governor of California, he had to reach out to people the way he reached out to guys who wanted bigger biceps and calves—one at a time; as a friend who understands and wants what you want; as a hero; and as a big, strong man who speaks the truth and will always look out for you. It's no coincidence that a state in terrible fiscal trouble turned to an individual of great physical power and personal force. That, too, is human nature.

Arnold likes to talk about a little brick-laying business he set up with his buddy Franco in their early days in America. That's mostly because he likes telling funny stories about it—two foreign muscle men hustling little old ladies to fix their chimneys, and so on. In fact, their deal didn't amount to much. Arnold made his money from bodybuilding. His mail-order stuff was a hit, and he did very well guest posing at contests and giving training seminars that I helped him set up. Almost every weekend he flew off somewhere to earn a few more bucks. Unlike other young guys, he didn't throw money away on fancy cars or silly things to show off his success. He put away every dollar he could. Meanwhile, he took business courses in college.

As soon as his savings built up, Arnold came to me for advice. He told me he wanted to use his capital to go into business and asked what would be the best kind of venture for him.

"Arnold," I said, "forget it. You already have a business—being a star."

I told him that running his own company would eat him alive. It would distract him and sap his energy. All the time, he'd have problems with this supplier and that customer, and the Harvard and Yale guys he hired to run things would talk down to him and give him grief.

"You don't need that," I said. "What you want to do is buy property. Find a building you like in a good area. Put your money down, and the property will increase in value. You just collect the rent, and you'll have the time to concentrate on your bodybuilding career and everything you want to do with your life."

Arnold used his money—$30,000 or so—and a $10,000 loan from me and bought an apartment building in Santa Monica. I got my money back within six months. In a few more years, Arnold had real estate investments worth millions.

More than anything, Arnold wanted to be a Hollywood star. After *Hercules in New York,* he played a gangland thug in a detective movie, the sort of bit part muscle men got all along. But then bigger things started to happen. Arnold was featured in a sort of art book about bodybuilding called *Pumping Iron,* by George Butler and Charles Gaines, a writer who loved and understood bodybuilding. This was the first high-class tribute to our sport from the outside. The book caught on with high-brow types, and Arnold later posed in a special art museum exhibition in New York City. Arnold got his first big movie part in *Stay Hungry,* based on a novel by Gaines. He played a guy much like himself, a European bodybuilder training in the U.S. He trained to act the same way he prepared for his bodybuilding contests, taking a crash course from the famous acting teacher Eric Morris. The filming of *Stay Hungry* started in the spring of 1975 and went on through the months when all the guys pushed to get ready for the Mr. Olympia contest in the fall, to be held in Pretoria, South Africa. Word went around that Arnold might not be in top shape for the contest because the movie work distracted him from training.

Arnold himself dramatized the situation by talking up Lou Ferrigno, supposedly his most dangerous rival. Lou later became famous playing the big green monster in *The Incredible Hulk* show on TV. He was a monster in real life, too—6 foot 5, with colossal muscle mass. I mean monstrous in stature only. Lou's a very gentle giant, a sweetheart.

In '75, Lou was something to behold onstage, but he didn't have the cuts and finish to take on Arnold. In truth, there was no threat to Arnold. And there wasn't any doubt about his condition. Because we kept in close touch, I knew Arnold was going to South Africa in absolutely top form. Predictably, he won in a walk, brushing off challenges from European sensation Serge Nubret, a Frenchman of African ancestry who had a V-taper to rival Sergio Oliva's, and a surprisingly good showing by Franco Columbu.

After his win, Arnold announced his retirement from competitive bodybuilding. Five years later he would make a surprise comeback, but I think he sincerely meant to quit. In a way Arnold never stopped winning in Pretoria. To this day people watch him train and beat the other guys in the documentary film about the '75 Mr. Olympia, *Pumping Iron,* made by the same two guys who put out the book. Butler and Gaines must have been very glad the only natural-born movie star in the contest won. I'm sure they counted on it when they decided to make their film.

After the '75 Olympia, Arnold went into partnership with Jim Lorimer of Columbus, Ohio, to put on bodybuilding shows. The year after he won Mr. Olympia, he co-produced it. For some years, Jim and Arnold put on Olympias, but then we all made a strategic decision to create two major annual events about six months apart. Every spring, Arnold and his partner stage the Arnold Classic in Columbus. The Mr. Olympia comes every fall.

After he got his start as a contest producer, Arnold's movies hit the screens. Critics praised his acting in *Stay Hungry,* and he won an award as best male newcomer at the Golden Globes. The movie didn't do very well, though. It was *Pumping Iron,* where Arnold didn't act at all, that propelled him toward stardom. People didn't care about the quality of any dramatic performance. They loved Arnold being Arnold.

Looking back, it's easy to think it was all a foregone conclusion, that Arnold was destined to reach the heights. But there are no foregone conclusions. Arnold made himself. He built his stardom the way he built his body, never sparing himself. Nobody but Arnold took Arnold to the top.

Just think about all his achievements in just seven years after he showed up in Miami, a kid from Austria who could barely speak English and didn't know how to act in polite company. He dominated our sport, showing power and perfection in muscular development like the world had never seen. He went to college. He acquired property. He got a start in movies and used his bodybuilding as a stepping-stone to stardom. He became a contest producer. A lesser man would have been all used up by any one of these challenges. But the guy never ran out of energy. He never quit charging ahead.

The Golden Age of Bodybuilding also was golden for me personally, because of my stage of life.

You don't hear it so much any more, but people used to talk about reaching the prime of life. They didn't mean youth or young adulthood. They meant the period when you come to a ripening and fullness. All your years give you knowledge and strength, but don't yet weigh you down and wear you down. And you're still a person of physical prowess—not as in youth, but the power of mind and spirit more than compensates.

Well, just then I was coming into my prime. I was in my fifties, and I felt fantastic. I could work other people into the ground. I could still throw around heavy weights that impressed even the champion bodybuilders.

At the same age a guy who didn't take care of himself—didn't exercise, didn't watch his diet, didn't work with purpose and conviction—would fall apart, old before his time.

Here's something you should consider: At the prime of life, you are your own creation. If you're strong and healthy, you worked for it. What powers you possess, you developed and earned. Of course you can't get away from genetics, which can hurt you or even kill you, but everything else is in your own hands.

I can't think of a better way to prepare for this stage of life than bodybuilding, which really builds your entire being. It preserves you from bodily decay, increases all your potentialities and powers, and keeps your spirits high. As Arnold said in the preface to this book, the muscles are there for the world to see, but bodybuilding does much, much more. I offer myself and my story as proof.

Not too long ago, Arnold sent me a thank-you note for a little gift I sent. In it he wrote, "Wouldn't it be great if we could go back to those golden years and freeze time?"

You bet it would be great to live in that wonderful time forever.

There's something I miss even more than my strength and vigor. Just talking about it to friends the other day, I almost broke down and cried. More than anything, I miss being with the guys—my guys, the bodybuilders.

This I know. If we did go back to the 1970s, Arnold would do one thing differently. He'd be more appreciative in public about all I did to help him. For many years now, Arnold has told anybody and everybody about my role in his life. For a while though, as he established himself outside of bodybuilding and became a Hollywood star, he had a hard time saying my name with gratitude and respect. Sometimes he didn't say my name at all.

Right before the '75 Mr. Olympia, *Sports Illustrated* ran a long profile, one of Arnold's first big write-ups in a mainstream magazine. In general, a pretty good story, I thought, except toward the end Arnold took some shots at me and my magazines. "Comic books," he called them and told the reporter they embarrassed him. He said he wanted to run his own magazines because he could do better.

Other Weider people had fits. Not me. I thought to myself, that's just Arnold. You can't take everything young guys say seriously because they like to shoot off their mouths. Besides that, I knew—probably more than Arnold himself knew—where such remarks came from. To truly come into his own, a man sometimes strikes out at those who helped him because a feeling of indebtedness threatens his sense of independence and personal power, and he can't be sure what's truly his. The situation also was a bit like what Freud wrote about—the son sees his father as a rival and wants to knock him out of power and take over. As son-figure and father-figure, Arnold and I had such psychological stuff. Because I had studied the human mind and seen more of life, I recognized it for what it was. And it didn't really bother me.

Later, however, came a slight that I had to answer in public.

It happened when *Pumping Iron* came out, and Arnold's star was on the rise. One night he appeared on *The Tonight Show* with Johnny Carson.

In general, I considered TV to be a complete waste of time, but that night I sat down and watched. It made me very proud to see Arnold dressed up and looking sharp and joking around like a showbiz pro. And my ears pricked up when Johnny Carson asked how Arnold came to America and if somebody helped him out and showed him the way to the top in bodybuilding. The way the questions went, I think maybe Carson knew something about me and wanted to hear the full story. I wanted to hear it even more. For some time I'd been asking Arnold why, in his interviews, he never put in a good word about me. He always told me that he never had the chance because nobody asked the right questions. Well, here was the question, and Arnold's big chance to set the record straight.

I about fell out of my chair when he said no, nobody helped him—he did it all on his own. With a perfectly straight face he told about coming to New York City on his own dime as a tourist. Somehow the producer of the Hercules movie saw him and was very impressed, and that's how he was discovered.

Hearing that cock-and-bull story, I felt very let down. Still, I might have let the whole thing slide except it happened in front of millions of people—and except for Betty's aunt, who didn't let anything slide.

Soon after the TV appearance, Arnold came over to the house and bumped into Annie.

"How's my favorite real estate lady?" he said. This was a standing joke because they always talked about property investments.

"Why did you lie?" Annie said, voice full of accusation.

Arnold, I'm sure, had no idea what got into her, not at first.

"On TV, you told Johnny Carson you came on a tour!" Annie said. "I sent you your ticket to America!"

Arnold said people wanted something more entertaining than what really happened, so he made up the story.

Betty was there, too.

Betty said, "Oh, Annie, he just wanted to be like Mark Twain. He said, 'Never let the truth stand in the way of a good story.'"

Arnold laughed and said, "Say that again, Betty. I love it!"

I missed most of this, thank God. On the other hand, what a thing to behold—a lady pushing 80, going after Arnold like a wild animal.

I expressed my own feelings in an editorial in *Muscle Builder/Power* headlined "Thanks is Not a Four-Letter Word." I wrote that stars add to their stature when they appear humble and express thanks to those who help them. I also wrote that Arnold and I were still good friends and that we worked together very often. I closed by expressing the idea that bodybuilding should be a character-builder in all of life. In Arnold's case, that turned out to be absolutely true.

Two signs of success I still didn't have: a briefcase and a personal secretary.

It bothered some people to see me carry paperwork to and from the office in bags and boxes, and now and again somebody gave me a briefcase, thinking I would change my ways. Once Betty gave me a really swanky case, which I tried but quit using. Regular executive-type briefcases weren't big enough for the loads of work I carried around. And they weren't built for the abuse I dished out.

Aunt Annie, God bless her, finally gave me something I could use. She saw a Samsonite commercial on TV and figured if people could throw the company's briefcases out of planes and run them over with trucks, they were tough enough for Joe Weider. Annie got me Samsonsite's biggest model, like a small-sized suitcase. I used that case for years and years. I'd still have it if it didn't get swiped at the Miami Airport.

The secretary was a lot like the briefcase. I didn't see the need, even with paper piling up at home and my office and people yelling that I needed somebody to help me get organized. Finally, though, I recognized that help really was necessary.

My pick for secretary was Anneliese Leyk, pushing 40 years old and from Germany. Much later, when she was like a member of the family, Anneliese said that she was extremely nervous at her job interview. She was somewhat frightened by my physical presence and forceful manner. A muscle-man executive was something new to her. She didn't know what to make of muscle men, period—

the guys around the office and the big pictures on the walls. But she took the job, which made me glad because I had a good feeling about her.

Of all the people I hired, Anneliese was one of the greats. Somehow we just clicked, like we were made to work together—the Polish-Canadian Jew and the German. She made my concerns her own and acted like company expenditures came out of her own pocket. And my God, was she Germanic—by the book, organized, with absolutely no tolerance for lack of discipline or laziness. I have to laugh thinking about her being scared of me, because people were scared of her. Besides being a fantastic secretary and bringing order out of chaos, Anneliese was like a watchdog, always vigilant and watching for trouble. She had a nose for sniffing out irregularities and monkey business like nobody I ever knew.

I entrusted Anneliese with things far beyond normal secretarial duties. In '75, I was too busy to take off and go to the Mr. Olympia in South Africa, even though it was a big deal for Arnold and I was to receive a special I.F.B.B. award. "If you can't go, send me," Anneliese said. At first she thought I was kidding when I said fine, buy your tickets. She went and accepted the award on my behalf.

Once I tried to advance her money to make a down payment on a house. She could pay me back later. "Nope," she said to me. "If I can't do it myself, I don't want it." The woman was proud, proud, proud. And there was no use trying to force a gift on her. When she put her foot down, that was that.

Betty got to love and appreciate Anneliese as much as I did, and she continued to work with us even after she reached retirement age and moved to Las Vegas. She worked right up to the point that cancer made her too sick, and then killed her. I'm glad to say we stood by her when things got rough, the way she stood by us. I think our support meant a lot because she never married and we were the family she needed.

My new helpmate at the office got there just in time, because things started to take off. Equipment sales were strong, and the Weider nutrition products flew out of the warehouses. Compared to today's sophisticated supplements—amino acids, creatine, herbal extracts, metabolytes—our stuff was still pretty simple. But it was the purest and best on the market, and I had a fantastic time with creative presentation and marketing. I taste-tested every product and worked as hard on the labels as I did on magazine covers. Besides the punchy and colorful graphics, I gave everything exciting names. "Weider Wildcats" was my favorite, with images of powerful cats to make the words come alive. Not long ago I wanted so much to see one particular label, which featured Betty and Frank Zane. I used to have the things by the thousands, but not one could be found here or down at the office. To get my label, I had somebody buy a mint-condition, unopened can of Weider Super Pro 101 on e-Bay. It cost $125!

We had a runaway hit in equipment—the Five-Minute Body Shaper—that became the best-selling Weider product of all time. It was ingenious, like a home gym you could hold in your hand. Basically, a Body Shaper consisted of two lengths of rope with loop-handles at their ends. Both ropes passed through little pulleys, which hung together from a small piece you attached to a doorknob. Lying on the floor, you put your hands in the loops at the end of each rope, feet at the other end, and worked the limbs in opposition. The Body Shaper functioned as a multi-position cable machine, with the resistance coming from the person exercising. Full motion gave full exercise benefits—unlike tensing muscles in a fixed position, as in isometrics or Charles Atlas' Dynamic Tension. This was no substitute for working with weights, but for those with more modest goals, like slimming and toning, the Body Shaper helped to do the trick.

At first I pitched ads to guys using bodybuilder endorsements, but then I realized the Body Shaper was more of a woman's product. It was small and non-intimidating. You could use it at home in privacy, then hide it away in a drawer. The exercises were as easy or hard as you wanted to make them. And it provided the benefits that most women wanted—trimming and sculpting, rather than building up strength and bulk.

I happened to be married to the ideal celebrity endorser. Betty, then in her forties but still the star Weider female model, had kept her famous hourglass figure and her ability to make people stop and stare. I made her image a central part of the Body Shaper's graphical presentation, designing a beautiful new box with a picture of her using the product. She also appeared all through the photo-illustrated instruction book.

Recognizing we could sell to a much wider public, we decided to make a TV commercial starring Betty. The producer loved her looks and her poise and professionalism on camera, but her brains got in the way. In everyday speech, Betty has perfect elocution and speaks in a thoughtful, precise manner. When she rehearsed her lines in her natural voice, the producer broke in and yelled, "Stop, stop! You're too elegant, too much of a lady. We are not selling Rolls Royces!"

The guy explained that Betty had to appeal to millions of everyday housewives sitting on their couches and eating potato chips. She had to come across like a friend, like somebody who could sit down next to them, with no barriers or social discomfort. If anything, they should feel smarter than her.

Betty, in other words, had to be the dumb blonde she was not. She tried and tried but couldn't hit the right note. You could see the producer getting exasperated.

We happened to be meeting at home, in the pool house, and our cat Tiger came through the room.

"Hi, Tigie," Betty said, "How are you doing? You want to be on TV?"

She used a voice she uses only with the cats, cooing and cute, like talking to a baby.

"That's it!" the producer said. "That's exactly what I want."

He told Betty to put Tiger up in the camera lens, mentally speaking, and speak her lines to the cat. Betty said she felt like a complete idiot, but she did what the TV guy said.

Who knows what would have happened if we rehearsed at somebody's office where there wasn't a cat.

Betty's commercial was a smash hit. Her lines—"I have a Weider body. Don't you want a Weider body, too?"—became famous, and people all over said them, trying to sound flirty and cute like Betty. She got invitations to appear on TV, including Johnny Carson's show. She turned the invitations down because she wasn't anything like the person in the commercial.

Body Shaper sales went through the roof. A boat-building company got mad at me because I used up the polypropylene rope that it needed, too. I must have sold 20 million units. The Body Shaper also became the centerpiece of our Betty Weider Body Persuasion line of exercise products for consumers, which were featured in the largest department stores around the country. We did more TV ads, too. That was our first play in products sold retail to the general population, and it did very, very well. You could say Betty Weider Body Persuasion took us from niche business to big business.

We should have been booming, but something wasn't right.

All along, Anneliese told me she didn't trust some of my top guys on the business side, who approved expenditures that didn't make sense, like a trade show display that was way too expensive, and huge, lavish parties that cost a fortune. I had my own reasons to be suspicious, but I gave the guys in question the benefit of the doubt. This is my nature. I am a trusting individual, and I always try to see the good in others. I keep seeing the good until the bad jumps out. I finally saw the light when the guys throwing company money around tried to talk me into taking a big bank loan we supposedly needed. They wanted me to guarantee the loan with my magazines. This gave me a terrific shock. I said no, absolutely not, I would not sign for a loan, and I would never, ever put my magazines—my babies, the heart and soul of the Weider enterprises and of all of bodybuilding—in jeopardy.

Finally I had to face the facts. Either I had guys who mismanaged company resources or I was getting flat-out robbed. It really didn't matter which.

It still makes me mad to think about what happened. I hate telling about it because I don't want people to think I was an idiot. I should have watched more closely. I should have counted the beans. I should have, except I couldn't be a bean-counter and fulfill my creative responsibilities. Always I had to be the voice of Weider, to create the look of Weider, to advance the cause of bodybuilding, fitness, and health. The magazines drove all our businesses, and they needed my constant attention, as did the ads, the product labels, and the new stuff coming out all the time. The bodybuilders, too, needed the Joe Weider touch, so we'd have the greatest possible champions to admire and learn from, who would use and endorse our products. Nobody in the world could do all that and count the beans.

So we needed somebody to come in, straighten out the books, and clean house. Ben happened to know the right man for the job up in Montreal. This was Allen Dalfen, a young man making a success of himself in the food business. He came up a lot like the Weider Brothers, the hard way, all on his own. More than that, he was a man of probity and character.

Before we could get a new regime, we had to get rid of the old one, starting with the top guy. Ben came down to Los Angeles to do the actual firing. He arranged things very carefully, the way he arranged delicate diplomatic meetings all over the world. Ben set up the meeting at a fancy restaurant, which lessened the chances that there would be some kind of scene or confrontation. As added insurance, Ben hired a security man who wore plain clothes and observed from a distance.

The security man watched the meeting, which went very smoothly, so much so that he misunderstood who was who. Halfway through lunch, he came over and said, "Mr. Weider, where's this nutcase I'm supposed to watch out for? Do you think maybe he won't show?"

The family still laughs about the security man's goof.

Why didn't I fire that guy myself? I didn't because I couldn't, that's why. I never could fire anybody. Not if they stole, were lazy or incompetent, or got screwed up on booze or drugs. Sometimes I was right to hang on to people, because they really were good and their problems didn't last. But it wasn't any different for me with crooks and back-stabbers. I couldn't get rid of them, either. When a person needed firing, I had somebody else do it.

I think I know why I never had the stomach to let people go. It goes back to 1935 in Montreal, when I was a kid out on the streets, wanting a job, needing a job, and there were no jobs to be had. Twice I walked around the city knocking on doors. Every "no," every turndown, made me feel more helpless, humiliated, more forlorn, and devoid of hope. Never did the world seem so cruel and cold. I never want to live through such a time again. I guess I don't want anybody else to live through it, either. On a deep, deep level, taking away a guy's job feels to me like killing him. That's just how it is, even with somebody who betrayed my trust. All my life I've been a tough guy and a fighter, but I cannot shut the door on another human being.

CHAPTER TEN

OSCAR'S GOLDEN KEY

Ben Weider

Defining Moment

The Olympic Dream started to become the Olympic Reality because of the timely intercession of Oscar State, the best friend I ever had and the best friend our sport ever had.

To tell the story, we must go back to the year 1968.

These days people take it for granted that one legitimate worldwide sports federation governs bodybuilding, but in the 1960s there were two international governing bodies. Besides the IFBB, the International Weightlifting Federation also sanctioned bodybuilding competitions, including its own Mr. Universe. In terms of athletic talent and quality of its competitions, IWF bodybuilding was not in the same league as the IFBB or, for that matter, our non-international rivals, Bob Hoffman's AAU committee in the U.S. and Oscar Heidenstam's NABBA in Britain. But the IWF itself commanded a great deal of respect. It was a long-established organization representing a sport of unquestioned legitimacy, which had been part of the Olympics since the revival of the Games in 1896.

Fortunately for both our sports, the weightlifting federation had a leader who recognized that the time had come for bodybuilding to stand on its own, fully independent and self-governing. This forward-thinking sports administrator was none other than Oscar State. Though his title was general secretary, he was *de facto* head of the IWF because the president took a less than active role in the federation's affairs.

It was in 1968 that Oscar took me aside and said, "Ben, I have some important news for you. The IWF is about to withdraw from its involvement with bodybuilding."

This news was a bombshell. It meant that the IFBB had an opportunity to consolidate a position as the one and only international federation for our sport. It also meant that a new group of national bodybuilding committees formerly under the IWF could be brought into our federation.

Here was a moment of great opportunity. But, as Oscar told me in no uncertain terms, it also had to be a moment of great change.

"Listen to me very carefully," my friend said. "You've got to start running the IFBB like a real sports federation. If you don't put your house in order, the IWF bodybuilding people won't take you seriously and join. And the Olympic Committee will never even consider your bid for recognition."

Oscar continued, "A federation cannot be a personal fiefdom. You must make it a democracy, and you and all of the federation executives must stand for election."

I knew he was 100 percent right, but it took a lot of discussion for me to fully accept what he said and act upon it. For more than 20 years I had been the IFBB's benevolent presidential dictator, free to make unilateral decisions for the good of the federation and care for and look out for it as I saw fit. I could comb the world for the best people to work with. If I liked you and trusted you, you were in, and if I discovered I was wrong about you, you were out. It was hard to give up such prerogatives and hard to think about losing the presidency of a federation I founded and worked so hard to build up, if the membership so decided.

"Ben, you have done wonderful work and laid a solid foundation," Oscar said. "Now it is time to build on that foundation."

I pondered his words and answered, "You are right, Oscar. How do we start?"

We rolled up our sleeves and went to work on a constitution. Oscar, who had just retired from teaching school, plunged into this project. With his extensive experience in sports administration, along with a head for detail and an incredible capacity for work, he drafted a document worthy of bodybuilding and equal to the best in all of organized sport. Because of all of the divisions and political complications in our sport, with the Arabs and Israelis at each other's throats, as were the black and white nations as well as the Communist and Capitalist countries, I decided to add a paragraph to our Constitution to prevent political and national disputes from entering into bodybuilding.

I am particularly proud of these sections from Article 7—General Provisions:

2. The IFBB forbids its membership from engaging in any racial, political or religious discussion, demonstration or act that may result, whether directly or indirectly, in the fostering of bias or prejudice between any of its members.

3. The IFBB does not distinguish or discriminate between individuals or countries for reasons of race, color, religion, or politics.

These provisions turned out to be vitally important in our dealings with certain oppressive governments.

Under the constitution, all IFBB officials would stand for election every four years, and each year the federation would convene an International Congress coinciding with the World Amateur Bodybuilding Championships. Year-round, an executive council would administer the federation and make decisions on its behalf. I, as president, would be obliged to discuss decisions and act with the approval of the executive council.

Through 1969 and into 1970, Oscar worked on the constitution, and he also created a rulebook for bodybuilding, up to the standards of other sports. He encouraged me to change the atmosphere and trappings of our competitive events. Among other things, he said we should drop all the "Mr." titles, Mr. Universe, Mr. World, Mr. Europe, and so forth.

"These are athletic competitions, not beauty pageants. We must present them in a serious manner," said Oscar.

Subsequently we did change our nomenclature, so, for example, our Mr. Universe contest became the World Amateur Bodybuilding Championships. The only remaining "Mr." is our Mr. Olympia, which somehow suits the grandeur of the event. Even Oscar never minded that.

In the autumn of 1970, 25 countries sent delegates who gathered at the federation's first thoroughly democratized International Congress, held that year in Belgrade, now in Serbia but then the capital of Yugoslavia. The delegates ratified the constitution and elected me president, as they have done ever since.

The IFBB now met the standards and technical requirements of international sports federations. I cannot overstate how important this was. It was as if Oscar handed me a golden key to open all the doors of international sport. Our sport and our federation would have kept growing without the changes that Oscar instigated, but we never would have gained acceptance and recognition from other sports organizations, including the Olympic committee. The popularity of bodybuilding, its merits as a sport, would not have mattered if our federation failed to meet accepted international standards.

During this period Oscar and I became best friends. Working together deepened our mutual respect and affection, and we became a team, second in my life only to the two-man team of my brother Joe and me. It wasn't our style to display our feelings, but Oscar and I were as fond of each other as best friends could possibly be. Our friendship was also as productive as any I know. Given his tireless work and numerous contributions, our members would have backed Oscar's bid for a high post in the IFBB. But, for the time being, Oscar was content just to be a member of our federation and work behind the scenes. He had a heavy load of other commitments and duties, especially with the International Weightlifting Federation.

Also in 1970, the year of the IFBB's transformation, Oscar's contributions to sport earned him recognition from no less than the Queen of England, who awarded Oscar the Order of the British Empire (OBE).

Federation of Federations

Almost immediately, the key Oscar gave us opened a door of great importance. Our federation now qualified for admittance to the General Association of International Sports Federations (GAISF), a sort of super-federation that worked closely with the International Olympic Committee. Formed in 1967 at Lausanne, Switzerland, home of the IOC, the GAISF was born out of the need for international sports federations to communicate and cooperate and represent their collective interests to the Olympic authorities. The GAISF membership included representatives of both Olympic and non-Olympic sports. Once again Oscar, who was very actively involved with the GAISF, paved the way for our success. He helped prepare our application for membership, then helped me to gather support for approval, which had to be ratified by the federation's members.

What a great day that was, at the 1971 GAISF Congress, when we were voted in as full members. I wrote in that year's IFBB annual report to our members, "The sport of bodybuilding is finally on the same level as hockey, skiing, weightlifting, swimming, track and field, and so forth." Adding to our happiness was Oscar's election to general secretary of the GAISF, which brought him to a new height of influence in international sport.

After IFBB membership was formally approved, I was asked to speak a few words. Standing before the representatives and delegates of so many major sports, I could not have been more proud. But then I noticed something very peculiar going on in the front row of the audience. While I spoke, a man whispered to the people around him and gesticulated. He lifted one arm and flexed, and then pointed to his biceps and pointed to his head. He did this repeatedly with a sneer on his face. The implication was clear: He meant that the muscles in bodybuilders' arms were the same as the muscles in their heads. Bodybuilding, in other words, was for dummies.

I didn't get angry or let the pantomime distract me. Instead I took a good look at the fellow and made a mental note of where he sat. During a break between meeting sessions I found out from others this was Lt. Col. Rudyard P. Russell, an Englishman who was president of the International Boxing Federation. I also learned that Colonel Russell had been sitting next to Sir Stanley Rous, then-president of the International Football Federation, and Mrs. Inger K. Frith, who headed the International Archery Federation.

During the break I spotted Colonel Russell and introduced myself. Acting as if I had not noticed his antics, I asked if he'd like to join me at a table for coffee and, perhaps, one of the delicious Swiss pastries that were being served. The Colonel accepted my invitation, and we sat down and began to chat. I talked about what an honor it was to be accepted by the GAISF membership, and I talked about our sport and its enormous popularity and continuing meteoric growth. As I spoke, Colonel Russell became increasingly attentive and respectful. When the break was over, he seemed sympathetic to our cause. If he wasn't a complete convert, he at least left the table with an open mind.

The Colonel turned out to be a friend and supporter. If I'd confronted him about his rudeness I would have created an enemy, most likely forever. Always I take the friendly approach first and avoid unpleasantness unless there is absolutely no alternative, which is really quite rare. A lifetime of meeting people and working with them has taught me this: The way to get people on your side, is to let them know you're really on their side, and the way to get them to see things your way, is to first see things their way.

I found myself in very congenial company at the GAISF meeting. The president, Tom Keller, head of the International Rowing Federation, understood the value of bodybuilding in sports conditioning. Once a competitive rower in the U.S., he had trained with weights to increase his strength and stamina in his own sport. At the meeting I established friendly relations with dozens of sports officials. From then on, GAISF membership worked wonders for our prestige. Leading figures who would not have worked with the IFBB beforehand suddenly began to cooperate on the basis of mutual respect, and we had new friends at the very top of international sport.

And there was much more involved than prestige. The GAISF recognized one, and only one, international federation from each sport. So by letting us in, it effectively closed out any potential rivals on the international level. Our position would give us many advantages in years to come, especially as we struggled for control of bodybuilding within the United States. At first our rivals didn't recognize the importance of our GAISF membership, but in the long run it made all the difference in the world.

Meeting the IOC President

GAISF membership also gave me new access to the top officials of the International Olympic Committee. This immediately became apparent in 1971 in Lausanne, when GAISF delegates and IOC executives enjoyed a dinner cruise together on beautiful Lake Leman, also known as Lake Geneva. At my table sat Lord Killanin of Ireland, a member of the IOC executive committee and a favorite to become president after the retirement of then-president Avery Brundage, who was an American. Without monopolizing his time, I informed Lord Killanin about our sport and our federation, and he seemed impressed with the progress we had made.

After dinner I had a chance to converse one on one with IOC president Avery Brundage. I'd already met him, briefly, but I had an important issue I wanted to bring up in private. My opportunity came when I saw Mr. Brundage standing by himself out on deck, getting some fresh air. I was pretty much terrified of approaching this great personage, the IOC president since 1952 and a giant in the history of sport, but I summoned my courage and asked if I might have a moment of his time.

"Sure, son, come on over," Mr. Brundage said and smiled. He was a somewhat stout but fine-looking man, with a receding hairline and glasses that gave him a professorial look. While some found him rather cold, I sensed an inner warmth and liked him immediately.

"What's on your mind?" the president asked me, and I began to tell him about something that troubled me a great deal. I had learned that Bob Hoffman was trying to prejudice the IOC against me and our federation. He did it through a proxy, Gaston Barahona, president of Mexico's weightlifting federation, who was also involved in Mexico's National Olympic Committee. In Switzerland, Barahona told anybody and everybody that I was not sincere in my efforts and that the IFBB was not a serious sports federation. I heard that he had badmouthed me to President Brundage himself. I was deeply concerned that Hoffman's stooge would poison these people's minds just when we were ready to ask for Olympic recognition.

I spoke no more than a few sentences before Mr. Brundage cut me short and then chuckled and put a hand on my shoulder.

"Son, I've been through this more times than I can count," he said in the tone of a kindly uncle. "I pay no attention whatsoever to malicious gossip. I make my judgments based on fact, and I've heard only good things about you and your organization. My advice to you is to keep up the good work and ignore the troublemakers."

I can't tell you how much those kind words, which I sensed were sincere, relieved me. We spoke for another moment, during which I told Mr. Brundage a bit about the IFBB and our future plans. He congratulated me on my work, and I excused myself.

That same evening I met many of the most important people within the Olympic movement, doing my very best to make a favorable personal impression and to show our sport and our federation in the best light. I ate, drank, and socialized with the likes of Count Jean de Beaumont of France; Clifford Buck, then-president of the U.S. Olympic Committee; Dr. Wlodzimierz Reczek, sports minister for Poland and that country's IOC member; Prince Alexander de Merode, who was president of the IOC's Medical and Doping Commission; Professor Giuseppe La Cava of Italy, then the president of the International Federation of Sports Medicine, and others too numerous to name. My friendships with those dignitaries, which began that night on the beautiful lake in Switzerland, would prove invaluable in the long, long quest for Olympic recognition.

The Game of the Olympics

Our first formal application for recognition appeared on the agenda of the 1971 IOC meeting. No action was taken, but I was thrilled just to know that we were in a position to make a credible bid. I met with President Brundage a few more times before he stepped down in 1972. Each time I brought him up to date on our progress and told him more about bodybuilding as an athletic pursuit. Once a champion in track and field, President Brundage seemed quite interested in bodybuilding both as a sport and as an activity with tremendous benefits for everyone. Here was a man reputed to be difficult and unyielding, yet he was listening carefully to me and nodding his head in agreement with many of the points I made. I felt confident that we were making progress, and I remember thinking to myself, "It's only a matter of time."

I might have been startled to learn that the "matter of time" would be 26 more years, but I would have forged ahead anyway. I have had, to date, more than 30 meetings with four IOC presidents, including two with the current president, Dr. Jacques Rogge of Belgium. Always the goal was the same, formal recognition of our federation by the International Olympic Committee, which would mean we belonged to the most elite group in all of amateur sports.

Recognition would not, however, guarantee inclusion as a medal sport in the Olympic Games. That comes later, if it comes at all. The ultimate dream is to see my sport become part of the Games, but I never made that a primary goal because so much is in other people's hands. Mr. Brundage, for instance, was quite resistant to adding new sports to the program because of concerns about what he called "giantism" in the Games. Nevertheless, it was perfectly reasonable and realistic to work for IOC recognition, which would be an unmistakable sign that the sports world had finally granted to bodybuilding the respect and honor it deserves.

I should explain a bit about the game of the Olympic Games.

First, a sport is not a sport just because many millions of people love it and participate in it. To be recognized as a sport by the IOC or any other legitimate body, a sport must be governed by an international sports federation, which is made up of at least 70 representatives of national sports federations on all continents, and run according to democratic principles and procedures set forth in a constitution. As I have written, the reforms instituted with Oscar's help brought us in line with other world-class federations and met the requirements of the IOC.

To succeed in obtaining recognition, I had to lobby all the IOC members I could. I had to make personal contact with them and do all I could to educate them about bodybuilding and our federation, making it clear we represented a well-run sport that rightfully belonged in the Olympic family. To this end I would devote thousands of hours, make more overseas trips than I can count, and spend millions of my own dollars. Expending almost as much effort and time were trusted colleagues such as Oscar State and Paul Chua, our vice president for Asia, an invaluable friend and ally since about 1960, who deserves much of the credit for our successes in Asia. The hero of our federation in Europe and Latin America has been Rafael Santonja, now my executive assistant. He is an indefatigable Spaniard who can fly halfway around the world, step off the plane, and start a grueling workday fresh and bright. Such lovers of bodybuilding as Paul and Rafael dream the Olympic dream and give of themselves unstintingly. There are others, too numerous to name, on whom we depend. Our efforts always have, and always will be, a matter of teamwork.

Before concluding this short Olympic tutorial, I want to re-emphasize a fundamental point: The Olympics quest involves only amateur bodybuilding. Our active amateur competitors number about a quarter million worldwide and compete in thousands of competitions all over the world. The U.S.A. alone has more than 1,000 amateur competitions a year. The top bodybuilding champions that Joe writes about in his part of this story are professionals. Though very much smaller in number than the amateurs, such stars are the names and faces that the world knows. Of course, they were once amateurs themselves, before turning pro and achieving fame and fortune.

Gift From Poland

In 1971 I received an invitation to return to Warsaw from Dr. Wlodzimierz Reczek, the chairman of Poland's State Central Committee for Physical Culture and Tourism, official designation of the Poland's Communist Sports Ministry. Mr. Reczek was also president of the Polish Olympic Committee. As I stepped from the plane in Warsaw, I was warmly greeted by Stanislaw Zakrzewski, president of the Polish Bodybuilding Federation, and an enthusiastic group of bodybuilders and fans. We had several minutes of handshakes and bear hugs, with smiles all around.

This reception proved that things had changed a great deal in Poland since my first visit in 1955. Indeed, there were signs of change shortly after my visit. In 1957, a slightly more liberal Polish Communist government allowed the startup of new magazines, among them *Sport dla Wszystkich,* "Sport for All," published by Mr. Zakrzewski, rightfully known as the Father of Polish Bodybuilding. He began to feature photos of American physique stars and training information, which spread the popularity of bodybuilding. In 1959, Poles got a look at international champions in the flesh when the International Weightlifting Federation's Mr. Universe contest was held in Warsaw in conjunction with the World Weightlifting Championships. There were ups and downs, but bodybuilding grew and was eventually accepted in a limited way by sports officials, who allowed bodybuilding in Poland's 300 government-owned gyms. All along, we tried to support Poland's courageous bodybuilders by providing our magazines, which were filled with photos of the outstanding champion bodybuilders and the latest instructional information.

It occurred to me, after I got off the plane, that the welcoming committee might be a sign of bigger changes to come. If something happened under a totalitarian regime, it usually meant that somebody powerful wanted it to happen.

My feeling was born out in my dealings with Sports Minister Reczek. He was a smallish man, a full head shorter than I, but large in vitality and his air of authority, which befit a man whose word was law in his country's sports. Minister Reczek attended a bodybuilding contest organized in honor of my visit. He was visibly startled by the enthusiasm of the 1,500 youthful fans who packed the stadium and gave noisy ovations as the various athletes took the stage. As I later learned, the minister had no idea that our sport was so popular among his nation's young people. Nor did he know how wildly enthusiastic fans could be. During the contest I watched him very carefully and saw that he kept smiling and nodding approval. When I went to the microphone and spoke a few words to the crowd, I turned in his direction and thanked him for lending us his support by attending. He beamed as the audience erupted in loud applause.

In a later meeting with Minister Reczek and members of the Polish Sports Committee, I explained that bodybuilding stressed discipline, clean living, and abstention from drugs, alcohol, and tobacco. At this the Minister became quite animated and friendly, saying that Poland's sports officials stood for exactly the same things. He surprised me by presenting me with a very important medal from his Sports Ministry. I, in turn, presented him the IFBB President's Gold Medal, one of our very highest honors.

Pleased by the sudden warmth between us, I said, "Mr. Minister, do your kind words and encouragement mean you will allow the Polish federation to officially join the IFBB?"

In silence the minister rubbed his chin with his fingers and raised an eyebrow. I assumed he was thinking of a diplomatic way to turn me down, but then he stood up and said, "Yes!"

Since he said it in Polish, I wasn't sure I understood.

"Does that mean 'Yes'?" I asked, hoping for affirmation from the interpreter.

"Yes!" Minister Reczek said in English.

I was so excited that I, too, rose. To the amazement of everybody present, including myself, I hugged the minister and then took his hand and shook it vigorously, thanking him over and over.

"This is the least we can do to support your sport in light of its popularity in our country," he said. "Bodybuilding deserves this recognition."

When I calmed down a bit, I was very embarrassed. "Mr. Minister, I beg your pardon," I said. "Please excuse my enthusiasm and emotion a moment ago. I was carried away."

He smiled and took my hand, saying, "That's perfectly all right. You've been working hard for this day to happen, and I admire and respect your dedication."

Thus Poland became the 70th nation to join the IFBB. I was so surprised—I should say stunned—at the sports minister's "Yes!" because I didn't expect to get his official approval so soon and so easily. For all I had known, Minister Reczek was yet another intransigent Communist sports official. Even if he favored bodybuilding, I thought he might have his hands tied by higher-ups in Moscow. But at that time the Polish people, even Communist government officials, had a new feeling of independence and a desire to go their own way, regardless of Moscow's wishes. One of the many ways that they showed the spirit of freedom and national pride, was by embracing bodybuilding. So our sport would be accepted throughout the Communist world. As oppressive regimes lost their grip, bodybuilding came out of the shadows. Where freedom went, bodybuilding went with it. It was just as I had predicted to the Soviet sports minister Nicolai Romanov in Moscow in 1955. Bodybuilding would prevail because the people wanted it.

Iraq

Middle Eastern violence and ill will against Jewish people never prevented me from making many wonderful friends in the Arab world. From the moment I first set foot in the Middle East in 1947, I became enamored of the Arab way of life, especially the politeness of the people and their code of hospitality. The Arab world has also been particularly fertile ground for the sport of bodybuilding. I think this is because strength sports, such as weightlifting and wrestling, have deep cultural roots here that go back to ancient times. And the Middle East has produced great IFBB champions such as the 1983 Mr. Olympia Samir Bannout, born in Beirut and called "The Lion of Lebanon" and the Egyptian Abdel Hamid El-Guindy, winner of the Amateur World Championship and other titles. Arab physique stars are major celebrities in their home countries, where bodybuilding is one of the top spectator sports.

I was very excited to be contacted by the Iraq Amateur Bodybuilding Association about holding our 1972 Amateur World Championships and International Congress in Baghdad. Immediately I put the wheels in motion to secure federation approval for Baghdad as a host city and start the advance work. For both professional and personal reasons I was eager to go to Baghdad. I believed holding our major annual events there would strengthen our sport and generate good will in the Middle East. And as a student of world history, I was extremely eager to see Iraq, once the ancient kingdom of Mesopotamia and, thousands of years earlier, one of the cradles of human civilization. I was also extremely eager to visit Ur in Iraq, the birthplace of the prophet Abraham.

But the current political climate was difficult, to say the least. All over the Middle East, hostilities simmered that would flare up into the 1973 Arab-Israeli war. Anti-Israeli feelings ran especially high in Iraq, along with anti-Semitic attitudes in general. I realized just how bad things were when I got a telex from the honorable Adman Ayoub Sebry Al-Azid, Iraq's minister of youth and sport and also the country's minister of security. Having discovered that I was Jewish, he very politely suggested that I send someone in my stead to our World Championships and International Congress because it violated Iraqi custom to invite a Jew. The minister's message stunned me, because it was the Iraqis who invited the IFBB and not vice versa.

To acquiesce was out of the question, but I didn't want to give up on Iraq. I sent the minister a carefully worded reply, explaining with the utmost courtesy that while I respected his customs and codes of conduct, I had to insist on respect for the rules of our federation, which explicitly stated that the president must be invited by a prospective host country to make an inspection tour and then to preside over our events. I had to stand by our rules, and if they couldn't be observed in Iraq, there was no choice but for us to go elsewhere.

After thinking over my message, the minister replied that I was most welcome to come providing that my route took me through a European country, and not Israel.

In this, and other similar dealings with nations that had discriminatory policies, my position was stronger because I could appeal to our constitution and rules, which were unmistakably clear. Without them, such disputes would have seemed much more personal. As it was, though, I referred to written words laying out policies that we could not violate.

Traveling alone, I made my inspection trip. I was greeted at the Baghdad airport by a large, enthusiastic contingent of the Iraqi bodybuilding community. Leading the group was Dr. Yousif D. Al-Naaman, professor and director of the College of Medicine at the University of Baghdad, who would chair the meeting of the IFBB Medical Commission at our Congress in Iraq.

Baghdad was a fascinating city, both very old and surprisingly modern, and my hosts pulled out all the stops to keep me comfortable and entertained. One group of sports officials invited me to a Baghdad nightclub. Walking to the club entrance I saw a military vehicle pull up ahead of us carrying a load of troops who jumped out and surrounded the club. Soldiers stood at the entrance, subjecting arriving patrons to thorough searches. Surprisingly, the soldiers let us pass untouched. This was very curious, but inside the club I got caught up in an unforgettable evening of good spirits and exotic entertainment, with traditional music and belly dancers and acts that included a fire eater. I felt like I'd stepped into the *1001 Arabian Nights.* As we left I saw the soldiers jump back into their vehicle, which pulled away just as we did. I asked one of my hosts what was going on, and he looked at the others in our party, then looked back at me.

"They were here to protect you," he said. "You are our honored guest and we want you to feel safe and happy."

Buttons in My Head

I don't know how great the risks to me really were, but I will say I had a sense of underlying danger in Baghdad, more than I felt in other Middle Eastern cities, although nothing bad actually happened. The authorities certainly took protecting me very seriously. I was attended at all times by three armed guards from the Iraqi Secret Service, none of whom could have been older than 25. Fortunately, since we were together day and night, they were very nice young fellows, and I respected them and treated them as if they were my own three sons. I had no doubt that they would have laid down their lives to save mine. Before I left, I wanted to show my gratitude to them and provide a token of our friendship. Someone had told me that a pen manufactured by the American company Parker was a high status symbol in Iraq, so I decided to buy three of the finest Parker pens as presents.

As we were saying our farewells, I wanted to present the pens to the guards, but they refused them.

The senior guard said to me, "Mr. Weider, you are the nicest man we have ever guarded, and we like you very much. But it would not be right for us to accept gifts for doing our duty."

I like to say that I have imaginary buttons in my head, which represent different people's cultures and countries. To solve the problem of the Parker pens, I pushed my Arab button so I could understand the situation in the guards' cultural world view.

Knowing full well that Arabs enjoy gifts, which they regard as an expression of respect, I therefore decided to tell the head guard, "You have mentioned, several times, that you like me and enjoyed guarding me."

All three nodded in agreement.

"If you have such feelings, why would you want to offend me by refusing to accept the pens, which I have offered in a spirit of friendship and good faith?"

Looking quite embarrassed, the guards stepped away and spoke together quietly. They came back, saying they would be very honored to accept my generous gifts. They said, once again, that I was the nicest man they ever had the privilege to guard, and that I'd always be welcome to come back to Iraq.

All my Iraqi hosts had treated me wonderfully, and I left with feelings of gratitude and affection.

At the opening of the World Amateur Bodybuilding Championships in Baghdad, I wanted to do something special to honor my hosts and all the Arab delegates and athletes and fans present. The moment was particularly ripe for a gesture of respect and friendship. Just a few months earlier, Palestinian terrorists had seized a group of Israeli athletes and coaches at the 1972 Summer Olympics in Munich, Germany. The whole world watched in horror as all the Israelis died in a hail of gunfire and grenades in a failed rescue attempt.

I decided to make a special gesture of friendship by delivering my opening speech in Arabic. I kept my intentions a secret, shared only with my dear friend from Lebanon, Malih Alaywan, now the IFBB vice president for the Middle East. Given that I neither spoke nor wrote Arabic, I asked Malih to translate my speech from English to Arabic, then write everything out phonetically. I rehearsed for hours each day while Malih coached me in Arabic word sounds, which are very difficult for non-speakers.

The World Championships, I should note, followed a very successful IFBB International Congress held in the Iraqi national parliament building, at which we had 50 countries participating. This made the competition the largest athletic event ever held in Baghdad. The evening of the World Championships, the air was electric, with the Al-Nasr Cinema filled to capacity. Iraqi president Ahmed Hassan al-Bakr was in attendance.

As I went onstage to make my opening address, Col. Abdul Hameed Al-Badri, president of our host federation, asked for a copy of my speech so that he could translate it from English for the audience. I didn't want him to know my plans to speak in Arabic, so I misled him.

"Colonel, it's a very short speech," I said. "I'll speak very slowly, and you can translate as I speak."

The lights dimmed and the house went quiet, and I stood in the beam of a single spotlight. As I began speaking in Arabic, the crowd roared its approval. Malih's coaching must have been good because afterward people came up and spoke to me in Arabic, convinced that I knew their language. That simple gesture opened the championships on a high note that continued through the evening. Our Baghdad events were among our most successful to that point. Afterward, the Iraqi Postal Services issued two special commemorative stamps, bearing beautiful images of bodybuilders. Those were the world's first bodybuilding postage stamps.

In the troubled times that followed, Iraqis continued to be bodybuilding enthusiasts. The sport did well during under the tyranny of Saddam Hussein. I have a letter, dated February 17, 2002, inviting me to make a seven-day visit to Iraq to tour the country and have meetings with the head of Iraq's ministry of sport and youth, who also led the country's National Olympic Committee. This high sports official was Saddam's son Uday Hussein, now deceased. I declined the invitation because of a shortage of time to prepare the trip. Even now, with the country war-torn and racked by violence, Iraqi bodybuilders organize competitions. I just received communications about major contests held in both Iraq and Afghanistan.

South Africa

The 1975 Mr. Olympia contest in Pretoria, South Africa, might be the most-watched competition in the history of our sport. It provided the climactic action in *Pumping Iron,* viewed by millions, which followed Arnold Schwarzenegger as he prepared for and then won his sixth consecutive Mr. Olympia title in Pretoria. This hit film gave the public at large a first long look at the world of competitive bodybuilding. It also put Arnold on the road to fame and fortune in Hollywood. All in all, *Pumping Iron* represented a dramatic turning point for both our sport and our first athlete whose name became a household word all over the world.

But the real drama, in my opinion, happened off-camera. It started in 1973 with correspondence from Dr. Piet Koornhof, South Africa's minister of sport and plural relations, expressing a desire to organize both the IFBB Amateur World Championships and our Mr. Olympia contest in Pretoria, his nation's capital.

I had a longstanding fondness for South Africa, which in 1947 became the first nation outside of North America to join the IFBB. But I also recognized that there were issues that made holding our events there problematic, to say the least. In 1948, the white rulers of the country instituted a system of rigid racial segregation known as *apartheid,* which legally guaranteed the supremacy of whites and the oppression of the country's African and non-white majority. I had profound doubts that South Africa could qualify as a host nation but decided it would be worthwhile to meet with Dr. Koornhof and hear what he had to say. So, I flew to South Africa.

Upon arrival, I was met by Lolly Bester, then the general secretary of the South African Amateur Bodybuilding Union. Although a female in a sport and subculture that was then almost exclusively male, Lolly was an assertive, capable administrator who had no trouble keeping bodybuilders in line. The next day,

Lolly accompanied me to a meeting with Dr. Koornhof, whom I found to be warm and friendly. Though he was tall and slim, he informed me in his Afrikaans-accented English that he was a former bodybuilder and still a great bodybuilding fan, which was why he dreamed of hosting our contests.

After more than an hour of friendly discussion, I came to the points that I was almost positive would rule out South Africa as a host country. I said we could not even consider holding the IFBB events in South Africa unless non-white athletes were permitted to participate as equals in absolutely every respect. They had to compete on the same stage at the same time, share the same hotels, restaurants, locker rooms, bathroom facilities, and transportation. Every athlete, regardless of race, had to receive equal treatment and equal access to everything. Though I personally found apartheid abhorrent, I didn't express myself that way. Instead, as in Iraq, I pointed out that discrimination was banned by the constitution of our federation, and a host country had to comply.

I didn't hold out a great deal of hope, because every single demand I presented broke South African racial laws. I was really asking the minister to suspend apartheid, the law of the land.

To my amazement, he did just that. Dr. Koornhof looked me in the eye and agreed unequivocally. Incredulous, I again ran down the list of our requirements.

Point by point, Dr. Koornhof agreed to everything.

"Mr. Minister, I'll need to have this in writing, so I can present it to the federation membership," I said.

"Of course. You'll have a letter from me when you arrive back in Montreal," he said.

"I am sorry, but I need a letter immediately," I replied, and explained. "I'm sure you understand that picking Pretoria as a host city is very controversial. Once word gets out, I'll have to prove that the federation is not compromising its principles and that our events will actually promote racial equality and not validate apartheid."

"When exactly would you like to receive your letter?" the minister asked.

"Immediately," I replied.

At that, Dr. Koornhof called for his assistant, to whom he dictated a letter. Some minutes later she returned with a document that Dr. Koornhof handed to me.

He paused to let me read it and then asked, "Does this meet your requirements?"

As a matter of fact, it did. I'll quote from it:

Dear Mr. Weider:

I wish to assure your members that I and my Department of Sport and Recreation stand firmly behind the S.A. Amateur Body Building Union and will give full support to this Union in organizing these Championships and that all athletes, regardless of racial, political or religious beliefs will be received on an equal basis and treated as sportsmen and friends... The same applies to all South African white and non-white participants who may qualify for participation.

With this letter in my hands, the contests in Pretoria were on.

Making that breakthrough in South Africa was one of the most thrilling moments in my entire career. All I had to use as leverage was our Constitution, but that's all it took. Once again the unsung hero was Oscar State, who crafted the documents that laid out our policies so well that we could make a small opening in the wall of apartheid, at least for a little while. It wasn't until the early 1990s that the system was finally abolished.

Our policies, so clear and ironclad, really were like a golden key. Not only did they open new doors for us, we could use them to lock trouble out. I remember an Arab military officer who insisted on taking Israelis to task for issues that had nothing to do with federation business. I politely explained that he was perfectly entitled to express his opinions, but he couldn't do it at our proceedings. Whenever disputes between nations threatened to creep into federation affairs, I put a quick end to the trouble by invoking the rules. As I wrote in an article explaining our stance: "We are strong believers that the United Nations was established to solve political, racial, and religious problems of the world, and that the sports federations should only be interested in solving sport problems."

Unexpected Honor

In 1975, in the midst of preparations for the championships in South Africa, which took more of my time and attention than usual, I received notice that I would be awarded membership in the Order of Canada, the highest honor for meritorious service to the nation and humanity. I received the award for my contributions to Canadian and international sport and fitness and for promoting international understanding through the medium of sport. I had hoped someday to be so honored, but I was very surprised it happened so soon. At the time the Order of Canada was still quite new, dating only to 1967, and there was a tremendously long line of deserving individuals waiting to receive the Order. Not only did the award validate my work, it meant that the committee that considered nominees found my character and my record to be above reproach.

Controversy Behind the Scenes

Between November 4, and November 11, 1975, Pretoria hosted the Amateur World Championships, the Mr. Olympia, and the IFBB International

Congress. Not surprisingly, the response was overwhelming in a country that had 400 first-class bodybuilding clubs, where Reg Park, who emigrated to South Africa from England, was a national hero. Seats sold out for the events, which were also televised. Thirty-three countries sent athletes to the World Championships, approximately one-third of whom were non-white, among them such greats as Robby Robinson and Chris Dickerson of the U.S. and Albert Beckles and Wilf Sylvester of England. Winston Roberts, a black Canadian originally from the Caribbean, was an integral member of the IFBB executive council and our general secretary, a position that brought him into constant contact with South African officials to ensure that everything ran smoothly.

I began my opening address with these words: "They said it could not be done," and spoke of the minor miracle we had brought about in South Africa. Dr. Koornhof gave an absolutely wonderful talk on the merits of our sport, proving that he really was a true believer in bodybuilding. To the athletes, he said, "In years to come, the invaluable role you, the bodybuilders, are playing in the quest for a really healthy world will be better appreciated. Yours is a very valid contribution to world health." Those words could have been spoken by my brother Joe. Arnold Schwarzenegger said Dr. Koornhof gave the most upbeat, optimistic speech about bodybuilding he had ever heard.

I found it ironic, to say the least, to be accused of racism at that event, which represented a major victory against racism. It happened, though. The trouble began brewing six months earlier, when I received complaints concerning a very popular and gifted French bodybuilder named Serge Nubret. Serge, who was black, came from the Caribbean island of Guadeloupe, considered to be part of France. Serge really had it all, wonderful build and good looks and charm, at least when you first met him. He seemed a likely candidate to become our next Mr. Olympia after Arnold left competition, as he was expected to do.

Unfortunately, though, Serge was his own worst enemy. I learned that he was appearing in hardcore pornographic films, which generated negative publicity for our sport in France and French-speaking nations around the world. Just then, we were trying to get the recognition and support of France's National Olympic Committee, so the timing could not have been worse. In Pretoria, this matter came up at a meeting of our executive council, where Serge presented his case.

I said to him, "Why are you making such films when you know it is detrimental to our sport?"

Serge answered, "I am showing the world bodybuilders are virile and attractive to women. Therefore, I am improving bodybuilding's image."

The delegates rejected this argument and wanted to suspend Serge. But I wanted to give him a chance to make amends. I told him the matter would be dropped if he apologized and promised not to appear in pornographic productions again. Serge, an extremely stubborn man, refused the offer, and, therefore, the executive council was obligated to suspend him from the IFBB for one year.

Serge did not accept his suspension gracefully. Instead, he became furious and decided to rent a large suite in his hotel, with a bar generously stocked with alcoholic beverages, and invited all the non-white athletes and officials present to an ad hoc nighttime meeting. Once the room was packed, and the drinks were flowing, Serge announced that I had suspended him because of his skin color.

"Ben Weider is a racist!" he declared with no mention at all of the charge that he made pornographic films that appeared in movie theaters. He told the people in the room that they should band together and demand his reinstatement, or they would return to their home countries. He believed this threat would upset and embarrass our host nation South Africa.

At three o'clock in the morning, Serge called up to my room and demanded that I come immediately and answer his charges. He said many delegates insisted on hearing my reply. I said I was too tired and offered to meet in the morning, but then the call had me wide awake and I decided I might as well meet my accuser. Before I left my room, I phoned Dr. Koornhof at his home and explained the entire situation to him. I asked him if, with a rebellion on my hands, I could solve the problem as I saw necessary. I also asked if it would embarrass him if some of the troublemakers left the country.

Dr. Koornhof replied that he had confidence in me and would respect any decision I made. If, in fact, some athletes wanted to leave, he said he would arrange air transportation for them the very next day.

So I went to Serge's suite with a fallback plan in case reason did not prevail. Walking into that angry, unruly bunch was like walking into a hornet's nest, with a good many of the hornets inebriated.

I said to the group that charges of racism were absurd, particularly after our fight against South Africa's racist policies. I said, too, that we suspended Serge because he appeared in pornography, which did grave damage to the image of our sport.

My words fell on some deaf ears, or, I should say, drunken ears.

Ms. Reiko Matuyama, president of the Japanese Bodybuilding Federation, normally a soft-spoken respectful woman, approached me in an absolute fury, saying, "You are a racist! Reinstate Serge Nubret immediately or I will fly home with my team tomorrow!"

Seeing that lovely little lady in such a drunken state appalled me. Ms. Matuyama had always been very dignified and polite in the Japanese manner and never drank alcohol, to my knowledge.

I said to her, "I am very sorry to see you like this, Ms. Matuyama. Formerly I had the highest respect for you, but now you are behaving like a drunken sailor. I am ashamed of you."

She was visibly upset by my remarks, and I did not see her again during the championships in Pretoria.

I then turned and addressed all present: "Before you make any decisions, you should demand the truth from Mr. Nubret about why he was suspended. If you still cannot accept the executive council's decision, we will arrange for your departure tomorrow. I'm going to sleep now. Do whatever you wish."

The next morning no one chose to leave. And Serge Nubret came to me asking quite nicely for permission to participate in the Mr. Olympia contest. I agreed to put off the suspension so he could compete. He really was one of the finest bodybuilders in the world, and the crowds loved him. And in spite of the trouble he stirred up, I liked him.

The public and press, with no idea what had transpired, saw nothing but a successful event, beginning to end.

Letdown in Lausanne

Socially speaking, I got off to a fine start with the new IOC president, Lord Killanin of Ireland, who took office in 1972. In contrast to his more serious and reserved American predecessor, Avery Brundage, Lord Killanin was a jovial person who enjoyed conversation and laughter. To me he seemed very friendly and supportive, and I got the idea that if we laid the groundwork correctly, he would favor the IFBB's bid for recognition. My friend Oscar State, a very well connected and respected figure in the Olympic movement, also believed Lord Killanin likely would smile on our request for recognition.

It was, in fact, Oscar who prompted me to ask the president the big question.

It happened in 1976, on an evening that was like a replay of the boat cruise on Lake Leman in 1971, where I first spoke one on one with Avery Brundage. Once again, we members of the General Association of International Sports Federations mingled with the top officials of the IOC on a boat excursion on the lake.

Oscar State and I had boarded the boat full of hope that the evening would be historic for both bodybuilding and our federation. We picked our way through the mingling sports dignitaries until we found ourselves seated at a table with none other than Lord Killanin. Also at the table was Sir Stanley Rous, head of the International Football Federation. Lord Killanin was extremely amiable. We ate, drank, laughed, and, most of all, we talked like old friends, discussing such subjects as art, culture, politics, and sport. I felt a deepening rapport with Lord Killanin and Sir Stanley Rous. Surely, I thought, men so cordial and warm to me would understand why bodybuilding deserved Olympic recognition.

Clearly Oscar felt the same way. He winked, leaned close, and whispered, "Now is the time, Ben. Ask the question right now." Though I was nervous, I had to agree with Oscar. The moment was right, the mood was right, so what was I waiting for?

"My Lord," I said to the IOC president, "will you support Olympic recognition for our sport of bodybuilding?"

With my words hanging in the air, Lord Killanin set down his fork, leaned back, and cleared his throat. Looking me straight in the eye, he said, in the most gracious tone, "Sure."

I felt giddy. My pulse raced. But then Lord Killanin spoke again.

"Over my dead body," he said.

Those four words still burn in my memory.

Though I was absolutely crushed, the words weren't as deliberately cruel as they might seem on paper. In the spirit of conviviality that reigned at our table, Lord Killanin couldn't resist making a joke out of our exchange. He really was quite a nice fellow, and our later encounters were always very cordial.

On the other hand, I could tell he meant what he said. He was dead set against IOC recognition for bodybuilding or any other new sports.

His position remained unchanged for the rest of his term as president, which ended in 1980. In other areas, though, we were in complete agreement. Lord Killanin was extremely concerned about the growing influence of international politics on the Olympic movement. The most horrific example was the kidnapping and massacre of Israelis at the 1972 Summer Games. And the disputes and political posturing that went on, with Arab countries and Israel at each other's throats and clashes between Communist and Capitalist countries, that finally culminated in the American boycott of the 1980 Games in Moscow. In 1976, African nations boycotted the Summer Games in Montreal because of objections to South Africa. Because I shared his distaste for politicizing sports, Lord Killanin and I had several agreeable discussions on the subject. But during his presidency, there would be no progress toward recognition of our sport.

Their Loss, Our Gain

For all his brilliance and the high esteem and respect he commanded throughout the world of sport, my dear friend Oscar State could be amazingly naïve. He was absolutely blind to double-dealing and underhandedness on the part of others. I think he found it impossible to imagine anyone, particularly in the world of sport, being less than honest and straightforward, as he always was.

Though I admired Oscar for his virtue, his naïveté sometimes drove me crazy, particularly in the mid-1970s when others in the International

Weightlifting Federation began political maneuvering against him. Oscar, in a way, was a victim of his own dedication and hard work. After years of giving the IWF his heart and soul, getting all its working documents and rules and operational procedures in perfect order, amateur weightlifting and its federation ran like well-oiled machinery. It was through Oscar's efforts that the IWF added many new member nations and became one of the largest sports federations in the world. At that point, certain individuals in the IWF decided to maneuver against Oscar and get him out of his executive position. Driven by intense jealousy and hunger for power, they conspired to get rid of Oscar, claiming that the IWF didn't need him any more. Everybody around Oscar could see that his position was in jeopardy, and we told him so.

"Watch your back, my friend," I would say. "There's a move afoot to get rid of you.

"Oh no, no, no, no. That's impossible. Why would anybody want to do that?" he'd say.

And I'd say, "Oscar, wake up. This is the real world."

He kept on saying "no, no, no, no" while his enemies conspired against him and finally deprived him of his post at the IWF. Even after he was out of his beloved federation for good, he didn't want to acknowledge that he might have been the victim of underhandedness.

But the IWF's loss was our gain, because from then on the IFBB had Oscar's complete attention. Though he already did yeoman work, he became a mainstay of our federation, and a familiar figure to the athletes and fans, who appreciated the touch of dignity and class he added to our competitions. Nobody who was there when he officiated will forget that dry, English-accented voice of his, as he issued directions to the athletes during posing and judging. He was able to give instructions in 16 languages. You can see Oscar at work at a women's bodybuilding contest in the documentary film, *Pumping Iron II: The Women.* One segment shows him minutely examining female competitors' bikinis to determine if the fabric met the specifications in our rules. That was Oscar, who did everything strictly by the book.

The only disagreements we ever had were brought on by his refusal to bend the rules, no matter what the circumstances. If an athlete arrived five minutes late for a weigh-in, Oscar would say, "You were supposed to be here at six o'clock. You weren't, so you can't compete." No matter if the fellow was likely to win, and a crowd favorite, and was late through no fault of his own.

In one such case, I said, "Come on, Oscar, we need to be a little flexible. The fellow just flew halfway around the world."

When I did insist on a bit of flexibility, Oscar always objected. I don't know how many times he told me that if we allowed a rule to be bent we would set a dangerous precedent, which others would want to follow. Bend often enough, and you might as well throw the rulebook out the window. Oscar observed protocol even in the way he dressed. For years he wore a red blazer to every contest, as if it were his official uniform, then later switched to a blue blazer.

Oscar had his quirks. One of them was writing out all his correspondence and work-related documents in longhand. I can still see him laboring for hours to write out his long reports after contests. We, at headquarters, would receive page after page of written matter in Oscar's longhand, which fortunately was neat and legible.

One of Oscar's rituals, on his trips to North America, was to buy an enormous load of donuts and take them home. His wife was the real donut lover in the family. Just before Oscar's departure he'd find the nearest donut shop and pick up four dozen in assorted flavors. He particularly liked Dunkin' Donuts. Upon arriving at IFBB events, he would invariably go to the nearest coffee shop and have a slice of apple pie. Usually he had his pie with Pamela Kagan, the IFBB's executive director, so the two of them could exchange information. No matter if it was Tokyo or Singapore at three o'clock in the morning, Oscar wanted his apple pie. If there was no pie to be had, he was sorely disappointed.

Oscar was one of the most focused, businesslike individuals I ever met, and absolutely incapable of making small talk. But he had a sense of humor, of the dry, British type. His jokes were so dry, in fact, that most people didn't recognize them as jokes.

Every organization could use an Oscar State. We were so very lucky to have him.

Forward Momentum

In the preceding chapter, Joe wrote about his Golden Age in California. In the same period I had my own sort of Golden Age, all around the world. Through the 1970s and into the '80s, things happened one after the other that were the result of work begun years previously. It was so gratifying and thrilling to see my efforts repaid by positive results, to the benefit of our sport and the many millions of people who learned about strength training and fitness and enjoyed the many benefits.

Lord Killanin's intransigence about recognition of our sport and others had one very positive effect. It led to the birth of the World Games, a sort of Olympics for sports that can't get into the Olympics. The movement to form an alternative quadrennial sports festival began with conversations I had with another very frustrated federation president, Don Porter, who headed the International Softball Federation. At a meeting in 1979 in Lausanne, he and I started talking, along with Hal Uplinger, a true enthusiast of international athletics who produced TV sports programs, including coverage of the Olympic Games. Don and I, tired of waiting for inclusion, decided our sports and others like them deserved Games of their own. Hal loved the idea of showcasing new sports, and we all got serious about pursuing our idea, so we started the movement to create the World Games. Years later, others claimed credit. However, as Don wrote to me in a letter, "It was you and I, initially with Hal Uplinger, that brought about the concept and creation."

The first World Games were held in 1981 in Santa Cruz, California, with 18 official medal sports and more than 1,200 athletes. Today the Games are many times larger and enormously popular, and they have the support and official recognition of the IOC. In fact Olympic Committee president Juan Antonio Samaranch opened the World Games in Lahti, Finland, in 1997.

The receptions we got from some of the countries that hosted our World Championships and International Congresses were truly amazing. The national media would cover everything, beginning to end, and generate enormous excitement. I found myself being entertained by countries' leaders as if I were a visiting head of state. I'll never forget a personal visit with president Ferdinand Marcos in his huge presidential palace in the Philippines, where we held our World Amateur Bodybuilding Championships and our International Congress in the fall of 1980 and many international events. I found President Marcos to be a very genial man.

"Mr. Weider, what is this physical fitness everyone talks about? Please, tell me in a few words what fitness is," the president said. I could tell he didn't take fitness very seriously.

I asked the president to stand and come out from behind his desk, and I pointed down a long hallway.

"Your Excellency," I said, "I would like you to run down and back, as fast as you can."

He did exactly that, and when he returned he was gasping for breath.

"That, sir, is what lack of fitness feels like. If you were fit, you wouldn't even be breathing hard, and you'd have more energy and stamina to complete whatever work you were doing."

President Marcos seemed to realize that he might, indeed, benefit from exercise. I had expected a very short, perfunctory audience, but the president didn't want to let me go. The Canadian ambassador to the Philippines, who accompanied me to the presidential palace, was amazed at how much time the president gave me.

President Marcos came to our World Championships meaning to make a polite, brief appearance, but then he became so engrossed that he stayed through the entire program. That wasn't the first or last time that a dignitary got caught up in watching a bodybuilding contest and stayed much longer than he or she intended.

The events in the Philippines turned out to be another great success. And the IFBB got another lasting gift from that country. My very good friend Gen. Carlos P. Rómulo, former Philippine foreign minister and a high official at the United Nations, once remarked to me, "Bodybuilding is important for nation-building." In a rather joking manner, I asked permission to use his words as part of the logo of the IFBB. He said with a smile, "Sure, sure, it's true. By all means you can use it." The words do, indeed, ring with truth about our sport. Bodybuilding does produce a strong, healthy youth, who eventually become stronger, healthier adult citizens, and thus produces a stronger, healthier nation.

The year after we held our events in the Philippines, we went to Egypt, which required a curious sort of negotiation. Normally, potential hosts boast about their great facilities and the attractions of the chosen city and the entire country. But as much as the Egyptians involved in our sport wanted to host us, the country's minister of youth and sport, the honorable Dr. Hasan, discouraged me.

"Mr. Weider," he said, "I regret to say that we have no facilities big enough for such a grand happening. What we can offer would be inadequate. Our theaters are so old and small they'll embarrass the country."

At that time Egypt did, in fact, lack the sort of large, new auditoriums and indoor meeting spaces that other countries could offer. But that didn't matter.

"Mr. Minister," I said, "allow me to differ with you. You have the biggest and most spectacular facility for our use that I've ever seen. Our members and athletes will be in absolute awe and return to their countries talking about the grandeur of Egypt. And people watching on television will want to visit as tourists."

"I know of no such place," Dr. Hasan replied.

"Sir, I think you do," I said. "Nobody thinks of the place as a theater, but it really is. I am, of course, talking about the Sound and Light Theater at the foot of the Great Pyramid and the Sphinx."

The "theater" I referred to was out in the open, where tourists sat and enjoyed nighttime displays of lights with music and amplified voices, some of them seemingly from the ancient past, explaining the history of Egypt. It was a terrific and educational show. Though the current set-up had only about 400 seats, I said to the minister that all he had to do was push aside some sand, bring more chairs and make the theater as big as it needed to be.

The Minister laughed and then with a smile on his face agreed, to the great delight of the other two men at our meeting, who were Abdel Hamid El-Guindy, president of the Egyptian Bodybuilding Federation and a former international champion bodybuilder and the Egyptian undersecretary of state, Yousef Kamal Abou Ouf, a former Olympic athlete who would head the committee that organized our events. Athletes from 41 countries competed in our championships, where the setting was beyond fantastic—perhaps the most spectacular site for a sports event in history. For me the place was full of meaning, because this was the spot where I first fell in love with the ancient splendor of Egypt and where I was feted at an unforgettable party as I said goodbye to my Egyptian friends at the end of my first trip there in 1947.

As important to me as the events themselves was the way our sport and our federation brought together people who might otherwise have been enemies. I remember watching our delegates together at our International Congresses. I saw people from countries that made war on each other, those whose peoples hated and persecuted each other, Jews and Muslims and Christians, blacks and whites, Communists and Capitalists, treating each other civilly, very often talking and laughing like friends. Those moments made me as proud as any of our big, public triumphs. I would see our members happy together, and think, "Our sport did that, and our federation did that." Those might have been my proudest moments, when I saw that our sport, which brings health and vitality to individuals, could also help to heal some of the wounds of the world. I deeply believe all sport has such power. This is the essence of the modern Olympic movement and a major reason why I devoted my life to promoting our sport and building our federation.

Late in 1983, I was very surprised to learn that I had been nominated for the Nobel Peace Prize for working for the betterment of mankind through international sport. I had no idea that such a nomination was in the works. Nor did I know the person who made it, professor Lee P. Anderson, chairman of the Department of Political Science at Northwestern University in Evanston, Illinois.

From Professor Anderson's written proposal to the Nobel Prize committee:

One man has achieved an outstanding accomplishment in uniting 120 countries into one overall sports federation using a cultural and recreational sports ideal. This ideal is to bring together human beings of all political, ethnic and civilized sociological backgrounds in health and peaceful self-comparison for growth and human progress. His name is Ben Weider...his life achievement, the International Federation of Bodybuilders.

Looking back, I see what a signal honor it was to be so nominated by a distinguished political scientist. It validated my work and that of everybody who worked for our federation.

Irreplaceable Loss

At the time of the Nobel Peace Prize nomination, I learned that Oscar State was gravely ill with cancer. He died in July 1984. His death cast a shadow on the months before and after it happened.

Oscar, characteristically, didn't seem to take his illness so seriously, certainly not as seriously as his work. Even when he was sick unto death, he carried a workload that would have worn down younger men in fine health. Oscar had no illusions about what was coming, but even the prospect of death didn't prevent him from putting forth 100 percent effort for the IFBB. What will have to be, will have to be, he said. He was a fatalist in the good sense of the word, in that he accepted the inevitable. And right up to the end, he went on working, which to him was the same thing as living.

The loss to our sport, and to all of sport, was immeasurable. I don't know of anybody who did so much, for so many people, for so long, while asking so little. By Oscar's own estimation he had traveled over three million miles on behalf of his two sports, weightlifting and bodybuilding. He attended or officiated at nine Olympic Games, two World Games, 21 regional games such as the Asian, Pan-American, and Commonwealth Games, 24 World Weightlifting Championships, 27 World Bodybuilding Championships, nine Mr. Olympias, two Miss Olympias, 51 international bodybuilding contests, and 101 weightlifting championships. Most of the heroic work he did for bodybuilding and our federation was voluntary. All Oscar wanted was for his expenses to be covered.

My personal loss was devastating. When I heard he was gone, I caught the first plane to London to join Oscar's bereaved family and his friends. I was honored to deliver a eulogy at his memorial service. Unbeknownst to me, his remains were cremated the day of the memorial and his ashes were scattered. I was very disturbed to know his body just vanished, and nothing physical remained. He was there, and then he was nowhere, just like that. But he was still with us, and always will be. To preserve his memory, the IFBB has an Oscar State Memorial Award. Each year it is presented to the most outstanding official and administrator within our federation.

Eulogy for Oscar State

Delivered by Ben Weider, July 11, 1984, London, England.

Today is one of the saddest days of my life.

Losing Oscar is like losing an arm, like losing a brother. Oscar's loss has thrown the entire bodybuilding world into a state of mourning. He was a pillar of strength and a guiding light for the 123 nations that are members of the IFBB.

Governments create holidays or special days in order to remember a special person, but I won't need a special day set aside to remember Oscar. I'll always remember him because he was my true friend, my teacher, my mentor.

Any time I needed advice, Oscar was there to give it to me.

Any time I needed assistance, Oscar was there to assist me.

Any time I needed guidance, Oscar was there to guide me.

Any time I needed Oscar, Oscar was available, not only to me, as president, but to all IFBB members.

Oscar was young at heart, untiring and energetic, a man at whom everyone marveled for his unceasing activity. He worked harder and longer hours than many members who were only 30 years old. Even last year in Las Vegas when he wasn't well, he would work until 2 a.m. and 3 a.m. without complaint. His work was his pleasure and his passion.

Oscar's contributions were recognized by the IFBB when he was presented with our highest award, the President's Gold Medal. He was also awarded the Order of the British Empire by Her Majesty the Queen for his contribution to sports worldwide.

Oscar was a man's man.

Paul Chua, as head of the Asian IFBB, representing 18 member nations, has flown in from Singapore to pay his respects and be with us today. Albert Busek, president of the German Amateur Bodybuilding Federation, has traveled from Munich to pay his respects. My brother, Joe Weider, who had firm commitments he could not break and was therefore unable to be present today, shares in our bereavement. He has asked me to convey to Oscar's family on his behalf, as well as that of the staffs of Flex *and* Muscle & Fitness, *his personal condolences.*

Oscar, though you are no longer with us, you continue to live through the legacy you have left behind.

May you enjoy peace in heaven.

CHAPTER ELEVEN

WEIDER'S WORLD

Joe Weider

When I was a kid, I knew that one day great changes would sweep the world and people everywhere would finally see strength training and fitness as shining hopes for humanity. I knew, too, this change would be a long time coming. I said to Ben that our beliefs and the Weider name would finally be widely recognized and honored in the 1980s. I wrote a letter to the same effect. That was in 1940. By my prediction we would wait 40 years for the Fitness Revolution.

I read once that it's a historical rule of thumb that revolutions simmer for 40 years before they break out. Forty years also happens to be the span of time that God made the Jews wander in the wilderness before he led them to the Promised Land. But my own observation and analysis led to my prediction. When I was a kid, the anti-exercise line came down from respected medical authorities, guys up in their years who had studied medicine before World War I, the Stone Age as far as exercise went. Those old men would have to pass from the scene to make room for new ideas. To really understand and believe in physical fitness, you must personally experience the benefits, so I knew we would have to wait until doctors and scientists and other leading individuals started to work out and spread the word. That I figured would not happen until the 1960s and '70s. After that, the truth would smolder and then suddenly burst out and spread like wildfire.

This is precisely what happened. In the early 1960s, President Kennedy told Americans to get fit. Scientists started looking at exercise in a new, respectful light and began to prove what we already knew, that fitness works wonders for physical health and longevity, and it's good for emotional balance and stimulates mental activity. In other words, it's smart to work out, and working out makes you smarter.

Running and jogging caught on after a couple of doctors who ran, Dr. Kenneth Cooper and Dr. George Sheehan, spread the word about their kind of fitness. Running wasn't new to us, because all along bodybuilders did roadwork for energy and endurance. People had laughed at runners the way they did at us, but then all the laughing died out. Sports coaches, the same guys who used to throw players who lifted off the team, saw the light and ordered their athletes to use the weight room. People afraid of barbells and dumbbells started training on fancy new weight machines that popped up in gyms. Trainers popularized aerobics routines that were like group calisthenics with music, and I promoted fast circuit training so people could lift with aerobic benefits. And the gym business went through the roof along with sales of anything related to exercise.

Others put forth all sorts of reasons for the great fitness boom of the 1980s and give credit to various individuals—among them Arnold Schwarzenegger. This confuses cause and effect, like saying that opening an umbrella makes the rain come down. With so many forces coming together, the boom was on its way with or without Arnold, or Jane Fonda and her aerobics tapes, or other celebrities and gurus who pushed fitness.

But would the boom have happened the way it happened—with the universal acceptance of training with weights—without Weider publications, products, and contests?

If you've read this far, you know that the answer is "no."

One sign of the changing times showed on the cover of my flagship magazine. In 1979, I retired the name *Muscle Builder/Power* because it was too narrow for new readers who were not dedicated bodybuilders and fans. I re-titled the magazine *Muscle: A New Body Image For You*. The following year I had something shorter and better; *Muscle & Fitness* said the right things to new guys who would not have picked up a plain old muscle magazine. The magazine's subject matter broadened along with the readership and included all things connected to the bodybuilding/fitness lifestyle. But nothing in the title or the content chased away my loyal bodybuilder readership. The guys stuck with the magazine and still do.

A few years after the name change, a trade magazine declared *Muscle & Fitness* to be the publishing miracle of the 1980s. By then, readership had jumped into the millions, and overseas editions spanned the globe. It's still the leader of the pack by far. I can't say the title made the magazine what it is, but it's hard, if not impossible, to have a great magazine without a great title. *Muscle & Fitness* holds the Weider record for longevity. No other title of ours has gone unchanged for 25 years. I wouldn't be surprised if it lasts another 25 years...or 100.

M&F is, of course, the continuation of my original magazine *Your Physique.* I love the idea of it living on and enriching the lives of people who aren't even born yet. We've already got three-generation Weider families. It fills me with pride to get letters from guys who read my magazines and work out, telling how their sons and their grandchildren follow in their footsteps.

Not long after that name change, I started kicking around titles for a new launch. Perhaps I maybe should call it a re-launch because it would pick up where my women's publications of the 1950s left off. The American News mess killed off *American Beauty* and *Figure & Beauty,* but I never stopped wanting to put out a magazine that would do for women what other Weider titles did for guys.

The readers were asking for women's coverage, too. Back in 1972, I ran a profile of Ann Mewshaw, a winner of our Miss Americana contest, which preceded today's more athletic IFBB women's events. Ann happened to be married to a bodybuilder and had interesting opinions about nutrition and other pertinent subjects. People wrote in asking me for more of the same. I ran a letter from a woman who wanted a whole new section devoted to women's training. I had to say "no," because I didn't have the money or staffers with the expertise to take on such an expansion.

Things had changed by the late 1970s, when we got involved in women's bodybuilding in a serious way. In 1979, I opened up a women's section in *Muscle Builder/Power.* In the introductory announcement, I wrote this: "It doesn't take an Equal Rights Amendment to convince us that women want to be bodybuilders, just like the men....Our intended expansion will accommodate them psychologically, socially, cosmetically, and editorially. They need us, and we need them. Welcome, ladies!"

The IFBB welcomed the ladies, too. In 1980, we staged the first Ms. Olympia. The winner, Rachel McLish, turned out to be terrific for the sport and for us—such an incredible looker and charmer. Honest to God, she took your breath away. Rachel had dark hair like a flowing mane and wonderful sculpted musculature that added to her beauty and grace. Also she was likable and a great spokesperson for her sport and sold my magazines like crazy. So did Cory Everson, another great beauty and winning personality who reigned as Ms. Olympia six years running, beginning in 1984.

In truth, we broke down gender barriers for the sake of men as well as women. I can't tell you how many times bodybuilders came to me and complained about how hard it was to meet nice girls. Gyms still were pretty much men-only, and most girls shied away from bodybuilders because they thought they were weird. Even the guys with girlfriends felt isolated and misunderstood because the girls didn't have a clue about bodybuilding. The men wanted women who shared their passion and spoke their language. The only solution was to inspire women to go to gyms and work out.

The example set by the Weider women of the 1980s did, in fact, help get millions of women into gyms. And our female champs stood as living proof of one of my deepest beliefs: Strength is beauty, and beauty is strength. This is as true for women as for men. After the world beheld our women, the ideal of femininity began to change. If you don't believe me, look at pictures of famous beauties from the past like Marilyn Monroe or Sophia Loren. By current standards they're too heavy, too soft. Many of today's female celebrities are more like Rachel or Cory than like the earlier beauty queens.

In my opinion, most of the current stars reveal too much of their anatomy in public. To their credit, though, they're also extremely fit. If a young star shows her bare stomach, she's probably got good ab definition and biceps development and nice shape and definition in the legs. Female athletes have changed, too. Take a look at the women in any sport. Most of them have terrific musculature. Could they get such bodies playing golf or tennis or swimming or running foot races? Not in a million years—they build themselves the Weider way, lifting barbells and dumbbells.

All these women the public admires—movie stars, singers, models, athletes—are bodybuilders. No other word fits. They use weights and resistance machines to improve the bodies they were born with according to their own particular needs and wants. The wonderful womanly attributes are there, but they're sculpted in muscle. And the muscle actually makes them more womanly, more sexy.

Most people agree with me here. If they didn't, they would pay their money to look at stars built some other way.

It goes without saying that the male body has been Weider-ized, too. In show business, in sports, in everyday life, guys are built like never before.

If I didn't feel my own sense of mission to spread the word about fitness and health to women, I would have picked one up from Betty. The lack of solid information about training for women made her so mad. Even with the whole world catching on to exercise, nutrition, and health, nobody took the women's side seriously. What little got published in magazines was mostly silly, fluffy stuff like fad diets and instant fixes that didn't do anything.

"Joe," Betty kept saying, "you have got to do something for women. We need to tell them, in an intelligent way, everything about the whole fitness lifestyle."

What Betty had in mind was much more mainstream and far-reaching than just bodybuilding for women. She wanted to create something for all the busy, intelligent, forward-thinking women who wanted to make exercise and good nutrition part of their daily lives.

I told Betty she was right, and we would do something. She and I began to talk about launching a revolutionary new women's magazine. We talked in great detail about how the magazine would look, the departments, and so on. This went on for a long time. As a matter of fact, we were already talking when the new women's section in *Muscle Builder/Power* came out and women's bodybuilding contests got going.

Now and again Betty got impatient and asked me why I didn't get going on the new magazine. What was I waiting for? What I was waiting for, I said, was the right person to put in charge. Where she was, I didn't know. But I'd know her when I saw her.

Where she was, was teaching and doing research in exercise science at UCLA and in Pasadena. Somebody told me about this fireball I had to meet, Christine MacIntyre. She was a professor with degrees from UCLA who promoted weight training as a foundation of women's fitness. She developed aerobics routines that incorporated light dumbbells and she got Pasadena City College, where she taught, to put in the school's first women's weight room. She also wrote textbooks and scientific papers and was a mover and shaker in various organizations promoting fitness.

This person sounded dynamic and interesting, but I gave no thought to teaming up until I met her. Then I flipped. Betty, who came to the initial meeting, was just as crazy about Christine. We looked at each other with expressions that said, "This is the one."

Christine was 40 or so, with the energy of three women half her age and full of ideas that lined up perfectly with mine. Christine believed in physical fitness and shared our dream to tell the world about it, and she especially believed in training with weights to build strength and re-shape the body. This distinguished scientist and educator understood and loved bodybuilding as truly and deeply as I did. If I dreamed up a perfect woman to head our new magazine out of thin air, I could not have done better. Christine, Betty, and I sat down at the big glass table out behind our house and started batting around ideas.

I could have hired any number of women away from major national magazines, but I could make an editor out of Christine a lot easier than I could make a fitness expert and true believer out of some New York City hotshot. In this respect, Christine was like all my people going back to such characters as Charlie Smith and Barton Horvath. I always favored knowledge of and love for bodybuilding over magazine experience. On the other hand, Christine broke the mold. She was the first of a new generation of editorial employees with advanced specialized educations. I couldn't have hired such people earlier, because they didn't exist. There was no such thing as an exercise scientist, and most educated people didn't want anything to do with my branch of publishing. After things changed, my life got a lot easier. I didn't have to worry about people like Christine screwing up the basics like spelling, grammar, and word usage, because they came to me literate and polished.

My diamonds weren't so rough any more, but I still found them where no other big publisher would look. Late in the 1980s, I hired Dr. Tom Deters, a chiropractor, who became editor of *Muscle & Fitness* and then advanced to executive vice president and group publisher. Vince Scalisi, another guy who edited *M&F* and rose higher, formerly worked at a bodybuilding fantasy camp and in our nutrition company. Barbara Harris, editor of *Shape* since 1987, came out of the fitness world, not publishing. Peter McGough, who edits *Flex,* left a career at a bicycle company in England to follow his passion for bodybuilding. All these people had a couple things in common:

1) They were bodybuilders and true believers in bodybuilding; and

2) They had a certain something that caught my eye.

We went around and around with two possible names for the new women's magazine: *Fitness and Shape.*

Fitness said what the magazine was about, but I worried it might scare some readers away because they'd think that they had to do something strenuous. And it didn't speak specifically to women.

Shape, on the other hand, rang like a bell. It expressed the reader's desire and goal, a better shape. It was feminine because people talk about women having a nice shape or being shapely. And *Shape* was a call to action: Shape up; get in shape. So it also sounded good to athletic types who wanted to train hard.

When one little word tells what your magazine is about and pulls in the readers you want, but doesn't push anybody away, and it's fresh and catchy and looks good on the page, you've got your title. *Shape,* if I do say so, is up there with greats like *Vogue, Newsweek, Glamour.* I made the title Weider's and nobody else's by making the "A" without a crosshatch, so it's like a "V" turned upside-down. It's hard to claim rights to a word, but the change made the word a graphic, which I could own. It suited my artistic sensibilities, too.

From Christine's editorial in *Shape,* Volume 1, Issue 1, September 1981: "I want to do for you the same thing I did for my family—get you started on the nutrition and fitness way of life."

She also wrote this:

The most avant-garde art form on the scene today is something Pablo Picasso never tried: the art of sculpting your own body. In layman's terms, weight training.Women all over the world are learning to tell their pecs from their lats. Better yet, they're learning to enlarge them or trim them to order.Want a slimmer waistline? Fuller breasts? Flatter stomach. By using the right weights the right way, you can customize your body...

From my publisher's note: "Our goals are high because we believe magnificence of body, mind, and spirit is your birthright. Our intention is to help you get the energy you need to get that birthright."

Publishers usually expect to pump big money into a new launch for years. At Weider in 1981, we didn't have the luxury. A few months in, and Christine had to cut her budget to the bone. She never faltered, though, because she believed so much in the mission and the future of *Shape*. An editor who didn't have her heart in the project would not have worked so hard.

The moral of the story is that passion is good business.

Shape got out of its tight spot, but still it didn't take off the way we knew it should. I thought things over and went to Christine and her staff and said they should put in more ladylike stuff—fashion, hair, makeup, and so forth. I told the art director and shooters to quit giving us girls in boring workout clothes and go down to the Fashion Mart and get the latest fashions from top design houses. As I said to the editors, what's the use of building a fantastic body if you don't know how to show it to best advantage? The fashion, all on its own, would sell Shape, because women will buy a magazine just to look at clothes. I also said to put celebrities on the covers posing with dumbbells and exercise equipment, the implication being that fitness is one of the secrets of the famous and beautiful. The women would naturally want to emulate the stars.

Not all of the stars were ready for the Weider message, though. I'll never forget shooting a cover with Joan Collins, who had a fit when we asked her to pose with little barbells. "I don't want to look like Arnold Schwarzenegger!" she was yelling.

After we made the changes I suggested, sales of *Shape* doubled, just like that. It took a few years more for sales to really take off, making *Shape* not only the biggest-selling Weider magazine, but the biggest fitness-and-health-related magazine in the world. U.S. circulation today is about 1.6 million, which means readership is pushing five million. These are audited figures, not me bragging, and they're for North America only. We put out editions all over the world. I saw last year that the South African edition was selling about 55,000 copies a month—more than North American sales of either of my muscle magazines 50 years ago when I was breathing down Bob Hoffman's neck. *Shape* has had an impact bigger than its numbers. I can't think of anything that did more to spread the word far and wide about fitness for women and give them tools to change their bodies and the know-how and confidence to use those tools.

Like our women's competitive bodybuilding, *Shape* helped redefine beauty and change how women look at themselves. Recently I got a letter from the editor of the Russian edition of *Shape* saying thanks for the amazing changes the magazine brought. Russian womanhood will never be the same, she told me. Funny, isn't it? My parents fled Europe because of unrest before the Russian Revolution. A hundred years later their son caused another revolution for the betterment of Russian women.

I wonder what Ma and Pa would think of that.

Shape broke ground in other ways. As our first shot into the mass market, it became the first Weider magazine to pull in significant ad revenues. The same year *Shape* came out, *Muscle & Fitness* opened up to outside advertisers, a very significant change. For 41 years, the ads in my muscle mags were practically all for Weider-brand products. As Bernarr McFadden once said, my muscle books looked like magazines, but really functioned as mail-order catalogs.

Mainstream advertisers still turned up their noses at bodybuilding, and the outfits buying ads mostly sold supplements and equipment just like the Weider companies. In other words, we made money helping direct competitors make money. This seems odd, I know, but it was good business, and it brought in more money to make bigger, better magazines, which in turn sold more of the other guys' stuff. Business isn't always dog eat dog. Sometimes it's the more the merrier. These days our competitors and our partners are often one in the same. They help the cause by providing ad revenue for the magazines and buying sponsorships and putting up prizes for the Mr. Olympia and other big IFBB events. The more they do for us, the more we do for them, and we all make out. "Leveraging relationships," the business school guys call it.

The fact that in '81 we had competitors who could afford to buy ads shows how much things had changed because of us—Weider made the markets that the other guys got into. Our supplement and equipment businesses outgrew mail order too, so now Weider was in stores all over, in big general retailers like Sears and sports stores and specialty nutrition shops.

All of a sudden we were big business. To me, the good news wasn't the sales volume, but what it meant. We bodybuilders used to live in a little world all unto itself, shunned by the rest of the world, but now bodybuilding was getting its due. The whole world was the Weiders' world.

The first time I went from one men's muscle magazine to two back in 1945, I did it because guys wanted more of what they were getting, and the magazines were pretty much the same. By 1983, something different was needed for hardcore guys who wanted rougher, tougher stuff focused on the top competitors and what they did to build their monster muscles. We launched a new book called *Flex*—another great title, no? In *Flex,* the bigger, the more extreme, the better. The tone, the look is very aggressive, with full-page bleeds of guys flexing hard and pumping monster weights, sweating and straining and making terrible faces. It's like you're in the gym and they're screaming in your face.

The same year that *Flex* came out, something happened that threw me for a loop. I got word that the Periodical and Book Association of America was about to name me Publisher of the Year for my contributions to the magazine business, expanding the fitness and health category and making fitness something all magazines now covered. In my business, this was the ultimate approval from my peers, like getting an Oscar. I remember saying to myself, "This can't be right, giving such an honor to somebody like me."

It seemed inconceivable that a guy who didn't finish grammar school and started with $7 and a homemade muscle magazine deserved a place alongside giants like Conde Nast and Henry Luce. I was proud and gratified, but the whole thing made me feel sort of odd. Instead of going East to accept the award, I made some excuse and stayed home. This happened many times. Whenever I could, I dodged going to ceremonies to receive special recognition and awards. Being singled out for attention and praise fills me with discomfort.

Maybe there's some complicated reason that only a shrink could figure out, or maybe it's my nature to be sort of shy. I shun big gatherings and events, which sometimes drives poor Betty crazy. More than once we got invitations to attend some special deal or another at the White House. I said no, we weren't going because I had too much work, and Betty said I was nuts to pass up a chance to meet and mingle with the president of the United States. I said to her, "Come on, Betty, he doesn't know me. If I don't show up, neither of us is going to miss a thing."

I have another issue concerning awards. If an organization heaps honors on you for doing something great, you know you did the guys in the organization a lot of good. Whether you did something great for the general benefit, you don't know. So I take such things with a grain of salt.

What I just wrote about being shy will raise some eyebrows. For more than 60 years, people have accused me of being a terrible egomaniac, a guy so crazy in love with himself he plasters his name and his image everywhere. In the 1980s, the *LA Times* ran a long feature story about me and the Weider companies. The writer claimed that I had a "Herculean ego" and pointed out that one issue of *Muscle & Fitness* that he went through contained at least 80 photos or graphical likenesses of me and more than 110 mentions of my name. The numbers were meant to prove the point about my big ego, but the only thing really big was the writer's ignorance. Professor Samir Husni of the University of Mississippi understood perfectly. Quoted in an article about me that ran in *USA Today,* he said that my name was my brand.

It couldn't be any other way in bodybuilding. A while back, I said that writing in my branch of publishing must be personal—me to you. Well, everything in bodybuilding must be that way—ads, marketing, product labeling, everything. The guys could not relate to a company. They needed a human being—a name, a face, a voice, a personality belonging to a guy they look up to and trust. Who could that be but Joe Weider? And I could never be plain, old everyday Joe, working on covers, tasting supplements, going home and petting the cat. I had to be Joe, the muscle man's icon, the supreme expert and champion of the cause of bodybuilding, working with all the top guys in the world and bringing them to the pages of my magazines. Bodybuilding is about getting bigger, so I had to be a little bit bigger than life.

What I did, philosophically speaking, was to create a Platonic ideal of myself and make exciting images of this ideal to catch and hold the attention of millions of people so I could educate them about bodybuilding and provide products they required. The ideal was a lot like reality, because I was a muscle man and I truly deserved my titles Trainer of Champions and Master Blaster. All my life I followed my own advice, working out and watching my diet and health, and I loved bodybuilding with all my heart. If I didn't walk the talk, as they say, people would have turned away from me long ago.

Since I had stuff to sell, it would have been very stupid not to promote it. I had to promote it by brand name, which was my name. But I know the difference between the guy in the Joe Weider logo and Joe Weider. A megalomaniac I am not.

When Arnold got out of the game and into movies, we still saw each other and he still asked me for advice. Back in 1980, he started work on *Conan the Barbarian,* the first movie he starred in. He came to me saying the producer, Dino de Laurentiis, wanted him to trim down because his muscles were too big for the movies. But I advised Arnold to flaunt his muscles because they set him apart and made him special. I said the muscles made him the first action hero who actually looked capable of heroics, and people would go crazy over him just as he was. Later I visited the set and watched him practice a scene where he picked up a log. Arnold just put the thing on his shoulder and casually walked away. I told him he should flex his muscles hard and dramatize the incredible power it took to lift the log, which only the mighty Conan—and the mighty Arnold Schwarzenegger—possessed.

Conan the Barbarian came out in 1982. On the day it opened, I drove by a theater and saw a line of great big bodybuilders that went down the street and around the corner. It looked just like the guys lined up outside one of our shows. I was so surprised I almost drove up on the sidewalk. "What the heck is this?" I said to myself even though I knew what it was. It was bodybuilding turning out for one of its own.

What the guys did for *Conan the Barbarian,* they would do for *Conan the Destroyer* and for Arnold's movies that followed. All over the world, muscle men would flock to see Arnold up on the big screen, like his success was a personal victory for each and every one of us. The guys gave Arnold a built-in audience, which, in my opinion, helped him in the early years of his career. People love to talk about how great Arnold was for bodybuilding. Well, that was a two-way street.

By 1983, Arnold was done filming the second Conan movie and looking for something bigger and better than ever. Boy, did he find it. In *The Terminator* he played a killer robot from the future sent back through time to the present. In the movie he just walks around and wipes out everybody in sight, showing no emotion whatsoever because he's a machine. It sounds crazy, but the part was absolutely perfect, like it was made for Arnold. His incredible body and inner strength projected menace, and the audiences were mesmerized. The studio bigshots saw Arnold's incredible drawing power, and his career went up like a rocket. Pretty soon he was Hollywood's No. 1 star.

Our great successes began to put a distance between Arnold and me that I didn't like. He was always somewhere shooting a movie, and neither of us had spare time. I think there was something else, too. Not that I ever was a barrel of laughs, but I got more serious and preoccupied as the Weider businesses grew. I had so much on my mind, and Arnold wanted no part of somebody else's seriousness. He liked people who added to his entertainment and *joie de vivre.* If you didn't do that, he didn't care so much for your company.

Mind you, I'm writing about Arnold more than 20 years ago when he was younger and completely focused on getting ahead in Hollywood. Age has opened his heart and deepened his feelings. And even at the time my feelings weren't hurt, because I understood Arnold. Still, I didn't like it. As anybody close to him will tell you, Arnold is a guy you miss. When he's gone, you wish he would come back.

This might seem crazy in connection with a world-famous muscle man and tough guy in the movies and governor of California, but Arnold's effect on people makes me think of a baby. A baby is like a magnet. As we get older we lose our energy and vitality, and a baby recharges us. Babies and kids always add energy, liven everybody up. They're the opposite of pain-in-the-neck grownups who wear you down and drain you of energy. Them, you're glad to get away from, but you want the baby to stay because he makes the weariness and cares of the world go away. The more cares you've got, the more you want to have the baby around.

Don't get me wrong—Arnold and I were not on the outs. Though we didn't see so much of each other face to face, we stayed on very good terms and we worked hand in glove. And my loss, in terms of contact with Arnold, turned out to be a gain for both me and Betty, because it brought a terrific young woman into our lives who works with us to this day.

The story shows, one more time, that if you make the right kind of impression on Joe Weider and he likes having you around, he'll figure out a way to make you part of the team. If you're not available or the timing is wrong, he'll wait until things are different.

This is, in fact, what happened with Charlotte Parker, who was Arnold's personal publicist all through his years on top in Hollywood. People in the know say she had a lot to do with Arnold's rise to stardom and that he was lucky to hook up with her. That wasn't luck; that was Arnold. He had a knack, like nobody I ever knew, for picking people who could do him the most good.

I got to know Charlotte in her role as a go-between for Arnold and me. From *The Terminator* on, the three of us had a sort of ritual. When Arnold had a new release coming up, he'd tell Charlotte to get hold of me to make arrangements for a cover and inside editorial attention. Always he took care of the Weider publications before anybody else.

Phone calls would have done the trick, but Charlotte took the trouble to come by. It was her nature to go the extra mile. I think, too, Charlotte liked to meet in person because we got along so well. She was only about 30 then, but it was like we knew each from way back. In a way we did. Charlotte's parents were Jews who survived the Nazi Holocaust, and like other children of immigrants—

like me—she grew up with one foot in the old country, one in the new, and she was steeped in tradition. Now and again we talked in Yiddish, which I had very little opportunity to do. Charlotte sometimes used Yiddish with Arnold, too, because it's so close to his native German. And Charlotte has a special warmth. She's a sweetheart, but also a go-getter, as is her partner Joel Parker. The two of them currently work with me and Betty. When they did publicity for the Mr. Olympia, Joel got us attention from the wire services and newspapers that we never had before. The Parkers also work with my nephew Eric Weider, CEO of our companies.

If you're a prize, the Weiders are going to catch you and keep you.

So who made out, Arnold or me, putting his movie stuff in my magazines? We both did. Arnold on the cover sold an issue like crazy, but then the magazines would put hundreds of thousands of *gluteus maximii* in the theater seats on the opening weekend. By the late 1980s, paid circulation of *Muscle & Fitness* was over a half-million and going up fast, and total readership was in the millions, all over the world. And we had power greater than other magazines. Our readers were much more likely than the readers of *Time* or *Newsweek,* say, to run out to see Arnold's new movie, because he was a still a brother of the iron. Often Arnold was a personal hero, too. Millions of guys in the 1980s got into bodybuilding 10 or 15 years earlier when they were mesmerized by magazine pictures of Arnold, the way I was once mesmerized by my hero John Grimek. Guys like that are Arnold fans and ticket-buyers for life. Since he went into politics, they're Arnold voters.

Twenty-some years later it still hurts to tell about this. I still feel the loss, and I still get mad that it happened.

One day in September 1987, we got word that Christine MacIntyre was dead. Early in the morning, a truck loaded with cement blocks went out of control and smashed into Christine's car and another woman's car. Both women died in the accident, which happened out on the Pacific Coast Highway in Malibu, where Christine lived. The accident didn't have to happen—the idiot in the truck had a load 15 tons over the legal weight limit. Christine left behind a husband and two children. For me, this was like losing a family member. Betty said she felt like her best friend died. We were afraid to tell Aunt Annie, who loved Christine, too.

Not long ago a woman at UCLA sent me a copy of a write-up she did about Christine and her contributions to athletics at the university and how popular she was. I told the woman that all she wrote was true—to know Christine was to love her—and I said that seeing Christine's picture in the article brought tears. She was such a wonderful woman. Open a copy of *Shape* and you'll see Christine's name on the masthead as founding editor. In that small way we honor her and say she'll always be with us.

Though her staffers were devastated, Christine's magazine did not suffer. Barbara Harris, another fitness expert and one of Christine's consulting editors, became editor. I took Barbara under my wing, and she turned out to be brilliant on the job and another true believer. Under her leadership, circulation shot up into the millions and *Shape* became the worldwide phenomenon it is. Barbara still runs the show at *Shape,* and we still stay in touch.

In the late 1980s, people started making a big uproar about anabolic steroids in sports—bodybuilding included—like this new, horrible menace dropped out of the sky. In fact, people who knew the score had been aware of steroid use in the U.S. for almost 30 years.

I should give a little background: People call them drugs, but steroids are not drugs like aspirin or antibiotics. They're synthetic hormones. Very simply put, a steroid is an artificial form of the male hormone testosterone, which makes a man a man. Among other things, testosterone tells the body to make more muscle, which is why men have more mass and strength than women. "Anabolic," the term commonly used with steroids, is just a fancy way to say something helps the body add new tissue.

Scientists figured out how to make steroids in the 1930s and explored ways for using them to help the weak and infirm. Like much of the world's evil, the use of steroids to enhance healthy people came from the Nazis and the Communists. Doctors played around with steroids in Hitler's Germany, and then the Soviet Union picked up where the Nazis left off and became the first country to use steroids to make athletes bigger and stronger. The difference showed very dramatically in the Soviet weightlifting team. Suddenly their guys were setting records and cleaning up at meets.

The first U.S. coach to catch on to steroids was none other than Bob Hoffman. A doctor with Hoffman's team figured out that the Soviets had a secret weapon and started pushing Hoffman to have his guys try steroids. Hoffman wasn't sure, but then the Soviets wiped the floor with everybody else at the 1960 Olympic Games. Guys at York tried steroids on their own, and their results made Hoffman a believer.

For once I'm not criticizing Hoffman. He couldn't stop what happened—nobody could. That genie was out of the bottle, and if his lifters didn't start using steroids, some other American athletes would have, because the Communists were using and winning in other sports, too. At first our athletes who got into steroids didn't even hide the fact. They weren't breaking any rules, and they weren't breaking the law. All the bans and prohibitions were in the future, and nobody had any idea there might be terrible dangers to athletes and their sports.

It didn't take long for some of my guys to start playing around with steroids. Being a purist and idealist about bodybuilding, I didn't like it, but like everybody else I was still a babe in the woods. You can see the naïveté and innocence in my old magazines. In 1963, we ran back-to-back articles pro and con. The pro writer actually took steroids to see what they did for him.

The con guy said you could do better using our protein supplements. I'm sure he meant well and believed what he wrote, but he was wrong. Steroids help guys put on lean muscle and get stronger, which is why professional athletes keep taking them, no matter what bans and laws are passed. As my brother Ben explains in his part of this book, amateur athletics are a different story, because it's easier to do thorough drug screening and enforce the rules when guys are scared of disqualification and money is not the name of the game.

Throw in millions of dollars and the chance to gain fame and power like gods on earth, and you've got deep, deep problems.

I didn't stay naïve about steroids for long, though, and my magazines issued some of the earliest warnings about the dangers of using them. This truly was a horrifying development. To me bodybuilding always was—and still is—about health and mental and spiritual uplift. This was a clean, innocent pursuit, and steroids were like the serpent coming into the Garden of Eden.

And I was heartbroken to discover that steroids had wormed their way into professional bodybuilding. Larry Scott, the first Mr. Olympia, our wonderful, clean-cut golden boy and my friend, said he had used steroids. He said it onstage in London when he announced his retirement from bodybuilding. Other people acted like he committed treason, but I think Larry tried to sound an alarm by being honest.

Nobody heeded the alarm, though. After that, my position with my top bodybuilders became like that of a father. My sons, those closest to me, like Arnold and Franco and Lou, knew I strongly disapproved of drug use and pretended they had nothing to do with drugs. Like a trusting father, I chose to believe them. Maybe this was innocence on my part, or maybe I just wanted to believe them. But I probably should have known better. Later Arnold admitted he used steroids, and these days he openly shares his regrets about it and warns young people not to make such a mistake.

God help us, the drugs Arnold and the others at that time took and the amounts they took are a joke compared to what's around today. People don't take one drug, they take many—"stacking," they call it—in amounts that can be deadly dangerous. Already we've had pro bodybuilders—young men!—suffer heart attacks and other serious medical conditions. Just recently, *Flex* ran a list of casualties, which include deaths. I don't want to blow things out of proportion—problems are few and far between, and ours is actually one of the safest sports in the world—but I wish there was no such thing as anabolic, performance-enhancing drugs in sports.

I hate drugs—truly hate them. But was it ever in the power of Joe Weider or Ben Weider or anybody else to wipe them out of professional bodybuilding? No. Top body builders are top body builders because they'll do absolutely anything to win. Anything. A study once showed that leading athletes would take a substance that made them winners—even if it killed them the day after they won! With that sort of psychology, do common sense, ethics, and concern for health stand a chance? Technology, so far, can't protect us, because for every new, improved kind of drug screening, there's a new way to beat it. In our experience, cracking down on the pros actually made things worse because it pushed guys toward stuff that doesn't show up on tests that can be far more dangerous than steroids—like human growth hormone (HGH).

The situation makes me think of a story from Greek mythology I read as a kid—the great battle of Hercules against the Hydra, a horrible monster that killed every warrior who fought it. It had a hundred heads, and every time one got cut off, two grew back in its place. Hercules won because he fought with both a sword and a torch that he used to seal the monster's wounds so nothing could grow. Hercules kept cutting and burning and cutting until finally the Hydra had no head. That, I believe and hope with all my heart, is our future. People in sports won't give up, and we'll cut and burn, and some day the monster will die.

Maybe I put off writing about this subject because it makes me so mad. I'm mad that there is such a problem and that it stains the name and honor of many sports, including ours. And I'm mad about the way bodybuilding gets unfairly singled out and criticized, as if all of bodybuilding, top to bottom, has been tainted and we're worse off than pro football, say, or baseball, or track and field. Such absolute nonsense—our problem is concentrated in the tiny percentage of bodybuilders who could profit from drug use, the top pro competitors. Because of Ben's efforts, our amateurs are as clean as any athletes in the world. And the vast, vast majority of people who lift to build their muscles wouldn't touch drugs.

Would you?

As for health problems and risks, other sports are far more dangerous. Think about the poor guys who drop dead in football practice from the heat or get their backs or necks broken. In a given year, more high school and college football kids get seriously hurt or die playing football, than the number of bodybuilders who have problems.

And even up at the top competitive levels, drugs have not changed the nature of bodybuilding. Take away steroids, and the same guys would still win. They would still be bigger than the winners from 10 years ago because they stay in the game longer and train more scientifically and eat better and use more advanced supplements. Would the guys be as big as they are without steroids and other substances that I hate to even think about? No, but the difference isn't as great as some would have you think. And the qualities of a winner are what they always were—good genetics, drive, discipline, self-sacrifice, and the smarts to train strategically and peak on contest night. Competitive bodybuilding is not competitive drug-taking. If I thought it was, even for a minute, I wouldn't want anything to do with it.

I'm still floored by the way we grew through the 1980s. In 1989, North American paid circulation of *Muscle & Fitness* broke 600,000, roughly seven times what it was in 1980. The increase was more like 10 times, if you include our *M&F* spinoffs for male readers, *Flex* and *Men's Fitness*. We took in ad revenues of more than $100 million—compared to zilch in 1980.

In that 10-year period, the revenues for all of Weider jumped by a factor of more like 100, from about $5 million in 1980 to the $500-million range. By any measure you can think of, the growth was out of this world. Previously, we rented out parts of our headquarters building to other companies, but now the place overflowed and we had to put people in neighboring buildings. Worldwide, Weider was up to about 2,000 employees. We acquired other companies and became, among other things, the biggest player in treadmill-type equipment. Our nutrition and vitamin companies put out more than 1,000 separate products.

I appreciated this success mostly because of the creative tools it provided. For once I had all the resources I needed to create the magazines of my dreams. I could use heavy, coated paper, put wonderful color all over the inside pages. Once in a while, for the sake of variety, I hired top-dollar photographers, the most prestigious names in the business. Top-flight people wanted to work for me, and we could tap PhDs and MDs for expert opinions and advice. The days of shame regarding muscle magazines and bodybuilding were gone. Celebrities wanted to be part of the action, and we ran covers of superstars like Clint Eastwood, Sly Stallone, Lauren Hutton, Brooke Shields, Linda Evans, and on and on.

The world never saw magazines anything like mine.

Everything changed—and nothing changed.

What didn't change was Joe Weider. This is true through my whole story. Fortunes went up, down, and up again, and I was still the same guy doing the same thing. Every day I gave my work my all, and I put the Joe Weider touch on everything—cover shots, ads, training materials, everything. If somebody brought in a new vitamin bottle and the label didn't thrill me, I'd send it back for more work and keep sending it back until it jumped up and said, "Read me! Buy me!" I taste-tested the supplements. I still went out on photo shoots and oiled up the guys.

You read right, a multimillionaire in his sixties putting oil on muscle men so they look perfect in pictures. Why did I do it? Because I took great care and did it just right. Others would slop too much oil on the chest, not enough on the arms, maybe overlook the back altogether. This seems like a small thing, but misapplied oil makes a picture that's less than great, which shortchanges the bodybuilder and the millions of people who pay to look at the picture.

For me, in my work, there are no small things.

Credit where it's due—I really appreciated having a good finances man, Allen Dalfen, watching the dollars come and go. He knew how to use money to make more money, and he kept everything and everybody on the up and up. For me, having such a guy watch my back was a tremendous relief, and we got to really like each other even though we often bumped heads.

It could be we liked each other better because of our differences and because we were true to our natures and our proper roles. Month in, month out, we had words about how big the magazines should be. I wanted more pages to put in more for the readers, and Allen wanted fewer to cut back on costs. Same with sponsoring bodybuilders and other issues, and the deal was always the same—I wanted to spend more, and Allen wanted to watch the bottom line.

You wouldn't think it of a bean-counter type guy, but Allen had a sense of humor. This shows in the way he once made a point about label designs. He was always after me to make my labels look more alike. He said they changed too often and were so distinct and different that people didn't recognize they came from the same company. We needed more consistency so buyers would always know at a glance they were looking at Weider. Or so Allen said. I thought he was just being cheap. For me labels were like a personal art form, and I put the same sort of effort into them as my magazine covers. Each one I took as a fresh challenge, and nobody had labels of such originality, beauty, and visual impact.

So I paid no attention to what Allen said about labels until one fine day the door to my office opened and Allen ushered in a line of the most beautiful young women, every one perfectly put together and lovely to behold—white, black, Asian, blonde, brunette, brown eyes, blue eyes, what have you. It was like the finalists at the Miss Universe pageant came for a visit.

Allen said, "Joe, I want you to take a very good look at these girls."

Like he had to tell me to look.

"They're beautiful, aren't they?" he said.

You bet they were. Then Allen asked if, based on their looks, I might think they were sisters, or cousins, or if they came from the same area.

How could I possibly think that?

"Joe," Allen said to me, "these girls are just like the labels you're putting out. They're gorgeous, but they come from all over. There's no relationship. If we're trying to build the Weider brand, shouldn't our products look like they belong to the same family?"

I had to laugh, and I had to give some thought to what he said.

The Bob Hoffman story ended with a strange and complicated legal case at the end of the 1980s that was like Hoffman's ghost rising and trying to make trouble for the Weiders.

Hoffman passed away in 1985, by which time he and York were shadows of their former selves. His flagship magazine, *Strength & Health,* outlived him by only a year, but his bodybuilding magazine, *Muscular Development,* survived, still published by York Barbell. In 1988, York sold the magazine to the guys who owned Twin Lab, a company making vitamins and sports nutrition products just like Weider. The deal meant we had a competitor with its own magazine.

Not long after that we stopped running Twin Lab's ads in Weider publications. I had my own good reasons for this, which had to do with the way Twin Lab treated the bodybuilders. The guys came to me very unhappy about the way the company put their pictures on its labels. The images showed body parts only, like an arm flexing, and you couldn't tell whose arm it was. This denied the bodybuilders valuable exposure.

Twin Lab brought a federal anti-trust suit against us, trying to force us to take their ads. Their claim, basically, was that nobody in sports nutrition had a chance without ads in *Muscle & Fitness* and *Flex,* and we kept their ads out in order to stay on top in the supplement industry, which we controlled like a monopoly. Our control was the crucial issue, and the whole case turned on whether we had more than 35 percent of the industry's sales. Twin Lab couldn't prove we did, so the case got thrown out. During the proceedings, I sent in a deposition so clear and persuasive that the judge was really impressed.

Hoffman must have been spinning in his grave. The owners of his old magazine went to court crying that Joe Weider had the only muscle magazines in the world that mattered. After a while, we made peace with Twin Lab when the ownership changed. However, one of the owners from the time of the lawsuit held on to *Muscular Development*. Things have calmed down, but for years he took shots at Weider magazines, especially *Flex,* in the most inflammatory language. I guess he hoped we'd make some kind of angry response, thereby calling our readers' attention to his magazine, the way my old rival Hoffman once gave me hell and provided a big boost when I needed it. The guy at *Muscular Development* should have known better. To us the attacks were like flies buzzing.

Our successes always contain the seeds of defeat.

Who said that? I did, and I keep saying it, because it's important to remember that success can be dangerous. It can fill you with false confidence so you think the next thing you try will be a success, too. It's even more dangerous when you're so carried away you decide you can take away somebody else's success and do it bigger and better. This is what happened to Vince McMahon, the king of professional wrestling, when he decided to move in on the Weiders and take control of bodybuilding.

My brother and I knew something was up in 1990, when McMahon showed up at bodybuilding events. Word went out that he was going to launch a magazine, *Bodybuilding Lifestyles.* At the time of the official announcement, he said there was absolutely no intent to form a rival federation or put on bodybuilding events.

I called McMahon and said that he might not understand what he was getting into and that only true believers, steeped in the sport, could hope to succeed in bodybuilding. I meant this as friendly advice because I was deeply impressed by what McMahon did with pro wrestling, taking it from low budget to the big time, creating spectacles and a whole new kind of entertainment. At that time some of the top-rated shows on network TV were his, featuring the stars of his wrestling federation. McMahon also made a killing in pay-per-view. In his field, the guy was a genius.

But then McMahon went on the attack. With the usual Ben Weider brilliance, my brother took care of McMahon's attempt to lure the best IFBB guys over to his so-called federation, the Worldwide Bodybuilding Federation. On my side, the bodybuilding side, I knew McMahon wasn't the big threat he might appear to be with all his money, his genius at promoting and staging big events, and his clout in TV. He might be a nuisance for a little while, but the brothers who truly loved and understood bodybuilding and bodybuilding itself had nothing to fear.

A friend of mine just found a videotape of the 1991 WBF World Bodybuilding Champs, staged at the Taj Mahal in Atlantic City. What you see is a bunch of second-string guys McMahon hired away from us at great expense. They came out in crazy costumes and put on little shows with lavish stage effects. There was some posing, but bodybuilding it wasn't. It wasn't wrestling, either. It was a multimillion-dollar flop.

McMahon was blind to the differences between his realm and ours, which are huge. You can be completely ignorant about wrestling and still get caught up in one of McMahon's shows, which are like comic books with flesh-and-blood characters. Bodybuilding is much more for connoisseurs. Mr. Olympia is a great show, which anybody can enjoy, but most of the people who buy tickets are true aficionados, like those who go to the opera or the ballet. Most are bodybuilders themselves. I truly believe we have the most educated fans, in terms of knowledge of the sport, in all of athletics.

The McMahon deal was an old, old story—an outsider sees all the muscles and doesn't see the brains. Bodybuilders are smarter than other people think.

I heard McMahon lost something like $20 million in a year and a half. Then he wised up and got out of bodybuilding. At the end, he did something unforgettable that showed class and dignity. He called up both Ben and me and conceded defeat, congratulating us on our successes, which he said were richly deserved. It was crazy, he said, to go up against guys like us on our own home ground, which we knew and loved better than anybody in the world.

McMahon had his son on the line listening in. He said he wanted the young man to hear what was said and learn something.

To me, he said he should have paid attention when I tried to warn him that he'd get into trouble in bodybuilding. And he said there's only one Joe Weider, and nobody else can duplicate what he has done. You had to be nuts to try.

He told Ben something similar, and we were both highly impressed.

Betty and I were happy and proud to see Arnold become a family man. All through the 1980s, he had gone out with Maria Shriver, a young woman we really liked. I started wondering what in the world Arnold was waiting for, but finally he popped the question, and in 1987 they got married. Like Betty and me, Arnold and Maria got married in the month of April. In fact, we celebrate our wedding anniversaries only two days apart—ours is the 24th, theirs the 26th.

We flew east and attended the wedding, which turned out to be one of the most glittering events of the year. Maria is one of the Kennedy clan, and we met her famous relations and other political bigwigs. Since she's a journalist, too, there were famous news people in attendance and Oprah Winfrey and other stars. Mingling with the *crème de la crème* were Arnold's bodybuilding friends. Franco was best man.

I felt privileged to be in such company, but the best part was seeing the bride and groom radiating happiness. Never have I seen Arnold so full of love and joy.

A while ago I wrote that Arnold made himself. But since they got together, I think that Maria had a lot to do with his success. Maria took some of the rough edges off Arnold and introduced him to the world of politics. But there's more to what she did: A good marriage gives a man a foundation on which to build his life and success, and a good woman provides a kind of stability and strength that a man lacks all on his own. I offer myself and Betty as proof. And couples, too, form important bonds. Arnold and Maria are like our children, and we get together with them whenever we can.

In the early 1990s, Arnold and I picked up where we left off before fame and fortune interfered. It happened pretty quietly and gradually, and nobody made a big deal. Now and again Arnold dropped in unannounced, without his family, for no particular reason except to hang around and visit. It wasn't like we saw each other all the time, but Arnold and I got to be pals again—better pals, I think, because we were older and wiser. I was very glad, and I could tell Arnold was, too.

All sorts of things happened in the course of the 1990s, good and not so good. My nephew Eric, Ben's son, joined us and took over the Weider companies, which got bigger than ever. But Joe was still Joe. I still had my magazines, and I still put oil on the bodybuilders at photo shoots. On the down side, I had a few medical problems. It happened that both Arnold and I had identical heart operations performed by the same doctor, to fix the same sort of heart-valve problems that we were both born with—what are the odds of that?

In 1998, Arnold absolutely floored me by telling the world the story that I wanted to hear him tell for 30 years. He spoke at a Hollywood gala, where he received the American Cinematheque Award for his brilliant career in movies. In his acceptance speech Arnold said he had to thank the man who brought him to America and gave him his start. Without that man, Arnold wouldn't be here, he said, and he told about me giving him a car and a place to live and helping with his schooling. He spoke so movingly and from the heart, and his words meant more to me because most of the stars and movie people in the crowd didn't know a thing about Joe Weider or bodybuilding. The event was broadcast on TV, so millions of people saw and heard.

CHAPTER TWELVE

REALIZING MY IMPOSSIBLE DREAMS

Ben Weider

President Samaranch

Just when the International Olympic Committee desperately needed an energetic and disciplined and forceful leader, it got one in the person of Juan Antonio Samaranch, who took office as IOC president in 1980. At that time, the IOC was in such desperate financial straits that many feared the Olympic Games might not survive. President Samaranch threw himself into the task of bringing the IOC back from the brink. As soon as he took office, he moved to Lausanne and became the committee's first president to treat his position as a full-time professional commitment, devoting to it all the time and energy that business and political leaders give to their jobs. This was a marked contrast to his predecessors, who were amateurs in the old-time sense—wealthy, high-born individuals who pursued their duties part-time and treated Olympism as a sort of exclusive international club. In their era, much of international sport was governed in this spirit of *noblesse oblige*. President Samaranch was himself an aristocrat, born into a wealthy Spanish family and granted the title *Marques de Samaranch,* but he was truly a professional in his work. And his professionalism would save the Olympics.

President Samaranch had been a government official and diplomat in Spain who in 1966 was appointed government secretary for sports. He was also a member of the IOC and president of his country's National Olympic Committee. In 1974 he became the IOC vice president. He rose in the ranks as a diplomat, becoming Spain's ambassador to the Soviet Union and Mongolia. Such successes showed President Samaranch to be an extremely sagacious and tough individual.

I made my first attempts to gain Olympic recognition under the Samaranch presidency with the backing of Walter Tröger, IOC member for Germany and chairman of the committee for the recognition of new sports. Walter, a robustly built man of middle height, was an extremely kindly and gentle man with a great strength of character and a deep belief in the sanctity and power of sport. Walter favored Olympic recognition for the IFBB, because he thought it was one of the best-run international sports federations. However, his position was actually rather contradictory, because he also believed that bodybuilding was not truly a sport. I found such a stance truly baffling. How could a rapidly growing branch of competitive athletics, with tens of thousands of participants and millions of fans, organized under an officially recognized international sports federation, be anything but a sport? On the other hand, I was very glad to have the support of such a strategically placed official in the Olympic Committee, and I was grateful for Walter's help in setting up my first meetings with President Samaranch. I also liked Walter personally a great deal. In fact, we became very good friends.

The first thing that struck me about President Samaranch was the way he commanded respect. He conducted himself with the utmost formality and decorum. He was one of the most reserved and in-control individuals I ever met. Although he appreciated a good joke, any sort of familiarity would have been out of the question. This made him quite unlike his immediate predecessor, Lord Killanin of Ireland. Of course Lord Killanin was also dead set against recognition for our sport. With President Samaranch I never sensed such intransigence, even though at our first meetings he showed absolutely no inclination to favor our bid for recognition. At the same time, however, he never closed the door to further discussion. And the respect he commanded, he also gave.

I knew, the first time I met him, that winning the favor of President Samaranch might well be the toughest challenge I ever faced. But I also sensed that I would someday succeed if I showed him the great respect that he deserved and did all I could to gain respect in his eyes. In that spirit I began a series of meetings that would continue for the next 20 years, which would foster my closest, best relationship, both professional and personal, with any IOC president.

One way I showed respect, which I know President Samaranch appreciated, was to take only as much time with him as necessary. Many people are drawn to the powerful and famous to no good purpose, seizing on any excuse to meet, dragging out conversations unnecessarily. But I never requested a meeting unless there was substantive information to bring to the president's attention. I always arrived fully prepared and then, often after only 10 or 12 minutes, I excused myself.

"Your Excellency," I would say, "I know you're an extremely busy man. I don't want to be rude, but I believe it is time for me to go."

This sent an important message: I considered President Samaranch's time highly important. This helped build our mutual respect.

In our early meetings, President Samaranch's answer to my request for his support for bodybuilding's recognition never varied, but hearing "No" repeatedly didn't anger or upset me. I simply looked forward to the next opportunity to meet. I can't say I discerned any signs of progress, at least for the first few years, but nor were there any signs of losing ground. I felt more encouraged than discouraged because the president never shut the door on me.

The U.S.A.

I was ever more convinced that the IFBB would ultimately succeed because the standing of bodybuilding and of our federation rose steadily in the world of international sport. By the beginning of the 1980s, we had more than a hundred member nations, and the great worldwide boom in bodybuilding and fitness in general was just getting into full swing. In 1982, the largest organization for amateur bodybuilding in the U.S. secured its affiliation with the IFBB and thus was officially recognized and authorized to control amateur bodybuilding in the U.S.A. Bob Hoffman and his faction had irrevocably lost their grip on U.S. bodybuilding, and all American bodybuilders could at long last enjoy all the benefits offered by their sport's only recognized worldwide federation.

Names of the groups involved in the story are a bit confusing, because the American group was called the National Physique Committee (NPC), not Bodybuilding Federation as in most of our member countries. The NPC designation dates to when bodybuilding was organized under the umbrella of the Amateur Athletic Union's weightlifting committee, which was, of course, under the thumb of Bob Hoffman. The National Physique Committee that in 1982 sought IFBB recognition and affiliation was, in fact, a reorganized committee completely independent of the AAU.

By 1982, the Athletic Union's NPC had already voted in favor of affiliation with the IFBB, but the new committee represented a clean break from the very troubled past. The trouble, I might add, was completely unnecessary. Progressive individuals had been trying to make peace between the IFBB and the AAU for years. In 1971, the Athletic Union's then-president Jack Kelly took it upon himself to heal the rift in bodybuilding. The situation really was ludicrous. To achieve international stardom, American champions had to compete in IFBB international competitions, by far the most prestigious in the world. This meant they had to switch allegiances from the AAU committee in the U.S., which was under Bob Hoffman's control, to the IFBB.

Jack Kelly, brother of the beautiful star and international celebrity Grace Kelly, recognized how silly this was and how detrimental to the sport. He also recognized how the IFBB's full membership in the General Association of

International Sports Federations validated our position as the only legitimate worldwide bodybuilding federation. In 1971, he invited me to his home in Philadelphia to meet with our opponents within the AAU. I was perfectly willing to try to find some sort of common ground, but the unfriendly AAU faction, led by Bob Hoffman's general manager John Terpak, would not engage in constructive discussion.

The Hoffman faction managed to forestall AAU affiliation with the IFBB for a few more years, but the writing was on the wall, and everybody but our opponents could see it. In the late 1970s, the barriers between the Athletic Union's Physique Committee and our federation came tumbling down. First the National Sports Act, passed by the U.S. Congress, mandated that the three sports then organized under the AAU's Weightlifting Committee—weightlifting, bodybuilding, and powerlifting—each become autonomous. After that, the AAU lifted the ban on its athletes participating in IFBB events, a huge benefit to the competitors. Then, the AAU committee voted overwhelmingly to affiliate with our federation. Finally, in 1982, members of that committee broke away and formed their own truly independent National Physique Committee, the U.S.A.'s own IFBB affiliate federation.

What was gained from all this? Basically, the strongest amateur physique organization in America now enjoyed full membership in our worldwide federation. And IFBB affiliation brought amateur competition in the U.S. up to our international standards. The change impacted a great number of bodybuilders. At the time of its reorganization and affiliation with our federation, the NPC had about 6,000 active competitors and almost 200 annual competitions.

From the NPC, we at the IFBB got something of great value. Jim Manion of Pittsburgh, Pennsylvania, chaired the committee and thus came into the ranks of our federation. A former competitor who won multiple titles, Jim is a tireless worker and true believer in bodybuilding. At first he held down a full-time job with a utility company while running the NPC. Now he holds some very important and active IFBB positions. He's still chairman of the NPC, now vastly larger than it was in 1982 with more than 40,000 paid members and up to 1,000 competitions organized each year. He also serves as the IFBB's assistant general secretary and vice president for North America.

Jim and I have a standing joke about our many years of working together. When he affiliated his National Physique Committee with the IFBB, more than one person said to him, "Are you crazy? You can't trust Ben Weider. If you hook up with him you'll be out within a year."

More than 25 years later, Jim is still waiting for me to make my move and maneuver him out. Of course this is just a private joke. I've placed my trust in Jim for more than a quarter-century, and he has never let me down. He's a straight shooter and does not suffer fools lightly.

The Fight Against Drugs

In the previous chapter, Joe gave his own observations and thoughts on the terrible scourge of anabolic steroids and other performance-enhancing drugs in our sport and in all other sports. I agree with him in every particular and every sentiment. I, too, despise the abuse of drugs, and wish with all my heart that drugs had never come onto the scene. And I have pledged to do everything in my power to stop their abuse. As I have laid out in numerous speeches, position papers, and our stringent drug-testing protocols and zero-tolerance rules and regulations, the IFBB's stance against drug use has been unequivocal since day one. The use of steroids and other such illegal substances in order to enhance performance, also known as "doping," is cheating. Period. Worse still, it endangers the user's health, not to mention his or her life. Bodybuilding is not body destruction.

As Joe has pointed out, administrators in amateur sport are in a much better position to institute effective anti-doping measures, as compared to professional sports where the situation is much more difficult to control. Soon after the IFBB became an accredited international federation in 1971, we formed a Medical Commission that began to study drug abuse and look for truly effective controls. By that time, the IOC had instituted some drug screening for Olympic athletes, but the tests then available were notably ineffective for detecting muscle-building hormones. Indeed, the IOC's first concerns about drugs had not involved steroids at all, but rather amphetamines used by endurance athletes such as cyclists.

By the 1980s, though, screening techniques improved, and we were ready to take action. At our federation's 1982 International Congress in Brugge, Belgium, I authorized a trial of drug-testing procedures at the 1983 European Championships under the direction of our Medical Commission chairman Prof. Dr. Ernst Jokl of the U.S.A., a distinguished researcher in the field of sports medicine. At the 1983 International Congress in Singapore, the delegates discussed the trial run of testing and then voted unanimously to begin mandatory drug screening at the 1985 Men's World Amateur Bodybuilding Championships to be held in Göteborg, Sweden. But then some valid concerns were raised about potential medical and legal problems at the 1984 International Congress in Las Vegas. I told our medical and legal experts to investigate and report on their findings at the 1985 Congress to be held in Sweden. The experts' reports answered the questions raised in Las Vegas to my satisfaction and that of all the IFBB delegates. Once again there was a unanimous vote to begin testing at the 1986 Men's World Amateur Bodybuilding Championships to be organized in Tokyo, Japan.

Never will I forget the great feelings of pride in our organization and our sport at the International Congress in Tokyo.

My brother Joe addressed an audience of our national members, supporters, and VIPs, saying, "I want to thank the delegates for their devotion to drug-free sport and for helping to make the drug testing a great success. I promise my continued support in this worthwhile endeavor."

Then I went to the podium and spoke. "The use of drugs in any sport to gain an unfair advantage over an opponent is not only reprehensible but dangerous to the health of the athlete," I said.

From then on anti-doping procedures would be part and parcel of a growing number of our international competitive events. Proof of the effectiveness of drug tests as a deterrent came just a year later. At our 1987 Men's World Amateur Bodybuilding Championships organized in Madrid, Spain, not one of the athletes tested positive for drugs. The IFBB took another important step by implementing drug testing at the Women's World Amateur Championships held in Reno, Nevada. Eventually doping controls would be implemented at all of our international amateur events and a growing number of national-level contests as well.

By this time Dr. Bob Goldman of the U.S., a staunch advocate of drug-free sport, chaired the federation's Medical Commission. To honor his work with us, we named Prof. Dr. Jokl the commission's chairman emeritus, and I presented him with the IFBB Gold Medal. Among Prof. Dr. Jokl's many contributions, it was he who introduced us to another distinguished medical researcher whose help was absolutely invaluable. This was Prof. Dr. Manfred Donike of Germany, chairman of the International Olympic Committee's Doping Commission, who worked directly with Prince Alexandre de Merode, chairman of the IOC Medical Commission. At the time, Prof. Dr. Donike was one of the foremost experts on doping in the world, with his own state-of-the-art research and testing laboratory in Cologne, West Germany. Through my efforts and that of my executive assistant Rafael Santonja, Prof. Dr. Donike became the special advisor to the IFBB Medical Commission.

Under Prof. Dr. Donike's direction we immediately brought our anti-doping protocols up to the IOC's Olympic Movement Anti-Doping Code. This code called for the sole use of its stipulated procedures in sample collection and control, use of IOC-approved doping control kits, and IOC-accredited laboratories for sample analysis. So now our anti-doping program was as good as any in the world. Prof. Dr. Donike's personal association with the IFBB also brought us instant credibility for our program in the eyes of the Olympic Committee. I well remember the surprise of President Samaranch upon learning that we worked so closely with Prof. Dr. Donike. The right thing to do, fighting drug use, also turned out to be the smart thing to do, in terms of advancing the great dream of Olympic recognition.

Later in the 1980s, Joe and I would campaign for new laws to criminalize the misuse of steroids and other such drugs. Joe ran editorials in his magazines urging readers to write to members of the U.S. Congress to ask for legislation adding steroids to the list of federally proscribed substances. Not only did the readers write to their legislators, they sent letters of support by the thousands to Joe's editorial offices. I was asked to present these letters to Congressmen in favor of new drug controls and went to Washington, D.C., with several thousand letters to show the extent of support within the bodybuilding community. U.S. Representatives Mel Levine and Henry Waxman of California and Ben Gilman of New York introduced me to some of the assembled Congressmen. Not long afterward, a new federal law made unauthorized distribution and use of steroids in the U.S. a federal offense on a level similar to the sale and use of heroin and cocaine.

Another Polish Surprise

More than 10 years after official recognition of our sport and the IFBB in Poland, bodybuilding was booming. In 1984, I received an invitation from the Polish sports minister Dr. Wlodzimierz Reczek, the same high official who had bowled me over in 1971 by his ready acceptance of both our sport and our federation in his country. Dr. Reczek wanted me to be a special guest at an important national sports festival familiarly known as the Polish National Olympics. The event, to be held that year in the city of Bydgoszcz, would include bodybuilding as a medal sport. I made the trip with my son Eric, then a 19-year-old college student and now the president and CEO of Weider Health and Fitness and IFBB general secretary. Eric also is publisher of his own group of magazines devoted to history, especially military history. Dr. Reczek greeted us warmly upon our arrival, and I told him how pleased I was at the progress that bodybuilding had made with his support.

In 1984, Bydgoszcz, a medium-sized city in north-central Poland, still showed a great deal of damage from fighting during World War II, some 40 years earlier, and there were many signs of stagnation and poverty. But the city pulled out all the stops for the opening ceremony held in its central square, which was packed with people. The dais was lined with numerous government and military officials. Having been asked to give an opening address, I went to the podium and spoke of the growing importance of bodybuilding and thanked everyone for supporting our sport.

I ended my speech by raising my hands over my head and shouting, "Long live Poland!" And the crowd went wild with jubilation. Keep in mind that Poland was still under Communist rule and Soviet domination, and such a statement was illegal.

At this time, shouting "Long live Poland!" would have landed a Polish citizen in jail, or worse. Making such a direct appeal to national pride, in front of a large audience with officials in attendance, was bold and provocative. The crowd's response was really a roar of defiance against the country's Communist regime and its Soviet overlords. After 40 years of occupation by a foreign army and oppression and poverty, the Polish people were full of the desire for individual freedom and self-determination for their country. I sympathized, and I wanted them to know it. Had I run for mayor of Bydgoszcz that day, I would have won in a landslide. Most of the leading newspapers reported on my speech the following day, and the publicity generated by the games was overwhelmingly positive.

Eric and I visited local gyms, jammed by young people who didn't seem to mind using the battered, primitive equipment available to them. In spite of widespread joblessness and poverty, Polish competitors and bodybuilding enthusiasts had achieved very good results. Both Eric and I were impressed by the quality of athletes at the bodybuilding contest held in Bydgoszcz.

One afternoon I had a most unusual experience. Eric and I were resting at our hotel when we heard a knock at the door, which I opened. Standing before me was a tall, strapping young man who looked to be about 19 years old. His eyes filled with tears as he stepped forward and gave me a powerful bear hug.

"Papa, papa!" the young man said, obviously feeling an excess of emotion.

Eric watched all this, looking absolutely baffled. Why on earth would this stranger my own son's age be calling me papa?

Believe me, I wondered the same thing. I invited the fellow into the room. He spoke just a bit of English, and we endeavored to communicate, both to show friendship and to solve the mystery of why he addressed me as he did. After several minutes he reached into his jacket and pulled out an envelope and very carefully withdrew a letter. The letter was from me, written 10 years earlier in response to a letter he had written expressing his interest in bodybuilding. At the time he was 9 years old, and I answered him personally and sent some of our magazines to encourage him. I had no recollection of that particular correspondence, which was one of thousands just like it. I sent magazines and a letter of encouragement to any person from any country in the world who wrote to me.

I read the letter and handed it back, and the young man put it away as carefully as if he were handling a priceless religious relic. I presented him with a Weider sweater and IFBB lapel pin, crest and tie, and, once again, he was overcome with emotion.

The story shows what a profound effect a bit of personal attention could have on a boy thousands of miles away and on the other side of the Iron Curtain. Obviously, bodybuilding was a very important part of that young man's life. The time and expense it took to answer his letter and send magazines paid off a hundredfold. No, a thousandfold.

But I still don't understand why he called me papa.

Bikinis in China

Bodybuilding had also come far in the People's Republic of China, to which I returned many times after my first visit in 1958. The intervening years had been difficult for bodybuilding and pretty much everything and everybody in China. Through the late 1960s and '70s, the so-called Cultural Revolution wracked the country with upheaval and violence. Chairman Mao's brutal purge of liberal elements brought untold costs in human suffering and death and destruction of property. Through it all, though, I kept contact with members of the Chinese Weightlifting Federation who tried to keep bodybuilding alive. One man in particular deserves credit for the survival of our sport. Regarded as the Father of Bodybuilding in China, his name is Prof. Lou Zhuo Yu. During the darkest and most dangerous days, when bodybuilding was forbidden, possibly on pain of being sent to a concentration camp by the young fanatics trying to stamp out all vestiges of Western culture, this hero taught bodybuilding in an underground gym. To him and others I sent photos, magazines, videos, reports and information on training and nutrition. Much later, at our World Championships in Shanghai in 1994, it was my great privilege and honor to meet with Prof. Lou Zhuo Yu at length and help him open a modern, state-of-the-art bodybuilding gym in thanks for his support of bodybuilding during the most difficult and dangerous times. I donated the exercise equipment free of charge to this hero of our sport.

In 1982, as China liberalized and opened up to Western influences, a national bodybuilding championship called the Hercules Cup was organized. In 1985, the All China Sports Federation invited me to the third Hercules Cup, to be held in Beijing. I went to China accompanied by two of my sons, Eric and Mark, who were, respectively, 20 and 19 years old.

Upon arrival, my sons and I received magnificent VIP treatment, passing quickly through customs and then being whisked to the Sheraton Group's Great Wall Hotel, offering all the comforts and amenities that travelers anywhere might expect. Clearly, this was a new China. It felt like the country had jumped ahead a hundred years in the 27 years since I first visited.

I met with Li Meng Hua, minister for sport and physical culture, who said that his government had mounted a number of campaigns to promote health and fitness. One was an effort to eradicate smoking. Another was to stop spitting in public places, a national bad habit that foreign visitors found particularly disturbing. I was impressed that the government campaigns seemed to have a major effect. I saw very few Chinese smoking and much less public spitting than I witnessed on my earlier visit.

I asked Li Meng Hua to attend the Hercules Cup with me, and he was delighted to accept. The contest filled the 3,000-seat Beijing Exhibition Center for three nights running. One hundred and ten male bodybuilders from throughout China competed, with individual posing routines performed to a very strange mix of music that included old American standards, Steven Foster tunes, Broadway hits, and other pop songs. Chinese television covered the event, and segments of the contest were seen even in Canada, broadcast by the Canada's largest television network CTV.

In a historic first, Chinese women bodybuilders gave a beautifully choreographed group exhibition. By our standards, their bodies were rather lightly muscled and smooth, but they were exquisitely well formed and feminine. The crowd responded with thunderous applause as the women, who wore one-piece bathing suits, went through their graceful moves.

Minister Li Meng Hua leaned close to me. "How lovely they are," he said. "I would like very much to see these women athletes organize within your great federation."

I said to him, "I, too, would like to see an IFBB national affiliate in your great country."

I went on to add, "However, our federation regulations would require that women bodybuilders be clothed differently."

"What do you mean?" the minister asked.

"The rulebook calls for the wearing of bikinis by female competitors," I said.

The minister sat back in great surprise.

"What does sex have to do with bodybuilding?" he asked.

"Sex has nothing to do with it at all," I said. "It's a question of being able to judge the muscularity and condition of abdominals and hips. Fat and inadequate muscular development can easily be hidden by a one-piece suit."

The minister thought for a moment and smiled, saying, "Mr. Weider, you have given me a very difficult task indeed. To bring the IFBB to China, as you and I both greatly desire, I must convince my superiors to change their thinking on this subject."

The minister explained to me that wearing bikinis would be strictly forbidden under current government strictures. The prevailing attitudes in China were very old-fashioned, even puritanical, about exposing women's bodies in public. But the minister would try to effect a change in order to accommodate our sport. There could be no doubt that we had a high-placed friend in China. The minister strongly supported bodybuilding and the IFBB.

Everywhere we went in China, my sons and I saw countless people jogging, doing calisthenics and practicing ancient physical disciplines such as Tai Chi and Wushu. Each morning people gathered to exercise in even the tiniest public spaces. One day Eric, Mark and I rose at five o'clock and went to a park near our hotel to participate. We worked out with a group for a half-hour, doing our best to follow the synchronized exercises, which really were stylized moves from martial arts. Afterward, everybody else hopped on bicycles and pedaled off to work, and my sons and I began our day feeling remarkably refreshed and relaxed.

In visits to state sport centers I saw children of very young ages in serious athletic training. The precious abilities of the children absolutely astounded me. One 8-year-old boy was the best table tennis player I ever saw. A Chinese coach explained the philosophy of early recruitment and grooming of athletically gifted youngsters. He said, "You don't wait until a child is 12 or 14 to teach him or her to read, write, or do arithmetic. No, you begin when they are young and most able to learn. The same thing should be true of athletics." Considering China's recent successes at both Summer and Winter Olympic Games, the efficacy of the system cannot be doubted. In an incredibly short time, China has become an athletic power to be reckoned with.

Before 1985 was out, China joined the IFBB, thus becoming our federation's 127th member nation. The following year the country's first women's bodybuilding championships were organized in Shenzen with the official sanction of our federation and the Chinese sports authorities. The event drew extensive national and international media coverage. Five thousand spectators and a big contingent of journalists watched 46 women competing onstage in bikinis, a first for China. True to his word, sports minister Li Meng Hua had managed to persuade his government to allow women to wear garments that met IFBB specifications. Since bikinis were not available in China, they had to be imported from Hong Kong.

Here, in the form of a two-piece posing suit, was an impossible dream come true. How incredibly far we had come. I first went to China because sports officials saw the value of bodybuilding as conditioning for other sports, but nobody thought that bodybuilding would ever be accepted as a sport in its own right. Now the sport and our federation had official approval and enormous support from athletes and fans. And the government bent its rules to conform to our rules, allowing women competitors the freedom to properly display the physiques they worked so very hard to build.

In 1987, the year after the historic women's competition, I received a telex from Dr. Chen An-Huai, president of the Shanghai Institute of Physical Education, informing me that the institute had made me an honorary professor. I was the first non-Chinese so honored. He invited me to address the institute's spring graduating class of 1,200, most of whom would coach or teach physical education. I was proud to address the graduates about the Weider Triangle of Peak Athletic Performance, conditioning, especially strength conditioning, training to improve sport-specific skills, and sound nutrition supported by vitamins and nutritional supplements. After my presentation, President Chen An-Huai awarded me an Honorary Professorship, the institute's highest honor for contributions to sports sciences.

The Chinese people proved to be true believers and true lovers of bodybuilding. This would become evident to all the world when we held our World Championships and International Congress in Shanghai in 1994. One man's epic journey to Shanghai symbolized the long, hard road we had all traveled to make that triumphal event for bodybuilding possible. Chen Gin, a young bodybuilding enthusiast, wanted so desperately to see the World Championships that he made the 2,500-kilometer trip from Ansun City to Shanghai by bicycle! Upon arriving, he asked for a special meeting with me, which I was delighted to grant. Chen Gin gave me a special flag from his hometown stamped with the postmarks of every town and village he passed through on the way to Shanghai. He presented this as proof that he had, in fact, made his incredible and arduous journey. This memento he gave to me in gratitude to me for bringing bodybuilding to China.

Progress

I met with President Samaranch more frequently than I had with any other Olympic Committee president. But I must admit, after a few years I became a bit impatient with the lack of progress in gaining the president's open support for Olympic recognition. Always the president treated me with the utmost courtesy and respect and listened attentively to whatever new information I brought to him. And as time went on, the unequivocal "No" of our initial meetings softened to a more diplomatic, "I will do what I can for you, Mr. Weider." Those words would have been much more encouraging if I saw that anything was actually happening. But, so far as I could tell, the president took no steps that would lead to recognition for us.

Whatever the evident progress, or lack thereof, I was fortunate to be meeting with the president at all in the early 1980s, when he saved the Olympics from financial ruin. Working day and night, he instituted fiscal reforms within the IOC and, most importantly, restructured the Games so they made money rather than losing it. In just four short years, he managed to turn things around. The 1984 Summer Games in Los Angeles made history by turning a profit of $200 million. Thanks to President Samaranch and his team of executives and officials, the specter of Olympic bankruptcy vanished.

Perhaps because the financial crisis was over and he could give more attention to other matters, my relationship with President Samaranch underwent a noticeable improvement. In 1985, we had a meeting memorable for its length and personal tone. I went to the meeting with Rafael Santonja, who subsequently would act as a liaison to President Samaranch and the Olympic Committee. I knew that President Samaranch was interested in adding to the collection of the Olympic Museum. With that in mind, I had purchased two very rare medals from the 1936 Olympic Games in Berlin and presented them to President Samaranch as a gift for the museum. The president was absolutely delighted. In a more relaxed manner than usual, Rafael and I sat in the president's office and talked for a long time.

The following year, Rafael and I were back in the president's office. In mid-conversation, the president stood and asked us to come with him downstairs. He conducted us to the building's basement, which was very interesting because it had been fitted out as an atomic fallout-proof bunker in the days when people feared imminent nuclear war. Now the IOC used the basement as a sort of library and archive. President Samaranch showed us many fascinating old documents.

Like many people in high-stress positions that require many hours of desk work, President Samaranch enjoyed working out to relieve physical stress and increase his energy. He took us into a little room set aside for exercise. I couldn't help but notice that IOC's little "gym" was rather poorly equipped and offered to properly fit it out so President Samaranch and his colleagues could enjoy complete workouts using up-to-date exercise machinery. I found President Samaranch to be trim and surprisingly strong and fit. He amazed me by repeatedly chinning himself on a pull-up bar, truly unusual for a man well into his 60s. This leader of world athletics was quite an athlete himself.

That was the first time we communicated on such a level, sportsman to sportsman. Heartened as I was by our new rapport, I still didn't see signs that the president supported bodybuilding and would push for our recognition, which would not come without his open approval and encouragement to the Executive Board and the general membership. But I just kept working harder, and the work brought many new breakthroughs within the Olympic Committee.

There are many gradations of Olympic recognition and participation short of full IOC recognition and inclusion in the Olympic Games. Each nation in the Olympic family has a National Olympic Committee (NOC), which could recognize our federation. More and more NOC's did just that, especially after we brought our anti-doping program in line with the IOC's requirements. And there were regional and continental organizations within the IOC. Those organizations held their own IOC-sanctioned sports festivals, such as the Pan American Games, Commonwealth Games, and Asian Games, which approached the Olympics in terms of number of participants and prestige in international sport.

The IFBB broke into IOC-recognized regional games at the Southeast Asia Games in 1987, held in Jakarta, Indonesia. At that event, which drew 3,000 athletes, bodybuilding had full inclusion as a medal sport. Of course I went to attend this wonderful and auspicious event. Watching our athletes compete for medals was a proud moment, indeed. Bob Hassan, president of the Indonesian Bodybuilding Federation and a member of the National Olympic Committee, a wonderfully warm and outgoing fellow, introduced me to many leading figures, some of whom would be important allies in securing full Olympic recognition for our federation. I had the pleasure of meeting Indonesia's President Suharto, who stated that bodybuilding was one of the most important sports for the youth of his country. Our inclusion in the Southeast Asia Games, a high honor in itself, also represented a significant step toward Olympic recognition. It meant we had solid support in the Olympic community in that part of the world. I left Indonesia on cloud nine.

The Long March to Moscow

The Soviet Union presented a uniquely difficult challenge. In 1955, when I first went to Moscow, I met resistance to the acceptance of bodybuilding as a sport that was quite unlike what I encountered elsewhere. On the one hand, the Soviets had a keen interest in bodybuilding as the foundation of good sports conditioning. In this respect, they were years ahead of the West. On the other hand, the Communist regime found the sport of bodybuilding itself unacceptable for reasons that had absolutely nothing to do with its athletic merits. Official opinion held that it was bourgeois, decadent, American, opposed to Communist ideology and a danger to youth. I ran into some of this sort of political-philosophical resistance in other Communist countries, but it wasn't so serious, and it was mostly gone by the end of the 1970s. By that time bodybuilding and the IFBB were going strong in Soviet-dominated nations such as Czechoslovakia and Poland, and even Communist China had begun to embrace our sport. However, ideology continued to be an obstacle with Soviet officials.

Some blatant propaganda disguised as journalism shows what the Communist party line on bodybuilding was. In 1979, Nicolay Kisseliov, editor-in-chief of the newspaper *Sovietsky Sport,* wrote a series of articles attacking bodybuilding. At that time more than five million copies of the *Sovietsky Sport* newspaper were printed every day and circulated throughout the Communist world. I can state with confidence that Kisseliov's articles followed the party line, because all major media outlets were very tightly controlled and subject to censorship.

Kisseliov's series included the story of a nice, well-behaved Russian boy who was a pure Communist at heart, hailed from a good Communist family, loved his parents, and excelled at school. But then this model youth fell into bad company and began training in an underground gym where he took up bodybuilding. The article reported that other bodybuilders encouraged him to take drugs that made him aggressive and hostile. Soon he dropped out of school and was expelled from his Communist youth organization. His life was ruined, and his parents' hearts were broken. Kisseliov's story was presented as a cautionary tale to prevent other young lives from being destroyed by bodybuilding. Every article in the series was full of such scurrilous nonsense, and they all made the point that bodybuilding, in and of itself, was a terrible danger to young Soviets.

Western newspapers, including the *L'Equipe* of France and the *New York Times,* published translations. The western press exposed the articles as propaganda and ridiculed them. Nonetheless, Kisseliov did damage to the image of bodybuilding in his own country where people could not get the whole story because of Soviet press censorship.

I decided to go to Moscow and confront Kisseliov face to face. At first he refused to receive me, but the Canadian Embassy in Moscow brought some diplomatic pressure to bear, and Kisseliov reluctantly agreed to meet. In Moscow we sat down together in his office, where he was flanked by two associates who frantically took notes like court reporters. Such was the climate of suspicion and paranoia that Kisseliov wanted witnesses and written proof that he did not diverge from the party line.

Point-blank I asked Kisseliov, "Why do you want to insult the Soviet Union?"

"What do you mean, Mr. Weider? Please explain yourself," he demanded, face reddening with anger.

I replied that readers all over the world laughed at his articles. By writing and publishing such patent rubbish he exposed his nation and Communism to ridicule.

Then, politely but firmly, I refuted the falsehoods contained in his stories. I issued a challenge to him to find one reputable Soviet physician or psychologist who could offer proof that bodybuilding was anything but beneficial to health.

"Prove that bodybuilding itself does harm, in any way, shape or form, and I will write a letter of apology that you may publish. Not only that, I will appear on television and apologize," I said. Adding, "However, if you accept my challenge and cannot back up your allegations, it is you who must apologize in public."

Understandably, Kisseliov did not accept my challenge. But he said he now understood bodybuilding better and would stop criticizing it. I left the meeting quite content with its outcome.

Such attempts to discredit our sport had little or no effect on Soviet bodybuilding, which grew in spite of official condemnation. A Soviet federation was organized, and Soviet bodybuilders competed in contests, which became commonplace. In the Soviet Union, I had the pleasure of meeting such pioneering spirits as Vasily Tchaikovsky, president of the Soviet Bodybuilding Federation, and his outstanding colleagues, Vladimir Shubov, Leonid Ostapenko, and Vladimir Dubinin, who would head the federation after Vasily Tchaikovsky moved to the United States. I also met Nina Koroviakina, an influential member of the Soviet Union's National Olympic Committee. She and I became friends, and she introduced me to such high sports officials as Anatoly Kolesov, deputy chairman of the

State Committee for Physical Culture and Sports, and Vitily Smirnov, president of the National Olympic Committee and a member of the IOC. Those two gentlemen became quite friendly and cooperative, and their support was instrumental in securing official Soviet recognition for our sport and the IFBB. Our great day of victory in Moscow came in August 1987, 32 years after I first went to the Soviet Union. For many of those years, I may have been the only person in the world who was sure that the day would come when our federation and sport were recognized in the bastion of world Communism, the Soviet Union. We returned the favor, granting official IFBB affiliate memebership in 1988.

Three years later the European Bodybuilding Championships were held in historic Leningrad, known before the Russian Revolution and after the fall of Communism in 1991 as St. Petersburg. It was indeed fitting that the Soviet Union would welcome worldwide bodybuilding in this lovely old city, which Russian Czar Peter the Great built as a sort of gateway city in order for his country to enjoy greater contact with European nations to the West.

The last sports minister of the Soviet Union I met, Nicolai Russak, surprised me. Since we had no previous contact, I didn't expect him to be very familiar with me or our federation, but he spoke at some length about how much he admired me for my dedication and perseverance and devotion to bodybuilders in his country. He presented me with an important Soviet medal for sports. I was told that no foreigner had received that particular medal before. I'm sure no foreigner received it afterward, either, because in a matter of months the Communist regime collapsed and the Soviet Union disintegrated into 15 independent states. Nearly all of them have joined the IFBB separately and become national members. The largest formerly Soviet republic, Russia, became a bodybuilding powerhouse and a host nation of our federation's World Championships and International Congress.

Up, Down, and Up Again

Although President Samaranch had yet to openly embrace our cause, there were other signs that we had increasing support within the corridors of power in Lausanne. In 1988, I was very pleased to receive a letter from Prince Alexandre de Merode, stating, "The IOC Medical Commission is most impressed by the steps taken by your International Federation to combat drug misuse in your sport." From the Medical Commission chairman and right-hand man to President Samaranch, this was a very high compliment.

I asked for and I received an even higher compliment in the form of an invitation from the president himself to make a formal presentation to the entire Executive Board of the IOC. This was a very rare privilege and a golden opportunity to state the case for the recognition of bodybuilding in person to the most influential leaders of Olympism in the world.

I arrived at Olympic headquarters in Lausanne on the afternoon of December 8, 1988, accompanied by Rafael Santonja and Albert Busek of Germany, the IFBB's vice-president for Europe. I had with me a written presentation, over which I had labored long and hard, and two videos beautifully produced especially for the Olympic Executives. One was a five-minute introduction to our sport, and the other starred my friend Arnold Schwarzenegger. In it he addressed the IOC executives, telling them all about bodybuilding, his own involvement in the sport, and why it deserved Olympic recognition.

When we arrived, the board was in session. Then came a break, after which I was called into the conference room. Rafael went in with me. Albert watched from a second-floor gallery where he could better gauge the response of everyone present.

Early in my speech I said to the IOC president and board, "To you, my being here may be another item on your agenda. However, to me it represents 42 years of hard, dedicated work. I will distill the 42 years of work into 15 minutes and trust my message will get across to you."

After a few minutes, I showed the videos. Arnold's onscreen presence enthralled President Samaranch and his executives. Arnold used his star power to wonderful effect, projecting a personality so powerful it seemed like he was physically present. In his closing remarks, Arnold stood amidst some of his many bodybuilding trophies and said, "There was one award I couldn't even begin to dream about. If the International Olympic Committee decides to recognize bodybuilding as a sport, maybe someday some young athlete training as long and as hard as I did can dare to have the Olympic Dream. Thanks for listening."

I then made the case for recognition point by point, with emphasis on our anti-doping program. In my concluding remarks I said, "Gentlemen, we deserve to be recognized because of the popularity of our sport all over the world and the prominence of our federation, which has millions of member bodybuilders worldwide. Please grant us this recognition and allow us to hold our heads up high as true sportsmen. Encourage us to continue the war on drugs. Please recognize these 42 years of work that I have contributed to this noble cause and grant us recognition."

I asked for questions, and President Samaranch inquired about the relationship between Prof. Dr. Manfred Donike and the IFBB. This gave me an opportunity to point out that the IOC's anti-doping leader was also our federation's special advisor and re-emphasize our commitment to keeping drugs out of amateur bodybuilding.

I knew the presentation had gone very, very well. Just how well became apparent when the entire Executive Board applauded me. I understand this had never happened before. If it had, it was an extremely rare occurrence. I walked out of the room on air, high as a kite. Out in the hall, Rafael and I shook hands vigorously.

"We're in," I said to my dear friend and colleague, and he concurred.

Then, however, Albert joined us and described what he witnessed after we left.

As soon as we were out of the room, President Samaranch turned to Prince de Merode, who sat next to him, and emphatically shook his head "No." The meaning was unmistakable. At this time President Samaranch did not favor our recognition. There would be no vote by the Executive Board and no action.

All the joy went out of me. I felt like I'd been punched in the stomach. After I got over the devastating disappointment, I remained mystified by what happened in the Executive Board meeting. It just didn't make sense. President Samaranch had gone out of his way to give me and bodybuilding a chance to succeed, and the board members clearly loved the presentation, so why did the president then respond so negatively?

I gave some thought to writing to President Samaranch himself for an explanation. Before I did it, though, I tried to get answers from friends who were present at the meeting. Kevan Gosper, a member of the Executive Board who was president of Australia's National Olympic Committee and vice president of the Olympic Committee for Oceania, wrote to me and put President Samaranch's "No" in an entirely new light.

As Kevan Gosper explained in his letter, the president really acted in my interest. He halted discussion of recognition for bodybuilding because there wasn't enough time remaining at the meeting for the Executive Board to give the matter proper attention. Without sufficient debate, our bid for recognition could have been dropped by default, which would be a serious setback. But the president effectively put everything "on hold."

Kevan also wrote as follows:

There is no doubt in the minds of the Executive Board members that your presentation was informative and convincing, and that you were able to present arguments demonstrating the internationalization, the commitment and the competitiveness of your sport. . . . If your presentation was not accepted by a lot of the members, your application would either have been quickly accepted or turned down. The fact that it wasn't is a good sign.

Kevan's very insightful letter lifted an enormous weight from my shoulders. I now understood that President Samaranch's "No" really meant, "Not now. We must wait until the time is right." The president, who already did me a great favor by allowing me to make my presentation, had just done me another favor that gave the bid for Olympic recognition a chance to be given a fair hearing and, ultimately, to succeed.

Here was a clear sign that I had gained an ally in the person of IOC president Juan Antonio Samaranch.

Kevan Gosper's words about the Executive Board members were also very encouraging. True, I needed more support, but I now knew I already had significant support, to the point that things were tipping in the balance.

Once I truly understood the situation, I realized that the tide was turning. Victory was not assured, but it truly was possible, and it was up to me and my colleagues to make it happen. I worked for Olympic recognition harder than ever.

Honor to Arnold

My brother Joe has already written extensively about Arnold Schwarzenegger. I would like to add a few words of my own about this extraordinary athlete and individual, to whom I would present the IFBB Gold Order Medal, proclaiming him the Best Bodybuilder of the 20th Century.

One of the many ways Arnold was, and is, bodybuilding's best ambassador to the world is evident in the story I just told about the presentation to the Olympic Committee Executive Board. Arnold, whose star was then shooting up in Hollywood, whose time and talent had become incredibly valuable, went to a good deal of trouble to produce his own video presentation to the IOC executives. He was very glad to do it. Indeed, he said he would have gone to Lausanne in person except that he had an unbreakable commitment to be present at the premier of a new movie. Upon my request, in 1994 Arnold agreed to invite President Samaranch and friends of the president's choosing to be honored guests at the gala London premier of *True Lies.* The invitation included use of Arnold's private jet so the IOC president and his party could make the trip to London quickly and in comfort. He and his friends would also be offered suites in the best hotel. The president did not accept this offer, but Arnold's generosity was unmistakable. Arnold remained fiercely loyal to bodybuilding and the IFBB and would do what he could to help our cause.

Though he last competed more than 25 years ago, Arnold is and always will be a proud bodybuilder and a staunch supporter of the sport and our federation. Even now as governor of the State of California, a state bigger and wealthier and more dynamic than most of the world's nations, he remains actively engaged in his sport. Arnold has attended the annual Joe Weider's Mr. Olympia contests countless times, giving the fans an enormous thrill. I know, from being with Arnold onstage and backstage, that he, too, is thrilled. He loves to be among bodybuilders because they are his people, his family.

The Weiders are Arnold's family, also. As both he and my brother Joe have written, their relationship deepened over the years from mentor-protégé, coach-athlete, to that of father and son. No son could be more loving and respectful and attentive than Arnold is to Joe, and it is a great joy to see Joe's happiness when

Arnold is with him. If Joe is the father, I am the uncle, and I am extremely pleased and proud to have Arnold in the family.

Eric

I was delighted that my son Eric chose to join the Weider company after he received his Masters of Business Administration degree from the University of Toronto in 1988, although he had a rather attractive alternative. Eric caught the eye of a recruiter for the Campbell Soup Company, which offered him a position. Though Eric wanted to come into the family business, he thought he might profit from experience elsewhere.

When Eric asked me what I thought, I told him what I had always told all my sons when they had choices to make.

"This is your decision," I said.

But then since he had asked for my opinion, I gave it. I said it used to be common practice for families in business to insist that their sons and daughters make a mark in other companies first. But I believed in Eric's case that did not make sense. His time would be much better spent learning our businesses from the ground up, rather than learning ins and outs of a company he intended to leave.

Eric came to the same conclusion and moved to California and began a sort of executive apprenticeship and crash course in the operations of the three branches of Weider Health and Fitness—equipment, sports nutrition, and publishing.

Eric's work turned out to be trial by fire because the early 1990s were extremely challenging years. Having gone from niche business to big business rather suddenly, we shot almost straight up to huge business. Our equipment branch, for instance, which began as Joe's backyard barbell business in Montreal in the early 1940s, became the largest in the world. By 1994 we were the largest maker of treadmills in the world, and we sold home gyms and weights under the Weider brand name and several others. As Eric learned, this huge business was also an extremely difficult business, involving expensive inventories of big, cumbersome products, fluctuating materials and manufacturing costs, and difficult and contentious dealings with retailers.

In 1994, we sold off the equipment division, and Eric, by then our executive vice president, was heavily involved in the transaction. Two years later he became CEO of Weider Health and Fitness. In 1997, Weider Nutrition International was listed on the New York Stock Exchange, with us retaining a majority of shares. Weider Nutrition remains a leader in its industry, selling supplements and high-performance foods under such famous brands as Tiger's Milk, Move Free, Schiff, and, of course, Weider.

Whether or not he were my son, I would be deeply impressed with any young man with the talent and capacity for hard work to take on such a load of responsibilities, heading an enormous and complex business enterprise in times of great challenge and change. Eric did so practically straight out of college at an age when others were still being groomed for corporate leadership.

I am proud, too, that Eric shares both my interests in history and his Uncle Joe's passion for putting out magazines. The two came together in 2004 when Eric created and launched *Armchair General,* a military history magazine that allows readers to make command decisions in situations faced by the world's greatest military leaders. Building on this publishing success, Eric recently acquired a group of 10 history and military magazines from the Primedia company and now has created his own media company called the Weider History Group. My other sons follow their own professional paths. I love all my sons dearly, but I'm writing about Eric here because he has a role in our story.

Slowly and Surely

Progress by the inch, over months and years, is still progress.

In the 1990s, I continued to do all in my power to achieve my dream of dreams—Olympic recognition for the International Federation of Bodybuilders. I met with IOC President Samaranch on a very regular basis, and the meetings became more enjoyable because I came to appreciate the president's company. The more time I spent with him, the more I recognized what a warm and friendly individual he was. Very simply put, we liked each other and became friends. Friendship didn't really change how we spoke and behaved. I still addressed President Samaranch in the proper manner—"Your Excellency"—and I observed the rules of decorum, as did he. Gentlemen of a certain age and level of accomplishment have no need to display their feelings to make them known.

I had no doubt that President Samaranch really wanted to see me succeed in my bid for official recognition. When he told me at the close of a meeting, "I will do what I can for you," I now knew that he would do just that. But even the Olympic Committee president could not force events. Many considerations were involved, some of which had nothing whatsoever to do with bodybuilding and our federation. It was up to me to keep working and preparing until the time was right.

Meanwhile, as ever, our sport and our federation progressed. The more nations of the world came into the IFBB, the more we strengthened our position. In 1995, we had a great coup on a small island in the middle of the Pacific Ocean. That year our World Amateur Bodybuilding Championships and International Congress were held on the island of Guam, a U.S. territory. Delegates and athletes from 56 nations participated in the event, a turnout that would have been impressive even in a more populous, easily reached venue.

Many people contributed to our great success in mid-Pacific, but the fellow who really made it possible was named Warren Langman, a resident of Norfolk Island, which is far smaller and more isolated than Guam. When I met Warren he gave me an enchanting account of the island nations of the Pacific, reeling off such romantic-sounding names as Bora Bora in Tahiti, Fiji, Tonga, Saipan, Samoa, and so on. Naturally I was eager to organize IFBB affiliates on every single dot of inhabited land, and I knew from my travels that many Pacific Islanders enthusiastically worked out with weights and built their bodies. Warren, a very optimistic and energetic individual, said an island federation could be very successful.

"You really think so?" I asked.

"Absolutely," he said.

"All right Warren, let's see if you can do it," I said.

I put it to him that way, as if I were challenging him to break a personal record for arm curls or the prone press, because I thought the sportsman in him would respond. I already knew that he had the right spirit, the energy, the enthusiasm for our sport and the region itself. I always prided myself on being able to recognize a person who could achieve the impossible. Warren rose to the challenge, and in two years had organized the South Pacific Bodybuilding Federation. As president of the federation, he traveled from island to island, lobbying Olympic officials to support recognition for the IFBB. The South Pacific federation became one of our best regional federations, and a year before the Guam World Championships, bodybuilders competed for medals in the IOC-recognized South Pacific Games.

I am so proud that wherever there are people on this earth, there are bodybuilders organized under the IFBB.

A Letter I'm Glad I Sent

After making so much progress with President Samaranch, something came up that I found troubling. And I felt compelled to answer what I felt were unfair conclusions about our sport. In 1997 a former champion bodybuilder named Bertil Fox returned to his native island of St. Kitts in the Caribbean. There he shot to death his girlfriend and her mother. Fox had found out his girlfriend had been unfaithful to him, so this was a crime of passion. But some members of the press sensationalized the murder as a case of "Roid Rage"—uncontrollable violent aggression supposedly brought on by abuse of steroids—which Fox supposedly took because he was a bodybuilder.

President Samaranch sent one of the more sensational clippings about the murder to my friend Dick Pound, a fellow Canadian very prominent in the IOC. The president wrote on the clipping, "Is this a sport we want to recognize?"

Dick showed the note to me, and I felt I had to write to President Samaranch. Very carefully I composed a letter in which I pointed out that people had been killing their lovers in jealous rages since time began, with no connection to steroids. Why pin the blame on steroids in this one single case and smear our sport? This was completely unfair.

I wrote very respectfully but forcefully, and before sending the letter, I showed it to my brother Joe.

"You'll make Mr. Samaranch angry at you if you send this," Joe said.

"I don't think so. I have something important to say, and he will respect me for saying it," I said.

"Ben, don't send it," Joe said.

I did send it, because I felt I had no choice.

I'll never forget what President Samaranch did the next time we met. He came close and looked me straight in the eye and spoke with great clarity and force.

"Mr. Weider," he said, "I respect you because you fight for your sport!"

I don't think anybody had ever dared to write Mr. Juan Antonio Samaranch such a strongly worded letter challenging his point of view. But he liked me better for doing it.

Phone Call at 3 a.m.

I knew a full year in advance that the request for recognition for our federation would be on the agenda of the meeting of the Olympic Committee's Executive Board held in conjunction with the 1998 Olympic Winter Games in Nagano, Japan. Because of the timing, though, I felt certain that the issue of our recognition would be put on the back burner. At Nagano, the board would be pressed for time and preoccupied with matters relating to the Winter Games. Even in much more favorable circumstances, our bid had been tabled for lack of time, and I had no expectation of meaningful action. At home in Montreal, I expected to follow the action and enjoy the excitement and spectacle of the Winter Olympics like any other sports fan.

But then, at 3 a.m. on February 1, 1998, I heard the phone ring. My heart raced. Very few people have my home number, and those who do wouldn't call at such an hour without an urgent reason. Experience teaches that pre-dawn calls bring either very good news or very bad. Since I wasn't expecting good news, I feared that the call would be bad news. But I picked up the phone and heard a friendly voice of a person within the ranks of Olympic officialdom who was calling from Nagano, Japan.

"Rejoice! Your perseverance had finally paid off," he said. "The Executive Board just voted for recognition of your federation. I knew you wouldn't mind if I woke you up to give you this news."

No, I didn't mind at all. My spirits soared. Never have I known such exultation, such joy, such satisfaction. My 52 years of blood, sweat, and tears had finally paid off. I never doubted that it would happen, but nothing could have prepared me for learning that my dream had been realized.

I felt like I could fly without a plane. Sleep was absolutely out of the question. I called my brother in Los Angeles to share the wonderful news.

"Joe, we finally did it," I said to the person I had admired most in my life, with whom I had worked ceaselessly and inseparably for more than half a century.

And then I called my son Eric, because he carries the torch that Joe and I lit into the future.

Neither Joe, Eric, nor I went to bed that morning. In a few hours, the sun would rise on a new era for bodybuilding and bodybuilders. We had earned for our beloved sport the highest honor it could receive, the ultimate seal of approval and legitimacy. I wanted to see the sun come up on this brand-new day and to paint a picture of it in my mind. My brother and my son did, too, and there was no sleep for the Weiders.

The next morning I received the following fax from Nagano:

Re: IOC Recognition,

Dear Mr. Weider, friend—

It is my pleasure to inform you that the Executive Board of the International Olympic Committee decided yesterday in its meeting in Nagano, to grant recognition to the International Federation of Body-Builders (IFBB) as a Recognized Federation, pursuant to Rule 29 of the Olympic Charter.

I should remind you that this recognition will be provisional for a two-year period. At the end of this period, the recognition will automatically lapse in the absence of definitive confirmation given in writing by the IOC. I would like to draw your attention to the fact that your doping regulations must be in conformity with the IOC Medical Code. We suggest that you consider having the IFBB adhere to the Court of Arbitration for Sport which has established itself as a most useful institution for the resolution of all forms of disputes relating to sport.

With regard to all practical matters resulting from the recognition decision, please let me know with whom our Sports Director should get in touch.

Finally, I should like to take this opportunity to congratulate you for all the efforts made in order to reach this goal, and to welcome you into the Olympic family.

Yours Sincerely,

Juan Antonio Samaranch

Marques de Samaranch

The president hand-wrote the word "friend" in the salutation, a gesture full of personal significance and meaning.

Solidifying Our Position

After telling my family, I called Rafael Santonja, who was absolutely key to this success. He was always there when I needed him and never let me down, and he was overjoyed to hear our news. I received numerous dozens of congratulatory calls and letters, and I was able to share my joy with the many, many individuals who helped bring our great success about. I did not do this alone. Believe me, a lot of people had a lot to celebrate after the news from Nagano arrived. So many gave so much of themselves that I couldn't even begin to name them and mention their important contributions in this space. To the end of our story I have appended an IFBB Roll of Honor listing key colleagues and supporters and highlighting their accomplishments. I urge you to spend some time reading it to better understand the mighty effort by a great number of people that was required to build our federation and improve it to the point that the IOC accepted our sport as a sport and recognized the IFBB.

Our athletes, too, were elated. As the news went out, bodybuilders the world over held their heads higher knowing they had a place of respect and honor in the world of international athletics. We did not rest on our laurels, however. If anything, our achievement spurred us to work harder. We continued to upgrade our federation's anti-doping program, now with the guidance of a new special adviser, Prof. Dr. Eduardo H. De Rose of Brazil, who had replaced Prof. Dr. Manfred Donike after he passed away. Dr. Eduardo De Rose was a renowned expert in the field of sports medicine and a member of the Olympic Committee's Medical Commission with special responsibilities related to the Committee's anti-doping program.

In 1998, Dr. Eduardo De Rose sent a letter to the IOC's Medical Commission chairman, Prince Alexandre de Merode, expressing his confidence in our commitment to making our sport drug-free. He wrote as follows: "When I was asked to replace Prof. Dr. Manfred Donike in this federation, I decided first to verify how they were dealing with the problem of doping, considering the stigma they have in the area. After attending two World Championships and one competition held by the IFBB, I was extremely pleased and satisfied by the professional and scientific way they handle their doping program..."

As Dr. Eduardo De Rose wrote in his letter, our anti-doping professionals were the very best, and all our protocols were up to standard. Under his guidance, we created our own 51-page anti-doping manual laying out even more stringent guidelines and procedures. As mandated in our manual, we initiated out-of-competition testing to help ensure that athletes remain free of drugs year-round. Effective January 1, 2000, every one of the 173 national federations of the IFBB was obligated to test for drugs at all national- and regional-level competitions, subject to penalties for noncompliance. Not many sports federations are tougher on drugs than the IFBB, and we get tougher each and every year.

I was very gratified at the ways in which President Samaranch himself honored our new status. I well remember a visit to his office in Lausanne with my friend and colleague Rafael Santonja of Spain when he called an assistant into his office.

The president said to the assistant, "President Ben Weider and his executive assistant Mr. Santonja are here. I want to know why the IFBB flag isn't flying out in front of the building. You know that is our protocol to fly the flag of a sports federation when its president is here. Why didn't you put it up?"

"Sir," the assistant said, "the bodybuilding federation has only provisional recognition…"

President Samaranch answered, "That's recognition enough for me. Please put the flag up."

"Yes, sir," the other fellow said.

President Samaranch accompanied us out of the building.

"Let's have a picture taken, with us in front of your federation's flag flying next to the Olympic flag. This will be a wonderful souvenir and a sign of your great achievement."

It was wonderful, indeed. I was gratified and touched when President Samaranch made such thoughtful gestures to me. Never will I forget the kindness and respect he showed to me and the IFBB. His Excellency Samaranch and I are friends to this day, and I respect him very much.

Building a Bridge With Bodybuilding

Never was the power of sport and the Olympic ideals more evident than on a trip I made in 1999 to the front lines of the long, bloody conflict between the Jewish State of Israel and its neighbors. On this trip I opened state-of-the-art gyms in both Tel Aviv in Israel and in Ramallah in Palestine. I donated both gyms in response to requests that came to me independently from Dr. Fawzi Khodari of Beirut, Lebanon, at that time the IFBB's liaison officer for the Arab countries, and Asher Frig, president of the Israeli Amateur Bodybuilding Federation. The rationale for the requests was exactly the same—youngsters in both Tel Aviv and Ramallah would benefit from new gyms open to them free of charge. I loved the idea of helping the young people and, more important, helping to build the desperately needed bridge of understanding and peace between Israelis and Palestinians.

It was the president of the Palestinian Bodybuilding Federation, Dr. Nazeh Abdel Rahim, familiarly known as Abu Jaffar, who oversaw the building of the gym in Ramallah, to be called The Ben Weider Academy of Physical Culture. Abu Jaffar, also a government official suggested that I, as a gesture of goodwill, send

Palestinian president Yasser Arafat a greeting for his 70th birthday. I did so, and received a very friendly reply inviting me to visit him in Palestine. That invitation was the impetus for one of my most amazing and rewarding adventures, dedicating Weider gyms given as gifts to peoples that had been in violent conflict for more than a half-century. Accompanying me to Israel and Palestine was my executive assistant, Rafael Santonja.

We flew into Israel where we were welcomed at the airport by both Asher Frig and Abu Jaffar and a party of Palestinians who went with Rafael, Luc, and me to Ramallah. Abu Jaffar did a brilliant job of organizing both our visit and the ceremonies for the opening of the Ben Weider gym. Thanks to him, I was received as a head of state. On the gym's opening day, Ramallah's narrow streets were hung with banners welcoming me and Rafael. The official ceremonies began with a military band playing Palestine's national anthem, and then more melodic selections as the program continued. Many speeches were made, and a dozen Palestinian bodybuilders showed off both impressive physiques and lifting techniques.

Our Palestine visit lasted a few days, and Abu Jaffar and his colleagues could not have made us more welcome or provided a more fascinating itinerary, which included many ancient places of great religious significance to Judaism, Christianity, and Islam. Our touring took us in and out of Israel and Palestinian territory through numerous military checkpoints. As we hurried to the Gaza Strip to make a scheduled appointment with President Arafat himself, Israeli soldiers held us up for a long time, eyeing our car suspiciously. I got out to explain who we were, and the soldiers immediately recognized me and told me with great excitement that they read Weider magazines, followed the Weider Training Principles, and used Weider equipment. They waved us on.

We went directly to President Arafat's headquarters in Gaza City and met with him for 35 minutes during which we never spoke of politics. President Arafat assured me that he exercised and watched his diet very carefully. I then presented him with the IFBB's Gold Order, which pleased him very much. In turn, President Arafat gave me a lovely mother-of-pearl depiction of the Christian Nativity. The Palestine National Authority controls Bethlehem, birthplace of Jesus Christ, and President Arafat gives that fine gift to visitors he especially esteemed. At our parting, the Palestinian leader took me by the hand and led me to the door, then stood waving goodbye. I also said farewell to my great friend and colleague Abu Jaffar, a fine administrator and tireless worker for bodybuilding.

Rafael and I then went to dedicate the Weider gym in Tel Aviv, where the city organized a wonderful welcoming reception with an orchestra and vocalists followed by a ribbon-cutting ceremony at the gym, filled with gleaming new equipment like a high-priced workout club. After the ceremony we enjoyed a lovely buffet. We were received with the same friendliness and enthusiasm and gratitude that we experienced in Ramallah, enemy territory in the eyes of many in Tel Aviv, just as Tel Aviv was enemy territory to the Palestinians. To us, though, the two gym-opening festivities were like mirror images of each other. In both cases politics were beside the point, and bodybuilding and fitness were all that mattered. I flew home happy in the thought that not only is bodybuilding good for nation-building, it is good for building bridges between nations.

Rewriting History

Just two years after IOC recognition of bodybuilding, came a sign that my other impossible dream, involving Napoleonic history, had also come true. Though the event involves a story I haven't told, that of my work to reveal the whole truth about Emperor Napoleon, both the long-hidden fact that he was deliberately poisoned and the great and noble achievements of his life, the realization of my two dreams are intertwined in my mind.

In the year 2000, I was awarded the Legion of Honor by France for my contributions to the understanding of Napoleon Bonaparte. Napoleon himself established the Legion of Honor in 1802 to recognize those who make extraordinary contributions to France. The country bestows no higher honor. Nor is there a medal more beautiful and prestigious in the world than the Legion of Honor.

I chose to receive the medal near Montreal on the island of *Ste.-Hélène,* French for St. Helena, the name of the South Atlantic island to which Napoleon was exiled, and where he was poisoned. France's Ambassador to Canada, Denis Bauchard, presented me with the medal. Also in attendance was my friend Prince Charles Napoleon, a direct descendent of Emperor Napoleon himself, who traveled from Paris to participate in this historic event.

Receiving the medal, I felt as if Napoleon were whispering in my ear, "Ben, I am proud of you." I was certainly proud to have helped the world better understand this iconic figure. In my acceptance speech I explained why I felt as I did about Napoleon and worked so long and hard to set the record straight about him: "When people ask me the reasons for my deep admiration of Napoleon, my answer never fails to surprise. It can be summed up in three words: liberty, equality, fraternity."

Liberty, equality, fraternity are the French Revolutionary ideals that Napoleon championed and fought to protect. They also sum up the ideals of the International Federation of Bodybuilders, which I used to bring people together in peace and brotherhood and health. In this sense my two impossible dreams are the same dream.

It meant everything to receive such an honor for my historical work in France where established historians and intellectuals fought tooth and nail to discredit me. They didn't want someone they considered an uneducated foreigner rewriting their own proud history, but the truth won out. As I write now, I recently received notice from a friend that the *Encyclopedia Britannica,* standard reference for the entire English-speaking world, is considering the murder of Napoleon as a historic fact. History has, indeed, been rewritten.

The same year that I received the Legion of Honor, the Olympic recognition of the IFBB was allowed to automatically lapse, due to technicalities. Had President Samaranch remained in office past 2001, I am absolutely positive our recognition would have become permanent. But under the new presidency of Jacques Rogge of Belgium, no action was taken to change the status of our provisional recognition, as required by the regulations. However, our position now is stronger than it ever was. Our federation is one of the largest in the world, with 173 member nations. We are participants in such IOC-recognized regional games as the Southeast Asian Games and Asian Games, both recognized by the Olympic Council of Asia. We also participate in the South American Games, Central American Games, and Caribbean Games, and also in the Arab Games, South Pacific Games, and the World Games, and we have the recognition of the Supreme Council for Sport in Africa, and the Pan American Sports Confederation. As I write, we look forward to full participation as a medal event in the upcoming Asian Games, the IOC sports festival second in size only to the Olympic Games. And we look forward to regaining our federation's full recognition by the International Olympic Committee.

Final Words

By now you should know that I am a very practical individual. Even though others thought my dreams were entirely unrealistic, I have dwelt in the real world and proceeded toward my goals in a very realistic manner.

Therefore, it has been difficult for me to come up with a satisfactory explanation for a strange occurrence in a television studio in Vancouver, British Columbia, in the 1980s.

I went to the studio to appear in a well-known talk show to discuss my discoveries about Emperor Napoleon and the manner of his death. As I sat in a backstage area waiting for my turn to go on camera, a fellow walked around me and was staring at me fixedly. His behavior, combined with the fact that he was a very eccentric-looking individual, made me quite uneasy.

I was about to ask him what he wanted when he approached and spoke up abruptly.

"Who is Anna?" he asked.

Anna, of course, was the name of my mother, Anna Weider.

"Who is Louis, and Philip?" he asked.

I was dumbfounded. This strange character, who introduced himself as a well-known psychic also appearing on the same show, had just named my father and my Uncle Philip.

"These people are very close to you right now,, and are looking out for you," the psychic said.

His words rattled me because he had absolutely no way of knowing the names of my family members.

However those names came into that man's head, they expressed a certain truth. As I wrote at the beginning of my story, most every day of my life I go back in memory to Colonial Avenue on the east side of Montreal. Something triggers a memory, and for a moment there I am, back where I got my start. And with me are the beloved people who gave me my start, my mother and my father, who taught their children, by example, uprightness and loyalty and discipline and honesty and industriousness. I was most fortunate to have had a third guiding light in my early years, my brother Joe, who inspired me and helped to put me on a path that led to my dreams.

Even though I know it's all absolutely true, because I witnessed it and lived it, I find this story of my brother and me rather incredible. It's hard to imagine that we got where we are from the start we had, in bad times with none of the advantages brought by money or education and the whole world opposed to our ideas.

I want you to know that you can do what we did. You can better yourself. You can educate yourself even if you can't go to university. You can live according to the truth, as you discover it, and you can work to make the world recognize and accept your truth. The Weiders' truths happen to involve bodybuilding and exercise and international sport and, in my own personal case, the truth about a great and misunderstood historical figure, Emperor Napoleon. Your own truth is for you to discover. But with the truth on your side, and the willingness to work as hard and as smart as you possibly can, you can do what we did. Really and truly, you can.

To my readers, especially young readers, I want to repeat a few simple messages that I once gave to the students attending a graduation ceremony at Concordia University here in Montreal, on the day I was presented with an honorary doctoral degree:

You can't wait for opportunity to come to you, because it won't. You've got to go get it. If you don't make things happen, they won't happen.

You can't accomplish great things all on your own. Clap two hands together, and you can applaud. Try it with one hand, and nothing happens.

It's okay if you reach for the stars. But don't forget to keep your feet on the ground.

VALEDICTORY

Joe Weider

Strive for excellence, exceed yourself, love your friends, speak the truth, practice fidelity, and honor your father and mother. These principles will help you master yourself, make you strong, give you hope, and put you on the path to greatness.
—*Joe Weider*

A year ago, Dr. Iain Kalfas at the Cleveland Clinic in Ohio performed surgery on my back to alleviate pain that had become unbearable. The trouble began in the 1990s with another back operation that went wrong, causing damage that compounded itself and brought on agony and debility that got worse and worse. I could have eased the pain with drugs, but I can't stand being doped up. So I searched the country for a top back surgeon with the know-how and guts to help me. Some guys were afraid to try because of the extent of my problems and my age. Some wanted to take halfway measures that wouldn't help a lot, but did not involve big risks.

I don't believe in halfway measures. Dr. Kalfas didn't, either. He said there was one hope for relief and regaining my vitality—a complete reconstruction of my spinal column. He didn't mince words about the difficulties and risks. The operation would last six or eight hours, and recovery would take more than a year. But Dr. Kalfas believed the odds of success were good and that the payoff justified the risks. Practically everybody around me said, "Joe, don't do it." They were scared I'd die or succumb to despair if nothing improved. I was much more frightened of doing nothing.

The back reconstruction went very well, but then post-op infections just about killed me. The doc had to open me up again, and over and over I went back into the intensive care unit. Dr. Kalfas said to Betty that my problems would have killed most strong, young guys in their twenties. And he told a friend of ours who visited that I was the toughest human being he ever worked on, bar none. My strength of body and spirit amazed him.

The doctor shouldn't have been so amazed—I'm a bodybuilder.

I knocked the germs and the Grim Reaper on their asses the same way I flattened that crazy, anti-Semitic, French guy my brother Ben brought to our front door in Montreal 70 years ago. Him I laid out with one punch. The germs put up more of a fight, but the end result was the same and so was the reason I came out on top. I had the power to win because I built my body.

I'm alive today, telling you my story, only because I am a bodybuilder.

When I was 13 years old, bodybuilding changed my life. In return, I dedicated my life to it. And it helped to save my life.

Bodybuilding is still saving my life. If I were not a bodybuilder, the long recovery and rehabilitation I'm going through might drive me crazy. Three months it took, just to get well enough to come home. Since then I've been working with a physical therapist who had to help me learn to stand up and walk, one foot in front of the other, like I never did such a thing before. Progress is slow, but I never quit trying, because long ago I learned the lessons of bodybuilding: determination, persistence, concentration and focus, and patience.

Bodybuilding teaches that you never get something for nothing. Even the smallest gains require great effort. Keep at it, though, and all the tiny gains add up and become astonishing.

These are, of course, the lessons a child must learn to grow up, which a grownup must take to heart to be a person of strength and character.

Lately my gains are adding up fast. And hallelujah, I remain free of pain for the first time in more than 15 years. A couple weeks ago, I went out and strolled down the sidewalk, something I thought I might never do again. The other day I woke up full of piss and vinegar like the old Joe Weider. I got my secretary on the phone and had her laughing so hard she couldn't even talk.

It's a miracle, nothing less—and so is bodybuilding.

When I say miracle, I mean it. When I was a kid, bodybuilding transformed my life. Every day since, I have seen it work miracles for others. A guy who was skinny builds some muscles where there used to be skin and bone. He looks in the mirror and says, "Hey, how about that," and walks out of the gym with new confidence, and a pretty girl gives him the eye for the first time in his life. That girl has her own miracle. She used to be overweight and sat home feeling sad and lonely and tried to comfort herself with food and put on more weight. But then she started working out and eating right, and now she's hot stuff. Is she thrilled? You better believe she is. Her miracle is no bigger, or smaller, than when a great bodybuilding champion finally breaks through a plateau that's been driving him nuts and adds a quarter-inch to his biceps—or when an old lady first picks up a two-pound weight at a physical therapy center. There is no such thing as a small miracle.

A gym is a place of miracles. People do things they once thought impossible—lifting heavier, squeezing out one more rep, finding discipline and willpower they didn't know they had. They're amazed at how good they feel and look, and they carry their new power into the world.

This is the miracle I wanted to give to the world.

And I want to give it to you.

The stronger you are, the more alive you are. This is more than a manner of speaking, because strength is life, and muscle is life. You're reading these words because the strongest muscle, your heart, beats in your chest. Muscles keep your head up and allow you to hold this book and turn the pages. They focus your eyes so you can see.

If you build your physical strength, you'll be more alert and better able to use your intelligence to consider my words and thoughts. The link between muscle power and brainpower isn't hype—it's fact, proven by science. It was known to the great thinkers who founded western civilization, the ancient Greeks. The Greeks had a motto: Sound mind, sound body.

All living creatures know something else about strength—it's one of life's great joys. Open the door for a house cat, and what does he do? He tears across the yard like crazy and then runs up a tree. There's no reason in the world for him to run and climb except that he's made to do it. You and I are like the cat. Our great physical abilities cry out to be developed and used.

Somehow people forgot the ancient wisdom about strength. By doing away with muscle-work and surrounding us with more food than we need, modern civilization makes people weak and unhealthy. But the weak cannot survive. A civilization cannot last when its people succumb to weakness.

If physical weakness is the problem, bodybuilding and fitness are the solutions. I meant just that more than 50 years ago when I wrote the last of my "Ten Predictions":

I PREDICT that bodybuilding will one day become one of the greatest forces in existence, and that it may be hailed as the activity that actually saved civilization from itself.

In 1950, people thought I was nuts, but I told the truth.

Back to Cleveland for just a minute...

Much of what I know about my hospital stay comes from other people like Betty, God bless her, who left my side only to sleep. My brother Ben visited, which meant the world to me. As I earlier wrote, Arnold also found time to visit, along with others too numerous to name.

I must rely on those people's memories because I spent so much time unconscious or with my mind wandering. Where my mind wandered, was back to my office. Other people told me I talked and talked about this cover shot and that headline and various bodybuilders I wanted in articles and pictures. My niece

Thresa came several times to Cleveland and sat by me for hours and hours. She says I stayed on the job day and night.

This shows, I think, how much I love my life's work, much of which was magazine work. I love magazines, every single thing about them—words, pictures, color, design, ads. I love the feel of paper and smell of ink. And I love what a magazine can do for people. There's nothing in the world like it. Nowhere else does a few bucks buy so much information and food for thought, entertainment and beauty. In my magazines, you also get a crash course in exercise and health and how to get more out of life. The cover prices are many times what they used to be, but the value is still amazing. Spend less than $5 on a magazine, and you get material worth a fortune.

Truth be told, I'd rather be putting out magazines than working on this book, but I no longer have magazines to put out. In 2002, we sold Weider Publications. This was a family decision, which couldn't happen if I said "no." Saying "yes" felt like tearing my heart out, but I thought and thought and realized it was time. When it's time, it's time.

In or out of the magazine game, I don't want to miss another Joe Weider Mr. Olympia.

In 2004, I had to miss the contest because it came right after my back surgery and I was still in the hospital in Ohio.

In 2005, I went back and forth about going to Las Vegas to see the contest and appear onstage, as both Ben and I traditionally do. I especially wanted to go because this was the 40th anniversary of Mr. Olympia, but I felt a little bit shaky, and I didn't want all my guys and the crowd to see the Master Blaster with his powers so diminished. As the contest day approached I was pretty sure I'd stay home.

In the meantime, Betty and I had an invitation to a private function in Malibu the weekend before the Olympia. Some of the biggest Hollywood celebrities and entertainment executives would attend. Betty was absolutely dying to go because Barbra Streisand was going to sing a few songs. Betty said we should go for my sake, too, because getting out does me good.

The party turned out to be very enjoyable. Streisand was great, and we sat at the same table with Arnold.

He said, "Joe, I'll see you next week at the Mr. Olympia."

I told him I wasn't going.

"What are you talking about?" he said, and I explained how I felt a little weak and under the weather.

"No problem," Arnold said. "I'll push you onstage in a wheelchair, and we can be at the podium together."

I said there was no way in hell I'd go out in a wheelchair, so he said I could hang onto his arm.

I tried to say "no," but Arnold said he'd carry me out if he had to.

Finally he said, "Joe, I'm not going to go unless you're there with me."

Arnold didn't know it, but his boyhood idol Reg Park gave me exactly the same ultimatum in 1951 at the NABBA Mr. Universe contest in London. The deal, as I wrote many pages back, was a little different. Reg insisted that I enter the contest with him and go onstage as a competitor. If I didn't do it, he'd pull out of the contest.

The guy didn't give me much choice, did he?

I am so glad I let Arnold strong-arm me. Just being backstage at Mr. Olympia was like a shot in the arm—the incredible competitors, bigger and better than ever; the crowd, 7,500 strong, which set an all-time record for attendance; and being with my brother Ben, champs from years past, and friends.

When the time came, I went arm and arm with Arnold out onto the stage, into the lights and waves of sound like I had never heard. Bodybuilders are a very loud audience, and that great big crowd raised the roof.

The plan was for Arnold to say a few words and turn the microphone over to me. He told the little story I just told about how he made me go to the Mr. Olympia. And he said he wanted to thank Joe Weider for creating this great contest in 1965 and making the sport of bodybuilding what it is.

People in the arena came to their feet. Above the roar I heard individuals shout, "Thank you, Joe." I had to stop and get control of my emotions before I could open my mouth.

These words I spoke: "I love you all. I was in love with bodybuilding since I was 13. You are my heroes. I wouldn't be able to do anything without you. God bless all of you. Long life. Keep up with your training."

I didn't say much, but each word carried all the feeling I possessed, from deep in my heart and from every fiber of my being. People jumped to their feet again and went crazier than before. I heard men and women shout, "I love you, Joe!" and "Thank you!" One bunch in the back chanted in unison, "We love you, Joe." As I later found out, Betty and Maria, the women Arnold and I love, cherish, and depend on, were hugging each other and shedding tears backstage.

I felt such waves of love and gratitude. I felt like all the years and love and effort I poured into bodybuilding came pouring back to me, right on that stage. Arnold seemed so happy for me, and we were joined by Mr. Olympias from years past. With the cheering going on and on, each of those greats and immortals took my hand and said, "Thanks, Joe." And I never felt prouder and happier.

ROLL OF HONOR

An entire book could be devoted to the following heroes of the IFBB. It took their passion, dedication, and tireless efforts to build our federation into one of the largest and best-run in the world, now with 173 member nations, and I am ever-mindful of the great debt owed to them.

Names appear in alphabetical order, not order of importance, which would be impossible to assign. In case I've forgotten anyone, I apologize in advance.

With gratitude and respect,

Ben Weider, CM, CQ, CBSt.J, PhD

Member of the Order of Canada, the Legion of Honor of France, commander of the Order of St. John, nominee for the Nobel Peace Prize, Colonel (Hon.) 62nd Field Artillery Regiment, Canada, and recipient of numerous international honorary degrees and orders

Dr. Tamás Aján, Hungary—president of the International Weightlifting Federation and a stalwart supporter of bodybuilding.

Malih Alaywan, Lebanon—IFBB vice president for the Middle East, patron of the IFBB, president of the Lebanese Bodybuilding Federation, and member of Lebenon's National Olympic Committee; a friend and ally since 1955, he played a key role in creating and consolidating support for bodybuilding in the Arab world.

Ch. Mohammed Amin, Pakistan—a pioneering leader of bodybuilding in Asia (deceased).

John Balik, U.S.A—publisher and editor of *Ironman* magazine, a great supporter of the IFBB, and contest organizer.

Togay Bayatli, Turkey—former president of the International Sports Press Association, member of the Turkish Olympic Committee, and great supporter of bodybuilding.

Monique Berlioux, France—former director of the International Olympic Committee and an early supporter of our sport and federation.

Prof. Dr. Friedhelm Beuker, Germany—secretary of the IFBB Medical Commission, whose work is important in our doping program.

Tony Blinn, Canada—chairman of the IFBB Technical Committee; our top troubleshooter for technical matters is also the webmaster of our highly successful site www.ifbb.com.

Julien Blommaert, Belgium—president of the Belgian Bodybuilding Federation and contest organizer, who was one of our federation's first top officials.

Albert Busek, Germany—IFBB vice president for Europe, who has been involved with the IFBB for over 30 years.

Aquiles de Cesare, Uruguay—IFBB vice president for South America.

Dr. Chen An-Huai, China—president of the Shanghai Institute of Physical Education and Sports, a great supporter of bodybuilding in educational system in China.

Robin Chang, U.S.A.—a highly dedicated IFBB official who produces Joe Weider's Mr. Olympia weekend, the top competitive event in bodybuilding; eats, sleeps, and lives the Olympia and deserves a great deal of the credit fo its recent spectacular successes.

Paul Chua, Singapore—IFBB vice president for Asia, president of the Singapore Bodybuilding Federation, top problem solver for Asia, unifier of the Asian countries, liaison with the Olympic Council of Asia, and responsible for the growth of the bodybuilding movement in Asia, who also works closely with the Arab Bodybuilding Federation; a friend and ally since the 1950s.

Rick Collins, U.S.A.—IFBB legal counsel.

Dr. Arpad Csanadi, Hungary—former president of the Hungarian Olympic Committee, former member of the International Olympic Committee, and one of the very early supporters of bodybuilding and the IFBB during the difficult days of Communist rule in Eastern Europe (deceased).

Prof. Dr. Eduardo H. De Rose, Brazil—special advisor to the Medical Commission of the IFBB; one of the world's most respected experts on doping in sports.

Prof. Dr. Manfred Donike, Germany—former special advisor to the IFBB Medical Commission and a key Olympic Committee anti-doping official (deceased).

Abdel Hamid El-Guindy, Egypt—former IFBB World Men's Amateur Champion bodybuilder, former president of the Egyptian Bodybuilding Federation, and promoter of bodybuilding in Egypt (deceased).

Gen. Sami Abou El-Mahasen, Egypt—former president of the Egyptian Bodybuilding Federation and a fabulous administrator and supporter of our sport.

Dr. Eng. Adel Fahim El Sayed, Egypt—IFBB vice president for Africa, responsible for organizing our sport on this challenging continent; involved in the Arab Bodybuilding Federation and plays a key role in expanding bodybuilding throughout the Arab world and president of the Egyptian Bodybuilding Federation.

Franco Fassi, Italy—IFBB patron and former president of the Italian Bodybuilding Federation; creator of the bodybuilding movement in Italy and a great problem solver.

Dr. Bob Goldman, U.S.A.—chairman of the IFBB Medical Commission; he plays a key role in the fight against doping in our sport.

Paul Graham, Australia—IFBB vice president for Oceana, which includes New Zealand and Australia; developer of our sport in both countries and a key contributor to bodybuilding for more than 30 years.

Kim Nam Hak, South Korea—IFBB patron, former president of the Asian Bodybuilding Federation, former president of the Korean Bodybuilding Federation, and one of the leading lights of bodybuilding throughout Asia.

Mostafa Hefzi, Egypt—IFBB patron and honorary chairman of the IFBB Judges Committee; a loyal and dedicated federation member for 40 years who has played a key role in strengthening the Judges Committee and publicizing our sport in Egypt.

Robert Helmick, U.S.A.—former president of the U.S. Olympic Committee and a supporter of bodybuilding (deceased).

Silvia Hernandez, Canada—financial comptroller.

Philip Hope, Cook Islands—IFBB vice president for the South Pacific, responsible for our sport across a huge geographical region.

Prof. Dr. Ernst Jokl, U.S.A.—One of the federation's earliest experts in doping and health and a leader within the world anti-doping community (deceased).

Pamela Kagan, Canada—IFBB executive director and veteran of 36 years of wonderful service to the federation; she communicates and solves problems with our 173 member nations.

John Kelly Jr., U.S.A.—former president of the Amateur Athletic Union who helped and supported the IFBB in the U.S. in our federation's very early days (deceased).

Toni Khoury, Lebanon—Member of the Lebanese Olympic Committee, member of the International Olympic Committee, and great supporter of bodybuilding.

Dr. Un Yong Kim, South Korea—former president of the Korean Olympic Committee and IOC member. His support for bodybuilding was invaluable.

Nina Koroviakina, Russia—top official of the former Soviet Union's National Olympic Committee; her involvement with the Soviet Sports Ministry helped bodybuilding to get official recognition in the Soviet Union (deceased).

Warren Langman, Norfolk Island—responsible for the organization of the South Pacific Bodybuilding Federation. His dedication and devotion has brought over 20 island countries into the IFBB.

Jim Lorimer, U.S.A.—one of the very best organizers of bodybuilding competitions; has organized IFBB contests for 30 years.

Loh Lin Kok, Singapore—IFBB legal counsel.

Prof. Lou Zhuo Yu, China—rightly known as the Father of Bodybuilding in China, he was very active during the early days when bodybuilding was outlawed by the Communist authorities of the People's Republic of China (deceased).

Jim Manion, U.S.A.—IFBB vice president for North America, president of the National Physique Committee; my top U.S. troubleshooter and right-hand man, under whose able leadership both amateur an dprofessional bodybuilding have exploded in popularity and importance. There are now more than 1,000 amateur competitions annually in the U.S, and more professional contests with prizes bigger than ever, that continue to increase.

Ferdinand Marcos, Philippines—former president of the Philippines, now deceased, and our sport's number-one supporter in his nation (deceased).

Peter McGough, U.S.A.—group editorial director of *Muscle & Fitness* and *FLEX* magazines, and a great supporter of our sport and federation; one of bodybuilding's most loyal representatives.

Sultan Mohamed Bin Mejren, United Arab Emirates—president of the Arab Bodybuilding Federation and a great supporter of bodybuilding.

Prince Alexandre de Merode, Belgium—former chairman of the IOC Medical Commission and advisor to the IFBB on doping (deceased).

Dr. Mahathir Bin Mohamad, Malaysia—former president of the Malaysia Republic and great supporter of bodybuilding.

Samih Moudallal, Syria—former president of the Syrian National Olympic Committee, active in the

IOC, and a promoter of the IFBB and the sport of bodybuilding.

Émile Muller, Canada—former official of the Czech Bodybuilding Federation under Communist rule and a pioneer Czech promoter and organizer of our sport.

Tom Ortega, Philippines—former president of the Philippine Bodybuilding Federation, which he founded; a great president, administrator, and contest organizer (deceased).

David Pecker, U.S.A.—chairman and CEO of American Media, Inc.; top business executive and close confidant whose valuable assistance and expertise has helped to make our biggest bodybuilding events standout successes; a great friend of bodybuilding.

Javier Pollock, U.S. Virgin Islands—IFBB vice president for the Caribbean; always in motion and always available to solve problems.

Don Porter, U.S.A.—president of the International Softball Federation, co-creator with Ben Weider of the World Games, and a big supporter of bodybuilding.

Dick Pound, Canada—president of the World Anti-Doping Agency, his organization plays a key role in our fight against drugs in sports.

Gen. Baktiar Rana, Pakistan—a top promoter of bodybuilding in Pakistan and throughout Asia (deceased).

Sandy Ranalli, U.S.A.—secretary of the IFBB Judges Committee, she plays an important role in developing judging in the U.S.A. and around the world.

Dr. Wlodzimierez Reczek, Poland—formerly his country's minister of sport and one of the early supporters of bodybuilding during the most difficult days under Communism (deceased).

Winston Roberts, Canada—one of the earliest IFBB executive council members, he has been involved with the federation for more than 30 years.

Gen. Carlos P. Romulo, Philippines—former foreign minister of his nation who suggested the IFBB credo, which states, "Bodybuilding is important for nation building," which appears in our official logo.

Dr. Tom Rosandich, U.S.A.—president of the United States Sports Academy and chairman of the IFBB Research, Exercise & Education Committee; important supporter of bodybuilding around the world.

His Excellency the Marques Juan Antonio Samaranch, Spain—president of the International Olympic Committee from 1980 through 2001 and now honorary IOC president for life; probably the number-one supporter of bodybuilding in the IOC.

Rafael Santonja, Spain—executive assistant to the IFBB president and president of the European Bodybuilding &

Fitness Federation; the number-one troubleshooter for the IFBB world wide, who travels continuously all over the world on federation business and lobbies and works closely with Olympic officials throughout the world to promote our sport and federation.

Pal Schmitt, Hungary—former president of the Hungarian National Olympic Committee, former member of the International Olympic Committee, and great supporter of the IFBB.

Chuck Sipes, U.S.A.—champion bodybuilder and worldwide representative and promoter of bodybuilding and our federation (deceased).

Arnold Schwarzenegger, U.S.A.—one of the most popular and influential bodybuilders of all time, all over the world; named "Top Bodybuilder of the 20th Century" by Ben Weider, president of the IFBB; Arnold always promoted bodybuilding and supported the IFBB and his contributions were of immeasurable value.

Oscar State, England—one of the early supporters of the IFBB, personal friend and confident to president Ben Weider, and creator of the IFBB Constitution, Rules, and other documents; his advice and guidance were critical to the acceptance of the sport of bodybuilding in the international sports community (deceased).

Stephen Stern, U.S.A.—IFBB legal counsel.

Maj. Hugh Storey, Malaysia—a top supporter of the IFBB in the early years (deceased).

Eva Sukupova, Czech Republic—chairwoman, IFBB Women's Committee; former amateur and professional athlete, and Ms. Olympia competitor.

Hitoshi Tamari, Japan—president of the Japan Bodybuilding Federation and IFBB patron; he is a great promoter of bodybuilding in Japan and Asia.

Vasily Tchaikovsky, Russia—first president of the Russian Bodybuilding Federation, administrator, and contest organizer.

Walter Tröger, Germany—president of the German National Olympic Committee, member of the IOC, and great supporter of the IFBB.

U.S. Air Force M. Sgt. Robert C. Wilkins, U.S.A.—a valuable and trusted troubleshooter and problem solver with superior organizational skills.

Eric Weider, U.S.A.—president and CEO of Weider Health and Fitness; dedicated his life to bodybuilding and worked behind the scenes to ensure success in numerous projects.

Joe Weider, U.S.A.—IFBB honorary patron; the Father of World Bodybuilding, whose name is recognized and revered the world over; top advisor, top contributor, key official; without him there would not be no

IFBB, no fitness industry, and no bodybuilding as the world knows it today.

Stanislaw Zakrzekewski, Poland—a great leader who led his country's bodybuilding movement in the toughest days under Communism (deceased).

Honorable Mention: IFBB National Officials

Pawel Filleborn, Poland
Axel Bauer, Austria
Stanislav Pesat, Czech Republic
Jose Ramos, Spain
Vladimir Dubinin, Russian Federation
Andrew Michalak, Poland
Penny and Jordan Leventelis, Greece
William and Wanda Tierney, England
Andrey Dolgokir, Ukraine
Erich Janner, Germany
George Katulin, Belarus
Zeki Yonat, Turkey
Dr. Hussein Omar Toga, Jordan
Eugene Koltum, Russian Federation

I wish to express my sincere thanks and heartfelt appreciation for the dedication, committment, support, and loyalty of the executive committees and other officals of the 173 national federations, as well as to those of our regional and continental affiliates.

International Olympic Committee Members and Officials

Mario Vazquez Raña, Mexico
Carlos Ferrer Salat, Spain
Dr. Julio Maglione, Uraguay
Nicole Hoevertsz, Aruba
Julia Rocha, Nicaragua
Willy Kalschmitt, Guatemala
Jorge España, Bolivia
Dr. Fernando Beltranena, Guatemala
Melitón Sánchez, Panama
Cornel Marculescu, Romania
Col. Antonio Rodríguez, Argentina
Danilo Carrera, Ecuador

For more information about the IFBB and Ben Weider's Napoleonic scholarship, visit these websites: www.ifbb.com and www.napoleonicsociety.com

ACKNOWLEDGMENTS

Of all those who helped me prepare material for this book, my wonderful wife, Betty, worked longest and hardest. With her it was a pleasure to revisit the past and share recollections. Betty also reviewed the manuscript and gave very helpful comments as did Charlotte Parker and Joel Parker and my friend and colleague Peter McGough, group editorial director for *Muscle and Fitness* and *FLEX* magazines. Dr. Terry Todd of the University of Texas at Austin helped with fine points concerning the history of bodybuilding and strength sports, and Alan Hustak of the *The Gazette* in Montreal helped verify details of Montreal life in my early years. The Weider photo archivist and our books photo editor David Marsh worked hard to locate many wonderful one-of-a-kind images for the photo pages. Both Harold Forsko and Peter Kennedy did a wonderful job of locating rare back issues of Weider magazines and other hard-to-find materials from the past, which I lacked because through the years I was always much more focused on the work at hand than archiving finished work. Thanks, also, to Laura Hohnhold and Ann Neilsen for reading and commenting. My dear sister, Freda Yankovsky, our family historian, helped bring back memories of our childhood. And I deeply appreciate others who took the time to talk over shared experience, both long ago and recent, including my niece Thresa Katz, Irving "Rusty" Halpert, René Leger, Vicky Uzar, Jimmy Breslin, Bob Delmonteque, Mel Sokolsky, Leroy Colbert, Larry Scott, Dave Draper, Arnold Schwarzenegger, Frank Zane, Vince Scalisi, Barbara Harris, Dr. Leroy Perry, George Lengvari, John Balik, Bill Dobbins, the late Tony Lanza, and the late Anneliese Leyk. My executive assistant, Celia Gigliotti, kept the appointment book and organized the many hours of meetings with others that this project took. Our transcriptionist Barb Krultz did a fine job of getting onto the page the many, many hours of interviews I recorded with our collaborator Mike Steere.

—Joe Weider

ACKNOWLEDGMENTS

Many thanks to my son Eric for creating the concept of this life story and inspiring us into making it a reality in this book. My son Louis, who has researched the Weider family history, contributed facts about our family history in Poland. My right-hand man in Europe, Rafael Santonja, and my left-hand man in Asia, Paul Chua, contributed their insights and expertise, as did our federation's executive director here in Montreal, Pamela Kagan. Tony Blinn, our IFBB webmaster, did yeoman work checking and rechecking the myriad names, dates and places in my account for accuracy. Thanks to Peter McGough, group editorial director for *Muscle & Fitness* and *FLEX* magazines, for sharing his reflections, particularly on the late Oscar State, to Winston Roberts of Toronto for talking about his memories of our federation in the 1960s and '70s, and to Julian Feinstein of the U.K. for sending us his 1984 in memoriam article on Oscar State. Alan Hustak of *The Gazette* in Montreal used his considerable journalistic skills on our behalf, to help nail down historical facts. My office staffers Jinny Addesa, Lorraine Dostie, and Rowayda Guirguis, did wonderful jobs handling phone calls, emails, faxes, and helping with appointment scheduling and travel arrangements connected to work on my portion of this book, as did Eric's executive assistant, Sari Kahn, in Los Angeles.

—Ben Weider

INDEX

T

U